Federalism and Local Politics in Russia

This volume, which includes contributions from internationally renowned scholars from America, Britain, Canada, Germany and Russia, examines federal, regional and local politics in Russia and assesses the impact of Putin's federal reforms on democratisation.

Many commentators have alluded to the unique nature of Russia's dual transition and its difficult task of simultaneously reforming its economy and polity. But there is in fact a third transition under way in Russia that is of no less importance, the need to reconfigure central–local relations and to create a stable and viable form of federalism. Federal states are much more difficult to set up than unitary ones, and forging a new federal system at the same time as privatizing the economy and trying to radically overhaul the political system has clearly made Russia's transition triply difficult. The book discusses how Vladimir Putin has re-asserted the power of the centre in Russia, and tightened the federal government's control of the regions.

It shows how, contrary to Putin's rhetoric about developing Russia as a free and democratic state, authoritarianism has been extended – through his reorganization of the Federation Council, his usurpation of powers to dismiss regional assemblies and chief executives, and his creation of seven unelected super-governors. The book explores a wide range of issues related to these developments, including a comparative study of Russian federalism and local politics, ethnic federalism, the merging of federal units, regional governors, electoral and party reforms, and regional and local politics. It also includes case studies of local and regional politics in specific regions.

Cameron Ross is a Reader in Politics in the College of Arts and Social Sciences, University of Dundee. He has published widely in the field of Russian politics particularly in the areas of regional and local level politics. His most recent books are: *Regional Politics in Russia* (2002), *Federalism and Democratisation in Russia* (2003), *Russian Politics under Putin* (2004).

Adrian Campbell is a senior lecturer at the International Development Department at the University of Birmingham. He has been involved in researching and consulting in local and regional government in the Russian Federation and the CIS since 1990. He recently co-edited (with Andrew Coulson) a volume on Local Government in Central and Eastern Europe, also published by Routledge.

BASEES/Routledge Series on Russian and East European Studies

Series Editor: Richard Sakwa
  Department of Politics and International Relations, University of Kent

Editorial Committee:

Julian Cooper, Centre for Russian and East European Studies, University of Birmingham
Terry Cox, Department of Central and East European Studies, University of Glasgow
Rosalind Marsh, Department of European Studies and Modern Languages, University of Bath
David Moon, Department of History, University of Durham
Hilary Pilkington, Department of Sociology, University of Warwick
Stephen White, Department of Politics, University of Glasgow

Founding Editorial Committee Member:

George Blazyca, Centre for Contemporary European Studies, University of Paisley. This series is published on behalf of BASEES (the British Association for Slavonic and East European Studies).

The series comprises original, high-quality, research-level work by both new and established scholars on all aspects of Russian, Soviet, post-Soviet and East European Studies in humanities and social science subjects.

1 **Ukraine's Foreign and Security Policy, 1991–2000**
  Roman Wolczuk

2 **Political Parties in the Russian Regions**
  Derek S. Hutcheson

3 **Local Communities and Post-Communist Transformation**
  Edited by Simon Smith

4 **Repression and Resistance in Communist Europe**
  J.C. Sharman

5 **Political Elites and the New Russia**
  Anton Steen

6 **Dostoevsky and the Idea of Russianness**
  Sarah Hudspith

7 **Performing Russia – Folk Revival and Russian Identity**
  Laura J. Olson

8 **Russian Transformations**
  Edited by Leo McCann

9 **Soviet Music and Society under Lenin and Stalin**
The Baton and Sickle
Edited by Neil Edmunds

10 **State Building in Ukraine**
The Ukrainian parliament, 1990–2003
Sarah Whitmore

11 **Defending Human Rights in Russia**
Sergei Kovalyov, dissident and human rights commissioner, 1969–2003
Emma Gilligan

12 **Small-Town Russia**
Postcommunist livelihoods and identities: a portrait of the Intelligentsia in Achit, Bednodemyanovsk and Zubtsov, 1999–2000
Anne White

13 **Russian Society and the Orthodox Church**
Religion in Russia after Communism
Zoe Knox

14 **Russian Literary Culture in the Camera Age**
The Word as Image
Stephen Hutchings

15 **Between Stalin and Hitler**
Class war and race war on the Dvina, 1940–46
Geoffrey Swain

16 **Literature in Post-Communist Russia and Eastern Europe**
The Russian, Czech and Slovak fiction of the changes 1988–98
Rajendra A. Chitnis

17 **Soviet Dissent and Russia's Transition to Democracy**
Dissident legacies
Robert Horvath

18 **Russian and Soviet Film Adaptations of Literature, 1900–2001**
Screening the word
Edited by Stephen Hutchings and Anat Vernitski

19 **Russia as a Great Power**
Dimensions of security under Putin
Edited by Jakob Hedenskog, Vilhelm Konnander, Bertil Nygren, Ingmar Oldberg and Christer Pursiainen

20 **Katyn and the Soviet Massacre of 1940**
Truth, justice and memory
George Sanford

21 **Conscience, Dissent and Reform in Soviet Russia**
Philip Boobbyer

22 **The Limits of Russian Democratisation**
Emergency powers and states of emergency
Alexander N. Domrin

23 **The Dilemmas of Destalinisation**
A social and cultural history of reform in the Khrushchev Era
Edited by Polly Jones

24 **News Media and Power in Russia**
Olessia Koltsova

25 **Post-Soviet Civil Society**
Democratization in Russia and the Baltic States
Anders Uhlin

26 **The Collapse of Communist Power in Poland**
Jacqueline Hayden

27 **Television, Democracy and Elections in Russia**
Sarah Oates

28 **Russian Constitutionalism**
Historical and contemporary development
Andrey N. Medushevsky

29 **Late Stalinist Russia**
Society between reconstruction and reinvention
Edited by Juliane Fürst

30 **The Transformation of Urban Space in Post-Soviet Russia**
Konstantin Axenov, Isolde Brade and Evgenij Bondarchuk

31 **Western Intellectuals and the Soviet Union, 1920–40**
From Red Square to the Left Bank
Ludmila Stern

32 **The Germans of the Soviet Union**
Irina Mukhina

33 **Re-constructing the Post-Soviet Industrial Region**
The Donbas in transition
Edited by Adam Swain

34 **Chechnya – Russia's "War on Terror"**
John Russell

35 **The New Right in the New Europe**
Czech transformation and right-wing politics, 1989–2006
Seán Hanley

36 **Democracy and Myth in Russia and Eastern Europe**
Edited by Alexander Wöll and Harald Wydra

37 **Energy Dependency, Politics and Corruption in the Former Soviet Union**
Russia's power, oligarchs' profits and Ukraine's missing energy policy, 1995–2006
Margarita M. Balmaceda

38 **Peopling the Russian Periphery**
Borderland colonization in Eurasian history
Edited by Nicholas B. Breyfogle, Abby Schrader and Willard Sunderland

39 **Russian Legal Culture before and after Communism**
Criminal justice, politics and the public sphere
Frances Nethercott

40 **Political and Social Thought in Post-Communist Russia**
Pxel Kaehne

41 **The Demise of the Soviet Communist Party**
Atsushi Ogushi

42 **Russian Policy towards China and Japan**
The El'tsin and Putin periods
Natasha Kuhrt

43 **Soviet Karelia**
Politics, planning and terror in Stalin's Russia, 1920–39
Nick Baron

44 **Reinventing Poland**
Economic and political transformation and evolving national identity
Edited by Martin Myant and Terry Cox

45 **The Russian Revolution in Retreat, 1920–24**
Soviet workers and the new communist elite
Simon Pirani

46 **Democratization and Gender in Contemporary Russia**
Suvi Salmenniemi

47 **Narrating Post-Communism**
Colonial discourse and Europe's borderline civilization
Nataša Kovačević

48 **Globalization and the State in Central and Eastern Europe**
The politics of foreign direct investment
Jan Drahokoupil

49 **Local Politics and Democratisation in Russia**
Cameron Ross

50 **The Emancipation of the Serfs in Russia**
Peace arbitrators and the development of civil society
Roxanne Easley

51 **Federalism and Local Politics in Russia**
Edited by Cameron Ross and Adrian Campbell

Federalism and Local Politics in Russia

Edited by
Cameron Ross and
Adrian Campbell

Routledge
Taylor & Francis Group

LONDON AND NEW YORK

First published 2009
by Routledge
2 Park Square, Milton Park, Abingdon, Oxon OX14 4RN

Simultaneously published in the USA and Canada
by Routledge
270 Madison Ave, New York, NY 10016

Routledge is an imprint of the Taylor & Francis Group, an Informa business

Typeset in Times New Roman by
Taylor & Francis Books
Printed and bound in Great Britain by
CPI Antony Rowe, Chippenham, Wiltshire

British Library Cataloguing in Publication Data
A catalogue record for this book is available from the British Library

Library of Congress Cataloging in Publication Data
Federalism and local politics in Russia / edited by Cameron Ross and
Adrian Campbell.
    p. cm. – (Basees/routledge series on russian and east european studies ;
51)
Includes bibliographical references.
    1. Central-local government relations–Russia (Federation) 2. Local
government–Russia (Federation) 3. Authoritarianism–Russia (Federation)
I. Ross, Cameron, 1951- II. Campbell, Adrian, 1958-
JN6693.5.S8F35 2008
    320.447'049 –dc22   2008018377

ISBN 978-0-415-43702-8 (hbk)
ISBN 978-0-203-89151-3 (ebk)

Contents

List of illustrations   xi
Contributors   xii
Abbreviations   xiii
Preface   xiv
Acknowledgements   xvi

1   Leviathan's return: the policy of recentralization
    in contemporary Russia   1
    VLADIMIR GEL'MAN

2   Between a rock and a hard place: the Russian
    Federation in comparative perspective   25
    MICHAEL BURGESS

3   Federal discourses, minority rights, and conflict transformation   54
    ANDREAS HEINEMANN-GRÜDER

4   Unification as a political project: the case of
    Permskii Krai   82
    OKSANA ORACHEVA

5   Putin and the election of regional governors   106
    DARRELL SLIDER

6   Electoral reforms and democratization:
    Russian regional elections 2003–2006   120
    ALEKSANDR KYNEV

7   Russian political parties and regional political processes: the
    problem of effective representation   150
    PETR PANOV

8   The representation of business elites in regional
    politics: étatism, elitism and clientelism   184
    ROSTISLAV TUROVSKII

9   The struggle for power in the Urals   207
    ELENA DENEZHKINA AND ADRIAN CAMPBELL

10 Local self-government in Russia: between
    decentralization and recentralization   227
    HELLMUT WOLLMANN AND ELENA GRITSENKO

11 Russia's elusive pursuit of balance in local government reform   248
    JOHN F. YOUNG

12 Vertical or triangle? local, regional and federal government in the
    Russian Federation after Law 131   263
    ADRIAN CAMPBELL

13 Municipal elections and electoral authoritarianism
    under Putin   284
    CAMERON ROSS

    Index   305

Illustrations

Figure

12.1   Robinson's (2002) Framework of State Transition in Russia.   272

Tables

4.1   Autonomous okrugs and their 'mother' regions   83
4.2   Timetable of regional mergers   84
6.1   Elections to the legislative assemblies of members of the RF on 7 December 2003 and 14 March 2004   125
6.2   Elections to the legislative assemblies of members of the RF in the second half of 2004 and first half of 2005.   127
6.3   Election to legislative assemblies of members of the RF during the second half of 2005 and on 12 March 2006.   132
6.4   Elections to legislative assemblies of members of the RF on 8 October 2006   143
7.1   The share of party deputies in 'second cycle' regional legislatures (in per cent)   158
7.2   The share of party deputies in 'third cycle' regional legislatures (per cent)   160
7.3   Effective number of parties in 'new generation' regional legislatures   166
13.1   Average turnout in Russian local elections 2004–05 (%)   291
13.2   Turnout (average per cent) and Votes Against All (average per cent) in the electoral districts of municipal raions in Saratov Region and Tula Region   293
13.3   Party membership of municipal councils and heads of municipal administrations in December 2005 (by type of municipality)   294

List of contributors

Michael Burgess University of Kent at Canterbury, UK

Adrian Campbell International Development Department, School of Governance and Society, University of Birmingham, UK.

Elena Denezhkina Centre for Russian and Eastern European Studies, School of Governance and Society, University of Birmingham, UK.

Vladimir Gel'man European University of St Petersburg, Russian Federation.

Elena Gritsenko Institute of Law and Public Policy, Moscow, Russian Federation

Andreas Heinemann-Grüder Bonn International Centre for Conversion, Republic of Germany

Aleksandr Kynev International Insitute of Humanitarian-Political Studies, Moscow, Russian Federation

Oksana Oracheva Ford Foundation, Moscow, Russian Federation.

Petr Panov Perm University, Russian Federation.

Cameron Ross Politics, School of Humanities, University of Dundee, UK.

Darrell Slider University of South Florida, Tampa, USA.

Rostislav Turovskii State University – Higher School of Economics, Moscow, Russian Federation

Hellmut Wollmann Humbolt University, Republic of Germany

John F. Young University of Northern British Columbia, Canada

Abbreviations

APR	Agrarian Party of Russia
ASSR	Autonomous Soviet Socialist Republic
CDU-CSU	Christian Democrats
CPSU	Communist Party of the Soviet Union
DPR	Democratic Party of Russia
ENP	Parties in Parliament Index
FOM	Public Opinion Foundation
FRG	Republic of Germany
FRS	Federal Registration Service
FSB	Federal Security Service
GRICS	Governance Research Indicator Country Snapshot
GRP	Gross Regional Product
RAO EES	Russian Electric Energy Company
KGB	State Committee for Security
LDPR	Liberal Democratic Party of Russia
NCA	National Cultural Autonomy
NPSR	National Patriotic Socialists of Russia
OPS	Social and Political Union
OVR	Fatherland – All Russia
PRES	Unity and Agreement Party
PRR	Party of Russia's Rebirth
RDP	Russian Democratic Party
RKRP	Russian Communist Workers' Party – the Russian Party of Communists
RPL	Russian Party of Life
RPP	Russian Party of Pensioners
RPRF	Republican Party of the Russian Federation
RSFSR	Russian Soviet Federated Socialist Republic
SDPR	Social Democratic Party of Russia
SPD	Social Democrats
SPS	Union of Right Forces
TSFSR	Transcaucasian Soviet Federal Socialist Republic
UR	United Russia
USSR	Union of Soviet Socialist Republics

Preface

The chapters in this volume describe and analyse how it was that the struggle for supremacy between federal centre and regions, so much a feature of the previous decade, should, starting from 2000 have been so rapidly resolved in favour of the Centre. However, although the Kremlin under Putin dominates the political space of the Russian Federation to a degree believed impossible by commentators in both Russia and the West even five years ago, the degree of effective centralization should not be exaggerated. Whilst the ability of regions to impose their will on federal policy, or to use the prospect for secession as a bargaining counter, has been largely eliminated (the recent agreement with Tatarstan notwithstanding, the capacity of the Centre to achieve its desired outcomes within regions remains weak), the appointment rather than election of regional leaders does not resolve the Kremlin's principal-agent problem, and administrative reform of regional and federal territorial bodies cannot by its nature bring quick results. Local government reform continues to be a complex and controversial issue with the recentralizing agenda of one group of policymakers at the Centre colliding with the sub-regional empowerment agenda of another.

Despite a major shift of power towards the Centre, the underlying question of Russia's regional structure still remains – how far it should abandon the asymmetrical ethnic/territorial dual system dating from the Stalin period and embark instead on the often advocated structure of a few large regions designed to facilitate economic development and planning. The practical and political problems facing the imposition of a single structure in place of, for example, the existing patchwork of North Caucasian republics, would be overwhelming. However, the announcement, in January, 2008, by the Minister of Regional Development, Dmitrii N. Kozak (whose Federal Commission in the years 2001–3 initiated many of the legal changes that were to consolidate the shift of power away from the regions) of the plan to establish 7–10 economic regions, running parallel to the existing regional government structure, represents an attempt to circumvent the problem by separating economic and political/administrative functions at the regional level. The evolution of regional policy in Russia is not therefore simply a matter of centralization or decentralization, but also involves a debate, at the highest level of government, over the purpose of regions – whether it be to faciliate control (as in much of the Soviet period, leaving aside Khrushchev's Sovnarkhoz experiment), to represent sub-national interests (or elites – as during the Yeltsin presidency) or to facilitate economic development strategy and planning (as seems likely under a Medvedev presidency). Either way, it is clear that, although the prospect of a slide into a 'Russia of the regions' has receded, the dilemmas around regional structure, centre–regional and regional–local relations will continue to be at the core of Russian federal policymaking for the forseeable future.

Acknowledgements

Cameron Ross would like to thank the publishers for their permission to include some materials from the article listed below in Chapter 13: Cameron Ross, 'Municipal government in the Russian Federation and Putin's "electoral vertical"', *Demokratizatsiya: The Journal of Post-Soviet Democratization*, Vol. 15, No. 2, Spring 2007.

1 Leviathan's return

The policy of recentralization in contemporary Russia

Vladimir Gel'man

On 13 September 2004, speaking in a television broadcast, President Putin announced a set of political reforms, the most important of which was the rejection of direct elections for executive heads of Russia's regions. From 2005, regional executive heads (henceforth 'governors' in this text, except in exceptional cases) would be confirmed in their post by regional legislatures, having first being proposed by the President of the Federation.

Putin's decision, taken in the wake of the tragic deaths of hostages in the North Ossetian town of Beslan, and announced as an anti-terrorist measure, provoked widespread criticism and was considered by a number of observers as one more step by the Kremlin towards the destruction of democratic institutions in the country. At the same time the switch (or reversion) to appointing rather than electing governors was the logical consequence of the policy of centralization which began in 2000. This policy was in many ways a reaction against the spontaneous and poorly managed process of decentralization in Russia during the 1990s. It included a comprehensive range of measures aimed at placing control over the main levers of power in the hands of the federal authorities (hereafter the Centre). These measures led to the recentralization of institutional regulation of the political 'rules of the game', recentralization of resources and administrative recentralization. The abolition of direct gubernatorial elections may be seen as moving the recentralization policy into a new qualitative phase.

What are the origins of the policy of recentralization in the Russian Federation? Which ideas and interests form its basis? How did these factors influence its course and results? How significant is recentralization for the political development of Russia and what is its future? These are the questions which this chapter shall address. In the first section we review the trend towards regionalization against the background of the transformations that were taking place in Russia during the 1990s and 2000s. We then consider the ideologies and interests of the political actors involved in recentralization after 2000, and their influence on the course of federal reforms in Russia, the policy that might be termed 'new centralism' (to distinguish it from 'old' soviet-style centralism). We then analyze this policy of 'new centralism' and its influence on the process of reform of the Russian state. Finally we draw conclusions on the meaning and significance of recentralization for the Russian political system.[1]

Federal Reform: the swing of the pendulum

Decentralization in Russia during the 1990s was anything but the result of a considered policy from the federal Centre. It was more a side-effect of the transformational processes that in Russia were accompanied by sharp inter-elite conflict, a severe and sustained economic collapse, and a serious falling away of state capacity. These processes did have their effects on Russia's regions, not directly, but rather through two closely related trends.

First, the decades of soviet (and pre-soviet) development had left their legacy in terms of centre–regional relations and in the development of the regions themselves. The soviet model of regional administration was strongly inclined towards hierarchical centralization of power and resources, held together by the vertically integrated structures of the CPSU and the USSR-level ministries and agencies, including the security sector (army, police and KGB). In the regions, depending on administrative status (republic, krai, oblast'), level of socio-economic modernization, pattern of settlement, sectoral economic profile and a number of other historically acquired factors, the conditions were created for particular types pf political and economic relation in the post-soviet period. Therefore the decentralization of the 1990s and the recentralization of the 2000s were path-depend.

Second, different critical junctures in the process of Russian transformation opened up different 'windows of opportunity' for political actors, the balance of forces between whom, and their motives, were to influence the character of Centre–regional relations.

This 'legacy' bequeathed a constraining framework which set limits to the changes that could occur in Centre–regional relations, but did not determine them: the vector of these changes was largely the result of specific steps taken by Russian politicians.[2]

The effects of path dependency and the influence of political actors on Centre–regional relations in the 1990s have been described in some detail in the literature. Commentators have noted the role of the ethnic model of federalism, established by the Soviet regime,[3] of disparities in socio-economic development between regions,[4] of the unintended consequences of the fall of the Soviet Union, which left in its wake ethno-political conflicts in Russia's regions,[5] and of the serious weakening of the administrative capacity of the Centre in its relations with the regions.[6] The struggle between elites at federal and regional levels for resources and spheres of influence, the Centre's attempts to win over the regions to its side in electoral campaigns,[7] and similarly the varying constellations of elites at the level of each region[8] have all left their stamp on these processes. In summarizing the evaluations of different commentators on Centre–regional relations in Russia in 1991–8, one may identify the following trends:

(a) Spontaneous devolution from the Centre to the regions of the most important levels of power, including:

- A range of powers in the field of institutional regulation, including the ability to pass regional legislation, some of which would contradict federal norms, and, in some regions, systematically avoid implementing federal legislations;[9]
- Administrative resources, including not only independent (i.e. without involvement of the Centre) formation of regional and local institutions of government, but also regional influence on the appointment of heads of federal agencies, including law-and-order bodies such as prosecutor's office and police, and in a number of cases their *de facto* subordination to regional political-financial (and sometimes criminal) groups;[10]
- Economic resources, including rights to property, were to a significant extent placed under the control of the regional administrations which thus gained a right of veto in Russian economic policy,[11] and similarly control over budget funds, the regional share of which rose to almost 60 per cent of the Russian state budget in 1998[12] due to the reduction in the share of financial resources under federal control.
- A growing asymmetry in relations between the Centre and regions and in the political and economic status of individual regions due to the conclusion of bilateral treaties between the Centre and the regions on the distribution of shared competences and powers (46 regions had signed such agreements by 1998), and due to exclusive rights being offered to ethnic republics (Tatarstan, Bashkortostan) or the concentration of a large volume of economic resources (Moscow).
- The loss of the Centre's levers of influence over regional political processes, which increasingly developed exclusively under the influence of the configuration of regional elites, in some cases forming closed regimes of 'regional authoritarianism' and the transformation of regional elites into leading actors on the all-Russian political stage, capable of deploying a 'group veto' in relation to federal elections, thereby necessitating further concessions from the Centre in terms of decentralization.

Most commentators have viewed these trends in profoundly negative terms, speaking of 'precipitous decentralization',[13] a 'destructive market',[14] 'negotiated federalism',[15] threatening the unity of Russia. The economic crisis of August 1998 demonstrated how significant Centre–regional relations were for the development of the country, and this created a demand for recentralization on the part of the federal elite.[16] The demand was to be fully satisfied – in contrast to the seven years of decentralization from 1991 to 1998, the following seven years up to 2005 were to be no less radical in the direction of centralization. The main results of this process were:[17]

- Recentralization of institutional regulation, including a series of federal laws that substantially curtailed the powers of regions, in parallel with a revision of regional legislation directed from the Centre;
- Administrative recentralization, as a result of which territorial branches of federal agencies were removed from subordination to the regions and control over them passed to the Centre or to the federal districts, which also had the task of political and administrative oversight over regional and local government on behalf of the Centre (the reversion to appointment of governors can be seen as part of this same trend);
- Recentralization of economic resources, leading to a weakening of the control over the regional economy previously exercised by regional elites, now more dependent on Russia-wide financial-industrial groups which functioned as conduits for federal power in the regions,[18] as well as an increased concentration of financial resources in the hand of the Centre due to the reduction of budget funds under regional and local control. In 2006 the federal share of the all-Russian budget rose to 66 per cent.[19] If at the end of the 1990s Russia had been the most decentralized federation in the world, then in the mid-2000s it occupied an average position among federal states in terms of the level of fiscal decentralization.[20]
- Equalization of the political status of the regions in relation to the Centre and to each other, due to the abolition of bilateral agreements (with the exception of Tatarstan where a new bilateral treaty was signed in 2007) and an almost complete end to the practice of giving exclusive rights to particular regions.[21]
- A sharp decline in the role of the regional elites in Russia-wide political processes against the backdrop of a substantial increase in federal influence over regional political processes, attained not only through administrative intervention by the Centre, but also institutional changes, leading in a number of cases to changes in the configuration of regional elites and transformation of regional political regimes.[22]

As with the decentralization of the 1990s, the recentralization of the 2000s was part of a larger-scale process of change at the level of the country as a whole. Consolidation of the state and restoration of its administrative potential, economic growth on the basis of raw materials, and the establishment of a mono-centric political regime, accompanied by de-differentiation and reduced fragmentation of elites and enforced consensus between the Kremlin and the economic and political actors subordinated to it – these are just a few of the aspects of the transformation that occurred within Russian after 2000.

The result is reminiscent of a pendulum swinging from one extreme type of consolidation (the Soviet political and economic system) to another (dominant power politics and state capitalism), passing through the equilibrium of democracy and a market economy.[23] In terms of Centre–regional relations, this pendulum, having started from a position of extreme centralization after a series of zigzag movements in the 1990s, reached the farthest point of decentralization during the of economic crisis in 1998, when there loomed the threat of extinction of the Centre as a significant actor. However, the pendulum then began to move swiftly in the opposite direction, passing the equilibrium between centralization and decentralization and reaching, by the mid-2000s, a new equilibrium of recentralization in the form of 'new centralism'.[24]

The establishment of the 'new centralism' of the 2000s was partly dependent on certain objective processes such as the formation of a nationwide market in Russia and the expansion of Russia-wide economic actors into the regions,[25] but to a substantial extent it was the result of political strategy. The development and realization of this political strategy depended on a constellation of political actors at the federal and regional levels, who represented particular ideologies interests and approaches. The interplay of these factors had many repercussions in terms of the course taken by the federal reforms of the 2000s.

Ideologies and interests

The question of why, after 1998, the direction of Centre–regional relations made a 180-degree turn may be separated into two parts. First, why did the Centre make such a decisive change in its strategy and how was it able successfully to introduce a whole series of federal reforms? Second, why did the regional elites, until 1998 active political rent-seekers in their negotiations with the Centre, so humbly agree with the imposition of new 'rules of the game'? It would be naïve to suggest that this turn-around was brought about merely by a change in the balance of power, which forced the regions to forgo continued decentralization and enabled the Centre to win back the ground lost in the 1990s. In considering Centre–regional relations, it is worth viewing these political actors as a coalition united by ideologies as well as by interests. Ideology in this context refers to the actors' perception of problems faced, their view of the existing social reality and the social reality they would prefer. The membership, resources and motivation of these coalitions changed radically in the 2000s.

In the 1990s the federal Centre consisted of a motley conglomerate of different organizations, clans and cliques entering into coalitions and conflicts among themselves and with regional elites. The interests and ideologies of these actors were markedly different. The divergence of interests lay in the attempt of some departments of state to centralize management, concentrating resources in their own hands (the Ministry of Finance was the clearest example of this) whilst other departments and politicians sought to pass onto the regions the responsibility for those problems, primarily social, that they themselves could not solve. Against the background of profound fragmentation of Russian elites, the divergence between their interests prevented the development of a coherent political strategy for the Centre and led to incongruent decisions being made.

Ideology was a major factor in the process of institution building in Russia, in terms of its positive and normative functions. It allowed actors, first of all, to minimize the amount of information needed for political decision-making (a particularly important advantage during a period of uncertainty and transition)[26] and, second, it enabled them to make judgements about how far existing institutions fitted their normative conceptions.[27] In this way the deployment of (applied) ideology in each sphere enables actors to take action on the basis of the information they have and to launch political strategies on the basis of particular ideological coalitions.[28]

In terms of decentralization and recentralization federal political actors demonstrated three main applied ideologies: (1) *managerial*; (2) *utilitarian*; (3) *self-governmental*.[29] These may be defined as follows: the managerial ideology is based on the normative conception of government as a unified corporation, of which regional and local institutions form the lower stratum. Accordingly, state policy on regions and municipalities is seen as a matter of administrative centralization. From the point of view of this ideology local and regional autonomy are permissible only insofar as they do not obstruct this; they are thus seen as deviations to be corrected. In practice this ideology finds its purest incarnation in the notion of the 'state vertical', that is a system where all state authorities at all levels are directly subordinated to the supreme authority, whether this is the tsar, general secretary or president. For adherents of this ideology regional policy is primarily about strengthening administrative controls over the actions of the lower levels of the governmental hierarchy. A significant proportion of senior officials at the federal level have been exponents of this ideology, as a rule veterans of Soviet-era *nomenklatura* or the security services, their ideal conception of government being 'good' Soviet practice, shorn of its characteristic deficiencies.

The utilitarian ideology is unconnected to the philosophy of the same name but refers to the notion of utility maxim. The normative conception of the functions of the State, including regional and local authorities, is exclusively linked to the imperatives of economic efficiency, understood from the standpoint of economic liberalism, minimizing the responsibility of the State in general and the federal state in particular, for the welfare of the population regionally or nationally. Regional and local economic or political autonomy are therefore permissible insofar as they further the cause of liberalization of the economy. Regional and municipal policy is therefore secondary to economic policy objectives and is thus subject to shifting priorities. In other words Centre–regional relations are purely instrumental according to this ideology. They may for example, be used to undermine enemies such as the (then) Communist Party, to 'shove' onto regional and local government the responsibility for carrying through unpopular policies necessary for the overall strategy. The exponents of this ideology in Russia were the 'young reformers' who moved centre stage in the 1990s.

Finally, the self-governmental ideology is founded on the normative ideal of representative democracy and civil society. Regional and local autonomy and the division of powers on the basis of the supremacy of law are the most valued (although not in themselves sufficient) principles of this ideology. They are seen as an organic part of the 'correct' form of local and regional government in the spirit of an idealized conception of contemporary Western practice, and decentralization (like recentralization) is also seen as an important element in a broader project of democratization of the political life of the country as a whole. Like the 'utilitarians' the 'self-governmentalists' came to power riding on the wave of transformation of the early 1990s and therefore also viewed the 'Soviet legacy' in wholly negative terms, although primarily on account of its undemocratic character. Exponents of this ideology at the federal level were found among those politicians termed 'democrats' – representatives of 'Yabloko', part of the Union of Right Forces and other liberal parties.

The differences between these ideologies as regards regional and local policy are derived from at least two bases: goals and means. At the level of policy goals the managerialists and utilitarians by and large gravitated towards centralization (the former everywhere possible, the latter everywhere where they thought it necessary); the self-governmentalists supported decentralization, as long as it did not hinder democratization. As far as means are concerned, if the managerialists considered the best way of dividing responsibilities between Centre, regions and municipalities was delegation of powers (both top-down and bottom-up), then the utilitarians, together with the self-governmentalists, advocated delimitation of competences between levels of government. Thus there arose the possibility of ideological coalitions with different configurations between interest groups (from the Ministry of Finance to 'oligarchs') and parties (such as the Communist Party of the Russian Federation) that did not have a clear ideological preference on this topic. It was precisely these circumstances that made possible federal policy in the field in the period 1991-8, although as a rule during this period the regional dimension was not a priority for federal-level political actors.

After the crisis of August 1998, the situation was substantially altered. First of all, the regional dimension of the political strategy became a priority due to the reaction of both the Centre and the regions to the economic crisis, and also due to the active part played by regional elites in the political struggle on the federal level leading up to the Duma elections of 1999. The loss of the Centre's capacity to manage the regions of Russia on the one hand and on the other the likelihood that regional leaders would undermine the position of the federal elite, created the 'demand for recentralization' on the part of disparate political forces. In other words the regional issue touched the interests of all federal-level actors and their very substantial ideological differences, against a background of great uncertainty, did not prevent unity of action by the Centre: its political course on this issue went from reactive to proactive. Second, there was a shift in the balance of power between the federal actors in the ideological coalitions concerned with local and regional policy. In the period 1991-8 it was the utilitarians who were the driving force behind reforms in this field, establishing coalitions now with the managerialists, now with the self-governmentalists and drawing other actors to their cause. After August 1998 the utilitarians' position came under pressure on account of the misfortunes of their economic policy. As a result the policy initiative passed to the managerialists, with the utilitarians now playing only a subordinate role. The self-governmentalists (whose influence on policy decisions had been very limited) were also invited to enter the new coalition, although their chances of influencing federal policy were slim.

As a result, after 2000 the managerialists were able to pursue their interests and ideology in the field of regional and local policy, drawing on the support of a wide range of federal elites,[30] and to launch a policy of recentralization without serious opposition from other actors (in contrast to the 1990s) – here the mass support enjoyed by the head of state was an important factor, and provided the window of opportunity that opened in 2000 for a radical shift towards recentralization.[31] The federal reform, announced by Putin in May 2000 was "doomed to succeed" insofar as it was (1) a key point in the manifesto of a strong and popular president; (2) supported by a wide albeit fragile consensus between the federal elite and ordinary citizens; (3) aimed not only at raising the administrative potential of the Russian state but at using this resource for carrying out the Centre's policy. The consensus attained between federal-level elites allowed the Centre to speak with one voice in its dealings with the regions and to formulate their shared interest in a policy of recentralization, brought about through maximizing federal control over resources whilst minimizing federal responsibilities. The fact that the managerialists dominated the coalition around the 'new centralism' meant that the reform was to bear their stamp, such that the new elites were in effect seeking, as Kathryn Stoner-Weiss put it, 'a Soviet solution to post-Soviet problems'.[32]

The stance adopted by regional elites also went through some changes. Although in the 1990s the regions were in a negotiating relationship with the federal centre, and could be seen to have a common interest in increasing the powers and resources available to regions, rarely was there collaboration between elites of different regions in such negotiations. Each governor was interested in solving the problems of their particular region, whilst there appeared to be no incentives for collective action to maximize regional power and resources. The asymmetry between regions limited the number of those leaders who were active in the process of regionalization and negotiations with the centre: (1) republics (20 out of 88 subjects of the Russian Federation, excluding Chechnya), (2) donor regions (those that were net contributors to the federal budget) – the number of these never exceeded 19, and only a few had the status of a republic.[33] However numerous the regions might be, the Federation Council, which was supposed to represent their interests at the Centre, lacked significant powers, and could not be see as an effective institution[34] – inter-regional coalitions emerged in an *ad hoc* manner and were short-lived as a result.[35]

The tone was set by a small minority of regional leaders (such as Moscow Mayor Yuri Luzhkov and Tatarstan President Mintimer Shaimiev). Taking part in these coalitions brought them extra benefits through selective incentives: for example when the electoral bloc 'Fatherland-All Russia' was being set up on the eve of the Duma elections of 1999, they played a leading role, supported by other regional leaders.[36] The majority of governors, lacking such incentives, but needing powerful allies in order to attain their own objectives (extraction of political rents) were drawn in by a kind of bandwagon effect. Their behaviour varied according to the fluctuations in the relationship between the Centre and the regions, whether it was decentralization, as in the 1990s, or recentralization, as after 2000.

It is not surprising that in setting the political course at the federal level the governors and their inter-regional coalitions were the junior partners of more influential interest groups. The same had happened with economic policy during the 1990s when the regional elites had been the allies of the oligarchs and the left (i.e. pro-market) factions in the State Duma.[37]

A similar bandwagon effect was set in motion during the federal elections of 1999-2000: as the campaign of the inter-regional bloc, OVR (Fatherland-All-Rusia), began to lose ground to that of the Kremlin-backed bloc 'Unity', so the regional elites began to desert to the camp of the victors, culminating in Unity's hostile takeover of OVR in 2001.[38] After their defeat in the Duma elections of 1999, the leaders of OVR no longer had the resources necessary to forge a coalition on regional policy. Thus when the Centre subsequently shifted away from its reactive regional policy towards an active political agenda it could apply the principle of 'divide and rule', without applying any special measures. Already in February 2000, before Putin's election as head of state, a proposal was circulated by the governors of Belgorod, Kurgan and Novgorod oblasts, calling for an amalgamation of regions to reduce their number to between twenty and thirty and to end gubernatorial elections in favour of their appointment from the Centre.[39] As usual in such cases, the governors concerned were not those who had been in the vanguard of regionalization. After 2000 the regional elites lost the ability either to formulate or to assert any collective interest and did little to hinder the Centre's policy of recentralization. Once again, just as in the 1990s, their preference was to negotiate with the Kremlin for individual deals to retain their previous status and resources but their negotiating positions proved weaker than in the past.

It is clear then that after 2000 the Centre found itself with an almost unique opportunity to bring about recentralization of power, due to a consolidated federal elite having put together an ideological coalition to further its unified interests, whilst the coalition of regional elites, united neither by interests nor by ideology, had to all practical purposes ceased to exist.

Means and ends

Thus the 'new centralism' became the most important project of the President's first term. The reforms in federal–regional relations served to achieve a number of objectives simultaneously: (1) reassertion of Russian state capacity through subordination of the regions to central administrative controls; (2) delivery of desired political outcomes at the national level through the support of loyal regional elites; (3) increased administrative efficiency through the acquisition of the resource base of regional elites, and the undermining of 'closed markets' in the regions (not least by these markets being taken over by Russia-wide corporations). The first steps in the implementation of the policy of recentralization included the following:[40]

- Creation by presidential decree of seven federal districts (*okrugs*), headed by appointed plenipotentiary representatives (*polpredy*), who were empowered to monitor regional compliance with federal normative acts and to coordinate federal agencies at regional level. This, combined with certain amendments to federal legislation (such as the law 'on the militia'), served to extract these federal services (ranging from the tax authorities through to branches of the Ministry of the Interior) from *de facto* (and in some *de jure*) control by regional elites and to re-establish them as exponents of central policy. Some of these services were reorganized at the level of federal districts. In addition, the *polpredy*, acting alongside the regional prosecutors (and supported by the Constitutional Court of Russia), carried through a targeted revision of regional legislation, which was largely (although not entirely) brought into line with federal norms.[41]
- Change in the composition of the Federal Council: instead of regional executive heads and chairs of regional legislatures it would be composed of people nominated by them. This meant a sharp decline in the influence of regional elites on central policymaking, even though regional executive heads were *ex officio* members of the president's State Council, since this was a purely deliberative body and met on an *ad hoc* basis under the control of the presidential administration. As a result, the Federal Council, which had relatively few powers in any case, lost any influence over political processes in Russia.[42]
- The President received the power, in certain circumstances (such as contraventions of federal law, confirmed by the courts), to remove elected regional officials from their posts and to dissolve regional legislatures. Although this power was never used in practice, the very threat of its use had a serious deterrent effect and reinforced the subordination of regional elites to the Centre.
- There was a recentralization of budgetary flows through changes in tax legislation, which substantially increased the amount and weighting of federal and shared taxes as opposed to regional and local taxes.[43] As a result, regional and local budgets became much more dependent on

central transfers than they had been in the 1990s. In addition, a redistribution of property in the regions took place in favour of a number of
Russia-wide financial industrial groups closely linked with the Centre.
Their active regional expansion in conditions of economic growth facilitated the removal from the economy of the administrative barriers that
had been erected by regional elites.[44] All these steps facilitated the vertical
integration of economic links and consolidated a single Russia-wide economic space although at the same time reducing economic competition
between regions.

Although at the level of policy formation the Centre's strategy may have
resembled a comprehensive set of measures for building an effective law-
based state and a modern market economy, the main mechanisms for its
implementation were selectively applied norms and sanctions and informal
methods of conflict resolution. On the one hand, the Kremlin would from
time to time rush to punish particular governors, as in the case of Alexander
Rutskoi, Governor of Kursk Oblast, who was disqualified from re-election
by a court decision, although many other governors had broken with impu-
nity the same law he was accused of breaking.[45] On the other hand, the
reward for loyalty of a number of governors was to be the removal of the
maximum term for most of them and the possibility of running for a third or
even a fourth term.[46]

In certain conflictual cases, where there was no possibility of attaining full
control over the political and economic situation in a region, the Kremlin
resorted to 'individual 'deals' with regional heads. The result of such deals
would be either the preservation of the status quo in terms of leadership at the
regional level, in return for what the Centre wanted in the elections for the
federal level – as took place in Bashkortostan in 2003, for example[47] – or, on
the contrary, the departure (to a senior post in Moscow) of the regional
leader who didn't suit the Centre, with the subsequent redistribution of
power and property going in the Centre's favour. An example was Yakutiya,
the head of which declined to take part in the election for a new mandate in
return for the post of deputy speaker in the Federal Council, after which the
Centre got its favoured candidate elected and reasserted its control over the
Republic's diamond sector, which in the 1990s had been virtually the patri-
mony of the Yakutian elites.[48] Similarly, the governors of the Maritime
Province and St Petersburg, although widely criticized for ineffective administration, both only left their posts to take up higher appointments as federal
ministers while their regional posts went to Kremlin loyalists.[49]

Selective sanctions and individual deals were logical enough in a context
characterized by widespread contravention of federal legislation and ineffective management, and these methods enabled the Centre to achieve the
desired results whilst minimizing its own costs of control.[50] It is not surprising that these measures met with support from the managerialists and utilitarians, but the position taken by the self-governmentalists was illogical. On

the whole they supported the strategy of 'the dictatorship of law', the consolidation of Russian state power regarding the supremacy of law, which had gripped all spheres of Russian politics during the 2000s: the policy of recentralization was no exception.[51]

The success of the first phase of the federal reform – the reassertion of central control over the regions – was evident even by 2001, and helped to usher in the second phase, involving the setting up of new mechanisms for ruling regions. The utilitarians prepared and introduced a series of institutional changes, with the aim of (1) securing the balance of power in favour of the Centre, maintaining the loyalty and malleability of the regions, preventing any possibility of any 1990's style 'landslip' toward decentralization, and (2) assuring the effectiveness of regional and local administration. In this direction the Centre took the following steps. First, to supplement administrative mechanisms, the Centre also used political institutions – parties and elections – to eliminate regionalism from the political life of the country, and the vertical integration of all regional political processes.[52] The law on political parties, adopted in 2001, forbade the registration of regional political parties, which were for the most part the political vehicles of the regional elites.[53] The Centre required the regions to introduce for elections to regional legislatures the mixed electoral system which had been used for State Duma elections in 1993-2003: no less than 50 per cent of seats must be reserved for federal party lists.[54] These measures were introduced to increase the influence of parties in general and the 'party of power', United Russia in particular, over the regional political process and regional administration.

Although these reforms were successfully brought into being, the consequences were ambiguous: on the one hand, the electoral success of United Russia became possible only through the patronage of regional branches of the 'party of power' by strong governors, but not the other way around;[55] on the other hand, United Russia managed to establish influential factions in a whole series of regional legislatures, controlling their agenda-setting and decision-making processes,[56] and after 2003 this process became irreversible.

Second, the Centre advanced the idea of reducing the number of regions in the federation that had been on the agenda since 2000. However, the radical plans for regional amalgamations were rejected by the presidential administration, because the utilitarians had an interest in getting rid of some weak regions but not in having to deal with strong regions. Therefore the process of amalgamation was carefully targeted and was directed towards the absorption of autonomous districts into the *krais* and *oblasts*, from whence they had emerged in the early 1990s (see chapter 4). Perm Oblast was reunited with the Komi-Permyatskii Autonomous Okrug, Krasnoyarsk Krai with the Yevenk and Taimyr autonomous okrugs, and Kamchatka Oblast with the Koryakskii Autonomous Okrug. It is only a matter of time before the Ust'-Ordynskii and Aginskii-Buryatskii autonomous okrugs are united with Irkutsk Oblast. However, the Centre blocked the proposal by a number of financial-industrial groups to merge Tyumen Oblast and the

Khanty-Mansiskii and Yamalo-Nenetskii autonomous okrugs; the economic potential of such a 'super-region' would have been too great.[57] Regional amalgamations have proved relatively successful and have allowed the Centre to reduce the costs of economic development in the regions.

Third, in 2001, under the influence of the utilitarians, there began the process of the division of what had been shared competences between the Centre and the Subjects of the Federation. This sphere, which according to Article 72 of the Russian Constitutions covers 26 fields (from education to ecology), was during the 1990s the subject of serious dispute between the Centre and the regions. Both Centre and regions were attempting to pass to each the responsibility for taking decisions on and financing these shared competences; the Centre and the regions proved unable to agree a common policy to resolve this 'joint decision trap'.[58] The Commission on Delimitation of Competences between Levels of Government, chaired by the Deputy Head of the Presidential Administration, Dmitry Kozak, proposed and passed through the State Duma a detailed plan delimiting the competences of the Centre, the regions and local self-government in all the areas of shared competences listed in Article 72. Kozak's plan foresaw the division of all spheres of responsibility and the assignation of financial responsibility for each to a particular level of government. For example the Centre would be responsible for higher education, regions for secondary education, and municipalities for primary and pre-school education.

The reform's trajectory was, however, to collide with other priorities within the overall policy of the Centre: the institutional changes initiated by the presidential administration contradicted the preferred approach of the Ministry of Finance, which was to concentrate financial resources at the Centre and partially restore the Soviet-era 'fan' model, whereby local and regional budgets are formed from above by transfers from the Centre. The conflict between the Presidential Administration and the Ministry of Finance appeared to echo, both institutionally and substantially, the stand-off between the Ministry of Finance and the Ministry of the Interior over the *zemstvo* reform of 1864-1905.[59]

In the absence of clear governmental accountability, the head of state may have the last word in such conflicts, but only in a case where the conflict touches on key points in the political agenda. The delimitation of competences between Centre and regions, despite all its significance, was not in 2002-3 such a priority for the Kremlin, and therefore the necessary amendments to the Tax and Budget Codes, which would have been essential to create the system of inter-budgetary finance in line with Kozak's plan, were blocked by the Ministry of Finance.

In 2004 the State Duma nonetheless passed a law containing the amendments to sectoral legislation necessary for implementing the Kozak plan, envisaging changes in the method of financing much of the state's social expenditure and, effectively, devolving responsibility for a wide range of social expenditure onto regions and municipalities. It was this set of amendments, known as Federal Law No. 122, that brought in its wake the monetization of social guarantees to many categories of Russian citizens (veterans, disabled and others). As a result of mistaken estimates about the amount of compensation necessary and inefficient methods of payment, the Law's entry into force in early 2005 was greeted by massive social protest, which only subsided after the Centre had transferred substantial extra funds to the regions. Without going further into the details of this policy, it is worth noting that shortcomings in the way the Law allocated competences to the federal and regional levels contributed to the failure of the monetization policy, and this was to put a brake on further major developments in the reform of the delimitation of competences between the Centre and regions, until the end of the electoral cycle in 2008.

Fourth, the Kozak Commission prepared a new Law on General Principles of Local Self-Government in the Russian Federation, adopted by the State Duma in October, 2003, in the face of objections from self-governmentalists and the 'Left' faction,[60] who saw the law as bringing about the *étatization* of local government in the spirit of the *zemstvo* counter-reform of 1890-2. The Law not only changed the structure and boundaries of local government, introducing multiple tiers, but substantially increased the numbers of municipalities. It changed the financing of local government in the direction of the 'fan' model referred to above, as well as introducing compulsory horizontal equalization between municipalities (distributing funds extracted from the better-off municipalities) and envisaging the possibility of *de facto* bankruptcy of municipalities, which could now be placed under external administration. The Law was criticized for placing more emphasis on making municipalities responsible for local questions rather than creating the conditions in which they could actually resolve these.[61] There were, however, more fundamental problems to be overcome before the Law was implemented – notably the establishment of new municipalities, boundary changes and the reform of local finance and the associated problems of inter-budgetary finance that had not been resolved by the Ministry of Finance or the regions. The entry into force of the new law was first postponed until the beginning of 2006 and at that stage neither the managerialists nor the regional leaders nor, in the end, the State Duma had any direct interest in the law's application. Thus, it was decided to let the regions decide their own timetable of implementation of the law over the period 2006-9[62] (see Chapters 10–12).

Overall, the second stage of the reform was less successful than the first: the Centre's policy was only partially implemented, and then not in the correct sequence.[63] It was at this point that the coalition that had been formed in 2000 in favour of recentralization fell apart. Insofar as the Centre had been able to fulfil successfully most of the objectives of the first stage of federal reforms, the perceived need for the recentralization seemed to have been exhausted, and some of the local self-governmentalists began to see in it a threat to the democratic gains of the 1990s. The regional dimension of the national policy also ceased to be a priority for the managerialists who were becoming more interested in preserving the status quo than introducing further reforms. Paradoxically, therefore, it was the early success of the recentralization campaign that hindered its further advance.

Against this background, the abolition of direct gubernatorial elections, although decided in the autumn of 2004 as a response to a very specific set of circumstances, was nonetheless a logical culmination of the policy of recentralization. Although, from the point of view of effective administration, it arguably added little that was new, its political consequences were quite predictable. First of all, the Centre minimized political uncertainty in the regions, which would otherwise have arisen from unpredictable results of competitive elections. In addition the increase in the political weight of the regional legislatures, which accompanied the weakening of the now appointed regional heads, served to strengthen the position of 'United Russia' (it was no accident that in the autumn of 2005 there was a decision to give the power of proposing candidates for the post of regional head to whichever political party had won a majority in the elections to the regional legislature). However, on a personal level little really changed in Centre–regional relations: in most regions the existing regional heads were reappointed. As of October 2006, previous incumbents had been appointed in thirty-four out of forty-nine oblasts,[64] although several were subsequently dismissed. In addition all the existing heads of republics were appointed to their posts. New leaders were only appointed in cases where the Centre had personal reservations about individual personalities (Ivanovo Oblast, Altai Republic) or where there was a serious conflict within the regional elite (Saratov and Nizhegorodskaya Oblasts) (see Chapter 5).

Appointment of a regional head 'from outside' (i.e. from outside the region) has been untypical, and has only occurred in a small number of cases (Ivanovo, Nizhegorodskaya, Kaliningrad Oblasts). This reflects not only a lack of suitable candidates at the Centre for regional posts, but also the Centre's tendency towards risk aversion, and a desire to maintain the status quo in Centre–regional relations, whilst holding the appointed regional heads responsible for the situation in the regions entrusted to them.

By the beginning of 2006 the policy of recentralization in Russia had been taken to its logical conclusion. If we leave to one side the unresolved problems facing federal policy in the ethnic republics of the North Caucasus[65] then it is possible to consider the vast majority of regions as fully subordinate to the Centre, politically, economically and administratively. What, then, does this 'new centralism' mean for Russian politics?

'New centralism': costs and benefits

At first sight the policy of recentralization may be seen to have resulted in the re-establishment of the managerialists' dream of the 'good' Soviet Union. Regional and local autonomy has been replaced by a system of controls from above; the vagaries of competitive elections have been eliminated not only by unequal electoral arrangements now in force in the regions, but also through the abolition of elections of regional heads; regional governmental institutions have taken their place in a Russia-wide administrative hierarchy and regional markets may in many respects be seen to have become part of a vertically integrated corporation headed by Gazprom. In terms of political status and administrative functions, regional executive heads had, by the mid-2000s, come to resemble the First Secretary of the *Obkom* (Regional Committee) of the Communist Party of the Soviet Union.

Comparing today's governors with the 'soviet prefects' (as the obkom first secretaries were described by Jerry F. Hough in his well-known study of regional government in the USSR),[66] enables a number of parallels to be drawn between the 'new centralism' and the Soviet model of government. Just as thirty–forty years ago, the Russian *oblasts* and *krais* are run by officials who are *de facto* central appointees but formally approved by the regional elite. Their fulfilment of the most important economic tasks – ensuring territorial development and the attraction of resources into the region – depends as in the past on their ability to exercise informal lobbying at the Centre. Their room for political manoeuvre in the region and beyond is constrained by the structure of powerful economic interests and the associated phenomena of 'regionalism' and 'departmentalism' at the regional level. Finally there is the tendency for regional authorities to become intertwined, as in the 'state corporatist' model, noted in several studies,[67] and which is not too distant from the system depicted by Hough. Of course, the parallels only go so far. The 'party of power', United Russia is not a reincarnation of the CPSU. The roles of Gazprom or power monopoly RAO EES in the regions and in the country as a whole is scarcely reminiscent of the All-Union ministries of the past, and the governors have not (yet) become 'post-soviet prefects'. Nonetheless, the 'new centralism' and the Soviet model of government do share a common foundation in the non-competitive nature of the political regime (both at the Centre and, even more so, in the regions) and the monopolization of the economy, now based not on central planning but on rent-seeking.

In this respect, the decision to abolish direct gubernatorial elections was not simply the product of a contingent political agenda, facilitated by circumstance (as in, for example, the proclamation of the federal reform as the Centre's reaction to the crisis of the 1990s). On the contrary, it was a strategic step, which was intended to reinforce the emergent system of political and economic relations between the Centre and regions. The Centre's orientation towards the (re-) establishment of a non-competitive institutional environment in politics and economics has led to the conservation of 'regional authoritarianisms' and 'closed markets' in the regions. All these phenomena are successfully accommodated in the system of 'new centralism': concealed behind the façade of a drive towards political and economic modernization in the regions lies a deepening of the clientelistic relations that flourished so markedly during the 1990s.[68]

In spite of the fact that the sustained economic growth that Russia has been experiencing would be seen, objectively, as favouring a major shift in the direction of decentralization (not least in fiscal terms[69]), in fact it is the opposite which has occurred. This is borne out by the following key examples (there are many more):

- The Centre's insistence on regulating all utility tariffs, rather than entrusting responsibility to the regions.
- Inter-regional budget equalization (the policy of negative transfers[70]), intended to redistribute budget funds from 'rich' to 'poor' regions.
- Repeated proposals from the federal centre to introduce temporary financial management of highly-subsidized region. The new Law on Natural Resources, which advocates the designation of such resources as exclusively federal, and the removal from the regional authorities of any decision-making role regarding the granting of licenses or control over the exploitation of mineral deposits.[71]

To some extent these measures were determined by the Russian 'political business cycle'. In the run-up to the federal elections of 2007–8 the Centre had an interest in being the main source of benefits for the regions and their voters, thereby assuring its desired election result,[72] whilst the governors would no longer have any such incentive, as they no longer depended on the preferences of voters. But, apart from such short-term effects it is worth considering some longer-term factors favouring recentralization in Russia. These have more to do with the increasing importance of natural resources in the country's overall economic development. Insofar as the country is increasingly dependent on energy-related exports, so the Russian elite has become more interested in concentrating the rents that may be extracted, and therefore in favour of long-term centralization. This has meant that the recentralization drive has continued right up to the end of the 2007–8 electoral cycle.

What are the consequences of 'new centralism' in terms of political transformation in Russia? One way of assessing this would be to compare the benefits (of reduced transaction costs in regional government) with the costs (in terms of greater central control). Standardization of institutional design significantly narrowed the scope for diversity of regional regimes and governmental systems. By the mid-2000s the Russian regions have undergone bureaucratic rationalization in the Weberian sense of homogenization of rules and procedures. However, this homogenization was not brought about through increased openness and transparency of policy and administration in notorious regional regimes such as those of Bashkortostan or Kalmykiya, but through the imposition of new 'rules of the game' on all regions without exception, regardless of results.[73] According to the Moscow Carnegie Centre, the decline in the quality of democratic (especially electoral) processes that occurred in Russian regions over the period 2001–5 occurred as a result of a fall in the average scores of those regions that had previously been considered more politically open and pluralistic.[74] Of course, dependence of political processes on electoral preferences does not in itself guarantee effective regional government – on the contrary the regions were also subject to political cycles, electoral populism and state capture by economic interest groups.[75] Nonetheless, the subsequent separation of governors from dependence on the electorate has meant there is even less incentive for effective regional government: accountability to the electorate has been entirely replaced by accountability to the federal authorities.[76]

At the same time the Centre proved unable to solve the principal-agent problem in its relations with the regions. It has no possibility of gaining an accurate assessment of the effectiveness of regional administrations (experience thus far has shown that the Presidents' representatives or the Ministry of Regional Development have insufficient capacity to perform this role), nor does it have workable instruments for improving the situation (beyond the power of appointment). In this situation the Centre is pursuing a dual course. On the one hand, it invests its resources in expensive but not particularly profitable initiatives aimed at securing control over the more problematic regions (the extreme case being the republics of the North Caucasus); one the other, it becomes hostage to systematic distortion of information by regional authorities and regional branches of federal services, all exclusively serving their own interests. This has given rise to massive abuse of power in the regions, which could become mere fiefdoms, delivered to the whim of their governors by informal agreements with the Centre, offering 'non-interference in return for loyalty'. The run-up to the federal elections of 2007–8 has brought this scenario nearer, to the degree that federal election results depend to a certain degree on the behaviour of regional elites.

One way of solving the principal-agent problem would be for the Centre to stimulate competition between different agents, thereby reducing the existing information asymmetry. In particular economic growth encourages regions to compete with each other to attract investment, including foreign direct investment.[77] However, if we leave out of the analysis the specialized sectoral profile or special geographical location of particular regions and look at regions overall, it is clear that the Centre is still, as in Soviet times, the main source of economic benefits, the distribution of which partly reflects political interests rather than the pursuit of greater effectiveness. In the 1970s, for example, the rapid development of automobile and aerospace manufacturing in Ul'yanovsk (which had previously seen only modest development) was driven by the Federal authorities' wish to create a 'shop window of socialism' in Lenin's home city.[78] For similar reasons, in 2005 the building of a Toyota assembly plant was launched not in Nizhnii Novgorod (at the site of the GAZ automobile factory, as originally discussed) but on a vacant site in a St Petersburg suburb that has become a showpiece for market development in Putin's home city.

The non-competitive political and economic environment draws the regional elites and the Centre into informal bargaining with each other, so that informational symmetry, far from being reduced, is actually increased. The development of alternative mechanisms for central control of regions, primarily via the penetration of all levels of the system by the 'party of power' United Russia, has yet to bring the Centre any substantial dividends in regional policy or governance. In principle, the Kremlin's drive to construct its power base in the regions and the country as a whole on party mechanisms rather than personalities is a rational strategy with reasonable chances of success,[79] but at the time of writing the balance between costs and benefits under the 'new centralism' remains as difficult as ever to ascertain

In place of a conclusion: out of the frying pan into the fire?

The transformation of Centre–regional relations in Russia in the 2000s may be summed up under the heading of 'out of the frying pan into the fire'. The pace and results of the recentralization policy in Russia was pre-determined by the genesis of 'new centralism' and the managerialist ideology that dominated throughout its creation and early stages of implementation. In the 1990s, after the collapse of the Soviet Union, the Russian government underwent such a high degree of fragmentation (not least regarding centre–regional relations), that the result bore comparison with the Hobbesian notions of the 'state of nature' and 'war of each against all'.[80] After 2000 the situation in Russia rapidly changed so that the more apposite comparison was with Hobbes's Leviathan: the country's fragmentation had been halted and reversed thanks to a reassertion of the administrative capacity of the centralized state.[81] The Centre, having lost control of the levers of power for a decade, was once again able to establish its supremacy over the regions, rising above them and drawing them in, just as in Leviathan. However, unlike with Hobbes's model, here it is not a question of sovereignty being delegated from below, on the basis of a social compact, but a victory by the Kremlin ruling group in a zero-sum game which has been implemented from the top down via an 'obligatory consensus' of clites. The fragmented and weak Centre of the 1990s was replaced after 2000 by a Centre that possessed sufficient administrative capacity to impose new 'rules of the game' on the regions.

However the low level of autonomy in Russian governance, the weak rule of law and the preference of Russian elites for rent-seeking from natural resources, all create the conditions for a predatory state[82] which has become a political instrument in the hands of the ruling groups, and is used by them for short-term ends. The presence of these characteristics of the Russian state creates new challenges for all dimensions of Russian politics, including the regional dimension. The Centre has succeeded in minimizing the autonomy of the regions, but it is not yet clear whether it will be able to derive any benefit in terms of the country's overall development, or whether there has merely been a division of power and property, for private benefit.

It is not given to history to operate in the subjunctive mood, and we cannot therefore know whether an alternative approach to that of 'new centralism' could, at the turn of the new century, have led to a more propitious outcome from the point of view of Russia's political development. For example, had the regional leaders' coalition OVR won against Unity in the Duma elections of 1999, the result would probably have been continued decentralization of the political structure and party system, placing in question the very survival of the Centre's administrative capacity. Such a turn of events could have been more dangerous than any 'new centralism'. It does not, however, follow that the centralizing political choices made by the Centre after 2000 (in particular the reform of the Federal Council and local self-government, and the abolition of gubernatorial elections) were strictly determined by past events. The 'Soviet resolution of post-Soviet problems' was facilitated by, on the one hand, the elimination of competition among federal elites and the subsequent monopoly of the Kremlin over policy and decision-making, and on the other hand, by the normative ideals and political thinking of the country's leadership. Therefore, as long as these two factors remain unchanged, no radical alternation to the policy of recentralization should be expected in Russia.

Decentralization in Russia in the 1990s flowed from the country's difficult adaptation to the major changes it faced – the collapse of the Soviet Union, market reforms and the creation of new political institutions. Its appearance may have been symptomatic of the prolonged growing pains of the Russian state that appeared to have dissipated after 2000. However, the cure may in time turn out to be worse than the disease, or itself cause more threatening chronic illnesses. The next few years will show whether the Kremlin's new Leviathan will bring forth effective and stable regional development or whether it will bring new problems for the country to overcome.

Notes

1 The author is grateful to Tomila Lankina and Lydia Galkina for their comments on an earlier version of the chapter.
2 Vladimir Gel'man, Sergei Ryzhenkov, Elena Belokurova and Nadezhda Borisova, *Avtonomiya ili kontrol'? Reforma Mestnoi Vlasi v Gorodakh Rossii 1991–2001*, Moscow, St Petersburg: Letnii Sad, 2002.
3 See Daniel Treisman, *After the Deluge: Regional Crises and Political Consolidation in Russia*, Ann Arbor, MI: University of Michigan Press, 1999; Alfred Stepan, 'Russian Federalism in Comparative Perspective', *Post-Soviet Affairs*, Vol. 16, No. 2, 2000, pp. 133–76.
4 Oksana Dmitrieva, *Regional Development: The USSR and After*, London: UCL Press, 1996.
5 Dmitry Gorenburg, *Minority Ethnic Mobilization in the Russian Federation*, Cambridge: Cambridge University Press, 2003.
6 Steven L. Solnick, 'Is the center too weak or too strong in the Russian Federation? in Valerie Sperling (ed.), *Building the Russian State. Institutional Crisis and the Quest for Democratic Governance*, Boulder, CO: Westview Press, 2000, pp. 137–56; Cameron Ross, *Federalism and Democratization in Russia*, Manchester: Manchester University Press, 2002; Kathryn Stoner-Weiss, 'Whither the central state? regional sources of Russia's stalled reforms', in Michael McFaul,

Kathryn Stoner-Weiss (eds), *After the Collapse of Communism: Comparative Lessons of Transition*, Cambridge: Cambridge University Press, 2004, pp. 130–72.

7 Treisman, *After the Deluge*; Anna Likhtenshtein, 'Parties of power: the electoral strategies of Russia's elites', in Vladimir Gel'man, Grigorii V. Golosov, Elena Meleshkina (eds.), *The 1999–2000 National Elections in Russia: Analyses, Documents and Data*, Berlin: Sigma, 2005, pp. 59–75.

8 Vladimir Gel'man, Sergei Ryzhenkov, Michael Brie, *Making and Breaking Democratic Transitions: The Comparative Politics of Russia's Regions*, Lanham, MD: Rowman and Littlefield, 2003; Grigorii V. Golosov, *Political Parties in the Regions of Russia: Democracy Unclaimed*, Boulder, CO: Lynne Reinner, 2004.

9 Sergei Mitrohkin, 'Predposilki i osnovniye etapy detsentralizatsii gosudarstvennoi vlasti v Rossii', in Galina Lukhterkhandt-Mikhaleva and Sergei Ryzhenkov (eds), *Tsentr – regiony – mestnoe samoupravlenie*, Moscow, St. Petersburg: Lentnii Sad, 2001, pp. 47–87; Stoner-Weiss, 'Whither the Central State?'.

10 Vadim Volkov, *Violent Entrepreneurs: The Role of Force in the Making of Russian Capitalism*, Ithaca, NY: Cornell Press, 2002.

11 Yakov Panne, 'Treugol'nik sobstvennikov v regional'noi promyshlennosti', in Vladimir Klimanov and Natal'ya Zubarevich (eds), *Politika i ekonomika v Regional'nykh Uzmerenii*, Moscow and St Petersburg, Letnii Sad, 2000, pp. 109–20.

12 Daniel Treisman, 'Russia renewed?', *Foreign Affairs*, Vol. 81, No. 6, 2002, pp. 58–72.

13 Mitrokhin, 'Predposilki i osnovniye'

14 Darrell Slider, 'Russia's market-distorting federalism', *Post-Soviet Geography and Economics*, Vol. 38, No. 8, 1997, pp. 445–60.

15 Leonid Polishchuk, 'Rossiskaya model' "peregovornovo federalizma": politico-ekonomicheskiy analiz', in Vladimir Klimanov and Natal'ya Zubarevich (eds.) *Politika i ekonomika v regional'nom izmerenii*, Moscow, St Petersburg, Letniii Sad, 2000, pp. 88–108.

16 Mitrokhin, 'Predposilki i osnovniye', p. 74.

17 For detailed analysis see Peter Reddaway and Robert W. Orttung (eds), *The Dynamics of Russian Politics: Putin's Reform of Federal-Regional Relations, Vol. 1*, Lanham, MD: Rowman and Littlefield, 2003; Peter Reddaway and Robert W. Orttung (eds), *The Dynamics of Russian Politics: Putin's Reform of Federal-Regional Relations, Vol. 2*, Lanham, MD: Rowman and Littlefield, 2005, pp. 123–43.

18 Christopher Speckhard, 'The Tie That Binds: Big Business and Center-Periphery Relations in Post-Soviet Russia', Ph.D Dissertation, University of Texas at Austin, 2004.

19 Ekaterina Semykina, 'Ochen' otritsatel'nye transferty', *Delo*, 14 November 2005. http://www.idelo.ru/395/9.html (accessed 16 October, 2006).

20 For comparative data, see Mikhail Filippov, Peter Ordeshook and Olga Shvetsova, *Designing Federalism: A Theory of Self-Sustainable Federal Institutions*, Cambridge: Cambridge University Press, 2004, p. 6.

21 Stoner-Weiss, 'Whither the central state?'.

22 See, for example, Kimitaka Matsuzato (ed.), *Fenomen Vladimira Putina i Rossiskiye regiony: pobeda neozhidennaya ili zakonomernaya?*, Moscow: Materik, 2004.

23 Vladimir Gel'man, 'From "feckless pluralism" to "dominant power politics"? The transformation of Russia's party system', *Demokratizatsiya: The Journal of Post-Soviet Democratization*, Vol. 13, No. 4, 2006, pp. 545–61.

24 Nikolai Petrov, 'Federalizm po-Rossiskiy', *Pro et Contra*, Vol. 1, 2000, pp. 7–33.

25 Natal'ya Zubarevich, 'Prishel, uvidel, pobedil? Krupny biznez i regional'naya vlast'', *Pro et Contra*, Vol. 7, No. 1, 2002, pp. 107–20.

26 Vladimir Gel'man, 'The unrule of law in the making: the politics of informal institution building in Russia', *Europe-Asia Studies*, Vol. 56, No. 7, 2004, pp. 1026–30.

27 Douglass North, *Structure and Change in Economic History*, New York: W.W. Norton, 1981, p. 49.
28 Paul Sabatier, Hans Jenkins-Smith, *Policy Change and Learning: An Advocacy Coalition Approach*, Boulder, CO: Westview Press, 1993.
29 Gel'man, Ryzhenkov, Belokurov, Borisova, pp. 46–8.
30 Anton Steen, *Political Elites and the New Russia: The Power Bases of Yeltsin's and Putin's Regimes*, London: Routledge Curzon, 2003, pp. 95–117.
31 John Kingdon, *Agendas, Alternatives, and Public Policies*, Boston, MA: Little, Brown, 1984.
32 Stoner-Weiss, 'Whither the central state?'.
33 Treisman, 1997; Stoner-Weiss, 'Whither the central state?'.
34 Thomas Remington, 'Majorities without mandates: the Federation Council since 2000', *Europe-Asia Studies*, Vol. 55, No. 5, 2003, pp. 667–91.
35 Vladimir Gel'man, 'Why it is so difficult to form a regional coalition', *Russian Regional Report*, Vol. 4, No. 16, 29 April 1999.
36 Anna Likhtenshtein, 'Parties of power: the electoral strategies of Russia's elites', in Vladimir Gel'man, Grigorii V. Golosov, Elena Meleshkina (eds), *The 1999–2000 National Elections in Russia: Analyses, Documents and Data*, Berlin: Sigma, 2005, pp. 59–75.
37 Andrei Shleifer, Daniel Treisman, *Without a Map: Political Tactics and Economic Reform in Russia*, Cambridge, MA: MIT Press, 2000, ch. 4.
38 Likhtenstein; Gel'man, 2006.
39 *Nezavisimaya Gazeta*, 22 February 2000.
40 Reddaway and Orttung, 2003.
41 For details see, Elena Chebankova, 'The limitations of central authority in the regions and the implications for the evolution of Russia's federal system', *Europe-Asia Studies*, Vol. 57, No. 7, 2005, pp. 934–9.
42 See Remington; Darrell Slider, 'The regions' impact on federal policy: the Federation Council', in Peter Reddaway and Robert W. Orttung (eds), *The Dynamics of Russian Politics: Putin's Reform of Federal-Regional Relations, Vol. 2*, Lanham, MD: Rowman and Littlefield, 2005, pp. 123–43.
43 See Kirill Fyodorov, 'Politicheskii kurs v sferye mestnovo nalogoblozheniya v Rossii', *Polis*, No. 4, 2003, pp. 71–81; Andrei Chernyavsky and Karen Vartapetov, 'Municipal finance reform and local self-governance in Russia', *Post-Communist Economies*, Vol. 16, No. 3, 2004, pp. 251–64.
44 Zubarevich.
45 Vladimir Pribylovskii, 'Triumphal'noye shestvie bashkirskoi izbiratel'noi tekhnologii', in Aleksandr M. Verkhovsky, Ekaterina V. Mikhailovskaya, and Vladimir V. Pribylovskii, *Rossiya Putina: Pristrastnyi Vzglyad*, Moscow: Panorama, 2003, pp. 160-3.
46 Petrov, 2003.
47 Vladimir V. Pribylovskii, 'Vybory: degradatsiya institute vyborov pri Putine', in Grigorii Belonuchkin (ed.), *Rossiya Putina: istoriya bolezni*, Moscow: Panorama, 2004, pp. 56–9.
48 Gel'man, 2002; Pribylovskii, 2003, pp. 167–8.
49 Pribylovskii, 2003, pp. 164–5; Pribylovskii, 2004, pp. 21–6.
50 For the arguments for this, see Ella Paneyakh, 'Neformal'nie instituty i formal'nie pravila: zakon deistvuyushchii vs. zakon primenyaemii', *Politicheskaya Nauka*, No. 1, 2003, pp. 35–52.
51 Gel'man, 2004.
52 Henry E. Hale, 'Party development in a federal system: the impact of Putin's reforms', in Peter Reddaway and Robert W. Orttung (eds), *The Dynamics of Russian Politics: Putin's Reform of Federal-Regional Relations, Vol. 2*, Lanham, MD: Rowman and Littlefield, 2005.

53 Grigorii V. Golosov, *Political Parties in the Regions of Russia: Democracy Unclaimed*, Boulder, CO: Lynne Reinner, 2004.
54 Petr Panov, 'Reforma regional'nykh izbiratel'nykh system i razvitie politicheskikh partii v regionakh Rossii, *Polis*, No. 5, 2005, pp. 102–17.
55 Grigorii V. Golosov, 'What went wrong? Regional electoral politics and impediments to state central in Russia, 2003–2004', *PONARS Policy Memos*, No. 337, 2004.
56 Aleksei Glubotsky and Aleksander Kynev, 'Partiynaya sostavlyauschaya zakono-datel'nykh sobranii rossiskykh regiononov', *Polis*, No. 6, 2003, pp. 71–87.
57 Paul Goode, 'The Push for regional enlargement in Putin's Russia', *Post-Soviet Affairs*, Vol. 20, No. 3, 2004, pp. 219-57.
58 See Fritz Sharpf, 'The joint decision trap: lessons from German federalism and European integration', *Public Administration*, Vol. 66, No. 3, 1988, pp. 277–304.
59 See Thomas Pearson, 'Ministerial conflict and the politics of zemstvo reform, 1864–1905', in Alfred B. Evans and Vladimir Gel'man (eds), *The Politics of Local Government in Russia*, Lanham, MD: Rowman and Littlefield, 2004, pp. 45–67.
60 Marina Liborakina, 'Atribut vertikali vlasti ili osnova grazhdankovo obschestva?', *K?nstitutsionnoe Pravo: Vostochnoevropeiskoe Obozrenie*, No. 3, 2003, pp. 144-51.
61 Tomila Lankina, 'President Putin's local government reforms', in Peter Reddaway and Robert W. Orttung (eds), *The Dynamics of Russian Politics: Putin's Reform of Federal-Regional Relations, Vol. 2*, Lanham, MD: Rowman and Littlefield, 2005, pp. 145-77.
62 Tomila Lankina, 'New system weakens municipalities', *Russian Regional Report*, Vol. 10, No. 17, 18 October 2005.
63 See the critical analysis by Chebankova, 2005.
64 Nikolai Petrov, 'Naznacheniye gubernatorov: itogi pervovo goda', *Moscow Carnegie Centre Briefing*, Vol. 8, No. 3, 2006; Vitaly Ivanov, 'O gubernatorskoi reforme –2', *Delovaya gazeta 'Vzglyad'*, 21 September 2006, http://www.vz.ru/columns/2006/9/21/49686.html (accessed 16 October, 2006).
65 This problem requires analysis beyond the scope of this contribution.
66 Jerry F. Hough, *The Soviet Prefects: The Local Party Organs in Industrial Decision-Making*, Cambridge, MA: Harvard University Press, 1969.
67 Natalya Lapina and Alla Chirikova, *Putinskiye reformy i potentsial vliyaniya regional'nykh elit*, Moscow: Institute of Sociology of the Russian Academy of Sciences, 2004, pp. 80-93.
68 Mikhail Afanasiev, *Klientilizm i Rossiskaya Gosudarstvennost'*, Moscow: Moscow Public Science Foundation, 2000.
69 Kenneth Davey, *Fiscal Autonomy and Efficiency: Reforms in the Former Soviet Union*, Budapest: Local Government and Public Service Reform Initiative, 2002; Semykina.
70 Igor' Ivanov, 'Den' donora: vedenie otritsatel'nykh transfertov stavit krest na "proekte Matvienko"', *Gazeta.ru*, 3 November 2005. http://www.gazeta.ru/comments/2005/11/03_a_467855.shtml (accessed 16 October 2006).
71 Marina Sokolovskaya, 'Nedra snova peretrakhnut', *Moskovskaya delovaya gazeta 'Biznes'*, 3 November 2005. http://www.b-online.ru/articles/a_8933.shtml (accessed 16 October 2006).
72 Andrei Scherbak, 'Ekonomicheskii rost i itogi dumskikh vyborov 2003', *Politicheskaya Nauka*, No. 2, 2005, pp. 105–23.
73 Aleksandr Kynev, 'Perekhod k smeshannym vyboram v regionakh – 'prinudi-tel'naya transformatsiya', *Polis*, No. 2, 2004, pp. 32–40.
74 Petrov, 2005.
75 Joel Hellmann, 'Winners take all: the politics of partial reform in post-communist transition', *World Politics*, Vol. 50, No. 2, 1998, pp. 203–34.
76 Polischuk.
77 Ibid., pp. 175–6.

78 Gel'man, Ryzenkov, Brie, pp. 189–93.
79 Gel'man, 2006.
80 Volkov.
81 Brian Taylor, 'Putin's state building project: issues for the second term', *PONARS Policy Memos*, No. 323, 2003.
82 North.

2 Between a rock and a hard place

The Russian Federation in comparative perspective

Michael Burgess

Introduction: taking stock of Russia's past

In a seminal article on comparative federalism published just over forty years ago, Anthony Birch observed that it was much better to approach the study of federal systems by trying first to identify the similarities between different systems than to begin with basic conceptual matters and definitions of federalism that served to underline their differences and made comparative analysis much more difficult to achieve.[1] In this chapter I want to follow the line of reasoning adopted by Nancy Bermeo who believes that institutions – and by inference federal systems – 'are best assessed from multiple vantage points' so that 'a fair analysis requires both comparative and historical perspectives'.[2] To be effective, comparative federalism must be rooted in historical analysis so that important legacies, which establish lines of continuity indispensable to our understanding of contemporary change, are acknowledged and incorporated in current explanations.

In the case of the Russian Federation, the Soviet legacy of federalism has to be confronted and addressed as a historical and ideological specificity before any meaningful comparative perspectives can be assembled. As we shall see, most of the current problems, stresses and strains together with the contemporary challenges, trends and developments in Russian federalism can be ascribed to this troublesome legacy. The Russian Federation that came into existence during 1991-3 emerged in the most difficult and unpromising of circumstances, which certainly did not bode well for future democratic stability. It was also built upon an extremely fragile foundation, one that replaced the former Soviet federal state structure cemented by a unitary centralized single party system, which effectively controlled all the institutions of policy-making and policy-implementation together with all the lines of political communication. It was, in short, a federal facade.

This means that we must be both careful and cautious in deciding precisely what comparative perspectives to choose. We are confronted by two conceptually and empirically distinct federations that existed in different historical epochs, one that endured for nearly seventy years, as the Union of Soviet Socialist Republics, the USSR (1922–91), and the other as its putative successor, the Russian Federation, formally for a mere fifteen years (1993–to date). There might be some lingering intellectual doubts about how accurate it is to construe the Russian Federation as the direct successor to the USSR but for our purposes in this chapter the period 1991–3 can be viewed as a convenient interregnum during which the preponderant Russian state re-emerged from Soviet disintegration and reasserted itself with mixed success *vis-à-vis* the remnants of the former empire both within and without Russia proper.

From this brief introductory survey we can appreciate that for many observers the comparison that is most relevant is not so much with other federations as with Russia's own past. In a sense it is impossible to compare it with federations outside Russia without first taking stock of its own albeit chequered federal experience. With this in mind the chapter will be divided into two main parts. The first part is itself subdivided into two sections, notably the enduring Soviet legacy of federalism in theory and practice followed by a second legacy, namely, the disintegration of the Soviet Union and the resurgence of Russia during 1991–3. We will begin with the Soviet legacy of federalism and we will examine the nature, meaning and political uses of this legacy and some of its implications for the Russian Federation. But we will also look subsequently at the USSR and the Russian Federation from the comparative perspective of the origins and formation of federations. This second section on the legacy of Soviet disintegration is important from the particular standpoint of its serious practical implications both for the Russian state and for the nature of Russian federalism. This approach, in turn, will enable us to place the Yeltsin era of Russian federalism that followed the initial federation building process (1993–2000) in an accurate historical perspective so that the succeeding, currently controversial, Putin era (2000–8) can also receive an even-handed contemporary assessment.

The second part of the chapter will briefly explore the Russian Federation from four distinct comparative perspectives, some of which emerge from the first part. These are identified in the following way: the federal bargain; historical legacies of centralization; ethnic diversity and multi-nationalism; and asymmetrical federalism. Together these four principal perspectives assist towards an overall assessment of the character and prospects for democratic stability of the Russian Federation from the standpoint of comparative analysis. The chapter will conclude with some thoughts and reflections about the extraordinarily difficult predicament that confronts political leadership in the Russian Federation in the new millennium. Let us begin our assessment with the Soviet legacy of federalism in theory and practice.

The Soviet legacy of federalism in theory and practice

What was the nature and meaning and what were the political purposes of the so-called 'Soviet legacy' of federalism? Article 70 of the Constitution of the USSR (1977) referred to the Soviet state in the following way: 'an integral, federal, multinational state formed on the principle of socialist federalism as a result of the free self-determination of nations and the voluntary association of equal Soviet Socialist Republics'.[3] But in contrast to the French, German and American Constitutions the Soviet Constitution was not drafted in reaction to the past. On the contrary, as its Preamble makes clear, it was drafted in continuity with the previous constitutions of the country. Consequently in order to trace the origins of Soviet federalism we have to go back at least to the Stalin Constitution, 1936 and the first Constitution of the USSR in 1924. Indeed, we can already identify the first step in the direction of Soviet federalism that foreshadowed the USSR and was consummated earlier in 1922 with the signing of the Treaty of Union among the Russian Soviet Federal Socialist Republic (RSFSR), the Ukraine, White Russia and the Transcaucasian Soviet Federal Socialist Republic (TSFSR).[4] The first documents of a Soviet federal or quasi-federal nature were the 'Declaration of the Rights of the Toiling and Exploited People' promulgated in January 1918 and incorporated later in the 1918 Constitution, and the resolution of the Third Soviet Congress on the 'Federal Institutions of the Russian Republic'.[5]

The original motive for the formal adoption of federalism first in Bolshevik Russia and then in the USSR was simple and straightforward: it was eagerly seized upon to prevent the secession of the nationalities, a phenomenon that returned to haunt both Boris Yeltsin and Mikhail Gorbachev over seventy years later. The threat of separation was a direct result of the post-revolutionary programme of national self-determination in Russia and the resort to federalism required Lenin to perform considerable ideological acrobatics to justify it in terms of established Marxist-Leninist theory. He quickly rationalized federalism as merely a transitional step to a real 'democratic centralism':

> In the example of the Russian Soviet Republic we see most graphically that the federation we are introducing will serve now as the surest step to the most solid unification of the different nationalities into a single, democratic, centralized Soviet State.[6]

As Vernon Aspaturian noted over half a century ago, this apologia of federalism emerged as one of the chief characteristics of Soviet federalism:

> only when it is realized that the Soviet Union regards federalism not as an ultimate end, but only a necessary, but temporary, expedient, to be given form but not substance, can one really understand the wide divergence between the theory and practice of federalism in the USSR.[7]

These words echo down the years. The immediate purpose of federalism was twofold: 'first, to prevent further separation and, second, to entice the already seceded border areas back into the Russian state'.[8] And once again these remarks are prophetic: they are imperatives that could conceivably refer to the Russia of the period 1991–3.

The nature of the Soviet legacy of federalism is one that was determined by its original purpose, namely, to rescue the Russian state from the imminent threat of complete disintegration wrought by Lenin's post-revolutionary support for national self-determination. Federalism was both salvation and solution, but it was initially only a short-term political strategy – a temporary expedient – designed to achieve immediate objectives. It was never intended that it should become an integral structural and institutional feature of any future Soviet state. Indeed, it had been categorically rejected by Marx, Engels and Lenin who collectively construed it as nothing more than a mere survival of feudal particularism. The temporary, however, became permanent because of the necessity to elevate the constitutional deception to a political myth and then to perpetuate it as a powerful ideological symbol of 'the free self-determination of nations' in a voluntary union of equal constituent republics. In this way the form took priority over the substance.

In these peculiar circumstances it is small wonder that political scientists in general and scholars of federalism in particular should view the Soviet legacy of federalism with both consistent scepticism and not a little intellectual disdain. It is easy to pour scorn on something that is so transparently a fake. A quick glance at the last Soviet Constitution of 1977 confirms this. Article 70 mentioned above is severely qualified by Article 3 which confirms the organizational basis of the Soviet state to be 'the principle of democratic centralism' while Article 6 alludes to the 'leading and guiding force of Soviet society and the nucleus of its political system, of all state organizations and public organizations' to be the Communist Party, the CPSU. If we add to these two articles that which deals with the role of the Supreme Soviet (Article 108), it is obvious that 'the highest body of state authority' that was 'empowered to deal with all matters within the jurisdiction of the Union' succeeded in fusing the legislative, executive and judicial branches of government rather than separating them.[9] This resulted in the most accurate description of the USSR as 'a multi-national unitary state'.[10]

But if it is clear that the USSR was not a federal state in the sense that federation is conventionally understood in the West, it is also true, as Filippov and others noted, that 'the mechanisms by which the union was sustained were not (at least following Stalin's death) wholly coercive and the federal aspects of its political processes were not entirely orthogonal to those of its democratic counterparts'.[11] This view of the USSR represents a useful corrective interpretation to the extent that it acknowledges a minimal degree of multi-level bargaining indicative of competing vested interests within the restrictive centralized Soviet polity, but it also compels scholars of federalism to reflect upon a particular aspect of this federal legacy. The federal credentials of the USSR have always been regarded as a sham and *prima facie* we would not expect such scholars to place the Soviet Union for comparative purposes in the same company as authentic established liberal democratic federations like the United States of America (USA) or Switzerland. This, however, is precisely what one leading scholar of federalism, William Riker, did during the Cold War years. Determined to promote the study of comparative federalism as a genuine objective political science inquiry in the early 1960s, Riker included the USSR in his seminal work and gave a conspicuous nod in its direction in an oft-quoted observation which contested the claim that 'federal forms are adopted as a device to guarantee freedom' and railed against the numerous writers on the subject who had committed 'this ideological fallacy'.[12] He believed that this falsehood derived from the mistaken assumption that confused the 'guarantee of provincial autonomy' in federation with 'the notion of a free society' when it was perfectly possible to 'convert the government into a dictatorship'.[13] As we will see later in the chapter, this assertion was itself erroneous.

In that same era another prominent scholar of federalism, Carl Friedrich, adopted a similar approach to the USSR, claiming that just because 'the formal federalism of the government structure is superseded and transcended by the integrating force of the CPSU ... does not mean, as is often asserted, that the federal system has no significance in the Soviet Union'.[14] His distinction between the form of the Soviet federal state structure and the substantive reality of Communist Party dominance implied that the structural features should not be dismissed as wholly inconsequential. State institutions played an important role that had practical consequences for the *operation* of the Soviet political system. Since 'uniformity was not the rule, with some republics managing to secure more autonomy than others', there existed differing 'degrees of regional independence and significant decentralization of authority'.[15] Indeed in the Brezhnev era (1964–82) Moscow 'prioritized considerations of social stability over economic or political reform' and pursued a 'federal compromise' with the provincial federal leadership that furnished them with 'a degree of power and patronage over their territories probably far more than at any time in Soviet history'.[16] Nonetheless, most scholars of federalism continued to treat the USSR as a special case, an anomaly, something that was in reality an empire not an authentic federation. And as an 'imperial federation' it was an impostor that could not be included in comparative federal studies.

In summary, then, the nature, meaning and purpose(s) of the Soviet legacy of federalism in theory and practice are interrelated in symbiotic fashion. The legacy constituted an integral feature of the revolutionary tradition that bestowed a historical legitimacy and an important ideological symbolism on the USSR. But as an imperial federation it has also had enduring implications for the Russian Federation, especially in terms of its centralizing propensities, its qualified liberal democratic credentials and its underlying authoritarian character. Let us turn now to the second legacy in our survey and assess the impact of the disintegration of the Soviet Union on the emergence of the Russian Federation.

The legacy of Soviet disintegration and the resurgence of Russia

This section of the chapter claims that the way the USSR collapsed in 1991 – the sudden and dramatic *manner* of its disintegration – had a direct impact on the formation and subsequent evolution of the Russian Federation. The chaos out of which the new federal state emerged in the years between 1990 and 1993 – the *context* of the transition – had important practical implications both for the Russian state *qua* state and for the *kind* of federation that it became. Consequently the period is characterized by two separate sets of events that are closely intertwined: the formal demise of the USSR and the resurgence of Russia. As we will see later, the relationship between these two sets of events has also had significant implications for the Russian Federation in comparative perspective.

The abrupt collapse of the USSR in 1991 continues to excite disputes and arouse controversies about how and why it occurred when it did. There exists a vast literature on these intimately interrelated arguments with many different competing explanations and I do not intend to rehearse them here. Instead we will engage with this literature only to the extent that it sheds light upon the argument advanced here. Most diagnoses, however, acknowledge with varying degrees of significance the emergence of reform communism that began in the mid-1980s, under Mikhail Gorbachev's leadership, as the principal source of change that served unintentionally to weaken the central institutional support system of the union to the point where it could no longer sustain the fundamental functions and policy priorities of a vast empire. Two summaries that succinctly encapsulate this broad generalization will be utilized here. Filippov et al. point to the impact of processes of liberalization and democratization that 'fundamentally altered federal arrangements that had prevailed for seventy years':

> The initial revision of statutory and constitutional arrangements initiated by Gorbachev upset the institutional status quo by shifting the arena of bargaining from within the Communist Party to previously unused or untested constitutional political structures. Those structures, whether good or bad as venues for bargaining, were not the institutions that either conferred legitimacy on policy or possessed legitimacy in their own right. Absent a set of common beliefs as to what institutions would coordinate or direct action within the union, the door was then open to a global renegotiation that not only encompassed the prerogatives of the union's constituent parts, but also the institutions that would link those parts to each other and to the centre. That, in combination with the authority and strategic position of those given formal voice by a partially constructed federalism that had earlier been designed to render a heterogeneous empire a single state, was the fundamental cause of the USSR's dissolution.[17]

Graham Smith summarized the circumstances that occasioned the demise of the USSR in a similar vein but with an added emphasis on 'ethno-federalism'. He described the unfolding of the Soviet Union as 'the geopolitics of defederation':

> What provided the necessary conditions for federalism to emerge on to the political agenda was the centre's eventual acknowledgement that socio-economic reform could not be effectively implemented without civil society's participation as catalyst in facilitating 'reform from above'. Having disabled the state-censored society through the twin policies of *glasnost* and democratization, the centre in effect purposely invited a multiethnic society to engage in the making of perestroika, without considering the likely implications of its actions. Consequently, the federal question became quickly bound up with 'a revolution from below' in which the ethno-regions came to shape the nature of the federal agenda.[18]

Both of these summaries share the conclusion that what happened was the politics of unintended consequences. The disintegration of the Soviet Union and the emergence of the Russian Federation were an accidental by-product of Gorbachev's reform communism. The mode of 'reform from above' provided the constituent ethno-republics with the opportunity – the institutional space – to seize the political initiative and set the pace in 'putting the issue of federation on to the reform agenda'.[19]

From the standpoint of political philosophy, ethics and political practice, Gorbachev openly repudiated what Richard Sakwa has called the 'emancipatory revolutionism of Marxian socialism' characteristic of the Soviet past.[20] But in seeking to address the yawning chasm that had opened up between 'the system's core and operating ideologies' by a 'cleansing process' that would remove 'the deformations and accretions of the operating ideology to allow a return to the core ideas', he took a calculated gamble. As Sakwa observed, Gorbachev's own 'antirevolution' was actually 'integrative', but 'the cleansing process came into contradiction with his integrative agenda, since integration in the event turned out to be something much larger than simply a return to core principles'.[21] In short, the intellectual basis of Gorbachev's reform communism was in tune with the modernizing pressures of the age but while the theoretical catharsis was long overdue its practical implementation harboured serious dangers for the future of the Soviet Union that he did not anticipate. Indeed, he badly miscalculated by overestimating the value and esteem in which the Union was held in the judgement of its constituent parts.

The lowering of the Soviet flag over the Kremlin for the last time occurred on Christmas Eve in 1991, but if we construe Soviet disintegration in terms of a process rather than a single date it began at least as early as June 1990 when Russia formally decoupled itself from the USSR and made its historic declaration of sovereignty. This event inaugurated a remarkable period of intensive constitutional and legal change that elevated sixteen ethnically defined autonomous soviet socialist republics (ASSRs) and four autonomous oblasts (AOs) to the status of constituent republics of what itself was in composition a federation, bringing the total number of 'ethnic republics' in Russia to twenty. The domino effect continued up until the summer of 1992 when the Checheno-Ingush Republic was split into Chechen and Ingush Republics, thus ensuring that, in Cameron Ross's words, 'the Soviet Union's hybrid ethno-territorial principle of federation was bequeathed to Russia'.[22] Meanwhile Gorbachev had been making last-ditch efforts to rescue the Soviet Union by cobbling together a new Union Treaty based upon asymmetrical relations with the three Baltic Republics – Latvia, Lithuania and Estonia – Georgia, Moldova and Armenia and varying degrees of federal relations with the rest of the imperial federation. The resulting nationwide referendum in March 1991 ended not with a triumphant bang but with a hollow whimper as six of the fifteen constituent Soviet republics simply refused to participate. A subsequent deal between Gorbachev and Yeltsin produced the so-called 9+1 agreement (referring to the leaders of the nine republics that did participate in the March 1991 referendum) in April but work on its completion was brought to a dramatic halt by the abortive coup of August 1991 that presaged the termination of the USSR in December.

The events and developments that occurred during the period 1990-3 in Russia and the USSR were apocalyptic. Together they represented two overlapping but distinct historical processes that occurred simultaneously and were tantamount to the chaos of destruction and reconstruction. With the disappearance of the Soviet Union – the unravelling of its empire into independent sovereign states – a resurgent Russia stepped into the vacuum created by imperial decentralization. Indeed, in many ways a large part of what we call the Soviet legacy *was* the resurgence of Russia. And these peculiar circumstances had important implications both for the Russian state and for the kind of federation that it became. In the first place it was obvious that what happened to the Soviet Union could just as conceivably happen to Russia. The collapse of communist party control allowed ethno-territoriality to become the driving force of Soviet imperial disintegration and this posed a similar threat to the territorial integrity of the new Russian state, especially in view of the territorial distribution of its own nationalities. Yeltsin, who in 1990 had actively encouraged Russia's autonomous republics to 'take as much sovereignty as they could swallow', found himself signing the Federal Treaty of March 1992, conceding greater powers to the republics and regions, in an attempt to rescue Russia from the same Soviet fate. Since these years were also characterized by Yeltsin's power struggle with Gorbachev followed by his fierce battle with the Russian parliament, it is easy to appreciate why it was also a period of weak central power that provided many opportunities for the republics to reassert their demands for national autonomy. The so-called 'parade of sovereignties' led to 'contract federalism' and 'the war of laws and sovereignties' that pushed the concept of asymmetrical federalism to its *reductio ad absurdum*.[23] The Russian state seemed to be in real danger of breaking up. Yeltsin's eventual defeat and dissolution of the parliament in October 1993 ensured that the constitutional consolidation of the state would be one that sought to rein in the recalcitrant republics and regions and subdue the assertive minority nationalities.

The Federal Treaty was not incorporated in the new Russian Constitution that was finally ratified in December 1993 because Yeltsin used his victory over the Parliament in October 1993 to claw back what he had been compelled to concede in March 1992. The new constitution therefore signified a presidential victory over parliamentary forces but it also bore the hallmarks of its creation. Andreas Heinemann-Grüder:

> The relative success of Russia's federalization … is based upon exclusive elite pacts between Moscow and the regions. The old elites in the centre and the regions recognized one another and assured one another of their status. … The executives in the centre and regions – both largely outgrowths of the old Communist power apparatus – remained unified in their interest in preserving power and strengthening the executives at the expense of legislatures. The centre–periphery pact is based upon a marginalization of legislatures, … on a disjunction between federalism and parliamentary democracy. Presidential federalism in Russia is therefore not only rooted in traditions of accumulating power at the centre but in the shared interest of central and regional elites in executive power concentration.[24]

The Russian Federation is 'a democratic federative rule of law state with a republican form of government' but it is a federal state with a presidential-prime ministerial form of government in which the office of the presidency is the primary constitutional and political force. The Russian president holds the reins of power and presidential leadership has been used to reinforce central state power. The *kind* of federation that Russia became therefore was determined by 'the context of transition' that 'played a conducive role in fostering federalization after the demise of the Soviet Union'.[25]

In summary, this brief sketch outline of Soviet disintegration and the resurgence of Russia have demonstrated how decisive the *manner* of the Soviet demise and the *context* of the transition in Russia were in determining both the federal outcome and the *kind* of federation that Russia has become. We will summarize the character of the Russian Federation in the conclusion to the chapter, but it is now time to place it in the context of comparative federalism and federation.

The Russian Federation in comparative perspective

Before we look in detail at our comparative perspectives, it is important first to note that they will be based upon the conceptual distinction between 'federalism' and 'federation', a distinction originally introduced into the mainstream literature by Preston King in 1982.[26] Consequently we must establish what we mean by federalism and federation and how these concepts will be used in what follows. I take *federalism* to mean the recommendation and (sometimes) the active promotion of support for federation. A *federation* is a particular kind of state. It is 'a distinctive organizational form or institutional fact the main purpose of which is to accommodate the constituent units of a union in the decision-making procedure of the central government by means of constitutional entrenchment'.[27]

The relationship between federalism and federation is complex because federalism informs federation and vice versa. And there are many federalisms that differ widely in their content. They reflect different constellations and configurations of cleavage patterns that reflect distinct values, interests and identities both in a territorial and a non-territorial sense. Like federation, federalism is rooted in context so that in order to understand each federalism we must locate the concept in its own distinct setting: historical, cultural, intellectual, philosophical, social, economic, legal and ideological. In this way we can begin to appreciate its huge multidimensional complexities. Federalism constitutes the socio-political reality of difference and diversity, of the variety of interests and identities that mobilize to seek genuine autonomy, representation and participation in federation. Federation, too, is similarly complex and contextual. As tangible institutional fact, it cannot be reduced to the mere end product of federalism. We do not move in a simple straight line from federalism to federation. Federation itself is governed by purpose, what King calls 'conscious self-direction'; it acts upon federalism, helping to shape and reshape both its expression and its goals. The relationship between federalism and federation is therefore symbiotic; each impinges on the other in an unending fashion.

The application of this conceptual analysis to the Russian Federation immediately calls our attention to the relationship between federalism, federation and liberal democratic constitutionalism. In the first place this particular conceptual approach would take issue with previous statements suggesting that the Soviet Union was 'a federation without federalism'.[28] On the contrary, the USSR certainly had federalism – in the sense defined above of its conspicuous ethno-territorialism as identity politics – which was, as we have seen, the very *raison d'etre* of federation in 1922. But it was not an authentic federal state. To adopt the structural trappings of a federation as an expedient without them being firmly embedded in a liberal democratic state that combined a written constitution with the rule of law and embraced local autonomy rooted in a division of powers between the central government and the constituent authorities, guaranteed free, fair and regular competitive elections based upon the secret ballot and political choice among freely formed political parties together with an independent judicial system and representative political institutions, was merely to construct a façade. Consequently the Soviet Union was an example of federalism without federation.

This conclusion has implications for the Russian Federation in the extent to which it has inherited any Soviet features, which serve to undermine or contradict the basic principles and practices of liberal democracy. States with authoritarian military governments or governments that use the coercive forces of the state to restrict the basic rights and freedoms of its citizens, control the media and intimidate opposition critics cannot be considered as genuine federations. In the mainstream literature on federal studies there has never been any doubt about these considerations.[29] There is admittedly a scholarly consensus about the doubtful credentials of 'federal democracy' in some federations, such as Malaysia, Mexico and Ethiopia, but this is a different matter. It is a world away from serious consideration of the USSR as a genuine federation. Where the Russian Federation presents scholars of federalism and federation with an awkward problem lies partly in its institutional design but chiefly in the *operation* of the federation. The written constitution entrenches the liberal democratic basis of the federation according to the recognized principles identified above but it must also *function* in accordance with these principles.

With these preliminary thoughts in mind, let us turn now to the four main comparative perspectives that we intend to utilize in our survey of the Russian Federation.

1 The federal bargain

We have already observed that Riker included the Soviet Union in his general survey of comparative federalism. The bedrock of his thesis about the origins and formation of federations resided in the notion of the 'federal bargain' whereby political elites willingly agreed to create a federal constitution. Riker also claimed that two preconditions were essential to federal state building, namely, the promise of territorial expansion and the existence of an external military threat. In his view the formation of the USSR in 1922 – later formalized with the constitution of 1924 – was just as much the product of the two preconditions that he identified as essential to federal state building as were to be found in the cases of the USA and West Germany. He deemed the period 1922–4 to be akin to a process of constitution-building that culminated in 'the bribe of federalism to meet the military threat'.[30] And in acknowledging that many scholars refused to classify the Soviet Union as a genuine federation, he simply dismissed this as 'the expression of American-Commonwealth mythology that federalism ought to prevent tyranny'. Indeed, since the Soviet Union exhibited many of the structural features of federation, the mere fact that it failed 'to prevent tyranny should not lead to casting it out of the class of federalisms. Rather it should lead to a re-evaluation of what federalism means and implies.'[31]

Given the ideological circumstances of the time, this conclusion about the USSR was all the more perplexing. Intellectually he seems to have been riding postilion. On the one hand the USSR was a valid federation, which was 'almost entirely indigenous', while, on the other, it was able to maintain 'the forms' of federation while converting 'the government into a dictatorship'.[32] Clearly the Rikerian federal bargain applied to the Soviet case was simultaneously susceptible to inordinate conceptual stretching and conspicuous empirical flaws. What, then, are the implications of Riker's federal bargain for the Russian Federation? How far do the so-called 'expansion condition' and the 'military condition' apply in this case? It is precisely here that the two Soviet legacies mentioned above come into play.

The period 1991-3 constituted the critical years of constitution-building in Russia and they were characterized by three sets of dramatic events that occurred more or less simultaneously and were interrelated in a highly complex and complicated way: the emasculation of the Communist Party (CPSU); the breakdown of the Soviet central command economy; and the territorial disintegration of the Soviet empire. The unmasking and subsequent resurgence of Russia that ensued created conditions that enable us to utilize Riker's federal bargain by adapting it to these unique circumstances. Smith claims that the Russian Federation is 'unique among federations in having been born out of the collapse of a federation, the Soviet Union' and he also adds that it is 'unique among post-Soviet states in opting for the retention of a federal structure'.[33] These statements are questionable because they take Soviet claims about federation at face value. While acknowledging the unique circumstantial causation of what we might call a 'process of federalization' in Russia, it would be more accurate to construe the federal constitution as having replaced a multinational unitary state by a multinational federation.

Heinemann-Grüder demonstrates that the Russian Federation emerged, albeit in unique circumstances, as the result of a federal bargain, 'a constitutional bargain among politicians'.[34] As we have already seen, he shows that 'the relative success of Russia's federalization' was based upon 'exclusive elite pacts between Moscow and the regions'.[35] But the new federation that was created in 1993 fits Riker's criteria only in a limited way. It can help to explain *how* rather than *why* the Russian Federation was formed. Since there existed no immediate external military threat to Russia, the main threat was internal from dissident republics and regions. Consequently one of the main driving forces behind the federal bargain was the fear of the break up of Russia so soon after the Soviet disintegration. This nightmare scenario constituted a sufficient condition for a new federal bargain to be struck and in this sense corresponds to Alfred Stepan's notion of 'holding-together federalism' whereby 'threatened polities' are transformed into federations.[36] In this regard it also has its counterparts in federal state building in India, Nigeria and Malaysia where the federal bargain was induced by similar fears and internal threats. In other words, Riker's federal bargain had to be modestly revised to allow 'the threat to come from prospective partners in the federation as well as from outside'.[37]

For comparative purposes it is also worth noting that although Russia remains unique among post-Soviet states in opting for a genuine federal state structure based upon a federal constitution, it is not the only post-communist state to do so. In December 1995 the Dayton Accord became the basis for a new federal bargain between Bosnian Serbs, Croats and Muslims in Bosnia-Herzegovina, a former republic in the six-state, two-province socialist federation of Yugoslavia.[38] Clearly Titoist Yugoslavia was no more an authentic federation than the Soviet Union, but the new multinational federal Bosnia-Herzegovina, like the new multinational Russian Federation, has a similar authoritarian communist past based upon formal single-party unitary governance. In neither case, then, was there a democratic federal political culture on which to build a genuine liberal democratic federation. The main difference between the *formation* of these two recent examples of post-communist federations is that the former was put together largely by the international community and in this regard might constitute a novel federal state.[39] We might also construe Cyprus and Iraq as contemporary examples of just this sort of novel international construction.

In summary, Riker's federal bargain can be adapted to explain how and why the Russian Federation was formed but only in a limited way. Federation came about as a result of territorial consolidation rather than expansion while the notion of a threat to the security of the state came from within rather than from without. Ultimately it is not the concepts of federalism and federation *per* se that require re-evaluation, but it is Riker's own notion of the federal bargain that needs to be revised and updated.

2 Historical legacies of centralization

In the study of comparative federalism and federation, it is customary for scholars to acknowledge and accommodate historical specificities prior to the search for patterns of regularities in political systems. In the specific context of the Russian Federation, we cannot avoid one of the most outstanding features characteristic of Russian history, namely, the overweening centralization of the state.

Russian autocracy dates back several centuries in the Romanov dynasty so that political scientists understandably dwell upon the historical continuities of centralization between the Russian state and the Soviet state. After the collapse of the USSR and the emergence of the Russian Federation, the historical legacy of centralization has weighed heavily upon contemporary attempts to transform Russia into a liberal democracy in conjunction with concerted efforts to introduce a working market economy. Indeed, it is now commonplace to construe the process of federalization as part of the larger process of democratization. Federation has not only kept the Russian state from falling apart, it has also served to promote liberal democracy. It is as much a cultural change as it is an economic transition. But the presence of the state that has been so ubiquitous in Russia's past – the deep-rooted tradition that all political authority and all lines of political communication must emanate from the centre – cannot be easily circumvented. The incorporation of federal principles and procedures in the Constitution of the Russian Federation cannot automatically erase centuries of centralist habits and practices. The relationships between the state, government, the economy and civil society are in constant flux but they still draw heavily upon the traditions of the past.

Nothing better expresses this hallmark of the Russian Federation than the institutional design of the state, a federation in which there is a 'unique coexistence of super-presidentialism and federal power-sharing'.[40] The concentration of executive power in the institution of the presidency that remains a symbol of Yeltsin's personal triumph over the parliamentary forces in the state is also an enduring historical legacy of the centralization of power in the hands of successive tsars and a long line of General Secretaries of the CPSU. In this light, President Putin is firmly cast in a dominant leadership role that stretches back to Brezhnev, Khrushchev, Stalin, Lenin, Nicholas II and Alexander I. These centralist presidential features include rule by decree, veto powers over the legislature, control over regional administrations, emergency powers and more recently a regression back to the appointment of governors. As Heinemann-Grüder has put it, presidential federalism is a governmental system that entails

> Conflict between centralism and regionalism as a systemic feature. ...
> The greatest danger for Russian federalism thus seems to flow from a presidentialism that attempts to be strong in implementation of legislation and executive power, but that cannot keep its promise, that is, a formal presidentialism without any corresponding power of redistribution and implementation.[41]

In this light the recent decision to extend central control over Russia's eighty-nine regions by terminating the direct elections of governors in favour of presidential nominees who must be approved by elected regional parliaments was indicative of the current determination to tighten the political grip of executive-presidential authority on the federal state.

Turning to look at comparisons, it must be recognized that all federations are constantly subject to the simultaneous push and pull of centralist and decentralist pressures and tensions. This is the very stuff of federalism and federation. It is also important to note that constitutional autonomy is more important than any particular division of powers and competences between the federal government and the governments of the constituent units. It is perfectly possible therefore to have federations that are either highly centralized or highly decentralized. Federations that share strong centralist characteristics with the Russian federal model are not hard to find. India, Malaysia and Nigeria each display a variety of strong centralist features and it is also worth underlining the contemporary unitary trends and developments that have been immanent in both the Federal Republic of Germany (FRG) since its inception in 1949 and in the Federal Republic of Austria since 1920.

In Germany the tendencies toward centralization have been largely inherent, implanted in the collective national consciousness, given the successive historical experiences of the Weimar Republic (1919–33), the Nazi dictatorship (1933-45) and the communist dictatorship in East Germany (1945–89). This historical specificity was given added practical stimulus in West Germany in the Basic Law (1949) through commitments to forge a uniform economic and legal order, and via policies aimed at ensuring uniform (now equivalent) living standards in all parts of the federal territory. Moreover, the sixteen *Länder* governments also participated in strengthening this process of notarization through cooperation with the federal government in Bonn. As Hartmut Klatt put it, 'the guiding principle of the unitary federal state' required that 'while institutions are federal, national and *Land* policies are oriented toward uniformity'.[42]

The post-war evolution of the FRG has been well documented to show that the three cornerstones of German federalism have been liberal democracy, uniformity and symmetry. Underlying pressures for centralization have been incessant from the outset and early developments in economic growth, financial planning arrangements, the party political framework and the agreements made between the Social Democrats (SPD) and the Christian Democrats (CDU–CSU) in the Grand Coalition (1966–9) 'gave unitarization and interlocking politics in the federal system its fundamental format' which has existed up until today. These cultural, socio-economic and party political features of German federalism that favoured increasing centralization were reinforced in the 1990s with the double impact of German unification that increased the size of the federation from eleven to sixteen constituent units, the Single European Act (SEA) that launched the single market and the Treaty on European Union (known as the Maastricht Treaty) that introduced the single currency, the euro, and the European Central Bank.[43]

Federal ideas and forms of social and political organization in Austria can be traced back to the Holy Roman Empire, the Habsburg Empire and later Austria-Hungary (the Dual Monarchy) in the wake of the *Ausgleich* (compromise) formed in 1867. This imperial past, the impact of two world wars and the peculiar social structure of Austria has set its seal on the nature of Austrian federalism and federation. Rather like Germany and Australia, it has evolved with a relatively homogeneous national political culture but a highly polarized and divisive social class basis to domestic government and politics. Shorn of its imperial territories, Vienna has dominated this rump state and it is widely regarded among scholars of federalism and federation as one of the most centralized federations in existence. According to virtually any yardstick of measurement from the constitutional distribution of competences and fiscal federalism to the institutional powers of the *Bundesrat* (Federal Council) and administrative autonomy in the constituent units, the

Austrian federation is highly centralized. As with all federations, there are ever-present efforts by the constituent units (the nine *Länder*) to put pressure on the federal government for decentralist reforms, but it remains the case that Austria is, like Germany, a unitary-federal state.

The historical legacy of centralization in many former British colonies that later became federations is also striking. Unlike Russia, India, Malaysia and Nigeria each owed their federal heritage to the devolution of British imperial power, but today their existence as highly centralized federations has in some cases developed to the point where their federal credentials have been brought into question. After the British left India in 1947, the imperial administrative legacy ensured that the federal idea began its life in a multi-lingual, multicultural and multinational federation with the notion of a strong central authority. The reasons for this are many and complex but they include the following: the British desire to bring together within a single constitutional system the parts of India under indirect rule – the princely states – and those under direct rule – the British provinces with representa-tive institutions; the British concern with Muslim anxieties that over-shadowed and subordinated issues of states' rights; the experience of partition in 1947 demonstrated the inherent dangers of separatism to those constructing the constitution and predisposed them to favour centralization; the national goals of economic development and modernization seemed to require a strong central authority capable of directing the economy; and the existence of a highly centralized hegemonic mass-based political party in the absence of a strong state and regional parties supported a centralized federal formula.[44] It is no accident that the Union government has very substantial powers, including the unitary powers of intervention and pre-emption in emergencies together with the power – as in Russia – to appoint the formal heads of the constituent states, the governors. These factors combined to produce a federation that possessed such a strong centre that one dis-tinguished scholar of comparative federalism, Kenneth Wheare, felt com-pelled to describe it as 'quasi-federal'.[45] Indeed, the term 'federal' was not used at all in the constitution.

In terms of centralization, Malaysia is even closer to the Russian federal model than India. Here the historical legacies of centralization are palpably clear: Malaysia has to be understood largely in terms of its overriding con-cern for order, stability and national unity in a society that can be described as multiethnic, multiracial, multilingual, multicultural and multinational.[46] In short, the high degree of social heterogeneity has placed a premium on national unity but this primary concern for the internal security of the fed-eration has led to repeated accusations of an 'overweening executive arm of government' so much so that 'the fine line between constitutional govern-ment and outright authoritarian rule has become even finer'.[47] The basis for criticisms like this derive from the many constitutional and legal procedures and practices that have clearly tilted the balance of power in the federation in favour of the federal government in Kuala Lumpur: Article 75 of the

Federal Constitution established the federal supremacy clause that has allowed the federal government to interfere in state legislation on almost any matter; Article 76 that permits the federal government to encroach upon state competences in pursuit of the uniformity of law; and Article 150 that provides the basis for proclamations of emergency granting both the parliament and/or the federal government virtually unlimited powers. To these must be added tight central control of the police and armed forces, surveillance of the media, influence on the law courts and evidence of political intimidation of legitimate opposition. Indeed, we could be forgiven for thinking that this is a broad-brush description of the Russian Federation rather than Malaysia.

Nigeria brings into focus yet another historical legacy of centralization in a federation and this is an example of a federal model that has recently emerged in 1999 in the wake of chronic constitutional, political and governmental instability that stretches back before its independence from the British in 1960. Among the lessons learned from its past failures has been the need to defuse tribal, communal and multinational conflicts by increasing the number of constituent units in the federation to thirty-six in 1996 and formally adopting in 1999 the institutional design of a presidential federation in the Federal Constitution of Nigeria that was intended to strengthen national unity and integration. Given that in four decades of independent statehood Nigeria has had six separate federal constitutions, the level of concern for the future territorial integrity of the country more than matches that of the Russian Federation. Consequently the promotion of a strong executive presidency bequeathed by the Nigerian military was the logical antidote to ethnic fragmentation. Rotimi Suberu summarized the legacy:

> The most widely lamented feature of the Nigerian federation involves the massive, relentless, and comparatively unprecedented accumulation of powers by the centre at the expense of the states and the localities … The process of hypercentralization in Nigeria … has been virtually preserved … as the framework for Nigeria's Fourth Republic. The repressive hypercentralization of that era not only put federalism virtually in abeyance … but also bequeathed a problematic institutional legacy for the succeeding federal democratic dispensation.[48]

This section has demonstrated that the Russian Federation can be usefully analysed and assessed from the comparative perspective of historical legacies of centralization in federations. It reveals that in this particular regard, Russia sits rather more comfortably among conventional federations if we utilize a spectrum or continuum of centralization–decentralization than we might initially have expected. Viewed from this angle, the Russian Federation under Putin's regime emerges as less exceptional and no more extreme in its predisposition toward centralization than many other federations.

3 Ethnic diversity and multi-nationalism

Up until 2005[49] the Russian Federation had a population of approximately 145 million citizens and its 89 'federal subjects' that comprised 57 territorially defined entities and 32 ethnically defined entities was largely a collective legacy of the old Soviet Union. Within the latter ethnic category were 21 republics and 11 national autonomies, making Russia a conceptual *melange* of ethnic and sub-state national identities. Heinemann-Grüder has claimed that 'the departure from a pure ethnofederalism and the avoidance of a pure territorial federalism are key achievements of federalization in Russia' and 'the combination of both principles seems to be the best variant for Russia'.[50] In this section we will construe the multiethnic and multinational composition of the Russian Federation as the federalism in the federation and address it from the standpoint of comparative federalism and federation.

Let us begin with Heinemann-Grüder's interesting comment about another historical legacy, namely, Russia's purported failure in the nineteenth century 'to develop an assimilative, homogenizing nation-state' and the Soviet Union's corresponding inability in the twentieth century to 'engineer a supranational, internationalist state'. These two failures, he suggests, served to de-legitimize 'compulsory assimilation as a means of integration'. What, then, were the implications of these circumstances for a federal Russia? Put in Heinemann-Grüder's own words, how did these 'successive failures of nation-state building become a pre-requisite for Russia's contemporary federalization?'[51]

The question is interesting in the extent to which it compels us to think deeply about the nature of Russia as a multiethnic and multinational state. In a sense the constitutional architecture and the institutional design of the Russian Federation themselves betray certain assumptions about its 'ethnonational' past, present and future. First, it is important to note that approximately 83 per cent of the total population is Russian so that we would need to determine the precise territorial distribution of the various primary ethnic identities and distinct self-conscious nations throughout the country. For example, Russia's 21 republics constitute just 15.7 per cent of the total population of the federation and in only seven of these republics does the indigenous population comprise a majority.[52] Second, we would need to detect the number and variety of similar identities existing as minorities within each of the primary ethno-national categories and how they were distributed. Third, we would need to understand how far elite representatives of each of these categories have already been successfully incorporated in the decision-making processes of their respective tiers of political authority. To paraphrase Heinemann-Grüder, it would seem that there was 'a comparatively high degree of "integral incorporation" of non-Russian elites into decision-making, and into the administration of their respective sub-national units'. Consequently past experience suggested that there were clear incentives for 'acculturation and assimilation' into the Russian polity and equally firm disincentives for secession. Moreover, the relationship between the core first-order titular ethnic groups and the titular ethnic communities in the second-order autonomous units (the autonomies inside the union republics) was pivotal. The desire by the latter to be protected from the former – as they had been in the USSR – ensured that federation provided an incentive and a political strategy to 'forestall a possible imposition of first-order titular group norms'.[53] Federal arrangements were therefore appropriate to provide the institutional and policy spaces for the recognition, autonomy and self-determination of distinct collective identities, including both territorial and ethno-national categories.

The Russian Federation could draw upon both the Soviet legacy of federalism and its own experience as the RSFSR – a federal incubus – within the USSR, but as Smith has emphasized, in some ethno-national areas 'the notion of federation retains a pejorative meaning associated with a highly centralized system of Soviet rule' and the new constitution has put in place 'political structures that resemble at best a highly centralized federal system'.[54] This raises questions about the utility of legacies in practical politics but it also calls attention to competing perspectives of federation. What does the federal experience have to say about ethnic diversity and multinationalism in Russia?

Comparative perspectives alert us to the fact that we are dealing with one of the most intractable political conflicts of our time: those that stem from rival national visions, whether within or between established states. Clearly federations that have significant patterns of cultural-ideological differentiation, as in Russia, require several different constitutional and political strategies in order to achieve successful accommodation. What might work in Tatarstan will not necessarily work in Chechnya. There are surprisingly few examples of genuine multinational federations to which we can turn for further enlightenment and investigation, but Belgium, India, Malaysia and Nigeria furnish us with some helpful comparative insights. There is, however, an assortment of special arrangements, procedures and practices that are collectively known as consociational democracy which have also traditionally been used in federations to help to facilitate difference and diversity, and they usually include at a minimum the following mechanisms: executive power-sharing, the use of the double majority; extensive proportional representation; and minority veto powers. The empirical evidence suggests that in multinational states the practice of conventional liberal democracy alone is not sufficient to achieve the sort of political accommodation so vital to sustaining legitimacy, order and stability.[55]

In Belgium a complex dynamic is at work which involves the management of a fundamentally bipolar polity in the north–south relations between Flanders and Wallonia, but it is made all the more complicated by the existence of Brussels situated just inside the Flemish boundary and a small German-speaking community of Belgians living inside Wallonia to the east. The Flemish constitute a majority of 58 per cent of the total population while the Walloons at 32 per cent are a large linguistic society to the south that accommodates about 67,000 German speakers in Eupen and Malmedy. On the face of it, this seemingly intractable combination of cleavage patterns in which territoriality, language identity and socio-economic disparities do not augur well for legitimate and stable liberal democratic rule is actually a highly successful multilingual federal polity. This is largely because of an innovative federal design that is ably complemented and buttressed by a range of consociational practices. While Belgium is territorially a small federation with a population of just over 10 million people compared with the giant Russian mosaic, its judicious use of constitutional, legal and political procedures, mechanisms and devices furnishes a battery of checks and balances that guarantee respect for the integrity of entrenched cultural identities and protect minority rights. The implications of this peculiar Belgian federation for Russia suggest that it is possible to forge a compound unity by integrating difference and diversity in the structures, institutions and practices of a liberal democratic polity that facilitates genuine ethnonational autonomy and internal self-determination.[56]

As a multilingual, multicultural, multinational federation whose population of just over 1 billion people makes it the world's largest liberal democratic federation, India is clearly more analogous to Russia in its territorial and demographic size and in the sheer scale of its diversity than Belgium. Language combined with regional identity has proved to be the most significant characteristic of ethnic self-definition, with Hindus unquestionably the dominant religious and linguistic social community. However, among the twenty-eight constituent units that constitute India today, the Sikhs in Punjab, the Tamils in Tamil Nadu, the Bengalis in West Bengal and the Nagas in Nagaland are a good representative sample of the strong sense of sub-state nationhood that exists. Jammu-Kashmir is of course a notable exception to the customary practice of political accommodation in India, and its frontier location with Pakistan has its counterpart in Chechnya as one of a handful of Russian republics situated on an outer border. Both cases of sub-state national identity are characterized by a complex combination of historical, territorial, religious, economic and international factors.

Like the Russian Federation, the idea of a strong centre in India has been driven largely by past fears of its possible disintegration, especially after the rupture with Pakistan, and as we have already noted above, this confers at least a partial legitimacy on federal government with a battery of strong constitutional powers designed to protect the security of the state. But it is also worth noting that ethnic diversity and multi-nationalism in India have been successfully accommodated, as in Nigeria, by the practice of creating new states out of existing constituent units and, more recently, by local government reform that introduced a third tier of government – the panchayats – enjoying formal constitutional recognition as another autonomous governmental form in its own right. The implications of federal rule in India for the Russian Federation, then, suggest that it is possible to secure the territorial integrity of the state by using coercive measures only sparingly while adjusting and adapting to ethnonational claims and challenges in the polity by promoting internal self-determination coupled with a vibrant local democracy.[57]

Malaysia also comes closer to both India and the Russian federal model in terms of its overriding concern for order, security, stability and national unity. And 'national unity' in Malaysia takes on a special meaning in a country of 20 million people of whom the Malays constitute approximately 59 per cent, Chinese 32 per cent and Indians 9 per cent. A combination of specific historical and economic circumstances have led to race, language and religion being formally consecrated in the federal constitution so that Islam is recognized as the official religion of the state and the majority Malay language is designated the national language of the federation. Moreover, it is also the case that the *Bumiputeras* (meaning literally 'sons of the soil'), who comprise the Malays and other indigenous or native peoples, are afforded a special recognition and status in the federation, an arrangement that dates back at least to 1948 and was intended to redress the economic imbalance between them and the non-Malays, especially the Chinese.[58]

The Nigerian federation shares a similar heritage of authoritarian government with Russia in that the coercive forces of the state have been used by political, economic and military elites to control civil society. In the first four decades since its independence from the United Kingdom in 1960, Nigeria has had six separate federal constitutions and long periods of military rule, the last one ending in 1999 with the imposition of another constitution that reintroduced a strong executive presidency as a variant of liberal democracy designed primarily as 'an antidote to Nigeria's ethnic fragmentation' but without either popular citizen consultation or the participation of the constituent units.[59] Indeed, the recent national elections in April 2007, the alleged corruption, intimidation and ballot rigging notwithstanding, were landmark elections reflecting the first handover of power from one civilian government to another in Nigeria's post-independence history.

Nigeria's three main nationality groups – Ibo, Yoruba and Hausa-Fulani – exist in conjunction with an estimated 200–400 'ethnic minorities', ranging in size from several thousand to a few million and comprising adherents to Christianity, Islam and traditional indigenous religions. With Nigeria's population estimated at approximately 110 million people who are distributed across thirty-six constituent units of varying territorial size, Suberu claims that any federal system in Nigeria must give adequate recognition to 'the multiplicity, complexity and latent fluidity of ethnic territorial interests in the federation'. Accordingly the operation of ethnic conflict management has been successfully achieved by a multi-state federation that has been able to 'fragment and crosscut the identities of each of the three major ethnic formations' so that the core population of each majority ethnic identity 'has been distributed among at least five states'. In this light, the creation of so many constituent units has served to subdue aggressive ethnic conflicts by confining them to smaller arenas and converting them into competitive distributive bidding in national politics.[60] Issues surrounding the economic viability of some small constituent units remain, as they do with Russia's eighty-five 'federal subjects', but there is also an important countervailing argument that this strategy enables federal systems to protect the numerous ethnic minorities from the direct hegemony of the largest ethnic groups.

These comparative perspectives of ethnic diversity and multi-nationalism in federations confirm that the ability of the Russian Federation successfully to accommodate this particular federalism in federation will be determined largely by how far distinct ethnic minority identities are protected from primary sub-state nationalities and how far primary non-Russian sub-state nationalities, such as the Muslim republics of Tatarstan and Bashkortostan and the poorer but culturally distinct republics of Buryatiya and Tyva, can reconcile their autonomy drives with the limits set by the federal constitution.[61]

4 Asymmetrical federalism

The notion of asymmetry in federalism and federation is not a novel idea. It has been implicit in the mainstream literature in studies of individual federations, such as Canada, Belgium, Germany and India, as well as in comparative surveys of federalism and federation for many years. References to the differential status and rights among the constituent units of federations and between them individually and the federation as a whole have appeared sporadically in this literature without attracting much scholarly attention, let alone controversy.[62] In the context of the Russian Federation, however, its dramatic appearance from the chaotic circumstances of the early years of the Yeltsin–Gorbachev rivalry has given it a bad name. From the standpoint of those, like President Putin, whose principal concern is to ensure that Russia does not suffer the same fate as the Soviet Union, asymmetrical federalism must not be encouraged. Indeed, in many cases it must be rescinded and symmetry restored.

The problem with asymmetrical federalism in Russia is that it is largely the by-product of Yeltsin's famous clarion call to the republics and regions to take as much sovereignty as they wanted. Consequently it has become associated in the minds of many Russians with the transition context – a period of chronic instability in which the territorial integrity of the state was threatened. The initial declarations of sovereignty in the USSR by Tatarstan and Chechnya in June 1990 presaged the so-called 'parade of sovereignties' by union republics, regions and autonomous republics that extracted a series of bilateral treaties and agreements from Moscow, giving rise to 'further asymmetries in Russian federal relations as forty-six other regions demanded and achieved bilateral treaties and agreements for themselves by 1998'.[63] Although never intended to violate the federal constitution, in practice many of these treaties and agreements did openly contradict it so that by the time

Putin was elected as president in 2000 there were many examples of regions legislating in flagrant opposition to the constitution and federal law. Yet asymmetrical federalism comes in various forms and packages, and need not be construed in such a negative light. Indeed, comparative perspectives demonstrate that it is used in most federations while in some it is actually indispensable as a foundation for the legitimacy, order and stability of the state.

No better example of asymmetrical federalism exists anywhere than that which has been in operation in Canada since the Canada Act (1867) created the first parliamentary federation based upon the Westminster model. It is important to note that from its inception Canada stands out as a federation in which not only was *de facto* asymmetry evident but *de jure* asymmetry was also consciously promoted. The former refers to asymmetrical relationships or practices that reflect and express socio-economic and cultural-ideological preconditions while the latter is formally entrenched in constitutional and legal processes so that constituent state units are treated differently under the law.[64] The principal though certainly not the only reason for inserting constitutional clauses that introduced *de jure* asymmetrical federalism in Canada was the existence of Quebec as the only province in the federation whose language was French. The initial list of asymmetrical provisions regarding Quebec focused mainly upon the protection of its language, education policy and the civil code, each designed to recognize its historical specificity not only in its language but also in its culture and social institutions. These provisions were also gradually extended to include a wider range of public policy areas, such as the Quebec pension plan and its participation (with federal government permission) in *la francophonie*, a loose international grouping of French-speaking countries.[65]

The Canadian experience with asymmetrical federalism up until recently demonstrates that concurrent pressures for both increased symmetry (outside Quebec) and asymmetry (inside Quebec) has sharpened internal tensions and conflict in the federation. However, it is also worth emphasizing that *de jure* asymmetrical federalism with particular respect to Quebec's place in Canada has served to integrate and accommodate it both as a province and as a nation. Moreover, the incorporation of *de facto* and *de jure* asymmetrical federalism in the constitution must also be seen to reflect the federal spirit that was predicated on a partnership of equality between anglophone and francophone interests which created the first federation based upon two distinct nationalities in the 1860s.

Belgium, Germany and India are federations that also exhibit various features of asymmetrical federalism but in different forms according to their particular historical specificities and the resulting constellations of cleavage patterns that exist in each case. In Belgium, for example, the 1993 federal constitution entrenched the regions and communities and enabled the tiny German-speaking community of Eupen and Malmedy to find its own institutional and policy spaces within the French-speaking Walloon Region while the special arrangements for the bilingual Brussels Capital Region – combining territorial and non-territorial federal elements – demonstrate the innovative strengths of asymmetrical federalism as part of a multi-polar response in the context of a multilingual federation with strong bipolar tendencies. In contrast, it may be recalled that the centralized 'unitary-federal' state of Germany preferred uniformity to diversity and that German society at large has always been suspicious of asymmetry as akin to inequality and injustice. Yet the German case has always exhibited a *de facto* asymmetry particularly regarding economic matters mainly as a result of German unification in 1990 and the impact of European integration due to the Maastricht Treaty ratified in 1993. The recent federal reforms in 2006, however, have signified a marked shift in the direction of a modest *de jure* asymmetry. Here the *Länder* have been given new powers designed to reduce uniformity by enabling them to deviate from federal legislation as well as from federal rules for the implementation of federal laws. Moreover, the end of 'framework' legislation (directives from the federal government), the reduction in the number of 'common tasks' (shared responsibilities), and concurrent legislation and the award of new, if modest, competences for the *Länder* have combined to give them more autonomy and in so doing brings the cherished mantra of *de jure* symmetry closer to the reality of *de facto* asymmetry.

In India it is safe to assume that the federation would not have survived intact without the implementation of both *de facto* and *de jure* asymmetry. If we take into account its colossal population of just over one billion together with its huge multilingual, multicultural and multinational complexities spread across twenty-eight constituent units, it requires little imagination to appreciate how far it could sustain long-term legitimacy, order and stability without the adoption of *de jure* asymmetrical practices. These are widely used and with considerable success: 'in a social system characterized by ... "asymmetrical obligations among unequals", special status and multilevel arrangements encountered no conceptual objections'.[66] The Indian constitution began with the assumption of asymmetry in the special status accorded to Jammu and Kashmir in Article 370, giving it a measure of autonomy that distinguished it from all other states, and since then it has not been hard to find concrete evidence of such flexible adjustment and adaptation to changing needs and demands not only in Assam, Punjab and Kashmir but also in Nagaland, Sikkim, Mizoram and Manipur. The delicate constitutional and political balance to be struck in such a huge country as India between constituent cultural-ideological identities, the territorial integrity of the constituent units themselves and the larger unity of the federation can therefore be viewed as 'an extended discovery of the minimum degree of uniformity necessary for maintaining a coherent union'.[67]

We can see from this short comparative survey of asymmetrical federalism that in many federations it is now regarded very much in a positive vein, bordering on virtue. In short, it has become a highly normative or prescriptive predisposition that reflects particular federal values, beliefs and interests that are, in turn, linked to fundamental issues of legitimacy, participation and overall political stability. The Russian experience of asymmetrical federalism therefore is in many respects both unusual and unfortunate although it certainly raises questions about the limits of asymmetry in federations. Clearly too much asymmetry could provoke serious conflicts and tensions in some federations and even encourage secession movements in others. Each case must be judged according to its own historical specificities, the constellation of cleavage patterns that give each its character and the peculiar circumstances that surrounded each case of federal state formation. It is now time to conclude the chapter with a summary of the Russian Federation in comparative perspective.

Conclusion: between a rock and a hard place

This chapter has looked at the Russian Federation from the standpoint of four principal comparative perspectives. These are the federal bargain, historical legacies of centralization, ethnic diversity and multi-nationalism and asymmetrical federalism, and each of these has been firmly located in the specific context of the Soviet legacy of federalism in theory and practice and the legacy of Soviet disintegration and the resurgence of Russia.

Our comparative survey has demonstrated that the Russian *federalism* – its socio-economic and cultural-ideological dimensions – in the Russian Federation sits comfortably in many respects with other liberal democratic federations on some perspectives, such as centralization and ethno-nationalism, but that it does not sit at all easily with the Rikerian notion of the federal bargain nor with the underlying normative assumptions characteristic of contemporary trends in asymmetrical federalism. The two legacies identified in our survey – what Stoner-Weiss has called 'dual transitions' – fit a modified path dependency argument that suggests they have effectively closed off some possible future scenarios and limited the likely Russian federal trajectory to what is currently dubbed a 'managed democracy'. Between a rock and a hard place, President Putin is himself a legacy of these legacies, cast in the invidious role of the villain – for some critics – trying desperately to hold the federation together by increasingly coercive and undemocratic means, however temporary they might be. Sakwa has argued that Putin's overriding aim was to 'make the federal system more structured, impartial, coherent and efficient' and that he was caught between the opposing models of reconstitution and reconcentration. The former is a law-based federal model while the latter is 'a more authoritarian attempt to impose authority over recalcitrant social actors in which it is the regime that is consolidated rather than the constitutional state'.[68]

These concluding reflections do not suggest that we should dismiss the Russian Federation as yet another post-communist failed federation. It is too soon to tell whether the contemporary trends in Russia will revert to a modified version of the old centralized autocratic Soviet rule or represent a new 'liberal-authoritarian' federal model further from the USSR but closer to Malaysia. From the standpoint of what Bermeo calls 'the grim reviews of federalism in post-communist states', it is at least clear that we must be very careful when we include countries like the Soviet Union, Yugoslavia and Czechoslovakia in any surveys of comparative federalism and federation.[69] The implications of failed federations in post-communist states for genuine liberal democratic federations are extremely limited, if not wholly irrelevant. As Bermeo remarks, 'in each of the post-communist cases, failed federalism was the legacy of imposed rule and of a past shaped by a dictatorial party'. She added that 'there are sound reasons to expect that an imposed federal system would be unlikely to last'.[70] And if the claim made by Valerie Bunce that 'territorially concentrated minorities in federal systems were the *only* minorities that challenged state boundaries in the new regimes of post-communist Eastern Europe' is empirically valid, it has no necessary implications for federation *per se*.[71] It is important to be clear about this. Federations are liberal democratic federal states – not dictatorships – and they are formed for a variety of purposes that can be distilled as combining 'unity and diversity' in many different forms. Federation *qua* federation, then, did not itself *create* the national entities in the East European states; they already existed and so-called 'ethno-territorial' units were deliberately organized along federal lines. This merely underlines the point that federations are not always appropriate and are certainly not panaceas for every political problem nor can we always prevent them from being used for illiberal purposes. But communist federations and military federations are essentially a contradiction in terms. Any serious comparative survey of the Russian Federation therefore compels us to confront the simple fact of the absence of a liberal democratic culture in Russia. As the Putin era indicates, rebuilding the Russian Federation will be an extremely difficult and dangerous balancing act. But one major advantage of the comparative approach is that it can expose federal facades for what they really are: impostors.

Notes

1 A. H. Birch, 'Approaches to the study of federalism', *Political Studies*, Vol. XIV (I), 1966, p. 3.
2 N. Bermeo, 'The import of institutions: a new look at federalism', *Journal of Democracy*, Vol. 13, No. 2, 2002, p. 98.
3 'Union of Soviet Socialist Republics 1977', Chapter 8, 'The USSR – a federal state', in S. E. Finer (ed.), *Five Constitutions: Contrasts and Comparisons*, Harmondsworth: Penguin Books, 1979, p. 165. The Stalin Constitution, 1936 described it in Article 13 as 'a federal state, formed on the basis of a voluntary union of the...Soviet Socialist Republics enjoying equal rights', 'Union of Soviet Socialist Republics, 1936', in Finer, p. 120.
4 See M. W. Graham, *New Governments of Eastern Europe*, New York: Henry Holt and Company, 1927, pp. 594–95.

5 For complete texts, see W. R. Batsell, *Soviet Rule in Russia*, New York: The Macmillan Company, 1929, pp. 79–82.
6 V. Aspaturian, 'The theory and practice of Soviet federalism', *The Journal of Politics*, Vol. 12, 1950, fn. 15, referring to Lenin's *Collected Works*, XXII, p. 26.
7 Aspaturian, p. 26.
8 Ibid.
9 'Union of Soviet Socialist Republics, 1977', Articles 3, 6 and 108 in Finer, pp. 149 and 175.
10 See L. G. Churchward, *Contemporary Soviet Government*, London: Routledge and Kegan Paul, revised second edition, 1975, p. 167.
11 M. Filippov, P. C. Ordeshook and O. Shvetsova, *Designing Federalism: A Theory of Self-Sustainable Federal Institutions,* Cambridge: Cambridge University Press, 2004, p. 89.
12 W. H. Riker, *Federalism: Origin, Operation, Significance*, Boston, MA: Little, Brown and Company, 1964, p. 13.
13 Ibid., pp. 13–14.
14 C. J. Friedrich, *Trends of Federalism in Theory and Practice*, New York: Praeger, 1968, p. 49.
15 Filippov *et al.*, pp. 92–3.
16 G. Smith, 'Federation, defederation and refederation: from the Soviet Union to Russian statehood', in G. Smith (ed.), *Federalism: The Multiethnic Challenge*, London: Longman, 1995, Ch. 6, pp. 159–60.
17 Filippov *et al.*, p. 92.
18 Smith, p. 162.
19 Ibid., p. 163.
20 R. Sakwa, 'From revolution to *krizis*: the transcending revolutions of 1989–91', *Comparative Politics*, Vol. 38, No 4, July 2006, p. 462.
21 Ibid., p. 465.
22 The detailed events and developments of the period 1991-93 that led up to the formal adoption of Russia's first post-communist Constitution in December 1993 are ably summarized in C. Ross, *Federalism and Democratisation in Russia*, Manchester: Manchester University Press, 2002, Ch. 2, pp. 17–28.
23 See C. Ross, 'Russia's multinational federation: from constitutional to contract federalism and the ""war of laws and sovereignties"", in M. Burgess and J. Pinder (eds), *Multinational Federations*, London: Routledge, 2007, pp. 108–26.
24 A. Heinemann-Grüder, 'Why did Russia not break apart? Legacies, actors, and institutions in Russia's federalism', in A. Heinemann-Grüder (ed.), *Federalism Doomed? European Federalism Between Integration and Separation*, Oxford: Berghahn Books, 2002, p. 153.
25 Ibid., p. 151.
26 See P. King, *Federalism and Federation*, Beckenham: Croom Helm, 1982.
27 M. Burgess, *Comparative Federalism in Theory and Practice*, London: Routledge, 2006, p. 2.
28 Heinemann-Grüder, p. 153.
29 Ronald Watts remarked that

> significant characteristics of federal processes include a strong predisposition to democracy since they presume the voluntary consent of citizens in the constituent units, non-centralisation as a principle expressed through multiple centres of political decision-making, open political bargaining, – ... the operation of checks and balances to avoid the concentration of power and a respect for constitutionalism.
>
> (*Comparing Federal Systems*, Montreal: McGill-Queen's University, 2nd edition, 1999, p. 14)

30 Riker, p. 39. For further details about the federal bargain, see Chp. 2, pp. 11–16. There is a critique of Riker's federal bargain in Burgess, pp. 76–101.
31 Riker, p. 40.
32 Ibid., pp. 14 and 38.
33 Smith, pp. 157 and 167.
34 Riker, 'Federalism' in F. I. Greenstein and N. W. Polsby, (eds), *The Handbook of Political Science: Governmental Institutions and Processes, Vol. 5*, Reading, MA: Addison Wesley, 1975, p. 113.
35 Heinemann-Grüder, p. 153.
36 A. Stepan, 'Federalism and democracy: beyond the US model', *Journal of Democracy*, Vol. 10, No. 4, October 1999, pp. 19-34. Stepan uses India as his brief case study but he also refers to Belgium (1993) and Spain (1978) in this category although the latter is not formally a federation.
37 See Birch, pp. 22–33.
38 See L. J. Cohen, 'Fabricating federalism in "Dayton Bosnia": recent political development and future options', in A. Heinemann-Grüder (ed.), pp. 116–45.
39 Bermeo claims to have identified a new kind of federation that she calls 'forced together federalism' which is characterized by 'outside actors and relates explicitly to system frailty'. She regards this as 'a slightly different concept' from Stepan's 'putting-together' federalism based upon coercion by a 'nondemocratic centralizing power'. See Bermeo, p. 108 and fn. 27, p. 110, and Stepan, p. 23.
40 Heinemann-Grüder, p. 155.
41 Ibid., p. 156
42 H. Klatt, 'Forty years of German federalism: past trends and new developments', *Publius: The Journal of Federalism*, Special Issue, titled 'Federalism and Intergovernmental Relations in West Germany: A Fortieth Year Appraisal', Vol. 19, No. 4, Fall 1989, pp. 186–7. See also his 'Decentralising trends in West German federalism, 1949–89', in C. Jeffery (ed.), *Recasting German Federalism: The Legacies of Unification*, London: Pinter, 1999, pp. 40–57.
43 A. Benz, 'From unitary to asymmetric federalism in Germany: taking stock after 50 years', *Publius*, Vol. 29, No. 4, Fall 1999, pp. 55–78.
44 For a detailed summary of these considerations, see Burgess, pp. 88–90.
45 K. C. Wheare, *Federal Government*, Oxford: Oxford University Press, 4nd edition 1963, p. 27.
46 See I. Bakar, 'Multinational federation: the case of Malaysia', in Burgess and Pinder, pp. 68–85.
47 H. P. Lee, *Constitutional Conflicts in Contemporary Malaysia*, Oxford: Oxford University Press, 1995, p. 120.
48 R. Suberu, *Federalism and Ethnic Conflict in Nigeria*, Washington, DC: United States Institute of Peace Press, 2001, pp. 173 and 197.
49 The Russian Constitution lists 89 federal subjects but in 2005 a process of merging federal subjects was implemented. There are now 85 federal subjects. See chapter 4.
50 Heinemann-Grüder, pp. 158–9.
51 Ibid., pp. 149–50.
52 See Ross, 'Russia's multinational federation', in Burgess and Pinder, p. 117.
53 Heinemann-Grüder, pp. 150–1.
54 Smith, p. 167.
55 See J. McGarry and B. O'Leary, 'Federation and managing nations', in Burgess and Pinder, pp. 180–211.
56 For a summary of the characteristics of the Belgian federation related to multi-nationalism, see Burgess, *Comparative Federalism*, pp. 115–17.
57 For a summary of the federal characteristics of India related to multi-nationalism, see Burgess, *Comparative Federalism*, pp. 88–90 and 123–5.

58 For a summary of the characteristics of the Malaysian federation related to multinationalism, see Burgess, *Comparative Federalism*, pp. 90–3 and 125–9.
59 Suberu, p. 198.
60 Ibid., pp. 3–6.
61 See K. Stoner-Weiss, 'Russia: managing territorial cleavages under dual transitions', in U. Amoretti and N. Bermeo (eds), *Federalism and Territorial Cleavages*, London: The Johns Hopkins University Press, 2004, pp. 301–26.
62 For an up-to-date summary of asymmetrical federalism in comparative perspective, see Burgess, *Comparative Federalism*, pp. 209–25.
63 Stoner-Weiss, p. 315.
64 These definitions and conceptual distinctions were published in the first comparative survey of asymmetrical federalism in 1999. See R. Agranoff (ed.), *Accommodating Diversity: Asymmetry in Federal States* Baden-Baden: Nomos Verlag, 1999.
65 The best survey of asymmetrical federalism in Canada remains D. Milne, 'Equality or asymmetry: why choose?', in R. L. Watts and D. M. Brown (eds), *Options for a New Canada*, Toronto: University of Toronto Press, 1991, pp. 285–307, but see also the more recent R. L. Watts, 'The Canadian experience with asymmetrical federalism' in Agranoff, pp. 118–36.
66 See B. Arora, 'Adapting federalism to India: multilevel and asymmetrical innovations', in B. Arora and D. V. Verney (eds), *Multiple Identities in a Single State: Indian Federalism in Comparative Perspective*, New Delhi: Konark Publishers, 1995, p. 72.
67 Arora, p. 78.
68 R. Sakwa, *Putin: Russia's Choice*, London: Routledge, 2004, pp. 235–7.
69 Bermeo, p. 106.
70 Ibid.
71 Quoted in Bermeo, p. 97.

3 Federal discourses, minority rights, and conflict transformation

Andreas Heinemann-Grüder

1 Introduction

What can be learnt from the various guises of federalism, particularly ethnic federalism, which have arisen in Russia following the dissolution of the Soviet Union? This chapter argues that the less the hegemonic discourses support a normative federal culture, the easier it is to undermine basic federal institutions. The thesis is discussed against the backdrop of changed perspectives on post-Soviet federalism. It is additionally argued that the recent changes in federal institutional arrangements affect the behavioural incentives of actors. As evidence of this thesis I provide an overview of federal arrangements, particularly the status of ethnic rights and ethnic regions, and their impact on conflicts with non-dominant groups. Finally, I argue that recent Russian experience demonstrates that the survival of a federation depends on the functioning of democratic regimes and federal parties. I examine patterns of interaction of federal arrangements with other segments of the political regime, particularly the concentration of powers in the central executive and presidency.

This study is part of a wider project, which examines the effects of ethno-federal arrangements on conflictual behaviour in Russia, India, Nigeria, and Spain. It is based on open and standardized interviews with the permanent representatives of ethnic republics in the central government; with deputies of the State Duma and the Federation Council, legal experts at the Constitutional Court, members of the presidential administration and the federal Ministry of Regional Affairs; with party officials of seven national parties, and thirty-one interviews with non-Russian deputies of regional legislatures in the republic of Bashkortostan, Adygeya and Kabardino-Balkariya. The interviews were conducted between December 2005 and November 2006.

2 Post-Soviet discourses on federalism

In post-Soviet Russia we can observe a change of the dominant topics to be found in the public discourse on federalism. Whereas Soviet federalism was perceived as a mere means of symbolically solving the 'nationality problem', the re-foundation of Russia was characterized by the takeover of federal principles in state construction. Federalism was understood as the voluntary covenant of the 'subjects' of the federation (Federation Treaties of 1992), an embodiment of the horizontal division of powers, of power division, an arena for inter-governmental bargaining, and as an instrument of decentralization. Some authors also linked federalization with democratization. Among the federal markers of the newly found Russian state was the recognition of the exclusive competencies of the federation, the combination of constitutional and contractual elements, the autonomy of the regions in realizing their exclusive and residual competencies, the formal equality of the regions vis-à-vis the central government and the tolerance of diversity in the organization of regional political regimes. Ethnic federalism additionally drew its legitimacy from the 'essentialist' characteristics and demands ascribed to ethnic groups or 'peoples'. In principle, the post-Soviet logic of ethno-federalism coincided with that of nationalism: self-determination was understood as discretion over a state apparatus and a specific territory.

In the 1990s, Russian discourses mostly criticized the deficiencies of the Russian Constitution of 1993 and the contradictory legal order, whereas Anglo-Saxon discourses – with few exceptions – viewed post-Soviet federalism with disdain. Federalism Russian style, it was claimed in the mainstream literature in the USA and the UK, would destroy the common market. Asymmetry would undermine the common legal sphere. The diversity of regional regimes had allegedly led to a federation of regional tyrannies.[1] Mikhail N. Afanasyev and Paul Goble attacked three 'myths' of Russian federalism: (1) it had not solved nationality problems but in fact made them worse, (2) federalism was not the purported twin of democracy. The call for more local sovereignty was authoritarian and, (3), the mistaken idea that the Russian government's weakness under Yeltsin resulted from federalism, whereas Putin's policies of de-federalization have strengthened the state.[2] The view that federalism promoted ethnic conflict and regional authoritarianism was also widespread in Russian studies, as seen, for example, in official textbooks and introductory studies on the political system. But only a few would side with the view that Putin's recentralization is a myth because it has not delivered the promised strengthening of state capacity (more on this below).

With the end of the Yeltsin era (1999) and the beginning of the Putin period the prevailing views of Russians also shifted. However, there are different 'schools' of thought – those that welcome Putin's re-centralization as a reconstruction of the legal order ('konets bezpredela'),[3] and others that sharply criticize de-federalization.[4] Finally, there are some authors of mostly non-Russian origin who fear that Putin's so-called 'harmonization' policy will lead to ethno-cultural homogenization and the dominance of ethnic Russians.[5]

Among the political elites and Russian scholars there is no longer a consensus on the founding principles of post-Soviet federalism. Since the end of the Yeltsin era most Russian authors highlight inter-governmental coordination problems, regional instrumentalism in exploiting federal arrangements, the alleged weakening of state capacity as a result of federalism, as well as the disintegration potential resulting from the socio-economic, ethnic and politico-institutional heterogeneity of the country. The assessment of de jure asymmetries, however, still varies among Russian authors. The constitutional underpinnings of asymmetry are often denied. The Constitution itself is somehow treated as a 'holy cow'. By contrast, extra-constitutional asymmetries such as the citizenship of republics, declarations of sovereignty, and bilateral treaties, are openly attacked – often from a different perspective from that found among scholars and experts of non-Russian origin.[6] It is probably not by chance that non-Russian experts more often defend federal principles against the predominant Russo-centric and centralist points of view.

In order to justify the new centralizing agenda, Putin's supporters have pointed to what they consider to be serious deficits of the federal system. With respect to ethnic federalism the following features were most strongly criticized: the sovereignty claims of the republics, contradictions between the Russian Constitution and the constitutions of the republics, the hierarchy among regions ('matryoshka federalism'), asymmetric regulations in bilateral treaties, the language legislation in favour of titular groups, and the large number of regions (originally eighty-nine) that allegedly led to heavy bureaucratization and poor performance of public administration.

Since 2005, at the latest, the improvement of the efficiency of inter-governmental relations has been top of the presidential agenda. The planned programme of administrative reforms for the years 2006-8 criticizes the duplication of functions and areas of responsibility among the federal administrations, the deficient delimitation of competencies and the lack of coordination, as well as a weakening of business autonomy. Russia is on the low end of the World Bank's 'Governance Research Indicator Country Snapshot' (GRICS), which measures the accountability of governments, political stability, effectiveness, regulative frameworks, rule of law and control over corruption.[7]

Since Putin's election as President in 2000 we have observed an expansion of étatist leitmotifs, anti-liberal platforms, a stress on an independent 'sovereign' path, a revaluation of Orthodoxy and the Russian ethnos as the state-forming group and gravitational centre for non-Russian people, and a rise in chauvinism and enmity against foreigners, combined with an intensifying Islamophobia. Instead of pan-Slavic and Soviet-imperial ideas, which were predominant among Russian nationalists up until the mid 1990s, there is now a focus on the Russian state and the resurrection of its power attributes. Although officially no Russification programme exists, it is easily discernible in practice in instances of Russophile chauvinism, onslaughts and pogroms against people from the Caucasus or Asians, on coloured people and other foreigners, in the countrywide enforcement of the Cyrillic alphabet, the demonstrated alliance of the state leadership with orthodoxy, and the collective expulsion of Georgians from Russian cities (in September 2006) in retaliation against the expulsion of three Russian spies from Georgia.

The Russian Minister of Interior, Rashid Murgaliyev, stated in November 2006 that there existed 150 extremist groups in Russia with some 10,000 members.[8] According to an opinion poll conducted in 2006, the trend of ethnic intolerance is flourishing among ethnic Russians: 62 per cent of Russians felt that certain ethnic groups should not be allowed to immigrate into their region, despite the constitutional guarantee of freedom of movement inside Russia. Only 24 per cent opted against such restrictions.[9] A poll of the Levada Centre conducted in September 2006 found that 57 per cent of Russians felt that an anti-Caucasian pogrom such as occurred in the Republic of Kareliya (August 2006) could also happen in their region. Fifty-two per cent agreed with the slogan of the racist 'Movement Against Illegal Immigration' (Russian acronym DPNI) – 'Russia for Russians'.

Putin and the Kremlin administration have repeatedly called for resistance against manifestations of extremism. Putin publicly criticized the President of Kareliya, Sergei Katanadov, for his initial inaction towards the violent onslaughts on 'Caucasians' in the city of Kondopoga.[10] However, government policy itself contributes to the growing ethnocentrism among ethnic Russians. In October 2006 Putin ordered the government to restrict the number of 'foreigners' permitted to work in Russian markets.[11] In a statement by Konstantin Romodanovsky, director of the federal migration service, the notion of 'foreigners' was defined as being different to the culture and religion of the Russian population, thus implicitly defining 'Russian' not as a notion of citizenship but of ethnicity. In other words, the entry of non-Russians to a market was to be limited, regardless of whether they had a Russian or 'foreign' passport.

Against a backdrop of rising tensions with Georgia, in September 2006 Putin declared that 'non-Slavs' 'dominated' the market places in most Russian cities, thus implying that not just 'foreigners' but people of a non-Slavic origin were to be targeted. There soon followed a wave of denunciations and closures of businesses of Russian citizens with Georgian names – a collective punishment.[12] Putin's own policy thus implemented the slogan 'Russia for Russians'.

The restructuring of inter-governmental relations corresponds to the centralist and Russo-centric creed – the strengthening of the regions' dependence on central government, the concentration of competencies at the centre, and the successive roll back of ethno-federal asymmetries. Officially, there is no farewell to federalism; the disempowerment of the regions is depicted instead as a strengthening of federalism. The type of federalism which operated under Yeltsin is held responsible for undermining the development of a uniform legal and economic sphere, for promoting corruption and ethnocratic misuse of power, regional authoritarianism and inefficient government.

Putin's centralization is portrayed as a strengthening of government perfor-mance. This line of argument is seconded by some Western authors, 'the advancement of a modern state would depend on the regulatory power of the central state towards its "periphery", on its credibility to threaten with sanctions and to enforce compliance'.[13]

As a matter of fact, the official conception of federalism has to some extent returned to the Soviet fig-leaf type of federalism – which acts as a symbolic reminiscence for those groups, which are not yet fully assimilated. The definition of regions as 'subjects' of the federation has been undermined by the Putin presidency – regions are treated as merely parts of an inter-governmental, administrative-territorial division of labour. Commentaries on the Constitution still speak of the right to 'self-determination' of the people, a concept that should also pertain to political self-organization at the sub-national level. However, normative regulations governing the work of the state apparatus, in force since 1999, speak of a uniform and undivided hier-archical administrative system.[14]

Recent commentaries on the Constitution stress territorial integrity, pro-hibition of secession, and uniformity of the executive system. One author-itative commentary on the Constitution declares that the federation is a union of 'states, state-territorial and national-territorial formations' ('obra-zovanii'). Regions are thus the constituent 'subjects' of the federation, but not specific national or ethnic groups. The federation might be a multiethnic state, but the people are neither constituent nor constituted by the Constitution as legal 'subjects'. Yet, the same commentary confirms that the republics represent 'states' and that their power as states derives 'from their people'. Evidently all citizens of a republic as a whole are treated as 'people', not just a specific titular ethnic group.

The constitutional literature seems to assume the dual nature of people as 'subjects' of the federation – on the one hand the multi-national people of Russia (one people) are the bearers of sovereignty of the whole Russian Federation, on the other hand the people of a specific region are treated as the 'sole and direct source of regional power'.[15] Accordingly, there are sev-eral people apart from the all-Russian people that are bearers of regional power, independent of their ethnic markers. The dispute and the confusion about divided or undivided sovereignty may sound like sophistry. Yet, the dispute on sovereignty is relevant because the dominant theory of undivided sovereignty legitimizes the quest for unlimited authority by the central government.

All people (nationalities) of the federation formally enjoy equal rights with respect to the structure of government and the development of their culture. Taken literally, this would imply a farewell to the idea of a hierarchy of people according to size or other markers. To treat the existing ethnic regions as a form of self-determination for all people living on its territory implicitly means a rejection of a differentiation between titular and non-titular groups.[16] However, the consequence of explicitly arguing against the factual

and de jure hierarchy among the ethnic regions is not drawn. Self-determination, an authoritative commentary of the Constitution claims, would have
to find its limits whenever the unity of the state, human rights or 'national
unity' were threatened.[17]

Federalism is ever more treated as a mere functional form of intergovernmental relations, thus replacing earlier ethnic-integrative justifications.
Federalism appears as a tactical and temporarily necessary concession to
noisy ethnic elites. As Irina Koniuchova notes, the fundamental idea of federalism as 'non-centralization' (as put forth by Danial Elazar), could only
work in stable states governed by the rule of law.

> Under conditions of legal nihilism, unstable political relations, the dis-
> integration of the legal system and its inefficiency, a matrix-model of
> federalism, in distinction to the preferred pyramid model, could lead to
> the destruction of the state and an imbalance of the state's power and
> relations.[18]

The language is awkward while the meaning is clear. One would have first to
provide the rule of law and stability through centralism, for only under such
circumstances could a state introduce 'non-centralization'.[19] Nonetheless,
this view does not give proof to the proposition that centralism is a guarantee
of the rule of law and stability.

Following the recommendations of the presidential commission under
Dmitry Kozak, the legal basis for centre–regional relations was systematized,
unified and centralized. As a result of this redistribution of competencies the
federation has approximately 700 areas of responsibility, the regions retain
some 50.[20] However, there are still many deficits, inconsistencies and contradictions.[21] The law 'On general principles of the organization of the legislative (representative) and executive organs of state power of the subjects
of the federation' still leaves open (although it has been amended several
times) the conditions under which the supremacy of federal law should be
executed. The implementation of norms of federal framework legislation in
the regions is a highly complex procedure.[22] Future constitutional amendments and federal constitutional laws will have to clarify the scope and
function of bilateral treaties, the 'state' character of the republics and the
relevance of the still valid Federation Treaties of 1992.

Contrary to the prevailing ethnic demobilization in domestic politics,
ethnic mobilization is used as an instrument in foreign policy. The Russian
policy towards the provinces of South Osetiya and Abkhasiya in Georgia is
to encourage their secessionist drive. The partial revision of Russia's former
stand on the independence for Kosovo has changed the government's
approach to post-Soviet secessionism too.[23] For a couple of years South
Ossetians have been provided with Russian passports, thus enabling their
claim to protection by Russia. The 'Public Chamber of Russia', the official
representation of 'non-governmental organizations', formed by a State

Duma Law on 16 March 2005, declared in December 2006 its willingness to support the secessionist regions of Abkhasiya (in Georgia), Transnistria (in Moldova), South Osetiya (in Georgia) and Nagorno Karabakh (in Azerbaijan). Ninety per cent of the people of Abkhasiya, Transnistria and South Osetiya have reportedly received Russian passports in recent years.[24] The rhetorical and political support for ethnic minorities beyond one's own state borders on the one hand, and the growing negligence vis-à-vis non-dominant groups in Russia itself on the other, would seem to be contradictory – both are the result of an instrumental policy on minorities and power calculus.

3 The hierarchy of ethnic groups

Russia is ethnically and regionally very heterogeneous. Some 170 different groups live in the federation. The autochthonous people of Russia came under Russian rule by the territorial expansion of the Tsarist Empire; other people belong to Diaspora groups who have a 'motherland' outside Russia.[25] Ethnic groups are categorized according to their size, settlement pattern, and the presence of a written language, the language tradition, the degree of national consciousness, and the active use of the 'mother tongue' as well as other languages.[26] The factual asymmetry of ethnic groups was translated into a de jure asymmetry of ethno-territorial regions and minority rights. However, it was impossible to create a complete or even far-reaching correspondence of objective criteria with the hierarchy of political or socio-economic rights. In practice, ethnic groups are actually not required to fit strict criteria in order to be recognized or afforded certain rights. At certain points in time former sub-groups of larger ethnic groups were recognized as independent groups. Thus, new ethnic groups emerged; others disappeared, as evidenced, for example, by the last countrywide census of 2002 – expected benefits obviously played a role in ethnic self-identification.

During the 1990s, out of 89 regions of the Russian Federation, 32 existed as ethnic autonomies – among them 21 republics, 10 autonomous districts (avtonomnyi okrug) and the Jewish Autonomous Oblast. Some of the republics were only elevated from autonomous districts to this status in the course of the re-foundation of Russia after the dissolution of the Soviet Union (Adygeya, Altai, Karachaevo-Cherkessiya, Khakasiya). Most republics and autonomous districts are strongly 'russified'. In some of the ethnic regions the proportion of autochthonous people is very small, for example in the case of Kareliya with a portion of only 9 per cent ethnic Karelians. At the time of the last census among the non-Russian ethnic groups were 41 'titular' ethnic groups, who individually or together with others provided the name for a region of the federation. The status as a 'titular' ethnic group does not necessarily coincide with a certain absolute or even relative size or any other structural characteristic.

Apart from the nominally strongest group of ethnic Russians (79.8 per cent) four autochthonous groups have more than one million people: the

Tatars (5 million), the Chuvashians (1.6 million), the Bashkirs (1.6 million) and the Chechens (1.1 million). Additionally, there are many people with a 'motherland' outside Russia, among them Ukrainians, Armenians, Azerbaijanis or Belorussians. Altogether these groups comprise 20.2 per cent of the populace of Russia. The cohort with a size between 0.5 and 1 million people consists of Germans, Udmurts, Mari, Kasakhs, Awars, Jews and Armenians. Twenty-two ethnic groups have a size between 100,000 and 0.5 million people, 28 groups a size of 10,000 to 100,000, and 24 ethnic groups comprise less than 10,000 people. Republics comprised of a majority of the titular ethnic group or groups include: Chechnya (93.5 per cent), Dagestan (95 per cent), Ingushetia (77 per cent), Tyva (77 per cent), Chuvashiya (68 per cent), Kabardino-Balkariya (67 per cent), North Osetiya-Alaniya (63 per cent), Kalmykiya (53 per cent), Tatarstan (53 per cent) and Karachaeva-Cherkessiya (50 per cent). All in all, in ten out of twenty-one republics the titular ethnic groups forms the majority. Among the autonomous districts, not a single one has a majority of the titular ethnic group.

Among the smaller populations there are the indigenous peoples of the far North, Siberia and the Far East – officially 45 registered peoples of roughly 275,000 individuals who are distributed over 27 regions. Ten of these indigenous peoples have an autonomous region of their own. The largest group are the Nenets (41,000), among the smaller groups are the Krymchaks and Oriks with less than 200 people each. The active command of the indigenous 'mother tongue' as a central feature of group identity is rapidly decreasing among the indigenous groups. Of the 28,000 Chants in Russia only one fifth speaks the 'mother tongue' fluently, whilst among the 2,900 remaining Teleuts only every tenth person speaks the 'mother tongue'.[27] The change of traditional ways of production, mixed marriages, migration processes and a constant assimilation contribute to the disappearance of traditional lifestyles, cultures, traditions and indigenous languages.

4 Conflicts among non-dominant groups

Conflicts with and among non-dominant groups in Russia can be found in various forms:

1 Conflicts between titular ethnic groups in autonomous regions and non-titular groups who feel politically under-represented or discriminated against in economic life.
2 Conflicts between non-Russian ethnic groups over the ethno-territorial boundaries inside or between autonomies, for example between North Ossetians and Ingushetians over the Prigorodny rayon, which is governed by Ossetians but mostly populated by Ingushetians.
3 Demands by ethnic groups, who are part of existing autonomies, for a territorial autonomy of their own, for example among the Nogay who are

scattered over Karachaeva-Cherkessiya, Stavropol Krai, Dagestan, and Chechnya.

4   Conflicts between migrants, descendants of deported people and refugees on the one hand and permanent regional residents – this conflict pattern pertains particularly to the Krasnodar Krai, the Stavropol Krai, the Rostov Region and several republics in the North Caucasus. In the Krasnodar Krai, for example, live some 16,000–18,000 Turkic Meskhetian, returnees or descendants of deportation under Stalin, some 10,000–12,000 of whom a residency permit was denied.[28] The OSCE, UNHCR and the Council of Europe try to assist the Meskhetians, and since 2004 several thousand have moved to the U.S.

5   The primarily socio-economic problems of small indigenous peoples, mostly in the high North and Far East, who do not feel adequately supported by the federal government and yet rather feel threatened by immigration or large business projects.

6   Conflicts between Russian and non-Russian groups that lead to an emigration of ethnic Russians. This pertains particularly to the Caucasian republics of Dagestan, North Osetiya-Alaniya, Kabardino-Balkariya, and Karachaeva-Cherkessiya, where, according to some observers, an anti-Russian policy of alienation takes place. Others hold that the emigration of ethnic Russians is mostly due to the catastrophic situation of the labour market.[29]

7   Violent conflicts with militants, first of all in Chechnya and emanating from there to North Osetiya, Dagestan and other North Caucasian republics.

8   The non-Russian minorities outside Russia who see an association with or inclusion into Russia as a way to secede from their current host country (South Osetiya, Abkhasiya).

9   Conflicts between Muslim groups, especially the official Islam and independent Islamic groups – these include the Wahhabites around Ahmed-kadi Akhtayev, moderate Salafites around Bagauddin Kebedov and radical Wahhabites around Ayub Omarov.

Russian observers perceive the situation in the North Caucasus as the most critical. Although the situation varies in the individual republics, there are overarching factors that could contribute to an escalation of conflicts: high unemployment, an extreme social polarization, a shift of Islamic elites from the 'official' Islam to autonomous Islamic leaders, a general change from Soviet to post-Soviet behavioural patterns, sharp tensions in multiethnic republics such as Kabardino-Balkariya, Dagestan and Karachaeva-Cherkessiya, as well as a high crime rate, corruption and sultanistic policy patterns. The central government seems increasingly perplexed. The preferred policy of nominating politicians loyal to Moscow – such as in Chechnya – does not take the local balance of power into account and often contributes to an increase in tensions. According to the former Duma deputy Vladimir Lysenko, the Caucasians oppose anybody imposed from above or outside.[30]

The conflict in Chechnya is certainly the most striking evidence of the inadequacies in the federal policy towards non-dominant groups. The inability to institutionalize conflict regulation, the rejection of negotiations with nationalist opposition, the excessive emergency powers of the President, the elimination of disparate regional regimes, miserable development impulses, the inefficiency of interregional redistribution and the unwillingness to cope with the Stalinist past, are amongst the most important deficits. In the last couple of years there has been observed a 'Chechenization' of the conflict.[31] Instead of direct rule, the Moscow leadership implants loyal collaborators – Chechen satraps reign. Chechen paramilitaries under Chechen president Kadyrov ('Kadyrovtsy') secure control, however, not as servants of the rule of law but as vehicles of personalized mastery. According to Human Rights Watch, the 'Kadyrovtsy' systematically torture and mistreat rebels or alleged supporters of rebels. Chechenization does not mean Russification, but a flexible mixture of central imposition, federal dependencies and rule by proxy – all this driven by power and cost calculations. Instead of the past cooperation with indigenous, old communist elites and the support of the established – but often corrupted – 'official' Islam, nowadays the younger, post-Soviet generation is co-opted, while the Russian government makes compromises on Islamic customary rules. The central government decentralized competencies to Chechnya and allowed for certain asymmetries in the Chechen Constitution and a bilateral treaty that had shortly before been portrayed as infringements on the unity of the legal system. Relative autonomy is offered in exchange for loyalty and the escape of the Russian government from being blamed for oppression.

Yet arbitrary control under Kadyrov increased rather than diminished. The everyday militarization and presence of security forces for domestic security actually expanded under Chechen rule. Human Rights Watch, the human rights organization 'Memorial', and the 'Nizhni Novgorod Committee Against Torture', report that illegal arrests, disappearances and torture by the 'Kadyrovtsy' and the 'ORB-2' attained a systematic character.[32] The European Court of Human Rights found the federal government complicit in the murder and abduction of Chechen civilians by federal troops over the period 2000–2.[33]

Over the last few years the Chechen conflict has been transformed. Islamic-fundamentalist groups with a pan-Caucasian agenda and scope of action are often replacing the former secular-nationalist rebels. Ethnonationalist justifications are substituted by a militant resistance that is religiously motivated and argues with anti-colonial slogans. Central military commands are substituted by decentralized, al-Quaida-like military networks. Extremist Chechens have expanded their field of operations from the republic of Chechnya to the whole North Caucasus.

Assessments of the virulence of inter-ethnic conflicts vary among Russian observers, yet they are all in all moderate in tone. The director of the secret service FSB, Nikolay Patrushev, declared in an interview for Izvestiya in mid December 2006:

The situation in this sphere, in the country as a whole, remains stable, although criminal incidents do sometimes take place in particular regions, involving local inhabitants and representatives of other nationalities. Examples are the clashes in Krasnodar Krai and Astrakhan and Novosibirsk Oblast in 2005 and the recent disturbances in the city of Kondopoga.[34]

Opinion polls, though evidence that the populace at large is less optimistic than the director of the FSB, do not show overt concern either. In 1996 12 per cent felt that a disintegration of Russia was the greatest threat to their nation, in 2000 10 per cent felt the same way, as did the same percentage in 2003; in 2005 this increased to 15 per cent but dropped to 13 per cent in 2006. According to another opinion poll of November 2006 that asked about the likelihood of secession, 9 per cent answered 'definitely yes', 32 per cent 'probably yes', 32 per cent 'probably no', 11 per cent 'definitely no' and 18 per cent 'do not know'.[35]

5 Minority protection

Minority rights are guided in Russia by international principles and norms, which follow from the signing of international conventions, and national legislation. The Russian Federation signed several international conventions concerning minority rights. Among them are the International Covenant on Civil and Political Rights, the International Covenant on Economic, Social and Cultural Rights, the International Convention for the Liquidation of all Forms of Racial Discrimination, the UNESCO Convention Against Discrimination in Education, the ILO Convention 111, the European Convention on Human Rights, and the Framework Convention for the Protection of National Minorities.

The Russian Constitution mentions minorities, but refrains from defining them. Article 26.2 of the Constitution proclaims everybody's right to declare his or her ethnic belonging, to use their 'mother tongue' and to freely choose the language of communication, upbringing, education, and of creative work.[36] According to the Constitution (Art. 72), the protection of the rights of 'national minorities' belongs to the joint competencies of the Russian Federation. However, my conversations in the State Duma, the Federation Council and the Ministry of Regional Affairs found evidence that specific federal assistance was only deemed necessary for indigenous small peoples and the ex-territorial 'national-cultural autonomy' (more on this below).[37]

The Russian-language legislation corresponds, by and large, to 'international standards', yet it is not sufficiently concretized. The 'Law on Education' (1992) foresees in general terms the protection and development of the national culture, regional cultural traditions and the characteristics of a multi-cultural state as well as the integration of individuals into the national and international culture.[38] Ethnic groups are also allowed to form associations, yet the Law 'On Political Parties' (2001) forbids the formation of parties on ethnic grounds. Contradictions between the formal equality of Russian citizens and the actual implementation of laws or the effects of inconsequential legal norms often allow for de facto discrimination of non-dominant groups. De jure there is a freedom of movement inside the Russian Federation.[39] *De facto*, however, this freedom of movement is restricted by the local registry offices – very often to the detriment of non-Russians.[40] The Law 'On Forcibly Displaced Persons' (1993) does not extend to Chechens because they are not recognized as victims of ethnic, confessional or political mistreatment.[41]

The indigenous people of the high North, Siberia and Far East are mostly nomads or semi-nomads, who are socio-economically disadvantaged, weakly integrated into the society at large, and badly prepared for the transition to a market economy. The declared aim is to protect them from forced assimilation as well as to assist their economic well-being.[42] In the past, the smaller indigenous peoples received material support mostly from the regions. Currently they chiefly depend on federal assistance. The indigenous people articulate requests for the preferential exploitation of their natural environment (mostly hunting and fishing rights), and they would like to preserve their traditional lifestyle, especially against the inroads of oil and gas companies. In the past they also demanded quotas for political representation in regional parliaments, in public offices and in the federal government, for example by asking to form a 'Public Chamber' of organizations of ethnic minorities.[43] The Soviet quota system for the promotion of ethnic minorities in higher education has been abolished, and an institutionalized system of 'affirmative action' no longer exists.[44] Yet the indigenous people are entitled to special representation in local representative bodies by the demarcation of electoral districts in their favour in areas of their compact settlements. The regions or bodies of local self-government may also introduce quotas for the representation of indigenous communities in their respective representative bodies or they may form specific consultative bodies in their respective administrations.[45] Traditional ownership of land or rights of land use is also recognized. The small indigenous peoples receive some assistance for the preservation of their way of production; they may also be granted preferential taxation rights and privileged use of public property. Representatives of indigenous people may participate in the elaboration of structural programmes that affect their traditional areas of living. Another law allows the indigenous people to form voluntary associations.[46]

De facto, however, the rights of indigenous people are far less protected than this list of rights would suggest. The principles of ascribing the status 'small people' or the terms under which individuals may belong to such a group are not clarified. The term 'traditional way of production' is also under dispute. The 'property rights' of individuals or indigenous communities with respect to land and soil are likewise contested. Even a minimal representation of indigenous people in local or regional representative bodies is not assured. Finally, the rights of indigenous people in case of a fusion of regions, especially the unification of autonomous districts with a surrounding region (oblast or krai), are not protected.[47]

6 'National-cultural autonomy' – no alternative solution in practice

The concept of 'national-cultural autonomy' (NCA) corresponds with the old idea, originally advanced by the Austro-Marxists Karl Renner and Otto Bauer, that juxtaposes 'personal autonomy' to 'territorial autonomy'. Underlying the NCA is the idea that ethnic groups form closed social units which embody political subjects – very different from the liberal conception that only recognizes concrete individuals as subjects of law, instead of abstract 'groups'. The Russian legislation on the NCA specifies that a 'national-cultural' group is only entitled to governmental support if it is organized and registered as a societal association. This means that ethnic groups are not per se a legal subject, but only as far as they voluntarily form an association. Ethnic groups are in this understanding just one societal interest or lobby group among many others.

In previous Russian debates the so called 'national-cultural autonomy' had three potential meanings – as an add-on to ethnic federalism, as an organizational model for ex-territorial, dispersed members of a titular ethnic group (for example Tatars outside Tatarstan), or as a total alternative to ethnic federalism. Since the mid 1990s, and increasingly since the de-federalization policies of Putin, the NCA is treated as a counter-concept to ethnic federalism. The justification is that titular ethnic groups only rarely form the majority on 'their' territory, and that the 'etatization' of ethnic groups would politicize ethnicity, discriminate against non-titular groups and potentially undermine the integrity of Russia.[48]

Additionally, the application of the law on the NCA specifies that a minority position is not sufficient for governmental assistance – it is dependent on a non-dominant status and 'objective' difficulties in realizing 'cultural tasks'. But how should these difficulties and injustices be proven? The Russian legislation further limits the entitlement to permanent residents of a certain area and only to members of one particular nationality (no joint NCA). Refugees are thus by definition excluded from the law on NCAs. In the meantime, the legal constraints are so severe that it is far easier to form a conventional association than a NCA.

Furthermore, the actual governmental assistance for the NCAs was decentralized and reduced to a minimum. At best, there exists in a limited number of regions some temporary programmes on radio and TV for minorities or 'consultative councils' in local governments. Fifteen years after the dissolution of the Soviet Union the 'national-cultural autonomy' is barely more than folkloristic symbolism. The NCA, originally portrayed as an alternative or addition to ethnic federalism, proved to be a mechanism for the de-politicization, control and inhibition of collective action by non-dominant groups.

7 The controversial status of republics

The existence of republics is for titular ethnic groups a demonstration that autochthonous people are not merely treated as 'small brothers' of ethnic Russians.[49] Conventional justifications for the reception of the status as a republic include traditions of settlement, the spiritual meaning of a given territory ('homeland'), and a 'making up' for past historical grievances or repression. In part ethnic symbolism also serves the preservation and development of a regional identity.

Republics are entitled to adopt constitutions of their own, which are not subject to approval by the Russian Federation. The republics have permanent representation vis-à-vis the President and the federal government. For a political culture fixated on symbols of power, titles such as 'President of the Republic' or other attributes of statehood provide a soft resource of power.[50] The republics are also allowed to introduce their own state languages. Additionally, they can sign international treaties as long as these are within the confines of the Constitution.[51] However, with the exception of a constitution and state languages, all other competencies are also shared by the purely territorial regions (oblasti and kraya).

In the republics usually one or several state languages exist of the titular ethnic groups. Among other things, this means that legal acts are published in these languages; education in these languages is promoted as well as their use in mass media and cultural policy. The promotion of titular languages and cultures is deemed to be essential – without the status as a republic it is feared that no governmental support of minority cultures would exist at all. Most of the republics support their Diaspora, e.g. members of the titular ethnic groups residing outside the republic.[52] A certain uniqueness of the republics also consists in the name, number of deputies and competencies of republican legislatures. In the republics, titular ethnic groups are usually over-represented in politics and administration.

Constitutionally, the republics are almost equated with other regions. Independent sources of political power are very limited. Republics can no longer claim sovereignty, although they are still deemed to be states. In Russian constitutional thinking, the concept of state – comparable to states in the USA – seems less disreputable than sovereignty.[53] Nevertheless, the highly symbolic dispute on sovereignty has political implications. The sovereignty declarations of the early 1990s were declared null and void and a right to secede explicitly denied. 'Self-determination' no longer involves sovereignty. The final decision-making power is held back for the central government. The exclusive sovereignty of the central government de facto implies pretence for absolute sovereignty. The relevance of retaining the status of statehood of republics may nonetheless create a better protection against dissolution than the mere territorial units, which are not seen as states.[54] But whether the ascription of statehood really protects against extinction remains to be seen.

Many republics are still better organized in promoting their interest vis-à-vis the central government than the oblasts, although distinct gradations exist. The permanent representations of republics in Moscow have formed an informal 'Council of Republican Representatives' that coordinates their approach to federal legislative initiatives or federal programmes. Tatarstan was traditionally the leader among the republics, followed by other donor republics such as Bashkortostan or Komi; at the other end we find recipient republics with minor mobilization potential.

The contraction of institutionalized access channels on the federal level and of independent sources of power, following Putin's reforms, changed the policy patterns of republican leaders. Since the turn of the century new patterns of conflict behaviour characterize the interactions between the republics and the central government. The judicial compromises, adopted mostly in the years 1991-3 in order to bridge opposite interests, have been entirely replaced by the supremacy of the central government. The concept of supremacy also replaces the former practice of antagonistic cooperation or competitive federalism. Tatarstan is no longer the leader with a following; it often stands alone. Due to the collection of 'compromising material' ('kompromat') republican leaders can be blackmailed. Since the abolition of the election of governors they now depend on the goodwill and the lending of power by the President. But Putin's declared 'dictatorship of law' is a potential threat rather than a practical guideline for the President's regional policy; it is retained for the case of disloyalty. The behaviour of the republican leaders is defensive and often subaltern, especially due to the deterring impact of the Chechnya policy and due to the general suspicion under which Muslim republics have been placed since September 11, 2001. Yet some of Putin's newly founded institutions – for example the federal districts – are often only accepted pro forma and silently boycotted; the Soviet practice of double speak has returned. The State Council, an organ created by decree in 2000 for the President's consultations with governors, only rarely serves as a forum for exchanges and deliberations; all in all it resembles more a venue for a Kremlin reception. Individual, bilateral and highly informal patterns of influencing the central government have replaced the past collective action. The lack of transparency of decision-making and the length of decision-making chains has grown tremendously. With the reduction of regional veto powers on the federal level the central government may have won autonomy in decision-making; however, the exclusion of regional leaders entails the risk of hidden exit. The demonstrative loyalty of the republican leaders is very superficial; it is determined by fears of being sanctioned, not by conviction.

8 Regional assessments of (ethnic) federalism

Between September and November 2006 we conducted interviews with non-Russian deputies in three regional legislatures – in Bashkortostan (10), Kabardino-Balkariya (11) and Adygeya (10) – in order to assess the current state of affairs in federal relations. The sample is small and cannot claim to be representative for all ethnic regions or ethnic groups. Non-Russian regional deputies were chosen because they were more likely to have views different from ethnic Russian politicians in the centre, although no comparison was undertaken. Two republics from the North Caucasus were chosen in order to assess whether the dominant perception of a special intensity of conflicts in the North Caucasus was reflected in the answers. In contrast to representatives of ethnic associations it could be assumed that the deputies represent their constituencies and have some knowledge of the federal institutions. Equally, in contrast to executive representatives dependent on the President, it was assumed that regional deputies are relatively more autonomous in expressing their views. Since the willingness to answer depended on the assurance of anonymity, no questions on biographical background were posed.

When asked how they generally assess Putin's reforms, a mixed picture emerged. Out of thirty-one respondents, only four had an explicitly positive view of Putin's reforms – they had strengthened the 'power vertical', and additionally some of their effect would not show immediately. The most vocal critique of Putin's reform came from the Bashkir deputies. The deputies from Kabardino-Balkariya, on the other hand, appreciated Putin's leadership capabilities and his military reforms. Some respondents paint a multi-coloured picture – the 'harmonization' of central and regional legislation is seen as positive, but not the abolition of elections to become governor. There is criticism that corruption and incompetence increased while the seven federal districts have by and large been unsuccessful.

Meanwhile, direct contacts with the central government have simply become more difficult. The centre had taken away almost all taxes from the regions, it is criticized, whilst none of Putin's reforms were carried through: for example, the local self-government was not advanced. The monetarization of welfare is very often sharply criticized. It is apparent that the absence of open resistance to Putin's reforms is not identical with approval; protected by anonymity, a high degree of dissatisfaction is expressed.

Do the non-Russian deputies, their respective republic and their people enjoy an equal access to the political system? The questions were aimed at the perceived discrimination or non-discrimination and the responsiveness of the political system. Roughly one third (10 out of 31) – mostly from Kabardino-Balkariya – stressed the possibility of initiating federal legislation by regional legislature, the representation of the republic and one's own ethnic groups in the State Duma and the Federation Council as well as in political parties. Two more highlighted the general possibility of representing ethnic and republican interests, but saw deficits in the actual implementation. The overwhelming majority of the respondents (19 out of 31) think that the ethnic regions are circumnavigated by the central government, that the city of Moscow would be preferred, and that access under Putin had deteriorated. The centre would not take regional authorities into account; the so-called 'harmonization' of republican constitutions was implemented at the expense of the ethnic regions.

A further question asked whether the status as a republic is seen as beneficial in receiving federal subsidies. Eight out of 31 respondents – equally distributed among the republics – thought that the status as a republic is beneficial. All others felt that the status does not pay off; the economic potential of a region or the relationship of the leadership of the republic with the federal government were more decisive. Very few felt that republics should not get any preferential treatment at all – but support should be needs-based, not status-based.

The deputies were additionally asked whether they would agree to changes in the current ethno-territorial make-up, either by splitting ethnic regions up or by merging them into larger units. Out of thirty-one respondents, four approved of a change of ethnic regions – that some ethnic regions with minimal autochthonous populations would only exist on paper as ethnic regions, for example the Yamalo-Nenets, the Khanty-Mansi, Komi or Kareliya, and that furthermore regions with a similar ethnic composition could merge. The overwhelming majority of the respondents, however, think that the ethno-territorial structure should be retained. Economically, a change of status could be reasonable, yet the republics were states, e.g. constitutive units of the federation. According to one respondent the ethnic 'subjects' of the federation were a guarantee for the preservation of different peoples.

The deputies were also asked whether each compactly settled group should have its own republic, district or at least rayon. Out of thirty-one respondents ten were more or less unconditionally in favour of such a territoriality of ethnicity. Seven respondents qualified the quest for an own territory – the individual situation should be taken into account, and any territoriality should not be at the expense of other groups. Ethnically close peoples could be unified into one republic, and ethnic rayons would be justified in cases of compact settlement with a minimum group size of 10,000 ethnically distinct residents. The duration of settlement should also be taken into account. Another respondent felt that ethnic groups would first have to deserve a territory of their own. Among the proponents of ethnic territories we may also count those who plead for the retention of the current ethno-territorial make-up, but who, given the potential for future conflict, were also against the formation of new ethnic units. Not a single deputy spoke out explicitly against ethnic territories.

The next question was linked to the former – how would the deputies assess the idea of replacing ethnic regions by governments (guberniya), such as occurred in tsarist times? All thirty-one respondents rejected this idea. Some responded that the guberniya would only result in more jobs for bureaucrats, and that the republics would lose their ability to support cultural policies. Federalism, it was also argued, would by definition consist of ethnic regions.

Federations need, at least in theory, neutral arbiters for conflict resolution, among them a Constitutional Court. The deputies were asked whether they perceived the rulings of the Constitutional Court on federal matters as just and fair. Only three respondents agreed unanimously with the rulings of the Constitutional court, almost half (15) responded that they did not know any of the respective rulings, while the rest saw the Constitutional court as prejudiced, under political orders, dependent on the Kremlin or that its decisions were not implemented. The Constitutional Court, in other words, is not seen as an institution relevant for federal conflict resolution.

With respect to the change to the Presidential nomination of governors in 2004, which replaced their direct election, the deputies were asked whether a nominated or an elected governor would have more influence. One third of the respondents (10 out of 31) support the nomination of governors by the President – they argue that Putin would only agree to those candidates already chosen by the regional legislature. Elections, by contrast, would offer more space for abuse whereas a nomination by the President would lead to fewer 'mistakes'. The President would consult before nominating a candidate, and ultimately a governor nominated by the President would have more influence. By contrast, nine deputies, equally distributed among the republics, reject the selection and confirmation by the President – only an elected regional leader would correspond to democratic norms and would feel responsible vis-à-vis the voters. The final third is undecided – whether through election or nomination, the decisive factor was the personality of the candidate. All in all, it is remarkable that only one third of the deputies criticized such a fundamental constraint on regional autonomy – a basic principle of federalism – that was caused by the abolition of gubernatorial elections. Previous disappointments with incumbents, the expected gains in terms of influence, and a personalized, not institutionalized, understanding of politics, as well as the elevation of regional legislatures who have the right to confirm the President's choice may play a role in this. It is clear that only a minority see the election of chief executives as a democratic value in itself.

The non-Russian deputies were asked furthermore whether they sense discrimination by the federal government or its subdivisions. They were asked to rank the presence or absence of such perceived discrimination on a scale from 0 to 5 (0 = absence; 5 = strong presence). The maximum value of 5 was given by five deputies, the minimal score of 0 given by ten deputies; the average of all scores is at 2.03. This therefore shows us that altogether discrimination by federal organs on ethnic grounds is not strongly felt.

Another question pertained to the assessment of quotas for ethnic minorities in the executive and legislative branches of the government. Eighteen out of thirty-one deputies felt that quotas should be preserved in order to represent the autochthonous population. Some added that quotas would not exclude professionalism. Nine deputies explicitly spoke out against quotas, stating that only professionalism or merit should count. The rest made no, or contradictory, statements. The plea of the majority in favour of quotas is somewhat contradictory to the low level of perceived discrimination. Ethnic minorities, especially titular ethnic groups, should obviously be represented independently of the demographic situation or electoral results.

The deputies were also asked what type of conflict regulation for conflicts between ethnic regions and the federal government would be the most effective. The answers varied and do not demonstrate specific preferences. Answers range from personal relationships to the President over arbitration, 'legal ways', negotiations, lobbyism, and cooperation with the presidential envoys – to judicial solutions in court. The deputies were further asked which ethnic conflicts they would see as the most urgent. The conflict in Chechnya and other conflicts of inter-ethnic relations in the Caucasus (especially between Ossetians and Ingushetians), Russian chauvinism, an anti-Islamic hysteria, xenophobia, skinheads and religious conflicts were mentioned most often. One third of the respondents stress conflicts that are related to enmity against aliens among ethnic Russians. The deputies were especially asked whether they saw the danger of an Islamic fundamentalism in the Muslim regions of Russia. Thirteen of the interviewees said such a danger would not exist; 'Islamic fundamentalism' was an artificial or conscientiously exaggerated problem. A group of equal size felt that the problem was serious or even very serious. The remaining interviewees felt that they could not judge this danger, or that the 'true Islam' was the real danger for Putin or republican presidents such as Rakhimov in Bashkortostan.

Finally, the deputies were asked what they expect for the future ('five years from now') – a stabilization or de-stabilization of their republic. Twelve interviewees (five from Adygeya) expected a higher degree of stability in the future in their republic. Six respondents expected a higher degree of instability due, amongst other reasons, to increasing political activity, which would replace the current political apathy. The rest felt insecure or mentioned factors that could influence stability ('it depends on the centre and president of the republic').

In contrast to the prevailing view that Putin's reforms are accepted, the non-Russian deputies articulate significant disagreements. A potential dissolution of their republic is seen as the most threatening factor. The unease about Putin is nonetheless less pointed than one would expect due to the streaky affinity of many deputies to democracy as a value in itself.

9 Federalism and democracy

To understand the de-federalization process under Putin, the debate on federalism and democracy is of particular importance. Here we find two opposite views. One camp sees federalism as a relative of democracy. Federalism would be a seedbed of democracy, as it would allow for more participation and accountability, stimulate civil society, add access channels for political participation, broaden sources of legitimacy, limit the 'terror of the major-ity', broaden citizenship by institutionalizing multi-ethnicity and provide for sub-national competition, thus stimulating local self-governance, innovation and efficiency. The counter-argument holds that federalism institutionalizes regional overrepresentation and undemocratic veto positions, preserves sub-national authoritarianism, promotes ethnocratic instead of democratic rule, exacerbates regional disparities, undermines the rule of law, and facilitates the rise of demagogues rather than encouraging democracy.[55] But if one looks at the empirical evidence in diverse settings, there is no inevitable link between democracy, federalism and the degree of sub-national autonomy. Especially in emerging and multi-ethnic federations, the integration of sub-national units or groups often took precedence over democracy. Two imperatives usually compete in these cases – integration and democracy. Federations generally tend to over-represent territorial units or ethnic groups on the federal level and thus contradict the democratic principle of 'one man one vote'. Regional autonomy may protect non-democratic regimes too, although federal democracy may cascade downwards as well. Federalism is probably a far too multi-faceted regime to attribute common effects to it.

Empirically, there are more authoritarian regimes among the republics and autonomous okrugs than among the purely territorial regions of the Russian Federation. The most critical cases are Bashkortostan, Kalmykiya, Chuvashiya, North Osetiya-Alaniya, Kabardino-Balkariya, followed by Tatarstan, Buryatiya, and other republics.[56] In particular the republics were very slow in the early 1990s in establishing post-Soviet, democratic regimes. Old elites effectively survived by virtue of holding positions in the unreformed Supreme Soviets in the republics.

> They acquired political resources that enabled them to remain in control of local power hierarchies after the Communist Party and its mechanisms of political integration collapsed. A shift to directly elected pre-sidencies, which occurred in the majority of the republics, did not elevate new elites to power either. Rather, they institutionally redefined the incumbent heads of republics and the existing power hierarchies.[57]

Initially, the retention of ethno federalism thus inhibited democratization of the republics.
Gordon Hahn implies

> that the authoritarian variant of ethnofederalism may have stabilized the regions, whereas democratization could have sparked ethnic mobiliza-tion ... Such mobilization, however, positive from the point of view of mobilizing civil society as a counter to state-dominated institution building, could prove to be not only a democratizing factor but also a destabilizing one to the extent that it mobilizes simultaneously several nationalities with conflicting interests in the regions.[58]

Hahn's argument sounds 'unconventional' by portraying past authoritarianism as a source of stability whereas Putin's alleged 'democratization' is seen as a potential source of instability. By implication one could assume that authoritarian ethnic federalism provides stability, whereas an equalization of the regional status and 'democratization' Putin-style holds the prospect of ethnic mobilization and instability. However, Hahn's argument is flawed in at least three ways. First, it associates authoritarianism with stability. Yet, the authoritarian rule in the ethnic regions is inherently unstable, because it is exclusive, dependent on the continuous provision of clientelistic favours, and it feeds corruption, extractive behaviour and kleptocratic rule. Second, Hahn identifies Putin's recentralization with democratization, particularly due to the expected increase in voter mobilization – an unfounded postulation, because with the nomination of governors, the most meaningful elections in the regions were abolished. Third, the argument implicitly repeats the old, empirically unproven claim that democracy is impossible in divided societies.[59] However, Hahn might be correct with his prediction that Putin's recentralization sparks a revival of ethnic mobilization and especially Islamism.

The imposition of uniform rules under Putin's presidency could be interpreted as a strengthening of the rule of law and of checks and balances. The argument in favour of re-centralization ultimately holds that only a single authoritative centre providing for rule of law, effective state administration, and determining the competencies and functions of the state could create the prerequisites of democratization.[60] However, the empirical record of more than five years of re-centralization does not confirm the expected strengthening of the rule of law, neither in terms of local self-government nor in terms of a protection of individual rights by the federal envoys acting as monitors and policy coordinators on Putin's behalf.[61]

Putin's re-centralization is based on the assumption that democracy and federalism are mutually exclusive. However, the substitution of regionally based authoritarianism by direct rule over the regions is unlikely to become a panacea for authoritarianism and ethnocracy. As Filippov and Shvetsova note, it is not only 'fundamentally inconsistent with democratic competition' but 'equally inconsistent with the non-democratic political competition which, even if democracy is abandoned, will arise sooner or later'.[62] In Soviet times centralism and authoritarian integration only functioned as long as the centre could enforce its policy and influence sub-national policy with ideological levers. Given the low degree of incorporation of non-Russian elites into the central government it is unlikely that non-Russian groups will *in toto* abandon their aspirations for self-preservation and territorial representation. Great-power chauvinism and xenophobia among ethnic Russians and parts of the Moscow elite may additionally estrange non-Russians and lead, at least in parts, to radicalization instead of the pluralistic sentiments or assimilation that prevailed in the first post-Soviet decade.

Putin's policy does not just curb the authoritarian policy styles of governors or republican presidents, it undermines the prerequisites for democratization. With the abolition of the federal power division, Putin undermines democratic institutions. De-federalization and de-democratization are mutually conducive. The equalization disempowers regional politics, reduces the division of powers, minimizes the representation and access channels of the regions in the federal system, increases executive accountability at the expense of democratic accountability, and identifies the 'centre' with the federation. The president nominates chief executives of the regions, the regional Duma will rubber-stamp the nominee, and if not, the president may install an 'acting governor' and threaten to dissolve the regional Duma. The president will have the right to fire a governor, but the regional Duma will not. Critics have pointed out that this practice violates articles 1, 3, 5, 10, 11, 32, 71, 72, and 73 of the Constitution, as well as several Constitutional Court rulings in which the court held that only the direct election of regional leaders can be considered to satisfy the requirements of the Constitution. However, the Constitutional Court, contrary to the opinion of leading Russian specialists on constitutional law, approved the presidential nomination procedure for governors. The chief executives in Chechnya and Ingushetiya have already given a preview of presidential appointees lacking legitimacy in the regions; one could even go as far as to say that Putin's reforms follow a model of Chechenization of federal–regional relations: additional control layers and buffer zones, and rule on the ground by proxy.

The past mix of confrontation and cooperation has changed due to the impact of Putin's re-centralization. The republics are more adaptive and cooperative, and less confrontational. However, Putin's policy not only consists of intimidation and confrontation; he has offered informal deals such as allowing the incumbent president to stay in power for a third term. In practice, Putin's 'dictatorship of the law' follows double standards. A law on regional bodies of government, adopted in October 1999, allows governors to run for a third and even fourth term – *de facto* in return for not obstructing the implementation of Putin's policies. The legal two-term limit only begins with the adoption of the law in 1999. The repenting presidents of Tatarstan (Shaimiev), Bashkortostan (Rakhimov), Kabardino-Balkariya (Kokov), Kalmykiya (Ilyumzhinov) and Dagestan (Magomedov) were allowed to run for a third term because they promised loyalty and offered favourable electoral outcomes for United Russia or Putin's second term as president. In these cases Putin preferred leadership continuity and loyalty to the 'rule of law'. Less submissive or subservient republican presidents – such as Nikolaev in Sakha and Spiridonov in Komi – were forced to leave office or were not allowed to run for a third term. In some of the Muslim republics of the North Caucasus, the federal government, on the grounds of countering fundamentalism or preventing Islamist counter-reactions, tolerated legislation contradicting federal laws or the Constitution. In Karachaevo-Cherkessiya, for example, a law was accepted on the grounds that it was supposed to counter Wahhabi fundamentalism. In Ingushetiya, a law allowing polygamy and elements of traditional justice was not rescinded. In Chechnya's constitution, even the notion of sovereignty and republican citizenship was permitted.

A loss of the Russian president's confidence may in future justify firing a governor. This opens up ample space for subjective judgement; it contradicts the conception of due process. The term of an appointed governor is no longer specified. The Russian president can nominate those who have already served two or even three gubernatorial terms — and this is the carrot which makes incumbents give in. The appointed governors may take back some of the duties transferred to the federal districts and thus be compensated for their loss of an independent source of legitimacy.

Putin's appointment of governors will restrict political access and expression, diminish popular control and accountability. It will provide institutional incentives for nepotism and corruption, and it is therefore likely to revive resentment and frustration.[63] Added to the changes in electoral and party laws, the political space open for contestation has been substantially reduced. If performance and efficiency depend on competition over strategies and outcomes, they must perforce suffer because loyalty trumps competition. Governors will no longer have to search for a local base, but instead demonstrate obedience and look for access to the presidential administration. The appointment of governors will change the whole architecture and patterns of political regimes in the regions. Furthermore, in the long run the Kremlin alone will be held responsible for mischief in the regions.

10 Conclusions

Do the recent developments in Russian federalism fit into a larger trend in the development of multi-ethnic federations? In principle, one can observe that de jure asymmetries seem to be more pronounced at the early stages of a federalization process in multi-ethnic states. Over time, they are mostly pushed back. This does not just hold true for Russia, but for Spain, India and Nigeria as well. At the outset, federalization processes seem to be characterized by a pointed juxtaposition of the central government and the regions which is transformed into differentiated regional attitudes vis-à-vis the centre.

The Russian case illustrates that different forms of instutionalizing ethnicity react to dynamically changing ethnic group characteristics. The Russian case also provides evidence that probably all attempts to institutionalize ethnicity are of a temporary nature. Any arrangement will have to react flexibly to changing socio-structural and demographic givens as well as shifting political identifications. The popular thesis according to which the institutionalization of ethnicity and the territorialization of ethnicity become a resource of a 'nationalizing nationalism' and a hardening of group boundaries is probably far too sweeping. The nominal discretion over a territory is by itself not proof of a self-fulfilling will to ethno-nationalist secession. The disposition over resources, dependencies on federal subsidies, expected benefits, demographic composition and the behaviour of potential allies are all factors that inform the mobilization of ethnicity.

The Russian case illustrates that institutional arrangements, particularly the provision of territorial autonomy, cannot prevent secular processes of assimilation; they can steer the process at best. After a phase of ethnicization of federalism, since the second half of the 1990s we have witnessed a phase of de-ethnicization – economic and political expectations supersede ethnic calculations. The de-ethnicization of federalism corresponds with a Russification of the state in the sense of an explicit and implicit preference for the attributes of the Russian 'lead culture' vis-à-vis non-Russian cultures.

The assimilation of non-Russians, either through Russification or the transformation of ethnic into civic markers of identity, will proceed quite heterogeneously. Some indigenous people will dissolve as a group in the foreseeable future. The territoriality of ethnicity may lose its salience as a result of social and spatial mobility too. A general expectation that ethnicity degenerates into an archaic, politically irrelevant residue or a folkloristic specialty is, however, unrealistic. Some non-Russian people will preserve their linguistic-cultural-religious uniqueness for decades to come. Despite the recent mergers of autonomous districts with surrounding regions, a radical reduction of the number of regions is unlikely.

A forced assimilation, marginalization or alienation of non-Russians would evoke counter-reaction and increase the conflict potential. There are no representative opinion polls on the degree of perceived or actual ethnic discrimination. The evidence is scattered and multi-dimensional – my interviews nonetheless confirm a high degree of nervousness among non-Russians about a growing chauvinist, xenophobic attitude. Non-Russian people, especially with a Muslim background, do not have a sense of being equal citizens.

In comparison to other multi-ethnic federations the conflicts over positive groups rights are relatively moderate. The possibilities to mobilize ethnicity for particular interests are indeed limited – ethnic cleavages cannot effectively be instrumentalized during elections because the electoral and party legislation forbids ethnic parties. The 'national-cultural autonomy', on the other hand, has been transformed into an instrument of depoliticizing ethnicity. The collective action of strong republics is much more difficult due to the effective 'divide et impera' of the central government. The radical reduction of access channels or institutionalized participatory rights vis-à-vis the central government leads instead to non-transparent, informal ways of pursuing one's interests, including clientelism and a policy of favours. Currently the assessments of the stability or instability of these patterns of centre–regional relations, and especially inter-ethnic relations, vary extremely. They range from 'stable' to 'extremely unstable'.[64]

The political infighting over the institutional structure and division of competencies is still not resolved. After a period of centralization a new reconfiguration of powers in favour of the regions may evolve. Yet, there is no inevitability; potential factors are the political mobilization in the regions and a visible weakening of the central government. The causes that led to the dissolution of the Soviet Union were systematic in nature. The Soviet federation broke apart due to the deficient societal federalism, the lack of a post-Soviet federal party system, and the inefficiency in overcoming inter-regional discrepancies, the weakness of the centre, nationalist transition strategies and the unstable combination of authoritarian rule with federalism. Some of these reasons could become virulent in Russia again. The official politics of history and culture, which are perceived by non-Russians as pro-orthodox, Russo-centric and blind with respect to past repression, could further alienate non-Russians. Democratization from below, on regional or ethnic grounds, could emerge. An increase in socio-economic disparities could stimulate new secessionist movements, especially in the North Caucasus.

In formal-institutional terms Russia is no longer a federation. The sources of Russian federalism are nonetheless deeper than Putin's instrumentalism seems to suggest. Putin's centralism is institutionally unstable, characterized by a permanent reconstruction and disrespect for constitutional principles; it repeats the mistake of a double subordination of the defunct Soviet system; it is systematically overburdened, almost unable to learn from mistakes, extremely personalized and exposes a low degree of predictability.

The autonomy and corporate self-organization of the regions is currently weak, and there are few veto points at the central level – this has opened a wide avenue for a presidential power grab. The Russian case demonstrates that authoritarian regression and de-federalization are mutually supportive. A system with an extreme concentration of unchecked powers in the presidency and a horizontally and vertically deficient division of powers is fundamentally opposed to federal principles.

Notes

1 Gail W. Lapidus, 'Asymmetrical federalism and state breakdown in Russia', *Post-Soviet Affairs*, Vol. 15, No. 1, 1996, pp. 74–82; Darrell Slider, 1997, 'Russia's market-distorting federalism', *Post-Soviet Geography and Economics*, Vol. 38, 1997, pp. 445–60; Steven Solnick, 'Russia over the edge: explaining the failure of liberal state building', *East European Constitutional Review*, Vol. 7, No. 4 (Fall), 1998, pp. 70–92; Kathryn Stoner-Weiss, 'Central weakness and provincial autonomy: observations on the devolution process in Russia', *Post-Soviet Affairs*, Vol. 15, No. 1, 1999, pp. 87–106; Cameron Ross, *Federalism and Democratization in Russia*, Manchester, New York: Manchester University Press, 2002.
2 Paul Goble, 'Three myths about Russian federalism', *Radio Free Europe/Radio Liberty Newsline*, 26 October 2004.
3 Irina A. Koniukhova, *Sovremennyi Rossiiski federalizm i mirovoi opyt: itogi stanovlenia a perspektivy razvitiia*, Moscow: 'Izdatel'skii dom Gorodets', 2004.
4 Nikolai Petrov, 'The security dimension of the federal reforms', in Peter Reddaway and Robert W. Orttung (eds), *The Dynamics of Russian Politics*.

Putin's Reform of Federal-Regional Relations, Vol. II, Lanham, MD: Rowman & Littlefield, 2005, pp. 7–32.

5 See for example Midkhat Farukshin (Kazan State University), 'New dimensions of regionalism and federalism: the case of Tatarstan', paper presented at the conference, 'The Russian Federation and the EU: New Dimensions of Federalism and Regionalism', University of Leuven, 8 November 2005.

6 For example, Rafael' Khakimov, Mikhail Stolyarov, Midhkat Farukshin, Suren Avakian, and Il'dar Gabdrafikov, to name just a few of experts with non-Russian origin and federalist convictions – this, however, does not mean that a non-Russian origin pre-determines federalist views, or vice versa.

7 *Kontseptsiya administrativnoi reformy v Rossiiskoi Federatsii v 2006-2008 godakh*, No. 1789-g, Goverment of the Russian Federation, 25 October 2005, www.worldbank.org/wbi/governance/bycountry.html.

8 *Johnson's Russia List*, No. 261, 20 November 2006.

9 *Interfax*, 17 November 2006.

10 *Johnson's Russia List*, No. 247, 3 November 2006.

11 *Interfax*, 16 November 2006.

12 Fred Weir, 'Ethnic cleansing in Russia. Putin stokes the flames of xenophobia', 15 November 2006 at http://www.inthesetimes.com/site/main/article/2887/.

13 Kathryn Stoner-Weiss, *Resisting the State: Reform and Retrenchment in Post-Soviet Russia*, Cambridge: Cambridge University Press, 2006), pp. 7–14.

14 See V. E. Chernik, *Konstitutsionnoe pravo Rossii*, Moscow: 'Yurist', 2004, pp. 200ff.

15 Viktor A. Cherepanov, *Teoriia Rossiiskovo Federalizma: Uchebnoe Posobie*, Moscow: 'MZ-Press', 2005, p. 173.

16 B. N. Topornina, *Konstitutsiia Rossiiskoi Federatsii. Nauchno-prakticheskii Kommentarii*, Moskva: 'Iurist', Izdanie tret'e, pod redaktsiei akademika Institut Gosudarstva i Prava RAN, 2003, p. 111.

17 Ibid.

18 Irina A. Konyuchova, *Sovremennyi Rossiiski Federalizm i Mirovoi Opyt: Itogi Stanovlenia Perspektivy Razivitiya*, Moskva: Izdatel'skii dom Gorodes, 2004, p. 43.

19 A similar view is the red string, in Richard Sakwa, *Putin: Russia's Choice*, London and New York: Routledge, 2004.

20 Milena V. Gligich-Zolotareva, *Pravovye Osnovy Federalizma,* Moksva: Iurist, 2006, p. 213.

21 Ibid., pp. 210f.

22 *Sobranie Zakonodatel'stvo 2000*, No. 31 (3205).

23 'Russia: Putin calls for 'universal principles' to settle frozen conflicts', *Radio Free Europe/Radio Liberty*, 1 February 2006.

24 'Public Chamber to Help Russians in Self-Proclaimed Republics'. *Johnson's Russia List*, No. 284, 19 December 2006.

25 I am using the term 'autochthonous people' because the term 'indigenous people' pertains in the Russian context only to the small people with a traditional lifestyle in the high North, Siberia and the Far East.

26 Olga Rom-Sourkova, *Die Sprachliche Situation in der Russischen Föderation*, Berlin: BWV Berliner Wissenschaftsverlag, 2004, p. 149.

27 Alex Rodriguez, 'Muted Voices, Compelling Cry', *Chicago Tribune*, 13 December 2006.

28 Alexander Osipov, *The Situation and Legal Status of Meskhetians in Russian Federation*, Moscow: Memorial Human Rights Centre, 2003; Oskari Pentikäinen, Tom Trier, 'Between integration and resettlement: the meskhetian Turks', *ECMI Working Paper*, No. 21, September 2004.

29 Ludmilla Lobova, 'Ethnopolitische konflikte im nordkaukasus: geschichte-gegen-wart-perspektiven', in Erich Reitter (ed.), *Jahrbuch für Internationale Sicherheitspolitik*, Wien: Verlag E.S. Mittler & Sohn, 2001, pp. 17–30.

30 Interview with Vladimir Nikolaevich Lysenko, Moscow, 6 December 2005.
31 Jeronim Perovic, 'The north caucasus on the brink', International Relations and Security Network, *ISN Case Studies* (Zürich), Vol. 1, No. 8, 2006.
32 ORB = Operational Investigative Bureau under the Chief Directorate of the Ministry of Interior for the Southern Federal District. On the above see Human Rights Watch, Widespread Torture in the Chechen Republic. Human Rights Watch Briefing Paper for the 37th Session of the UN Committee Against Torture, 13 November 2006.
33 Andrew Osborn, 'Kremlin was complicit in Chechen murders', *The Independent*, 10 November 2006.
34 *Izvestia*, 16 December 2006. Translated in *Johnson's Russia List*, No. 282, 17 December 2006.
35 Leonid Sedov, 'Map of hopes and fears – political sentiments of Russians: regional cross-section', *Nezavisimaya Gazeta*, 11 December 2006, in *Johnson's Russia List*, No. 278, 12 December 2006 (a sum of over 100 per cent of the individual answers resulted from the rounding up partial results).
36 See B. N. Topornina, *Konstitutsiia Rossiiskoi Federatsii. Nauchno-prakticheskie Kommentarii* (Moskva: 3rd edition, Iurist, 2003), pp. 510f.
37 Interviews with Mansur A. Ajupov (8 December, 2005), Deputy of the State Duma, Committee for National Affairs; Aleksandr V. Nikonov (8 December, 2005), consultant to the State Duma Committee for National Affairs; Svetlana Smirnova (7 December, 2005), deputy of the State Duma from Chuvashiya; Gennadii Oleynik (13 December, 2005), member of the Federation Council; Svetlana A. Bastanzhieva (12 December, 2005), Ministry of Regional Development.
38 Zakon No. 3266-1 'Ob obrazovanii', 10 June 1992.
39 Zakon No. 5242-1 'O pravde grazdan RF na svobodu peredvizheniia', 25 June 1993.
40 An overview of minority rights legislation is provided by Doris Widra, 'Legislation of the Russian Federation Concerning Ethnic Minorities and its Shortcomings', at: http://www.eawarn.ru/pub/Projects/TacisProjecdts/Widra.htm.
41 http://www.legislationline.org/?jid = 42&less = false&tid = 143.
42 Vladimir A. Kryazhkov, *Status Korennykh Malochislennykh Narodov Rossii. Pravovye Akty*, Moskva: Assotsiatsiia korennykh malochislennykh narodov severa, sibiri i dal'nego vostoka Rossiiskoi Federatsii, 2005.
43 Interview with Professor Vladimir Kryazhkov, Consultant at the Constitutional Court of the Russian Federation, Moscow 12 December, 2005.
44 Interview with Genadii Dmitrievich Oleinik, member of the Federation Council, Head of the Committee for Affairs of the Far North and Small Peoples?, Moscow, 13 December 2005.
45 Zakon 'O garantiyakh prav korennykh malochislennykh narodov Rossiiskoi Federatsii', 30 April 1999.
46 Zakon 'Ob obshikh principakh organizatsii obshin korennykh malochislennykh narodov severa, Sibiri i dal'nego vostoka Rossiiskoi Federatsii', 20 July 2000; a listing of rights of indigenous people is found in Kryazhkov, esp. pp. 19ff.
47 Ibid., pp. 45–7.
48 See in the following Aleksandr G. Osipov, *Natsional'no-kul'turnaya avtonomiya: Idei, Resheniya, Instituty* (Sankt Peterburg: Tsentr nezavisimykh sotsiologicheskikh issledovanii, 2004).
49 Interview with Minister Mikhail Stolyarov, 7 December, 2005, Deputy Head of the Permanent Mission of Tatarstan in Moscow.
50 Interview with A. I. Grigorev, Deputy Head of the Permanent Mission of Chuvashiya in Moscow, 8 December, 2005.
51 *Konstitutsiia Rossiiskoi Federatsii: Nauchno-prakticheskie Kommentarii*, pp. 464f.

52 Interview with A. I. Grigorev, Deputy Head of the Permanent Mission of Chuvashiya in Moscow, 8 December, 2005.
53 On the various conceptions of sovereignty in republican constitutions and the rulings of the Constitutional Court of Russia see N. M. Mirichanov, *Federalizm, Etnichnost', Gosudarstvennost': Novyi Kurs Rossiiskoi Vlasti*, Moskva: Arba T-XXI, 2002, pp. 170–80.
54 Viktor A. Cherepanov, *Teoriya Rossiiskovo Federalizma*, Moskva: MZ-Press, 2005, p. 167.
55 William H. Riker, *Federalism: Origin, Operation, Significance*, Boston, MA: Little Brown, 1964, p. 111.
56 Kelly M. McMann, Nikolai V. Petrov, 'A survey of democracy in Russia's regions', *Post-Soviet Geography and Economics*, Vol. 41, No. 3, 2000, pp. 155–82.
57 Grigorii V. Golosov, *Political Parties in the Regions of Russia: Democracy Unclaimed*, Boulder, CO: Lynne Rienner Publishers, 2004, p. 163.
58 Gordon M. Hahn, 'The impact of Putin's federative reforms on democraization in Russia', *Post-Soviet Affairs*, Vol. 19, No. 2, 2003, p. 142.
59 M. Steven Fish, Robin S. Brooks, 'Does diversity hurt democracy?', *Journal of Democracy*, Vol. 15, No. 1, 2004, pp. 154ff.
60 Hahn, p. 148.
61 Emil Pain, 'Reforms in the administration of the regions and their influence on ethnopolitical Processes in Russia, 1999–2003', in Peter Reddaway and Robert W. Orttung (eds), *The Dynamics of Russian Politics. Putin's Reform of Federal-Regional Relations, Vol. II*, Lanham, MD: Roman & Littlefield, 2005, p. 356, and Tomila Lankina, 'President Putin's local government reforms', in Reddaway and Orttung, pp. 145-77.
62 Mikhail Filippov, Olga Shvetsova, 'Federalism and democracy in Russia.' Paper prepared for the conference 'Postcommunist State and Society: Transnational and National Politics', Syracuse University, 30 September–1 October, 2005, p. 19ff.
63 Robert Bruce Ware, 'Russian democracy', *Johnson's Russia List*, No. 8395, 4 October 2004.
64 'Stable' according to Koniucheva, p. 14. The opposite assessment ('extremely unstable') is represented by Gligic-Zolotareva, p. 214.

4 Unification as a political project

The case of Permskii Krai

Oksana Oracheva

Federalism as a political institution is rightly seen as the most appropriate way of accommodating a country's size and internal diversity. Harmonization of important political and cultural differences through the creation of a tiered system of government is considered to be one of the fundamental tenets of a federal political system. In multi-ethnic states, federalism also plays a key role in protecting the rights of ethnic minorities and territorial communities.[1]

The Soviet Union provides an example of the co-existence of different types of territorial communities within the same country. The USSR was a multi-layered federation within which another federal body, the Russian Republic existed. Moreover, it combined two different principles that formed the federation – territorial and ethnic. After the breakdown of the Soviet Union in 1991 Russia inherited the federal structure that had been codified in the 1978 Constitution. Federalism has been seen in a positive light as a way to hold the country together.

Until 2005, the Russian Federation consisted of twenty-one republics[2] based on the ethnic principle; six krais and forty-nine oblasts that are purely territorial in character; ten ethnically based autonomous okrugs (see Table 4.1); two federal cities, and one autonomous oblast.

The Constitution also institutionalized the formation of compound subjects of the federation, i.e. constituent units of the federation which are situated within larger constituent units – similar to the traditional Russian doll ('matryoshka'). As Gordon Hahn fairly points out, 'Russia, the core of the USSR's "internal empire", mirrors its predecessor not only in its territorial, ethnic and confessional incongruence but its weak asymmetrical, "nation-territorial" administrative structure.'[3] Even though the status quo was preserved and confirmed by the Russian Constitution of 1993, the issue of Russia's state territorial structure and the institutionalization of federal principles have never been far from the top of the political agenda.

Yeltsin's successor Vladimir Putin, on the contrary, is replacing federal mechanisms by those associated with a unitary state. The foundation of seven federal districts,[4] the reconfiguration of the Federation Council, appointment of regional governors, centralization of the decision-making

Table 4.1 Autonomous okrugs and their 'mother' regions

Name of the Autonomous Okrug	'Mother' Region	Okrug's Capital	Area (sq. km)	Okrug's Population/ (Place Within the Russian Federation)
Aginskii Buryatskii	Chita Oblast	Aginskoe	19,000	72,213/(84)
Chukotskii	N/A	Anadyr	737,700	53,824/(85)
Yevenkiiskii	Krasnoyarsk Krai	Tura	767,600	17,697/(89)
Khanty-Mansiskii	Tyumen Oblast	Khanty-Masiisk	523,100	1,432,817/(36)
Komi-Permyatskii	Perm Oblast	Kudymkar	32,900	136,076/(82)
Koraykskii	Kamchatka Oblast	Palana	301,500	25,157/(88)
Nenetskii	Arkhangel'sk Oblast	Naryan-Mar	176,700	41,546/(86)
Taimyrskii	Krasnoyarsk Krai	Dudinka	862,100	39,786/(87)
Ust'-Ordynskii Buraytskii	Irkutsk Oblast	Ust'-Orda	22,400	135,327/(83)
Yamalo-Nenetskii	Tyumen Oblast	Salekhard	750,300	507,000/(72)

Source: Compiled by the author.

processes, and changing political rhetoric are not the only signs of defederalization. The tendency to revise the state administrative structure by reducing the number of federation subjects fully fits with this approach. There have been numerous initiatives aimed at reducing the number of subjects of the federation through regional mergers. Some of them have come into being (see Table 4.2 for the mergers' timeline), others (such as the mergers of Tyumen Oblast and Yamalo-Nenetskii and Khanty-Mansiskii autonomous okrugs, or the mergers of Arkhangelsk Oblast and Nenetskii Autonomous Okrug) have been more problematic, and the final outcome is still unclear.

However, mergers of federal subjects have required amendments to federal legislation. In December 2001, the constitutional Law, 'On the Process of Accession to the Russian Federation and Foundation of a New Constituent Unit of the Russian Federation', was adopted.[5] This law regulates the conditions and procedures for mergers. According to the law, only neighbouring federation subjects are permitted to initiate merger procedures. There are two possible outcomes of a merger: two federation subjects (A and B) could merge and create a new subject of the federation (A + B = C), or one subject of the federation could incorporate another without creating a new subject (A + B = A). The law also requires federation subjects interested in a merger to hold a referendum, but only the President can place before the State Duma the draft law required to institute a new merged subject of the federation.

The main thrust of this chapter is an examination of Putin's new policy of merging federal subjects with a focus on the first new federal subject to emerge from such a merger, Permskii Krai. The choice of this particular case

Table 4.2 Timetable of regional mergers

Merging subjects of federation	Name of the new subject of federation	Referendum date	Merger Law Adoption	Transition period	Date of the new subject of federation formation
Perm Oblast Komi-Permyak Autonomous Okrug	Permskii Krai	7 December 2003	26 March 2004	26 March 2004–31 January 2007	1 December 2005
Krasnoyarsk Krai Taimyr Autonomous Okrug Yevreiskaya Autonomous Oblast	Krasnoyarskii Krai	17 April 2005	14 October 2005	14 October 2005–31 December 2007	1 January 2007
Kamchatka Oblast Koryak Autonomous Okrug	Kamchatskii Krai	23 October 2005	15 July 2006	15 July 2006–31 December 2008	1 July 2007
Irkutsk Oblast Ust'-Ordynskii Autonomous Okrug	Irkutsk Oblast	16 April 2006	11 January 2007	11 January 2007–1 January 2009	1 January 2008
Chita Oblast Aginskii Buraytskii Autonomous Okrug	Zabaikalskii Krai	11 March 2007			

Source: Compiled by the author.

is not random. Implementation of the idea to reduce the number of federation subjects only took place with the merger of the Perm Region and the Komi-Permyak Autonomous Okrug. Decision-makers today see this merger as an example of a successful unification. The process of creating Permskii Krai led to the adoption of a new legal framework at the federal level.

I see the merger of the Perm Oblast and the Komi-Permyak Autonomous Okrug as a complex elite project that needs to be evaluated from both a political and an economic perspective In this chapter I define political and economic criteria and indicators of unification, discuss the main instruments used, and assess unification practices and procedures. The political and economic outcomes of the unification project will be evaluated against the declared set of objectives. I also look at possible implications of the upcoming mergers for the future of federalism in Russia. In order to evaluate the process of unification it is first necessary to look at the historical framework within which it has occurred.

Unification as a project – theoretical framework

According to President Putin, 'unification is not an end in itself',[6] it should be aimed at improving the social and economic conditions of the region. Summarizing the arguments in favour of unification, Putin stated at his annual press conference in 2007:

> any territorial changes, whether mergers or separations, can only go ahead if this is the will of the citizens. Local laws allow for different procedures, but they are all based on the region's citizens expressing their will. The mergers that we have seen between regions took place because many regions proved economically unviable. .. and were unable to deal with their economic and social problems. In cases where regions wish to merge in order to improve their situation and be able to resolve their problems more effectively, we support such mergers.[7]

Therefore, the principal goal of unification, as it was articulated by the state, is to improve the economic situation in the less developed subjects of the federation using the donor regions as a power locomotive. Explaining the economic costs and benefits of unifications, Putin argues that:

> the budgets of the regions that are subsidized by the federal budget will obviously benefit from such mergers, but this does not mean that, at the same time, the budgets of donor regions or regions with better economic results will suffer. As a rule, these self-sufficient regions will actually get an added benefit in the form of access to infrastructure, access to mineral resources and the possibility of carrying out major joint investment projects. This will give the federal authorities the possibility of

making more effective investments in regional support and regional infrastructure programmes.[8]

To be fair, differences in population density, income level, access to public services such as health care, education, transport etc. exist within all countries, not only within those which have huge territories and different climate zones. Russia is no exception. Thornton Matheson is right when he points out that, 'Russia's 89 regions differ starkly in terms of their economic endowments due not only to the natural diversity of Russia's immense territory but also to the spatial concentration of sectoral investment under Soviet central planning.'[9] As a result, regional development was, and still is, characterized by a high level of specialization. For example, in the early 2000s fuel production comprised 88 per cent of the total industrial output in the Khanty-Mansiskii Autonomous Okrug; in Vologda region iron and steel production constituted 60 per cent of the regional output; in Komi Republic fuel production made up 56–60 per cent of the regional output; and in the Krasnoyarsk Krai about 67 per cent of regional output was concentrated in non-ferrous production.[10] Merging subjects of the federation fully fit in with this trend in regional development. Regional infrastructure, delivery of public services (healthcare, education, sanitation, etc), per capita income, also differ significantly from one subject of the federation to the next. For example, in 2003 only 8–11 per cent of the populations of the Khanty-Mansiskii and Yamalo-Nenetskii autonomous okrugs lived below the poverty line, while in the Ust-Ordynskii Autonomous Okrug and the Republic of Ingushetiya 83 per cent were living in extreme poverty.[11] Moreover, one could observe even greater differences at the local level where most resources are concentrated in regional capitals and a few other cities, whilst other areas remain underdeveloped. As Vladimir Leksin indicates, in Russia,

> asymmetry along meridian and latitude lines, within large and small regional units, between urban and rural settings that have been determined by past practices, has now been exacerbated by new practices of resettlement, and economic and infrastructural disparities. ... Russia is doomed to asymmetry.[12]

However, some of these problems could be successfully addressed by employing different fiscal federalism mechanisms, especially by the distribution of government transfers to those subjects of federations that have special social needs. Current debates on the role of fiscal instruments also focus on issues of efficiency and equity. While among other things, efficiency is related to the 'delivery of services by the appropriate tier of government', 'fiscal equity considerations suggest that like individuals should be treated in a like manner'.[13] Fiscal federalism is usually seen as the instrument of levelling up regional economic and social development to ensure the delivery of standard public services across the country. However, the costs of such delivery will also differ depending on the demographic and social composition of the region, the regional geography and climate.

Federal subjects in contemporary Russia have a relatively short list of local taxes – only three tax revenues are fully allocated within regional budgets, namely: the property tax on organizations, the transport tax and the tax on the gambling industry. Some other taxes (e.g. the profit tax, income tax, etc.) are distributed between federal and regional budgets in differing proportions. Recent developments of fiscal federalism in Russia have been aimed at budget centralization to bring them into line with the current levels of 'political centralization'. As Rostislav Turovskii stresses, this policy of the centralization of budget revenues is clearly illustrated by changes in the distribution of one of the key taxes – the value-added tax (VAT). In 1997–8 25 per cent of VAT revenues were received by regional budgets. From the second quarter of 1999 the regional share decreased to approximately 15 per cent. Since 2001 the regions have received zero revenues from VAT; 100 per cent of VAT revenues are now centralized in the federal budget.[14] Moreover, the government is centralizing some other taxes and excise duties, such as the tax on mineral production and tobacco. By centralizing taxation revenues the federal government claims it will be able to redistribute financial resources more fairly between regions.

To decrease the sharp abnormalities between regional finances the federal government adopted the federal programme, 'Reduction of differences in the social and economic development of the regions in the Russian Federation (2002-10 and up to 2015)',[15] which aims to reduce the 'development gap' between the leaders and the economically less developed regions. One of the goals of the federal programme is to decrease by 2010 the number of regions that have fallen below the average level of economic development by 25 per cent, and to reduce by 15 per cent the number of people living below the poverty line. Overall regional economic differences are set to decline 1.5 times; 18.7 per cent of the funds used to implement this programme will come from the federal budget, 22.9 per cent from regional budgets (subject of federations) and 58.4 per cent from off-budget sources.

However, by calling for mergers of the less developed, if not to say, undeveloped subjects of the federation, with those which are considered to be rich donor regions, the Russian state has created a new method of levelling out regional differences. To sum up, mergers are aimed at improving the social and economic situation in 'problematic' regions through the use of the funds of donor regions, rather than the federal budget.

Prerequisites for mergers

There are several prerequisites that regions should satisfy in order to start the unification process. First, only neighbouring regions are entitled to merge. Second, mergers must be 'approved' by the popular will of citizens through a referendum. Third, the federal Centre (e.g. the President) has to approve each merger which then must ratified by a special merger law.

A number of political, economic, social and ethnic/cultural indicators allow us to evaluate the effectiveness and results of the merger process. Political indicators include: (1) changes in the decision-making process as a result of the merger, (2) the appearance of new political institutions, (3) changes to existing political institutions, (4) gains and losses of political elites in the merging subjects, and (5) the level of protection provided to national minorities within the new territorial unit. Institutional aspects of the political indicators include: the activities of 'old' and 'new' institutions during different stages of the merger process, the organizational structure of new political institutions and their reflection of the goals of the merger process, and the ability of political institutions to successfully achieve the stated goals of the merger.

Among the economic and social indicators are: levels of economic compensation for the merger and their time frame, appearance of new economic projects as a result of the merger, encouragement of new short and long-term investment opportunities for the less developed subjects that merge, development of the regional infrastructure, and changes in the quality of life of citizens in the merging subjects. One could assume that positive social and economic changes would take place in those regions that had positive trends before merger. However, Vladimir Leksin makes the important point that it is difficult to determine to what extent positive economic developments are the result of the merger itself and not other extraneous factors, and to what extent a merger is useful for a wealthy donor region.[16]

Cultural indicators relate to the changes in the cultural/ideological environment in the merging subjects, the creation of a new territorial identity alongside the preservation of existing ethnic identities of national minorities.

The Perm region and the Komi-Permyak Autonomous Okrug – historical framework

The Perm region is located in the Urals and could be described as a region at the edge of Europe, as the Ural Mountains divide the European part of Russia from Siberia. The regional capital, the city of Perm, is located in the middle of the region on the banks of the Kama river. The city received its name after the Finno-Ugrian *pera ma*, meaning 'distant land'.

The Komi-Permyak Okrug is situated in the northern part of the Perm region. The small town of Kudymkar that used to be a village is now the Okrug's capital. The Okrug is composed of seven districts (raions) (including the city district of the Okrug capital) situated on the upper Kama river basin. The Okrug received its name after the Komi-Permyak ethnic group. This group along with the linguistically closed Komi-Zyryans belongs to the Finno-Ugrian group. The Komi-Permyak Autonomous Okrug is one of just two okrugs in the Russian Federation where the titular ethnic group makes up the majority of population (according to the 2002 census Komi-Permyaks constitute 59 per cent of the Okrug population).[17]

The Komi-Permyak 'national' Okrug was founded on 26 February 1925 as a part of the Urals Oblast. Even though the Okrug was the first to be founded it was an uneasy arrangement. The issue of the institutionalization of a Komi-Permyak national identity goes back to 1921 when the Komi Autonomous Republic was founded. Even though there was agreement that there should be some territorial institutionalization of the Komi-Permyak national identity, there was no consensus among the Bolshevik party elite as to whether Komi-Permyaks were to be part of the Komi Republic or institutionalization could take a different form. In the end, the idea to unite two close ethnic groups in one administrative and territorial unit did not receive enough support from the party elite. Therefore, the first territorial unit in the newly created form of a national Okrug was founded.[18] The foundation of the Komi-Permyak National Okrug was the starting point in the history of compound territorial units within the Soviet Union (it is symbolical that the Okrug was also the first one to merge and disappear). In 1977, all the Okrugs in the Soviet Union, changed their title from 'national Okrugs' to 'Autonomous Okrugs'. The Komi-Permyak Okrug did not miss out in the process of the levelling up of their status during 'the parade of sovereignties' in the early 1990s, and in 1993, the Komi-Permyak Autonomous Okrug became a fully-fledged subject of the federation. At the same time, the Komi-Permyak Okrug never completely broke away from its 'mother' region. In 1994 the Okrug adopted its Charter reconfirming its status within the Federation. Article 1 of the Charter stated that the Komi-Permyak Autonomous Okrug was a fully-fledged subject of the Russian Federation.[19] At the same time, article 8 proclaimed that the Komi-Permyak Autonomous Okrug was an integral part of the Perm Oblast. Relations between the Okrug and the Oblast were regulated by the Federal Constitution, the 1992 Federal Treaty, Federal laws, and special bilateral treaties signed between the Komi-Permyak Autonomous Okrug and the Perm Oblast.[20]

The Perm Oblast Charter also stated that the Perm Oblast acknowledges the rights of the population of the Komi-Permyak Autonomous Okrug, their right to self-determination and development of their language and culture, respecting their traditions and customs (article 6, part 1).[21] The Charter declares that the region would not interfere in the Okrug's internal affairs (article 6, part 3).[22] The only instrument that institutionalizes relations between the Okrug and the Oblast is the bilateral treaty (article 6, part 2).[23] The Perm Oblast law, 'On the Administrative-Territorial Structure of the Perm Oblast', also confirmed that administratively the Komi-Permyak Okrug was an integral part of the Oblast and that administrative boundaries between the Okrug and Oblast were set as of 1992.[24]

In 1996 a tripartite agreement was signed between the Komi-Permyak Autonomous Okrug, the Perm Oblast and the Russian Federation which defines their spheres of competence and responsibility.[25] Therefore, one could

argue that by the mid-1990s Oblast–Okrug relations were finally institutionalized. Being part of the Oblast, the Komi-Permyak Okrug was always
involved in Oblast politics: the Okrug had two deputies in the Perm Oblast
assembly and participated in the Perm Oblast gubernatorial elections.
Traditionally the Komi-Permyak Okrug and the Oblast had very strong
political, economic and cultural ties that were not destroyed by the fact that
the Okrug became a fully-fledged subject of the Federation. Even before the
merger about 80 per cent of the Okrug's industrial enterprises were structural
units of Perm Oblast's enterprises; the Perm Oblast factories processed
almost 90 per cent of the timber produced in the Okrug, etc.

In 1997 the author interviewed members of the Perm Oblast Assembly,
including those who represented the Komi-Permyak Autonomous Okrug.
Questions were asked about centre–Oblast relations, Oblast–Okrug relations,
and on their prospects for the future. It was interesting to observe the differences in approach as regards prospects of closer relations between the
Okrug and the Oblast, or the Okrug's eventual reintegration into the Oblast.
A majority of deputies, who represented districts within the Oblast, expressed satisfaction with the status quo or were not supportive of any administrative changes. At the same time leaders of the Perm Oblast Assembly
believed that greater cooperation between the Okrug and the Oblast would
be beneficial not only for the economically depressed Okrug, but for the
Oblast as well. Not surprisingly, deputies representing the Komi-Permyak
Autonomous Okrug strongly supported greater integration of the Oblast into
the Okrug's economic affairs, and believed that the Okrug would definitely
benefit economically from a merger.

Starting the merger process: external imposition or initiative from below?

The Oblast and Okrug elites, politicians and business people had discussed
the idea of reintegration before it became a part of the nationwide political
agenda. In 2000, Yuri Trutnev, during his successful gubernatorial electoral
campaign, made it one of his key initiatives. Nevertheless, the implementation of this initiative was impossible without the further development of
federal legislation.

Article 66.5 of the Russian Constitution states that 'the status of a component of the Russian Federation can be changed by mutual consent of the
Russian Federation and the component of the Russian Federation in accordance
with federal constitutional law.'[26]

One of the major requirements to start the merger process is to get popular support from the citizens in a referendum. According to the referendum
that was held on 7 December 2003 in the Perm region and the Komi-
Permyak Autonomous Okrug, about 90 per cent of those who took part in
the referendum in the Komi-Permyak Autonomous Okrug voted in favour of
unification with the Oblast, while in the Perm Oblast about 85 per cent of

voters supported the idea of merger.[27] Such support for unification did not come as a surprise. The unification campaign had actually been conducted for quite a long period of time, even though officially it started just one month before the referendum. But an analysis of the regional press demonstrates that only the views of those who fully supported the merger were fully represented in the mass media.

One would have expected at least some opposition in the Okrug that was losing both its political independence and institutionalized ethnic territorial community. However, such opposition was very weak and given little voice. Even one of the opposition leaders, the former chairman of the Okrug Legislature, Ivan Chetin, did not fully disagree with the concept of unification but insisted that the full conditions of the merger, including the Okrug's special status, should be clarified from the very beginning. The low level of opposition to the merger can be explained by a number of factors.

First, the pro-unification campaign was very proactive if not to say aggressive and gave very little chance for the opposition to fight against the mainstream – press, TV, radio, visits of federal politicians, discussion clubs, cultural events, show business star tours, etc. – everything was working in favour of unification. The circulation figures of *Permskii Krai*, a special newspaper fully devoted to the unification process, were very high – about one million copies.[28] The campaign even became part of the education process – schoolteachers were asked to talk about the common history and culture of the peoples living in Perm Oblast and the Komi-Permyak Autonomous Okrug, so that children would be aware of the referendum and prospects for unification, and discuss such ideas with their families.[29]

Second, one should consider that the political culture of the Komi-Permyak rural population is dominated by passive loyalty to government, which is hardly compatible with the open expression of opposition to official power. Moreover, long before the merger was put on the political agenda the Okrug's population clearly expressed the view that they were not interested in autonomy as such, but were more interested in being part of a larger community.[30]

Third, the propaganda in favour of unification almost entirely rested on economic arguments – there was widespread dissemination of economic data showing the economic gains, which would flow from the merger, while other more sensitive political issues were not given so much publicity. The Oblast and Okrug elites made full use of a document that lauded the economic benefits of the merger. According to the 'Prognosis for Socio-Economic Consequences of Unification of the Perm Region and the Komi-Permyak Autonomous Okrug', the merger would lead to the construction of an additional 225 km of roads, a rise in the Okrug's per capita income from 2,575 roubles to 2,812 roubles in 2006, and the average wage would rise from 3,912 roubles to 4,578 roubles.[31] Such positive economic data was naturally very attractive to the citizens of the Okrug.

Thus, long before the referendum there was a general consensus that the populations of both the Oblast and the Okrug would support the merger. Approval of the merger required 50 per cent plus 1 vote.

Regional elites worried about low turnout for the referendum utilized their 'administrative resources' to achieve the desired result. Some of the methods used clearly violated the citizens' rights to freely express their opinions. The Perm Oblast Centre of Human Rights noted the following violations: employees were required to present a written confirmation of participation in the referendum at their workplace, hospitals refused to admit people for regular treatment without an absentee ballot, the day of the referendum (Sunday) was made a working day and all employees were obliged to come to their workplace with an absentee ballot to vote collectively.[32] Such techniques enabled regional elites to control the process of voting and to ensure that enough people came to the polling stations and that they voted the 'right way'!

The referendum in fact completed a set of negotiations that had begun much earlier. A number of very important agreements were made between the Oblast and Okrug political elites on the one hand, and the federal centre on the other. Those agreements included, but were not limited to: (1) the preservation of a special administrative status for the Komi-Permyak Okrug, (2) the maintenance of special bonuses for citizens of the Okrug living in the Northern territories, (3) the establishment of a transition period, and (4) a continuation of the practice of providing financial aid to the Okrug through federal transfers.

The economic legacy of unification

Natalia Zubarevich identifies two major principles that an economic justification for mergers would have to be based on:

- 'mother' regions should be able to lead the development of the new subject of the federation because of their higher economic potential and ability to apply an effective model of modernization (positive condition);
- Okrug elites are unable to improve the socio-economic situation and to overcome economic gaps (negative condition).[33]

On the surface the Perm region and the Komi-Permyak Autonomous Okrug's merger fully complies with the above arguments. The Okrug occupies 20.5 per cent of the total territory of the Perm region while only 5.1 per cent of region's population is concentrated there. The Komi-Permyak Okrug has a very low population density of just 4.6 people per sq. km. – that is, four times lower that in the Perm region. Moreover, the Okrug has very low urban density of 26.0 per cent, which is the lowest in the European part of Russia. The population is unevenly spread throughout the Okrug territory and this has also been a contributing factor to the Okrug's slow economic development.

Moreover, the Okrug's economy has been almost exclusively based upon timber production (in 2004 timber production occupied 61.6 per cent in the Okrug's industrial output).[34] The timber industry went through a phase of rapid development in 1950s–1960s. However, the Okrug never had any pulp and paper mills and timber was always transported outside the Okrug's boundaries for processing. As a result in 2005 only 16 per cent of timber was processed in the Okrug itself.[35] As the Okrug's road system was, and still is, underdeveloped, the Kama river and some other smaller rivers became the major source of timber transportation. However, in the 1980s and 1990s the timber industry began to decline and many timber factories were closed with the loss of thousands of jobs. With new laws against using rivers for timber logging, the industry now faces a further decline. Today one can see many former timber areas where there is far more poverty now than there was in the 1990s.

By the mid 1990s, the Komi-Permyak Autonomous Okrug was still one of the least developed of Russia's territories. The Okrug has the lowest living standard of all the regions of the Volga (Privolzhsky) Federal District. Whilst in 2002 industrial production in Perm Oblast was 45,5000 roubles per capita, it was only 3,400 roubles per capita, in the Okrug. Total investment volume per capita (of large and medium size businesses) in the Oblast was 12,7000 roubles while in the Okrug it is was 3,1000 roubles.[36] In 2004 federal budget subsidies covered more than 80 per cent of the Okrug's budget deficit. Federal transfers are the main sources of social development and investment. The Okrug still has one of the highest poverty levels in the country. The average salary in the Okrug is only 50 per cent of that in the Oblast.

One of the ways to overcome the deep economic crisis has been to focus on subsistence farming: 99 per cent of potatoes and vegetables and up to 65 per cent of meat and milk are produced on individual plots.[37] Most of the agricultural products are consumed within the Okrug's territory. The development of subsistence farming has helped the promotion of other areas of agricultural development such as flax production which had almost disappeared, and this has led to an improvement in the job market.

The demographic situation in the Okrug is characterized by a continuous natural population loss due to the high level of the death rate, and the low level of the birth rate – in addition to migration dynamics. For example, in 2004 migration outflow was 129 people (2,103 people arrived and 2,232 left the Okrug territory). The major migration trends are between the Okrug and the Oblast (84.0 per cent of those who arrived and 76.0 per cent of those who left, migrated between the Okrug and the Oblast territories).[38] It is important to stress that the previous existence of two different subjects of the federation has no influence on current migration trends. According to research conducted by local Kudymkar Company 'Vektor' in 2005 (after the merger was completed) more than 50 per cent of the Kudymkar population expressed a desire to move outside the Okrug boundaries. Moreover, 90 per cent of students who are studying in the Okrug would like to leave the town, and the Okrug.[39] There is a clear trend showing that the most educated and active part of the Komi-Permyak Okrug population would like to migrate, as the Okrug social and economic conditions are unsatisfactory. And one should accept that any economic development would be problematic without sufficient development of human capital.

At the same time, unlike the situation in the Chukotka AO (which has maintained its status as a fully-fledged subject of federation) and Yevenkiya AO (which has merged with Krasnoyarsk Krai), political elites in Komi-Permyak Okrug have been unable to offer attractive economic packages to attract industry to the territory. The presence of better business conditions in Perm Oblast (where there is low level of profit tax – 20 per cent instead of 24 per cent) has resulted in the inevitable migration of Okrug businesses to the Oblast, thereby reducing the Okrug's budget revenues.

Those who put forward economic justification for the merger claimed that after it was completed, the social and economic situation in the Okrug would dramatically improve. According to the 'Prognosis for Socio-Economic Consequences of Unification of the Perm region and the Komi-Permyak Autonomous Okrug', adopted by the Perm regional legislature, one of the major goals of the merger is to recover those mechanisms that would allow the regional economy to function effectively thereby improving the living standards of citizens who reside in both the Oblast and the Okrug. Several strategies were recommended to achieve this goal: the complex use of natural resources, the formation of a competitive economy, the development of small businesses, structural reorganization of the Krai's economy, and investment in infrastructure, etc.[40] However, it is still unclear what mechanisms should be used to achieve the stated goals. During the current transition period, during which time the Okrug has benefited from substantial economic support form the federal budget, there has been no pressing need to enact such radical reforms.

It was agreed that in 2004-6 the federal budget would support a number of very important infrastructure projects, including: construction of a railway line between Grigorievskaya station and Kudymkar (so far the Okrug has no rail connection with any other regions, the nearest railway station is about 100 kilometres away from the Okrug capital); the construction of roads as part of the North corridor connecting Perm, Kudymkar and Syktyvkar, including the bridge over the Kama river; and the building of a gas pipeline from Ocher (Perm Oblast) to Kudymkar.[41] Later, some new projects were put on the agenda – there was a revival of the Belkomur project (a railway corridor that connects Kudymkar with the White Sea via Syktyvkar and Arkhangelsk)[42] and the construction of a nuclear power station.

However, it is difficult to assess to what extent these economic goals could be achieved by the merger of a poor Okrug with a much richer Oblast. Despite the deep economic crisis the Okrug's economic development in 2001-4 was characterized by some growth – a 12.6 per cent increase in industrial production.[43] However, many projects, which were offered, now look unrealistic. The construction projects guaranteed by the federal centre have slowed down. Perm Krai managed to attract the interest of some Finnish investors to support its biggest investment project – the construction of a new pulp and paper mill (the total project will cost about 700 million dollars) but it is highly unlikely that the new mill will be located in the Okrug.[44] The Belkomur project that was part of the compromise agreement[45] between the Oblast and the Okrug during merger negotiations has not received sufficient interest from the key Joint Stock Company, 'Russian Railways', which is not willing to support such an unprofitable project. Construction of a nuclear power station seems to be very speculative, as the Okrug doesn't have enough infrastructural and human resources to back it up. Both projects cannot be realized without significant federal support. Therefore, the question arises – what are the economic gains of the merger if all the really significant projects are fully dependent on federal support?

According to the newly adopted consolidated budget of the Perm Krai for 2007, the Komi-Permyak Okrug is due to receive 500 million roubles of extra support, which constitutes a 50 per cent increase. If the Okrug retained its status as an independent subject of the federation the increase would be much smaller, between 8 and 11 per cent. Such an increase reflects the Okrug's special status within the newly formed Krai, and the need for levelling up, as the average increase for other territories within the Krai is 20 per cent. However, while the Krai budget is willing to support the Okrug's development, the Okrug itself has very limited capacity to 'absorb' the money by offering new investment projects and infrastructural development.[46] At the same time the budgetary redistribution within the Perm Krai budget that is aimed at decreasing intra-regional differences (providing more financial resources to the Komi-Permyak Okrug) would decrease the positive outcomes of the merger, as this redistribution would be at the expense of other territories within the Perm Krai.

Therefore, the first joint-budget is based upon a typical mechanical redistribution and does not offer a new institutional framework to bolster the Okrug's sustainable development. Moreover, the increase in transfers from the regional to the Okrug's budget is seen as a temporary solution and will have a short-term economic effect on the Okrug's development if any. Thus, the economic indicators do not provide us with a clear answer regarding the economic gains and losses arising from the merger.

Unification as an elite project

On the surface Perm and Komi-Permyak elites initiated the process of unification, but one could argue that this initiative was encouraged by the Presidential Administration. President Vladimir Putin offered unconditional support to the process as the merger fully complied with his major goal – the building of a 'power vertical', with regional enlargement as a key component of his centralizing policy. Moreover, Putin openly demonstrated his support for the merger, and even visited Kudymkar (the capital of the Komi-Permyak Autonomous Okrug) in October 2003. Putin's visit raised the profile of the political campaign. The Governor of the Perm Oblast, Yuri Trutnev, confirmed this fact, and even more clearly expressed his opinion on how this support should be used: 'This is a very unique moment. The president and his administration are interested in unification and we should use their support to promote our own goals. We could receive additional financial support through unification.'[47]

Economic justification for unification also contributes to the argument that the merger was more of an elite project. The Komi-Permyak political elite was opposed to the merger before certain guarantees were received. For example, in 2002 the Komi-Permyak Okrug Governor, Gennady Saveliev initiated a campaign of collecting signatures against the referendum, and about 15,000 signatures were collected. However, later he denied his personal responsibility for the initiative[48] and headed the process of unification in the Okrug. The Perm Oblast elite finally got the Okrug's support after some very important concessions were made:

(1) The more democratic merger formula (A + B = C) was adopted. In comparison, Krasnoyarsk Krai's merger with the Taimyr and Yevenk autonomous okrugs was based on a different formula (A +B + C = A), which did not create a new subject of the federation.
(2) The agreement legally confirmed the Okrug's 'special status' within the new region (Krai).
(3) The Oblast and Okrug executive powers effectively restricted the rights of the Oblast and Okrug legislatures. During the transition period neither legislature could adopt new laws or any other legal norms or initiate impeachment procedures against the Governor. The Okrug administration also received the right to appoint members of the administration without consultation and approval from the Okrug Legislative Assembly. Thus, the Okrug elite was able to maintain its powers, at least during the transition period and,
(4) The Okrug was to continue to receive both direct and special transfers from the federal budget in 2006, and via the Perm Oblast budget in 2007–8. In 2009 a new joint-budget of Perm Krai would be created.[49]

There were some obvious political losses for the Okrug, such as a loss of seats in the Federation Council and the State Duma. It was assumed that after the merger new Perm Krai representatives would be appointed/elected to these bodies, but for the Okrug political elite it was a clear loss. Moreover, the Okrug political elite didn't manage to negotiate special Okrug representation in the Perm Krai regional assembly. According to the agreements the Okrug retains only two seats. In contrast, the Koryak Okrug political elite, after its merger, managed to negotiate ten seats in the new Krasnoyarsk Regional Assembly. However, the Perm Okrug political elite considered that the gaining of 'special status' was a major political gain of the merger. They believed that this would allow them to maintain their political power or even increase it. There was also a belief that the Okrug political elite would improve its public image by supporting the merger.

To conclude, the negotiations were successful for the Okrug and the Oblast, as both parties managed to gain significant benefits from their support of unification. A former Perm Oblast governor, Yuri Trutnev, who pushed the merger, was appointed the federal Minister of Natural resources at the time when the unification process had become irreversible.

Ethnic and cultural dimension of the unification

However, the merger has not led to the adoption of legislation which would guarantee the protection of the Komi-Permyak ethnic identity, language and culture, which was one of the reasons why the Okrug was created in the first place. A series of interviews with members of the Okrug administration and those working in education, including the Okrug institute for the retraining of schoolteachers, conducted by the author in December 2004 and November 2005, demonstrates a serious concern on their behalf about the future of the Komi-Permyak language, the development of ethnic culture and the practical substance of the Okrug's special status within the region. The existing programme on the development of inter-ethnic relations in the Perm region supports a number of initiatives to promote ethnic culture, such as: the regular monitoring of ethno-social problems; the carrying out of ethnological, linguistic, and folklore research in the Okrug; and the creation of the 'Institute of Language, Culture and History of Komi-Permyak People', in Perm. However, such a list of activities tends to demonstrate that the Komi-Permyak people are now considered to be just one of the many ethnic groups that live on the territory of Perm Krai, and that they do not enjoy any special treatment compared with the other minorities (Tatars, Bashkirs and others).

It is too early to say what the implications of the merger may be for Komi-Permyaks in the spheres of language, culture and education. However, neither Federal Constitutional Law nor regional acts (including the Krai's draft Charter) and agreements pertaining to the merger contain any concrete references to the Komi-Permyak language and culture – nor do they establish any guarantees for the Okrug's educational and cultural institutions, which used to receive their funding from the Okrug budget. However, in Kudymkar there is an ethnic publisher, an ethnic theatre and an Institute for the Retraining of School Teachers.

Moreover, the Okrug has four branches of higher education institutions (one should stress that only one of them represents the Perm Oblast higher education institutions, while others came from Udmurtiya and Yekaterinburg), two technical schools and five vocational schools. It is unclear what support those educational institutions would receive after the merger. As Yuri Shabaev speculates: 'most likely vocational training would be fully done in Perm'.[50] The Perm Krai Governor has already noted that the Krai will reserve fifty publicly funded slots at Perm higher education institutions for graduates of Okrug schools.[51] Even though vertical educational migration is a positive trend from the personal development point of view, it would not necessarily help to develop the Okrug's human capital, as it is unlikely that the return rate to the Okrug would be very high.

It is unlikely that all these facilities can be financed from the municipal budget, and there are no guarantees that Perm Krai will finance them from its budget – as to federal subsidies, the Okrug will definitely lose them. Besides, after the merger, schools in the Komi-Permyak Okrug will have to adopt the same regional component that is shared by schools all over the Perm Krai, and there are no guarantees that it will address specific needs of Komi-Permyak people.

One may assume that the ignoring of ethnic issues in the process of unification was not accidental because the entire nationwide campaign of regional unification would appear to be aimed at the goal of eliminating the ethnic element from Russian federalism.

The Komi-Permyak Okrug – special status

According to the initial agreements between the Oblast and Okrug political elites, the Komi-Permyak Okrug should receive special status within the newly merged subject of the federation. This special status was even mentioned in the federal law, 'On the Foundation of the New Subject of the Russian Federation as a Result of the Merger of the Perm Oblast and the Komi-Permyak Autonomous Okrug', that institutionalized the foundation of the Perm Krai. As article 4 part 2 of the Law states, 'The Komi-Permyak Okrug forms the Krai's administrative and territorial unit with a unified territory and a special status that is defined by the Perm Krai Charter, in accordance with the federal legislation.'

However, the federal law 'On General Principles of the Organization of Local Self-Government', adopted on 6 October 2003, stipulates that the territory of any federal subject is subdivided into municipal districts. However, the Komi-Permyak Okrug consists of six municipal districts each of which contains other types of municipal units – municipal settlements and the capital city. According to the federal law there should be a two-layer municipal structure (settlement and district levels). According to the Law, boundaries of a municipal settlement should be set up according to criteria which facilitate a one-day walking distance access to the centre of the municipality, and boundaries of the municipal districts should be set up within a one-day round trip using transport to the centre of municipality.

There is a clear contradiction between the promise of special status and the actual federal legal framework. According to the Perm researcher Kochev,[52] there are two possible scenarios for how this special status could be realized within the current federal legislation on self-government organization. The first scenario is based upon a two-layer government system, with the first layer being a state power and the second one being local self-government. This scenario is less favourable as it would lead to unnecessary duplication of functions. The second scenario is characterized by a one-layer government system, whereby the Komi-Permyak Okrug would become a unified municipality. In this case the state functions would be realized at the Krai level and the Okrug status would lose its special meaning. Statements by Oleg Chirkunov, who is the first Governor of the unified Permskii Krai, have only added uncertainty to the issue as he had no clear vision of the Okrug's special status. In his early interviews on the Okrug's future within the Krai, he discussed a number of different possible scenarios, confusing both the Krai and the Okrug political elites.[53]

The new Krai Charter should have resolved the issue of special status. However, the first draft, which was published in January 2007, demonstrated that all issues related to the Okrug's special status remained unresolved. It stipulates that the Komi-Permyak Okrug remains as a unified administrative territorial entity with the town of Kudymkar as an administrative centre. The Okrug administration represents the state power and it is an integral part of the Perm Krai administrative structure. The head of the Okrug administration receives the status of a minister of the regional government. Thus, the Charter provides a duplication of state functions at the Krai and Okrug levels. Moreover, originally it was agreed that the head of the Okrug's administration would receive the higher status of vice-governor, but the first draft of the Charter diminishes his/her role to that of an ordinary minister who will need to defend the Okrug's interests before other ministers with the same administrative status.

The draft Charter also gives a choice of organizations of self-government within the Okrug's territory. First, its states that the Okrug consists of different types of municipalities, that is municipal settlements, municipal districts and town district. Here the charter changes its grammatical tense from the 'imperative' to the 'subjunctive'.

There are gains and losses in any of the choices of municipal structure. If the Okrug becomes a single municipality then the municipal districts would have to give up their current status and become municipal settlements. This is the most favourable solution for the Okrug elite, but not for the municipal bureaucracy that would loose its power. Moreover, there is a problem with the rule regarding a one-day walking distance access to the centre of municipality and with the town Okrug of Kudymkar. If all municipal districts retained their present status then the Okrug's special status would become meaningful, as there would not be any joint Okrug budget, but the Okrug administration would not be accountable to the Okrug's population for their actions and all cooperation would be inter-municipal.

Thus, the form of the Okrug's special status remains unclear. Even though the charter has a special chapter on guaranteeing the preservation of the ethnic identity of the Komi-Permyak people its content is too broad and declarative. It states that the Perm Krai authorities should set up the conditions for preservation of the Komi-Permyak language and culture. In addition the Okrug administration participates in the development of federal and regional programmes in the area of language and culture preservation, develops folk crafts, and funds the Krai educational and cultural institutions tasked to maintain and develop ethnic identity. However, the special chapter doesn't explain who funds such activities and, moreover, the funding is not secured (by guaranteed inclusion of a special line in the regional budget).

The chapter on social and economic development of the Komi-Permyak Okrug is even less detailed and contains only general wording on the inclusion of the Okrug's social and economic development goals in the social and economic development programme of the Krai. The Okrug's municipalities enjoy the same rights and privileges in inter-budgetory relations as all other municipal units within the Krai territory. Again, adoption of such clauses weakens the essence of the Okrug's special status.

Once it became public, the draft Charter was heavily criticized by numerous members of the political elite and some changes were made to the draft. It was agreed that there should be a special description of the Okrug's social and economic development goals and that policies on the preservation of a Komi-Permyak ethnic identity should be more precise.

The Charter was finally adopted by regional assembly on 19 April 2007.[54] There were only two readings instead of three, and the Charter was adopted in a hurry. As a result the major governing document still contains many ambiguities. The Charter (article 37) stipulates that the state power on the Okrug's territory should be executed by the Krai state institutions, and a special governing body should be founded – the Ministry for Komi-Permyak Okrug Affairs. However, its major role (article 40) is: to create conditions for the Okrug's economic and social development; to coordinate work of different territorial units of the Krai governing institutions in relation to the Okrug affairs; to promote special federal and regional programmes at the Okrug's territory. Article 42, which specifies issues relating to the preservation of a Komi-Permyak ethnic identity, also remains vague and does not specify funding guarantees. The only real advantage given by the Charter (article 44) is the maintenance of a higher level of guarantees (in comparison with the other Krai territories) that were adopted before the merger, to speed up Okrug's social and economic development, and to improve living conditions during the three-year transition period. The key issue of the Okrug's place within the new system of local self-government remains unresolved.

A third possible scenario that the Okrug political elite is backing is to have a three-layer system of local self-government.[55] This scenario maintains the status quo, as all the Okrug's political actors would be able to keep their powers. But such a scenario contradicts federal legislation, and therefore requires changes at the federal level. However, as it is the federal centre that monitors and even controls the merger process, and to date it has not offered any changes that could resolve this situation, one can assume that this is the least likely of the scenarios to be implemented.

Perm Krai as a merger model?

As all laws related to merger were passed with amazing speed, there was no opportunity to review them closely to ensure that all of the new legislation is consistent with the Constitution and existing legal norms. As Milena Gligich-Zolotareva points out, if one considers the foundation of Perm Krai as a model project that should be followed by other federal subject, 'then it is quite possible that they will sooner or later reach constitutional and legal deadlock. One should not reform federative relations on a basis that is defective from the constitutional point of view.'[56] Two years after the adoption of the federal law that legally founded the new subject of the federation, changes are needed, including new mechanisms for the appointment of the new governors.

Indeed, the pilot unification process has not proved as flawless as the federal centre has tried to suggest. Certain commitments that were crucial at the time of the initial negotiations have still not been fully met. The Okrug's population is dissatisfied with the slow pace of changes in the economic situation and the rapid increase in the degree of uncertainty. Even the Okrug elites have expressed their anxiety about the merger. Gennady Saveliev (when he was still the governor of the Komi-Permyak Okrug) articulated these fears during Prime Minister Mikhail Fradkov's visit to the region in September 2005. As a local paper concluded, 'neither for him [Saveliev] or the citizens of the Okrug does the unification of the two regions now look so optimistic'.[57]

Even though the unification rationale is formulated as economic expediency it should be viewed as primarily a political project, which was initiated by federal Centre. As the Perm Region and the Komi-Permyak Autonomous Okrug merger demonstrated, the regional elite viewed the unification project not only as something desired by the population, but as the federal Centre's business project. In this view all financial arrangements, privileges and transfers are seen as a price the federal Centre pays for getting a better-off region to merge with a less developed subject. As Natalia Zubarevich rightly concludes, 'the most obvious outcome of the merger is the image one: federal subjects with extremely unfavourable social and economic indicators will now disappear from regional statistics'.[58]

Based on lessons learnt by the merger of Perm Oblast and the Komi-Permyak Autonomous Okrug, the law 'On the Process of Accession to the Russian Federation and Foundation of a New Constituent Unit of the Russian Federation' was amended to ensure greater representation of the federal Centre and regional executives in the merger process. For example, the amendments stated that a referendum on unification cannot be held without presidential approval, as the President needs to issue a decree to initiate a referendum. Moreover, according to new amendments, the role of regional assemblies in the process of unification has significantly decreased, as it is the governors of the merging regions who are charged with placing such mergers on the political agenda. As governors are now appointed by the President, such changes have moved the regional population further away from the decision-making process, and turned questions regarding mergers into projects, which are to be decided exclusively by elites.

Another important additional factor to be considered is that the recent unification projects can be seen as a silent revision of the ethnic dimension of the Russian federation. All mergers, and the unification of the Perm region and Komi-Permyak Autonomous Okrug again is very illustrative, have resulted in the disappearance of some 'ethnic subjects of the federation'.

With other mergers now in place one should ask whether the Perm Oblast and the Komi-Permyak Autonomous Okrug can be viewed as a 'merger model'. There is no straightforward answer to this question. On the one hand, the formation of Perm Krai started the process of the mergers and brought to the surface some of the ambiguous legal issues and procedures (appropriate changes were made into the federal legislation). It also secured the role of certain political institutions and actors in the process. It was agreed that the merger was not to be initiated at the grassroots level, but nonetheless was required to gain popular support through a referendum.

At the same time the specific political and economic gains and losses will differ significantly from merger to merger, thus demonstrating that elite negotiations play a significant role in the merger process. Moreover, the economic gains from mergers are rapidly decreasing as the centre is shortening the unification transition period and speeding up the creation of joint-budgets in the newly merged subjects. Moreover, by adopting changes to the Russian Federation Budget Code that significantly limit federal budget support to compound subjects, the federal centre has sent a political signal that it intends to push for the elimination of all of the compound federal subjects through the merger process.

Notes

1 Some authors argue that federalism helps to protect ethnic minorities within multinational federations. This argument is developed by Will Kymlicka, 'Western political theory and ethnic relations in Eastern Europe', in Will Kymlicka and Magda Opalski (eds), *Can Liberal Pluralism Be Exported? Western Political Theory and Ethnic Relations in Eastern Europe*, Oxford: Oxford University Press, 2001, p. 29.

2 Fifteen republics (Bashkortostan, Buryatiya, Chuvashiya, Dagestan, Kabardino-Balkariya, Kalmykiya, Kareliya, Komi, Mari El, Mordoviya, North Osetiya-Alaniya, Tatarstan, Tyva, Udmurtiya, Sakha) are former Autonomous Soviet Socialist Republics (ASSR) that existed within the RSFSR. Four republics (Adygeya, Altai, Karachaevo-Cherkessiya, and Khakasiya) appeared after the upgrade of the status of autonomous Oblasts. Two republics (Chechnya and Ingushetiya) are the result of the breakdown of a former Chechen–Ingush ASSR.

3 Gordon Hahn, 'Reforming the federation', in Stephen White, Zvi Gitelman and Richard Sakwa (eds), *Development in Russian Politics*, Basingstoke: Palgrave Macmillan, 2005, p. 148.
4 Seven federal districts were created by a presidential decree of 13 May 2000. Each federal district unites several regions and is headed by a presidential representative.
5 'O poryadke prinyatiya v Rossiskuyu Federatsiyu i obrazovaniya v ee sostave novogo b'esub'ekta Rossiskoi Federatsii', 17 December 2001. http://vff-s.narod.ru/fz/kz/01_06.html
6 *Rossiskaya Gazeta*, 19 April 2005. http://www.rg.ru/2005/04/19/sibir-referendum.html.
7 Transcript of Press Conference with the Russian and Foreign Media. 1 February 2007. Round Hall, the Kremlin, Moscow. http://president.kremlin.ru/eng/speeches/2007/02/01/1309_type82915type82917_117609.shtml
8 Transcript of Press Conference with the Russian and Foreign Media. February 1, 2007. Round Hall, the Kremlin, Moscow. http://president.kremlin.ru/eng/speeches/2007/02/01/1309_type82915type82917_117609.shtml
9 Thornton Matheson, 'Does fiscal redistribution discourage local public investment? Evidence from transitional Russia', *Economics of Transition*, Vol. 13, No. 1, 2005, p. 142.
10 See, *Rossia Regionov: v kakom sotsialnom prostranstve my zhivem?*, Nezavisimyi Institut Sotsialnoi Politiki, Moscow, 2005.
11 Ibid., p. 54.
12 Vladimir Leksin, 'Prostranstvo vlasti i mir cheloveka', *Mir Rossii*, No. 1, 2005, p. 40. http://www.ecsocman.edu.ru/images/pubs/2007/02/06/0000301904/2005_n1_p3-61.pdf
13 Ross Williams, 'Fiscal federalism: aims, instruments and outcomes', *The Australian Economic Review*, Vol. 38, No. 4, 2005, p. 352.
14 R. F. Turovskii, *Politicheskaya Regionalistica*, Moscow, 'Izdatel'skii Dom GU VSHE', 2006), p. 551.
15 http://www.programs-gov.ru/ext/142/content.htm
16 Vladimir Leksin, 'Prostranstvo vlasti i mir cheloveka', *Mir Rossii*, No. 1, 2005, p. 47, http://www.ecsocman.edu.ru/images/pubs/2007/02/06/0000301904/2005_n1_p3-61.pdf
17 http://www.perepis2002.ru/ct/html/TOM_04_03_4.htm
18 See, for example, S. V. Kurenkova, 'Iz istorii voprosa: obrazovanie Komi-Permyatskogo Avtonomnogo Okruga – pervogo natsionalnogo okruga v Rossii (K 80-letiu obrazovaniya SSSR)', at http://politarchive.perm.ru/pls/gopapo/page.show_page?p_page_id = 118&p_detail = Y
19 *Ustav Komi-Permyatskogo Avtonomnogo Okruga* (Charter of the Komi-Permyak Autonomous Okrug). Adopted on 19 December 1994. Chapter 1. http://www.legislature.ru/ruconst/komiperm.html#1
20 *Ustav Komi-Permyatskogo Avtomnogo Okruga.*
21 *Ustav Permskoi Oblasti* (Charter of Perm region). Adopted October 6, 1994. Chapter 1. http://parlament.perm.ru/laws/ustav.html
22 *Ustav Permskoi Oblasti.*
23 *Ustav Permskoi Oblasti.*
24 Law, 'Ob Administrativno-territorialnom delenii Permskoi Oblasti'. Adopted on February 22, 1996. As amended on May 7, 1997. http://www.permreg.ru/region/laws/?document = 42
25 'Dogovor o razgranichenii predmetov vvedeniya v polnomochii mezhdu organami gosudarstvennoi vlasti Rossiskoi Federatsii i organami gosudarstvennoi vlasti Permskoi Oblasti v organami gosudarstvennoi vlasti Komi-Permyatskogo Avtonomnogo Okruga ot 31 Maya 1996 g.', *Rossiiskie Vesti*, 25 July 1996.
26 I quote the English translation of the Russian 1993 Constitution as provided in, Richard Sakwa, *Russian Politics and Society*, London: Routledge, 1996, pp. 395–429.
27 *Rossiiskaya Gazeta*, 9 December 2003.

28 Sergey Ilyin, 'Prikamskii plebistsit: missiya vypolnima', *Novyi kompanion*, 2 December 2003. http://nk.permonline.ru/articles.php?newspaper_id = 513&article _id = 14089

29 *Radio Svoboda*, 22 November 2003. http://www.svoboda.org/programs/CH/2003/ CH.112203.asp

30 *Perma*, 24 February 1995.

31 'Prognoz sotsial'no-ekonomicheskih posledstvii ob'edineniya Permskoi Oblasti i Komi-Permyatskogo avtonomnogo Okruga.' Prilozhenie k postanovleniu Zakonodatelnogo sobraniya Permskoi Oblasti ot 05.06.2003 No. 849.

32 'Pravozashchtniki zhdut ot vlastei publichnogo vystuplenia', http://www.prpc.ru/ actual/komi/nw031203.shtml

33 Natalia Zubarevich, 'Ob'edinenie avtonomnykh Okrugov: preimushchestva i riski', http://atlas.socpol.ru/overviews/social_sphere/ukr.shtml#health

34 Official site of Komi-Permyak Okrug, http://Okrug.perm.ru/econ.php?id = 88&doc_id = 173

35 Official site of Komi-Permyak Okrug, http://Okrug.perm.ru/econ.php?id = 88&doc_id = 324

36 Natalia Isaeva, 'Sozdanie Permskogo Kraya: problemy i dostizheniya', http:// www.kazanfed.ru/publications/kazanfederalist/n17-18/18/

37 http://Okrug.perm.ru/econ.php?id = 94&doc_id = 196

38 http://Okrug.perm.ru/info.php?id = 36&doc_id = 226

39 *Perma*, 5 March 2005.

40 'Prognoz sotsial'no-ekonomicheskih posledstvii ob'edineniya Permskoi Oblasti i Komi-Permyatskogo avtonomnogo Okruga', Prilozhenie k postanovleniu Zakonodatelnogo sobraniya Permskoi Oblasti ot 05.06.2003, No 849.

41 'Prognoz sotsial'no-ekonomicheskih posledstvii ob'edineniya Permskoi Oblasti i Komi-Permyatskogo avtonomnogo Okruga', 15 February 2003. http://Krai.perm. ru/doc/doc_03_06_13.asp

42 Belkomur is a railway construction project that plans to connect the White Sea, Komi and the Urals. The project has two sections. The northern section passes through Arkhangel'sk Oblast and the Komi republic, while the southern part transverses the Komi republic and the Perm Krai (including the Komi-Permyak Okrug territory). The project began in 1996 but was suspended in 2002 due to financial difficulties. As a result, out of the planned 1311 km of railway line, only 580 km (Syktyvkar–Arkhangelsk part) were constructed. Expenditure for the Southern section from the construction budget (Perm Krai only) is 37.83 billion rubles. It is planned to apply for federal investment funds to support the completion of this part of the project. The Perm Krai administration hopes to restart the construction project in 2008, the construction would be realized in six years, the payback time would be nine years.

43 http://Okrug.perm.ru/econ.php?id = 88&doc_id = 173

44 Arkadii Zakharov, 'Pervyi Blin', *Ekspert Ural*, Vol. 22, No. 194, 13 June 2005, http://www.expert.ru/printissues/ural/2005/22/22ur-upol/

45 Minister of the natural resources Yuri Trutnev (former Perm Oblast governor) has promised his full support to the Belkomur project. This was part of the compensation package promised to the Komi-Permyak Okrug for its support of the merger. See, *Permskii Obozrevatel*, Vol. 6, No. 308, 19 February 2007, http://www. permoboz.ru/txt.php?n = 4903

46 'My budem zhit teper po novomy', *Kapital Weekly*, http://www.kapital.perm.ru/ number/details/1640

47 Valerii Tsygankov, 'V Permskii Krai zamanivayut rublem', *Nezavisimaya gazeta*, 27 June 2003.

48 See, for example, http://www.rvs.perm.ru/numbers/3_04/3_sav.htm

49 For more details, see the federal law 'On Foundation of A New Subject in the Russian Federation as a Result of the Merger of the Perm Oblast and Komi-Permyak Autonomous Okrug.' Adopted on 24 March 2004, and amended on 5 July 2005.

50 Yuri Shabaev, 'Etnosotsialnye posledstviya ob'edineniya regionov (iz opyta formirovaniya Permskogo Kraya)', *Sotsiologicheskie Issledovaniya*, No. 3, 2006, p. 67.

51 http://www.perm.ru/news/news_more/?id = 8589

52 V. A. Kochev, 'Obrazovanie novogo sub'ekta RF – Permskovo Kraya: pravovye aspekty', L. A. Fadeeva (ed.), *Politicheskii Al'manakh Prikamia*, Perm: Izdatel'stvo 'pushka', 2005, pp. 228-41.

53 See, for example, Oleg Chirkunov, 'Mogu pozvolit sebe roskosh govotit pravdu', *Novyi Kompanion*, 2 August 2004, http://www.Krai.perm.ru/pressa.asp?id = 666

54 Ustav Permskovo Kraya, http://www.perm.ru/region/laws/

55 *Kommersnt-Prikamye*, 1 July 2004.

56 Milena Gligich-Zolotareva, 'Novye tendetsii zakonotvorchestva v sovremennoi Rossii', *Kazanskii Federalist*, Vol. 2, No. 10, Spring 2004. http://www.kazanfed.ru/publications/kazanfederalist/n10/4/

57 *Gorodskaya Gazeta*, 27 September 2005, http://www.berezniki.ru/topic/gorod/050927_4/print

58 Natalia Zubarevich, 'Ob'edinenie avtonomnykh Okrugov: preimushchestva i riski', http://atlas.socpol.ru/overviews/social_sphere/ukr.shtml#health

5 Putin and the election of regional governors

Darrell Slider

Perhaps the most significant change made by Vladimir Putin to the Russian political system was his decision in September 2004 to end the popular election of regional executives. The consequences of this decision are potentially far-reaching and represent nothing less than the dismantling of what little remained of Russian federalism and democracy.

Putin announced his decision in the immediate aftermath of the Beslan school tragedy, in which over 300 hostages lost their lives. On 13 September 2004 Putin spoke before the Russian government and leaders of the regions and argued that terrorists sought to bring about the collapse of Russia and its government. Citing article 77 of the 1993 Constitution, Putin called for the creation of a 'unified system of authority', which should function as a single, integral hierarchy. This new 'executive vertical' would require replacing popular elections with a process that would involve both national and regional organs in the selection of regional executives. Putin proposed that this should be achieved through the election of governors by regional assemblies, with the candidate or candidates to be nominated by the Russian president.[1]

The law implementing this decision was passed by the Duma and Federation Council in December 2004.[2] When the law was adopted it became clear that the assemblies would not have a choice of candidates selected by the president; they could either accept or reject his single nominee. Furthermore, if the regional assembly voted against his choice twice, the president had the power to dissolve the assembly and name an acting governor. In essence, then, the system of popular elections was replaced by presidential appointment of governors.[3] Regional legislatures were put in the position of approving Putin's candidate or face dissolution.

Regional elections 1991–2004

The first elections to regional executive posts sanctioned by Boris Yeltsin took place in 1991, at the same time as the election of Yeltsin as president of the Russian federation. As an 'experiment' mayors were elected in the two largest Russian cities, Moscow and Leningrad.[4] Both cities were firmly in the hands of Yeltsin allies, the liberal academics Gavriil Popov and Anatoly Sobchak, and they won election easily. Sobchak took credit for proposing the idea to Yeltsin.[5] In the lengthy interview that Vladimir Putin gave in advance of the 2000 presidential elections, he also took some of the credit for initiating elections for regional executives in Russia. Putin reports that he successfully convinced Leningrad city council members in 1991 to create the post of mayor, thus opening the way for popular election to the post.[6]

The first election of a president of an ethnic republic within the Russian federation took place at the same time in Tatarstan, without the approval of the Russian authorities. These elections were initially encouraged by Gorbachev's team, in part as a way of undermining the authority of the Russian president, Boris Yeltsin.[7] Ethnic republics tended to be dominated by the communist-era nomenklatura, and they sought legitimacy through elections that would buttress their influence vis-à-vis the new, reformist Russian leadership. Rather than risk a confrontation, Yeltsin allowed republics the right to elect presidents by popular vote. The Tatarstan precedent was soon followed by other Russian republics, including Chechnya which elected the separatist leader Djokhar Dudaev in October 1991.

In other regions, regional chief executives—soon informally called 'governors'—were appointed by Yeltsin. For years after Russia became independent, Yeltsin resisted calls from regional elites to allow elections. His purpose was to hold on to an important source of political leverage in the regions, at least temporarily. From the perspective of Yeltsin's advisors, it was feared that regional elections would result in the victory of Yeltsin's opponents. Retaining the power of appointment—and dismissal–would give Yeltsin at least temporarily the ability to influence the most important question of political authority in the regions. Yeltsin began to sanction regional executive elections on a case-by-case basis in 1993, while other regional leaders in Bryansk, Chelyabinsk and Amur held elections without Moscow's approval. Beginning in 1995–6 the election of governors became the standard practice for all regions, and by October 1997 all regions had an elected executive.

These elections reflected and corresponded in time with Yeltsin's declining political authority, and they had the effect of speeding up the reduced control of central authorities over the regions. The elections had a mixed impact on Yeltsin's political power. On the one hand, elections meant that it became almost impossible for Yeltsin to remove a governor or republic president from office. On the other hand, Yeltsin reached an understanding with most regional leaders that led them to support him in disputes at the national level. In part they played this in their new status as members of the upper chamber of the national parliament, the Federation Council.[8] With the obvious exception of Chechnya, the deals made with the non-Russian ethnic republics precluded efforts to break away from the Russian federation. Republics generally had more autonomy that other regions; in other words, the emerging Russian federal system was asymmetrical. Treaties were concluded on a case-by-case basis that gave regions such as Tatarstan and

Bashkortostan additional powers. Many regional leaders used their considerable influence over local politics (known in Russia as 'administrative resources' which included control over courts, police, media, election commissions, regional financial and economic assets) to help insure that Yeltsin was re-elected in 1996.

Nevertheless, the regional elections that took place in the Yeltsin era showed signs of Russia's progress toward a more democratic system. Andrew Konitzer has argued that the second round of gubernatorial elections in the late 1990s showed important advances in Russian democracy, as voters held leaders accountable for economic conditions in their regions.[9] It is also the case that growing pluralism at the regional level was developing enough to prevent the centre or regional incumbents from determining the outcome of every election. Many of Yeltsin's appointees did not win election when elections were introduced. The Kremlin had limited success in getting its favoured candidates elected. According to the Panorama research group, of fifty-five governors elected between September 1996 and October 1997, only twenty-two were supported by the coordinating council headed by Yeltsin's aide Sergei Filatov.[10]

Gubernatorial elections in the first years of the Putin presidency were increasingly subject to Kremlin interference. A number of 'electoral technologies' were applied that in effect took the decision-making out of the hands of voters and put it squarely in the Kremlin.[11] In several prominent cases, sitting governors or other leading candidates were forced off the ballot (Alexander Rutskoi in Kursk, for example, and candidates in Pskov and Arkhangel'sk) or pressured not to run. The complexity of the machinations and/or negotiations required to perform these operations in a large number of regions may be one reason for shifting to a simpler control system. It is also the case that in some regions the Kremlin's substantial efforts were to no avail, and voters chose another candidate. Andrew Konitzer found that between 2003 and 2004, the new 'party of power' United Russia was much more effective in mobilizing political assets for its candidates: in forty-three races thirty-five of the candidates supported by United Russia won.[12] Nevertheless, eight losses were far too many for the Kremlin to accept. Given the mindset of the Putin administration, elections introduced an element of unpredictability that complicated their efforts to run the country from the centre.

One initial response by the Russian authorities to the unpredictability of regional elections had the effect of making regional elections more democratic: in April 2003 the election law was revised to require a second round of voting if no candidate received over 50 per cent in the first round. Prior to this, most regional elections were held under a first-past-the-post system. In elections, which frequently featured a large number of candidates, this meant that winning candidates often had only a small share of the total votes cast. Two candidates with a pro-Kremlin stance, for example, could split that electorate and lead to an opposition victory. The run-off system made such an outcome less likely. In the final analysis, though, the solution to regional instability that was more amenable to Putin and his advisers required circumscribing democracy, not expanding it.

The decision to end gubernatorial elections

In the debates surrounding the decision to rescind the popular election of regional leaders three major arguments have been made in support of the measure, the first two explicitly and the third—and perhaps critical one–behind the scenes.

1. *Weak federal control over the regions.* The lesson taken from Beslan was that there was a need to further strengthen the top-down control in the executive, what in Russian is called the 'vertical of power' (*vertical' vlasti*). In fact, Putin had been dramatically reducing the power of regional leaders since the beginning of his first term in office.[13] While Beslan appears to have been used as a convenient excuse to do something that the Kremlin had long wanted to do for reasons unrelated to that tragedy, there were events in Beslan that provided confirmation to some that a new policy was needed. Dmitry Rogozin, then head of the party Rodina, was present in Beslan on 3 September and witnessed a confrontation between the then presidential representative in the Southern Federal District, Vladimir Yakovlev,[14] and North Ossetian President Dzasokhov. According to Rogozin, the two men could not reach agreement on 'who would lead the parade', in other words, on who would take charge at the command centre that was responsible for making operational decisions.[15] Yakovlev was the only representative of the Kremlin present at the time, but Dzasokhov claimed that it was he who had the ultimate authority to determine what was in the interests of the people of North Osetiya-Alaniya. The poor coordination of the response to the hostage-taking is widely considered to be a major cause of the chaotic storming of the school and the loss of the lives of over 300 hostages.[16] By making all regional governors part of the president's team through the power of appointment, governors would now be subject to greater central control and accountability. In a book that was written to justify the Kremlin's new policy, it was argued that in the aftermath of Beslan the public demanded further centralization of decision making in order 'to oversee everything that was happening in the country and answer for it.'[17] The incompatibility of this conception with Russian federalism should have been apparent from the outset; the ultimate goal seems to be a system that is 'federalist in form, unitary in content'.

2. *Flawed elections.* Elections in regions were not democratic, but increasingly dominated by financial groups and/or criminals. As a result

governors were often beholden not to the people but to special interests. This also contributed to the election of governors who were divorced from national, Russian interests. This argument had some validity, but a more honest analysis would have included the distorting role played by the Kremlin and its surrogates in regional elections. It was also disingenuous, in that the Kremlin had done so little to improve the quality of regional elections under Putin.

Putin's own experience as a campaign manager for the 1996 election of his boss and mentor, St Petersburg mayor Anatolii Sobchak, evidently soured him on the reality of Russian regional elections. According to Putin, Sobchak faced an opponent, Vladimir Yakovlev, who was funded by an anti-Sobchak faction in the Russian government in Moscow.[18] Sobchak, by contrast, lacked the funds needed to hire a professional campaign staff.[19] The defeated candidate, Sobchak, described the 1996 St Petersburg election in the following terms: it was

> a signal of how the genuinely democratic expression of the will of the population can be distorted with the help of so-called election technologies, the massive buying of voters, unleashing compromising materials, and the shameless interference of law enforcement organs in an election campaign.[20]

Behind some of the criticism of regional elections is the belief that voters in Russia's regions are not ready for democracy; they too often vote for candidates for the wrong reasons. The most widely cited proof for this argument was the recent election outcome in Altai Krai. A television comedian who became popular for portraying an alcoholic, Mikhail Yevdokimov, was elected governor of the region in April 2004 in a close race with the long-term head of the region, Alexander Surikov. Another way of putting it was that voters in the regions did not always vote for the candidates who were favoured by the Kremlin

3. *The term limit dilemma.* Governors and republic presidents who were coming to the end of their last terms in office would be forced out, opening up the possibility of substantial changes in Russia's regional leaderships. The dilemma this posed for the Kremlin may have been, in fact, the strongest motivation for ending the election of executives in the regions.

In 1999 Yeltsin signed into law a measure that limited gubernatorial terms to two. Under Putin, in early 2001 the question was revisited and the law was interpreted to mean that the counting of governors' terms would begin from their first election after the law was adopted in 1999. Not coincidentally, the new interpretation came into effect just as Tatarstan's Shaimiev was ending his second term as president.[21]

Shaimiev, in fact, had already registered as a candidate for his third term despite the fact that it was against federal law at the time. The Kremlin viewed Shaimiev as having single-handedly suppressed separatist sentiment in his republic, and the prospect of trying to find a replacement was a daunting one.

Putin's 2004 decision on ending regional elections (and, as a consequence, term limits) coincided with the approaching end of Shaimiev's and other governors' third and last term (second term under the new interpretation of the law). The impending forced retirement of leaders in a large number of critical regions over a relatively short time frame was undoubtedly an important factor enticing the Kremlin to cancel elections. While Putin and his team had an interest in replacing certain governors, others were seen as vital to regional stability and had proven to be loyal to the Kremlin when needed. Most importantly, they assisted the Kremlin's party, United Russia, in the December 2003 Duma elections, and also made sure that Putin won a first-round victory in his re-election in March 2004. Of particular concern were the leaders of the major ethnically non-Russian republics such as the republics of the North Caucasus, Tatarstan, Bashkortostan, Tyva, and Kalmykiya.

Reaction to the new system

The willingness of the Kremlin to reappoint the majority of sitting governors helps explain why so many of them were quick to endorse the changes proposed by Putin. There were exceptions—governors who resisted the changes and even challenged them. One group of opponents were those governors most likely to be dismissed in the near future, or at least not reappointed when their terms expired: Butov in Nenets AO; Vladimir Tikhonov in Ivanovo, Yuri Yevdokimov in Murmansk. Other regional leaders initially opposed Putin's new steps, and in public pronouncements. Shaimiev, who was not just president of Tatarstan but a leader of United Russia, argued that the measure as proposed contradicted the principles of federalism, especially the power to disband regional assemblies, and should be restricted by a specified time limit.[22] Several other regional legislatures also unsuccessfully attempted to amend the draft of the law on the new procedures, in order to eliminate the presidential power to dissolve regional legislatures.

Despite the Kremlin's claims that the public demanded the new steps to increase regional leaders' accountability, Russian public opinion on Putin's initiative was divided. VTsIOM, which had been taken over the previous year in a Kremlin-inspired change in owners, reported that in September 2004, 55 per cent of the population opposed a change that would lead to Putin appointing mayors or district leaders. The polling group apparently suppressed the results they had obtained on appointing governors.[23] In September 2006 the same polling group found that 45 per cent supported

Putin's new powers to appoint governors, while 27 per cent were opposed and 28 per cent had difficulty answering. (The poll also found that 51 per cent supported as candidates people from the region, even if they lacked management skills, while 37 per cent would support a candidate with proven skills from outside the region).[24] A more independent polling body, the Public Opinion Foundation (FOM), found in September 2004 that 37 per cent of respondents expected negative consequences from presidential appointments, while 28 per cent expected a positive outcome.[25] By December 2004, when the new law was adopted, 36 per cent foresaw more positive consequences from presidential appointees, while 29 per cent expected negative consequences.[26] Attitudes become somewhat more negative during the first year of implementation. FOM reported in November 2005 that 34 per cent approved the presidential appointment process while 36 per cent disapproved.[27]

The constitutionality of Putin's new policy was in dispute as well. The 1993 constitution was vague on issue of how organs of power are formed, since it predated most elections of regional executives. Nevertheless, the constitution gave regions the right to 'form their own organs of state power' and placed the formation of these organs exclusively in the hands of the regions; it was not in the list of functions to be shared jointly by federal and regional levels. In December 2005 the Constitutional Court upheld the legality of Putin's new procedures in response to a challenge by a voter from Tyumen' oblast that was joined by the Union of Right Forces.[28] The court argued that the constitution should be interpreted 'in the socio-historical context which is developing' and that the president, as 'direct representative of all of the people', could add to his constitutional powers simply by the passage of a law.[29] In other words, the Constitutional Court gave Putin free reign to interpret the constitution 'creatively'.

The new system in practice

The new process by which governors were appointed was far from transparent. A direct role in the choice of candidates was supposed to be played by the presidential representative (in Russian abbreviated as *polpred*) in the federal districts.[30] They were required to provide the presidential administration with the names of at least two candidates for the top post at least ninety days before a governor's term expired. The Kremlin's role in the process appeared decisive, in fact determining who would be on the 'short list' of candidates to be considered—and often deciding in advance who would be the ultimate winner. The presidential representative not only was sometimes excluded from this process, but at times was the last to find out about the Kremlin's choice.[31] A former governor, Sergei Sobyanin of Tyumen' oblast, was named head of the presidential administration in November 2005. Reports suggest that the decisive role in determining the preferred candidate for regional executives was played by the deputy head of the administration, Vladislav Surkov, and the presidential aide responsible for personnel, Viktor Ivanov.[32] Candidates on the short list were usually brought to the Kremlin for interviews, including an interview with Putin.

Rather than accept that the previous popular elections meant that sitting governors should remain in office to the end of their terms, a procedure was established that allowed governors to seek a 'vote of confidence' from Putin that could lead to reappointment. Behind the scenes bargains were struck between governors and the Kremlin on when would be an appropriate time to ask for reappointment. In most cases, the public announcement that a governor would seek reappointment meant that the issue had already been decided.

Regional legislators were presented with Putin's choice by the polpred and often had the opportunity to discuss the options in advance with the presidential representative. In February 2007 Putin reported that for several regions, which he did not name, 'I had to change my initial opinion when deputies of the legislative assembly said "We respect you ... even love you, but we will not vote for the potential candidate who you want to propose."'[33] One of these cases was undoubtedly that of Nizhnii Novgorod, where Putin was prepared to reappoint as governor Gennadii Khodyrev. Khodyrev had long ago dropped his communist affiliation and had joined United Russia. His reappointment was strongly opposed, though, by the presidential representative, Sergei Kirienko, and a majority in the regional assembly.[34]

Once Putin nominated his choice from the candidates presented to him, the process worked in a way that he would describe as '*effektivnyi*'—in every case Putin's choice has been endorsed on the first vote and nearly unanimously in every case. In this, Putin has been aided by the increasing dominance in the regions of the political party United Russia. By the end of 2006, United Russia had a majority of seats in the assemblies of two-thirds of Russian regions.

Another factor that helped many governors retain their posts was the problem of where to find people to take their places. Unlike the Central Committee of the CPSU, the Kremlin had no cadre reserve system for officials at this level. And, as some joked at the time, there simply weren't enough Leningrad KGB officers from the 1970s (a key component of Putin's inner circle) to fill eighty-nine regional posts. An alternative approach for determining candidates was suggested by the dominant Russian political party, United Russia. It proposed a new procedure which would give the party that 'won' regional elections to the legislature the right to suggest the candidate. The assembly would then vote on whether to submit the candidacy to the president. The president would then review the selection and formally nominate the candidate to the legislature. Putin signed this amendment into law in January 2006. It begs the question, though, of how decisions are made in the party that wins. If that party happens to be United Russia, the decision is in fact made by the party's central leadership, which in turn takes instruction from the Kremlin. Another issue is what constitutes 'winning' a regional election in a proportional party vote system. The winner of a multiparty contest may be far short of obtaining a majority of seats in the assembly. The first region in which the majority faction nominated a candidate was the republic of Adygeya in late 2006. In fact, the nominee, while approved by United Russia in the region, was proposed to the party by the presidential representative.[35]

Putin's appointments and non-reappointments in the first two years of the new system provide some clues as to the real reasons behind the end of elections. The chief emphasis was on continuity and stability, rather than a radical change in the existing cohort of governors. Of the first forty-eighty governors appointed, thirty-three were reappointments. There were enough exceptions, though, to make it difficult to define a pattern.

The law allowed the president to dismiss sitting governors with the vague justification that they had 'lost the confidence' of the president. In one early case a governor was removed for what was deemed incompetence. In March 2005 Putin fired the governor of Koryak AO, Vladimir Loginov, for failure to prepare his region for winter. (To what extent this power was truly new can be questioned. Even in his first term Putin was able to pressure even a well-entrenched governor, Yevgenii Nazdratenko, to give up his post as governor of Primorskii Krai to head the fisheries ministry in Moscow.) Mikhail Yevdokimov in Altai Krai, the former television comedian, was neither removed nor reappointed by Putin. In August 2005 Yevdokimov was killed in a car accident.

Only one governor was removed for alleged criminal offences. In July 2006 the last governor to be popularly elected (in January 2005), Aleksei Barinov of Nenets AO was dismissed by Putin. Barinov had been charged in May 2006 by prosecutors in Arkhangel'sk oblast with fraud in a case that dated back to before he became governor. The very first governor to be reappointed, in February 2005, was Sergei Dar'kin of Primorskii Krai. Perhaps of all governors he is the most often suspected of having ties to criminal groups that control a substantial portion of his region's economy. In a number of other cases, the initiation of criminal prosecutions did not lead to removal from office (these regional leaders included Butov in Nenets AO, Platov in Tver', Lisitsyn in Yaroslavl', Shpak in Ryazan', Titov in Samara, Lebed' in Khakasiya, and Mashkovtsev in Kamchatka), though the prosecutor's pressure undoubtedly sent a strong message to the incumbent to demonstrate his loyalty.

Putin's choices showed no sign that he had any interest in fighting corruption and political stagnation at the regional level. Many of the reappointed governors had remained in office for several terms and entrenched themselves in both the administrative apparatus and among regional economic elites. Yegor Stroev, for example, was among the reappointed governors. He was the only governor who had served as a member of the CPSU Central Committee and Politburo in Soviet times and was still governor of

Orel oblast when he turned 70 in February 2007 (in Russia the usual retire-ment age for men is 60).[36] In a notable case of nepotism, Stroev appointed his daughter to be senator from the region. And according to the head of the small business-lobbying group in the region, 'only businesses connected to Stroev, his family or close associates have the chance to develop in our region'.[37] Moscow mayor Yuri Luzhkov had been in office since 1992.[38] He is the only mayor in the world whose wife (Yelena Baturina) is a billionaire, all 'earned' of course by her construction company while Luzhkov was in office and mostly through projects that were directly under the city's control. Among the longest-serving executives were a number of leaders of ethnic republics, including Bashkortostan, Tatarstan, Tyva and Kalmykiya. All had been republic presidents since at least 1993. Mintimer Shaimiev, one of the first to be reappointed, also turned 70 in 2007 and had been Tatarstan's leader since 1991. Bashkortostan's president Murtaz Rakhimov, 71 when he was reappointed in 2005, was widely viewed as perhaps the most author-itarian regional leader, and he managed to put his son in charge of an important conglomerate in the region's energy sector.

A number of regions had governors who were either members of, or had close ties to, the KPRF. The fates of these 'red governors' varied under Putin's new system. Several who never managed to establish a good working relationship with the Kremlin were forced out, including Vasilii Starodubtsev of Tula, Vladimir Tikhonov of Ivanovo, Nizhnii Novgorod's Gennadii Khodyrev, and Petr Sumin in Chelyabinsk. Others who had been supported by the KPRF in the past, however, were reappointed – Nikolai Vinogradov of Vladimir, Viktor Shershunov of Kostroma, and Yuri Lodkin of Bryansk.

There were several cases in which Putin's approach could be summarized as, 'the new governor should be anyone except the old one'. Thus, the replacement of an incumbent resulted in surprising nominations of candi-dates with no political and little administrative experience. When Boris Govorin's term in Irkutsk expired, he was replaced by Alexander Tishanin, whose entire career had been spent in the railroad sector. Tula oblast's 'red governor' Starodubtsev was replaced by Viacheslav Dudka, who had been deputy director of a mechanical engineering office. The long-time governor of Saratov oblast, Dmitry Ayatskov, was replaced by Pavel Ipatov, at the time director of a nuclear power station. In these and other cases, one pur-pose was apparently to avoid selecting anyone with close ties to one of the rival political factions in a region. In three regions former aides to Moscow mayor Yuri Luzhkov were brought in to serve as governors: Mikhail Men' in Ivanovo, Georgii Boos in Kaliningrad, and Valerii Shantsev in Nizhnii Novgorod. The successor Putin named to take the place of Yevdokimov in Altai Krai was Alexander Karlin, who had worked in a minor capacity in the presidential administration as head of the civil service department.

Non-Russian republics seemed to warrant far more attention from the Kremlin's decision-makers, perhaps because of the potential for ethnic con-flict. Appointments of new republic presidents resulted in leaders with political experience that was higher by several orders of magnitude than that of most new governors. In North Osetiya-Alalniya after Beslan, Alexander Dzasokhov was replaced by the head of the republic legislature Teimuraz Mamsurov. The Dagestan leader Magomedali Magomedov retired and was also replaced by the speaker of the parliament, Mukha Aliev. When the long-time president of Kabardino-Balkariya, Valerii Kokov, resigned due to a serious ailment, he was replaced by a member of the State Duma and successful entrepreneur, Arsen Kanokov. As factions began to divide the Chechen leadership in early 2007, Putin pressured the elected president, Alu Alkhanov, to resign in order to make way for the then prime minister of the republic Ramzan Kadyrov.

Implications for Russian federalism and democracy

Putin's elimination of gubernatorial elections fits a pattern of reducing the scope for independent institutions; checks and balances are viewed as obstacles to efficient, accountable decision-making. For the Kremlin, federalism and democracy are luxuries that Russia cannot afford at its current stage of political development. In its place the Kremlin is proposing a Russian form of democratic federalism that is neither democratic nor federalist.

In an interview on the American CBS news program '60 Minutes' in May 2005 Putin was asked whether ending elections was not a step away from democratic principles. He rejected this view and argued that other democratic federalist systems chose governors through appointments from the centre. Putin pointed to India and said

> India is called the largest world democracy. But their governors have always been appointed by the central government, and nobody disputes that India is a large democracy ... The principle of appointing regional leaders is not a sign of a lack of democracy.[39]

In point of fact, federalism makes little sense without the popular election of regional executives. If regional decision makers are appointed and subject to removal from the centre, they can hardly be viewed as having regional interests as their first priority. In India, which has a parliamentary form of government, the post of 'governor' is not the main locus of executive power in a state; Indian states are run by the party or coalition that controls the state legislative assembly. The Kremlin has also at times pointed to Nigeria as an example of a federal system without regional elections, yet here too the reality is that it was the dictator Sani Abacha who suspended gubernatorial elections after his 1993 coup. When democracy returned to Nigeria in 1999, the new constitution again provided for popularly elected governors.

Putin's new system, if carried to its logical conclusion, would eliminate all elections for executive posts below that of Russian president, including those not just for governors, but for mayors and other municipal leaders.[40] Putin would appoint governors, and governors would appoint mayors and lower-level officials. In his September 2004 speech Putin called for governors to play a greater role in formation of local organs of power. Ultimately, the result would be a system under which the only elections would be for pre-sident, the Duma, regional legislatures and municipal councils. Combined with the increasing emphasis on proportional representation by political parties as the basis for creating legislative bodies, one could imagine Russian elections in which the only name of a person listed on a ballot would be for the office of president.

The ideas of democracy and federalism that are a major part of the Russian constitution provided a framework that, if allowed to develop, would give the system built-in 'safety valves' that would make it easier to weather periodic crises. The path to a more democratic Russia would be to reform those elements that would strengthen democracy and federalism, such as clarifying the budgets and responsibilities of the centre and the regions, strengthening national institutions, and creating a system of inde-pendent courts. Many analysts questioned the Kremlin's assumptions about Russia and the wisdom of the new strategy. One could argue that excessive centralization and the consequent deferral of many key decisions to the centre makes Russia more, not less, vulnerable to collapse. Instead of increasing accountability in the regions, it has the effect of making the centre responsible for everything. Governors, who were just beginning to be accountable to voters, were now accountable only to Putin.

Notes

1 V. Putin, 'Vystuplenie na rashironnym zasedanii Pravitel'stva s uchastiem glav sub'ektov Rossiskoi Federatsii,' 13 September 2004. From the presidential site http://www.president.kremlin.ru

2 The law was passed by a vote of 372 to 60, with only the KPRF and independent deputies opposed.

3 Putin in his public appearances has consistently rejected this characterization of the new system, insisting that the election of governors by regional legislatures is the essential element of the new procedure.

4 Moscow and Leningrad, later renamed St Petersburg, had the status of regions ('subjects of the federation'), rather than cities within regions.

5 See A. Sobchak, *Iz Leningrada v Peterburg: Putshestvie vo Vremeni i Prostranstve*, Kontrfors: St. Petersburg, 1999, p. 143.

6 Vladimir Putin, *Ot Pervogo Litsa*, Moscow: Vagrius, 2000, p. 104. In the book Putin mistakenly places these events in 1992 rather than 1991.

7 The Soviet leadership was encouraging the republics within Russia to join the new union treaty autonomously from the Russian federation. See the material pub-lished by the Gorbachev Foundation, *Soiuz mozhno bylo sokhranit'*, 2nd edn, Moscow, 2007, pp. 235-9.

8 Starting in 1996 governors were automatically given seats in the upper chamber, which also provided them with immunity from criminal prosecution. Under Putin, regional leaders were removed from the Federation Council and replaced by their

appointed representatives, a group much more willing to take instructions from the Kremlin.

9 Andrew Konitzer, *Voting for Russia's Governors*, Washington, DC: Woodrow Wilson Center Press, Johns Hopkins University Press, 2005, pp. 82–8.

10 Grigory Belonuchkin, *101 fakt o Rossiiskoi Federatsii*, Moscow: Panorama, 2006, p. 145.

11 Cameron Ross, 'Federalism and electoral authoritarianism under Putin', *Demokratizatsiya*, Summer 2005, Vol. 13, No. 4, pp. 347–71.

12 Konitzer, p. 225.

13 The most complete analysis of these measures is Peter Reddaway and Robert W. Orttung (eds), *The Dynamics of Russian Politics: Putin's Reform of Federal–Regional Relations, Volume II*, Lanham, MD, Boulder, CO, New York, Toronto, Oxford: Rowman & Littlefield, 2005.

14 Putin had pressured Yakovlev to leave his post as St Petersburg governor to become deputy prime minister and then presidential representative in the Southern Federal District. This step eventually allowed Putin to appoint Valentina Matvienko as acting governor, and she won election to the post in October 2003. Later Yakovlev returned to Moscow as head of a new ministry for regional economic development.

15 Rogozin interviewed by Vladimir Solov'ev on the programme 'Apel'sinovoi sok', NTV, 26 September 2004.

16 Yakovlev was quickly replaced as presidential envoy (by long-term Putin ally Dmitry Kozak) and after a few months Dzasokhov was forced into early retirement from his post of North Ossetian president.

17 Vitalii Ivanov, *Putin i Regiony: Tsentralizatsiia Rossii*, Moscow: Evropa, 2006, p. 200.

18 Yakovlev had served as Sobchak's minister for communal services; the presumed support he received came from Yeltsin aides in the so-called 'party of war', Alexander Korzhakov and Oleg Soskovets.

19 Putin, pp. 105–7.

20 Anatolii Sobchak, *Diuzhina Nozhei v Spinu*, Moscow: Vagrius-Petro-N'ius, 1999, p. 106.

21 Rostislav Turovskii, 'Putinskaia piatiletka v regional'noi politike, ili beg po krugu', http://www.politkom.ru , 28 December 2005.

22 Vera Postnova, 'Rech' idet o likvidatsii national'nykh respublik', *Nezavisimaya Gazeta*, 27 October 2004.

23 Results reported in, 'Bol'shinstvo rossiian za vybory merov and senatorov', *strana. ru*, 22 November 2004.

24 'Gubernatory Rossii: poderzhivaem mestnykh', VTsIOM press release No. 536, 20 September 2006, from the website http://www.wciom.ru.

25 Georgii Satarov, 'Piramida sizifa', *Novaya Gazeta*, 4 October 2004.

26 'Reforma regional'noi vlasti: monitoring', FOM website, http://www.fom.ru, 9 December 2004. 36 per cent had difficulty answering.

27 'Izvmeneniia v protsedure izbraniia glav regionov', FOM website http://www.fom. ru, 24 November 2005.

28 Among national political actors, the main opponents of Putin's plan were the KPRF (though it had traditionally favoured centralization and restrictions on the powers of governors), as well as the extraparliamentary parties Yabloko and the Union of Right Forces.

29 'Ot Konstitutsii ostanetsia trukha', *Vlast'*, 26 December 2005.

30 Presidential representatives in federal districts began functioning in 2000; they are chosen by the president and report to his administration. The districts and post of polpred were created by decree and are an extra-constitutional institution.

31 See the discussion of Kvashnin's role as polpred in Siberia in Andrei Riskin, 'Shchupal'tse prezidenta', *Nezavisimaya Gazeta*, 18 September 2006.

32 Natal'ia Melikova, 'Fenomen Sobianina', *Nezavisimaya Gazeta*, 13 November 2006 and 'Kak vybiraiut novykh gubernatorov', *Nezavisimaya Gazeta*, 31 August 2005.

33 'Stenograficheskii otchet o press-konferentsii dlia rossiiskikh i inostrannykh zhurnalistov', 1 February 2007, http://www.president.kremlin.ru.

34 'Nizhegorodskomu gubernatoru predlozhili uiti po-khorshemu', *Kommersant*, 25 April 2005.

35 'Edinaia Rossiia' odobrila vybor Dmitriia Kozaka', *Kommersant*, 11 October 2006.

36 Stroev had been first secretary of the Orel oblast committee of the Communist Party from 1985 to 1989 and Governor since 1993.

37 Francesca Mereu, 'Governors Facing a Struggle for Survival', *The Moscow Times*, 18 March 2005. The quote is by the head of the Orel office of the group Opora.

38 Luzhkov's term ends in December 2007, but he has indicated that he will ask to be reappointed.

39 'Putin Defends His Democracy', Putin interview telecast on 8 May 2005. CBS News website, http://www.cbsnes.com/stories/2005/05/06.

40 If extended to mayors, this would violate the provisions of the European convention on local government to which Russia has agreed to adhere.

6 Electoral reforms and democratization

Russian regional elections 2003–2006

Aleksandr Kynev

For Russia the years 2001-6 were years of all-encompassing political reform that fundamentally changed not only the federal but also the regional political process. The main features of the reform that affected the political process in the regions were:

- election of at least half the deputies to regional parliaments through a proportional electoral system (this rule became obligatory for elections held after 13 June 2003);
- changes in the composition of the Federation Council, the upper house of the Federal Assembly (from 2001, instead of the governors and chairmen of regional legislative assemblies who were members of the Federation Council as part of their position, two representatives were appointed from each region, one by the governor and one by the legislative assembly, and in this way the heads of the regions lost their parliamentary immunity);
- the gradual raising of the threshold for party lists to 7 per cent;
- a ban on the existence of regional political parties, followed by a ban on the formation of pre-election blocs (so that parties unable to meet the 7 per cent threshold would be prevented from joining forces);
- the abolition of direct gubernatorial elections.

All this had major implications for how Russia functioned as a federation, and for how regional political systems and regional political parties operated. Citizens, parties, regional political elites and, arguably, society as a whole, did not have time to become accustomed to each change before it was succeeded by a further redrafting of the rules regarding political and electoral processes, and, by extension, the system of interaction between different levels and branches of government. In the period 2001–6 the rules for regional elections were tightened almost annually. Thus the main features of these electoral reforms were, overall, standardization of electoral and party legislation, a minimization of the degree of permissible variation in the rules for holding elections in different regions and the full introduction of parties at elections accompanied by a simultaneous sharp strengthening of state control over political parties.

For President Putin's administration electoral reforms in the Russian regions were just as integral an element in the construction of the 'vertical of power' as the reforms that preceded them: reform of the power structures (reforms that removed the power structures from the control of the regional government bodies and made them totally subordinate to the president and the leaders that he appointed) and of the allocation of economic powers between the centre and the regions (the cancellation of the principle of 'two keys' in the matter of the exploitation of natural resources, etc.).

In addition, those who advocated standardization of regional electoral legislation cited clear 'deviations' in the electoral legislation of such regions as Kalmykiya, Tyva, Ingushetiya and others, to prove how essential it was. In the framework of the new law on political parties, which made parties increasingly dependent on the state authorities, the party vertical centred on Moscow, no less than the executive vertical, was to be set to work 'reinforcing the country's unity' and strengthening internal cohesion.

The ruling elite gradually learnt how to engage with a new area of public life, political parties, and the federal bureaucracy mastered the techniques of electoral engineering, thereby creating a model consisting of an increasingly managed party system and limited political competition.

On the one hand, the multi-party system had become an integral part of the country's political system after the reforms of the 1980s and 1990s. In particular, Article 13 of the Russian Constitution enshrines the acceptance of political variety, a plurality of parties. At the same time the generally accepted principles and rules of international law and the status of international treaties signed by the Russian Federation (Part 4 of Article 15 of the Constitution) are a component of the national legal system. The rules enshrining the multi-party system are contained in the Declaration on Criteria for Free and Fair Elections adopted in Paris in 1994, the Universal Declaration on Democracy adopted in 1997, and also in documents signed by the Russian Federation and adopted by the Conference on Security and Cooperation in Europe,[1] which took place in three stages: in Paris in 1989, Copenhagen in 1990 and Moscow in 1991. Thus the existence of a multi-party system forms part of the international obligations that they took on.

On the other hand, the state bureaucracy's apparently instinctive inclination towards complete control over public life, part of the Soviet institutional legacy, drove it to search for levers by which the new political system could be directed and this led to its discovery and 'seizure' of those rules from various electoral models that offered the potential for manipulating the electoral process whilst maintaining the external aspect of a multi-party and competitive system.

The result is a system of limited party competition, in which parties are placed under actual state control and citizens have almost no ability to unite freely in political parties. This is the result of an attempt to assure the formal existence of a multi-party system but to use various manipulatory mechanisms to subvert the meaning that such a system traditionally has in developed democracies.

This phenomenon may be explained by reference to the concept of historic institutionalism. Thus, according to Peters, an initial institutional choice (of both a structural and regulatory nature), made in the historical past for some individual feature or overall system, will have a profound effect on all subsequent political decisions.[2] Hence the country's historical and institutional past places unavoidable and insurmountable limits on any attempts at electoral and political reform; it has a specific effect on the actual results of the application of one or another form of electoral mechanism. Thus, in a country where a party like the CPSU dominated for seventy years, any subsequent attempt to create a mass party with a strictly fixed membership will inevitably lead to the creation of bodies like the Communist Party of the Soviet Union. Chernomyrdin's words – 'here any party will end up as the CPSU' – perfectly encapsulates this phenomenon. If no attention is paid to the country's institutional inheritance when adopting the most important laws, then the intended result of their adoption will be considerably distorted. One could assume that the establishment of a super-presidential form of republic in 1993, with very weak representative governing bodies and where the power of the president is almost as absolute as the power of the CPSU during the Soviet period, would make the establishment of state control over public institutions just a matter of time.

1 The reforms of December 2003–May 2005: approval of the new electoral system in regional elections

As has already been mentioned, the effective implementation of the new electoral system for regional assembly elections started on 14 July 2003. Elections to regional legislative assemblies during this period can be broken down into three groups:

- combined with elections to the State Duma on 7 December 2003 (seven regions)
- combined with the presidential elections on 14 March 2004 (six regions)
- held at various times between September 2004 and May 2005 (19 regions); these elections were held after the initiative of the Russian President in September 2004 to abolish the direct election of governors

Thus between July 2003 and May 2005 thirty-two electoral campaigns took place under the new voting system for elections to regional legislative assemblies. A mixed voting system was used everywhere, with the exception of the Sverdlovsk Oblast where, as previously, one chamber (the Chamber of Representatives) of the Legislative Assembly was elected entirely using the majority system and the other chamber (the Regional Duma) was elected entirely by the proportional system (with half the membership being re-elected every two years). The ratio between the proportional and the majority parts varied across the regions from 50:50 (in most regions) to 7:5

in the Koryak Autonomous Okrug (hereafter, AO). The number of deputies elected under the proportional system ranged from six (in the Chukotka Autonomous Okrug) to fifty-five (in the Kabardino-Balkar Republic).

The first elections to be held under the new system, the elections of 7 December 2003, were the most significant, and their results were in many ways connected to the federal campaign for the elections to the State Duma. The resources of the regional elites were scattered and the system for regional elections was new, and consequently there were electoral blocs almost nowhere (apart from the elections in the Ul'yanovsk Oblast, where they played a considerable role); the results for the parties were relatively close to the federal results. United Russia dominated in all seven regions, but performed worst of all in the Ul'yanovsk Oblast.

The largest number of lists, nine, was registered in the Ul'yanovsk Oblast, and there were only four in Mordoviya, six in the Vologda and Volgograd Oblasts, Ingushetiya and Kabardino-Balkariya. And this is despite the fact that there were twenty-three lists in the elections for deputies to the State Duma. Five parties entered parliament in Ingushetiya, four in the Ul'yanovsk and Vologda Oblasts (but for the 8 per cent threshold it would have been five in Vologda), three in the Volgograd Oblast and Kabardino-Balkariya (but for the 7 per cent threshold it would have been four in Volgograd), two in Mordoviya and Kalmykiya (but for the 10 per cent threshold there would have been four parties in Kalmykia). Thus, with the 5 per cent threshold a two-party system could have benefited only Mordoviya, and all the other regions would have had four or five parties in their parliaments. The most active were the supporters of United Russia: they put forward lists in all seven regions. The CPRF took part in elections in six regions (all apart from Ingushetiya), the Party of Russia's Rebirth (PRR) and the SPS participated in five regions, the LDPR, Yabloko and the APR in four, and the Russian Party of Life (RPL) in three. One should note in particular the energy of the APR, RPL and PRR, which had not managed to achieve any great success at federal level. Moreover the PRR and RPL, which had formed a single list for the elections to the State Duma, were not able to form electoral blocs in one single region. Other 'small' parties hardly figured in regional elections: the Party for Peace 'glittered' in Kalmykiya and Ingushetiya[3] as a virtual regional party for Aushev, and the 'Greens' put forward a list in Kalmykiya and were the founders of the Ulyanovtsy bloc. The Party for Peace and Unity, the Social Justice Party, the For Holy Russia Party and the Party of National Revival all made one attempt each to participate in regional elections.

The elections of 14 March 2004, when presidential elections did not require a major diversion of the resources of specifically regional elites, were marked by a clear increase in political competition at proportional elections and a further erosion of the direct participation of federal parties in the elections. On this occasion ten lists were registered in the Yaroslavl' Oblast (an eleventh list, United Russia – Za Yedinuyu Rossiyu, withdrew voluntarily), nine in Tatarstan and the Sverdlovsk Oblast, seven in Karachaevo-Cherkessiya, six in the Altai Krai and only three in the Ust'-Ordynskii Buryatskii Autonomous Okrug.

Only three parties, United Russia, the CPRF and the LDPR, put forward lists in all the regions where elections were taking place on 14 March 2004. United Russia and the CPRF entered regional parliaments everywhere and the LDPR entered in four out of the six regions (the party lost in Tatarstan and the Ust'-Ordynskii Buryatskii AO). It is worth noting that, in comparison to federal voting, the indicators for United Russia fell in Altai Krai and Yaroslavl' Oblast, places where elections were most genuinely competitive. In Altai Krai United Russia list gained 24.43 per cent of the vote for the Council of the Krai, compared to 29.96 per cent in the elections for the State Duma, and in Yaroslavl' Oblast it was 25.98 per cent instead of 36.25 per cent. United Russia's indicators rose in places where there had been attempts to use force to influence the electoral process: Tatarstan (69 per cent instead of 60 per cent) and the Ust'-Ordynskii Buryatskii AO (58 per cent instead of 47 per cent). There were slight increases in Karachaevo-Cherkessiya (55.87 per cent instead of 50 per cent) and the Sverdlovsk Oblast (38.24 per cent instead of 34.7 per cent); competition between the lists was also less than in the elections to the State Duma and consequently there was a minimal dispersal of votes.

Regional blocs achieved considerable success in Altai Krai (For Our Altai – Communists, Agrarians and NPSR! and Supporting the President – for the Region's Development), the Yaroslavl' Oblast (Motherland and Truth, Order and Justice) and the Sverdlovsk Oblast (Union of Ural Public Employees and others). In other words, the regional parties that had been banned by the law were effectively resurrected at the elections under the guise of regional pre-election blocs.

Special mention should be made of the participation in elections for legislative assemblies in three regions (the Yaroslavl' and Sverdlovsk Oblasts and Tatarstan) of the bloc called Rodina (Motherland). In fact this bloc came second in the elections in the Yaroslavl' Oblast. Problems occurred everywhere in using the name of the party when registering the lists. There were attempts to register two blocs under this name in the Yaroslavl' Oblast, and two 'Rodinas' were set up in the elections in the Sverdlovsk Oblast. In Tatarstan the Party of National Revival and the Socialist Unified Party of Russia 'Spiritual Heritage' set up the Rodina (Republic of Tatarstan) Bloc. Originally the Party of the Russian Regions, the third founding party of the federal Rodina, was also to have been part of the bloc, but it decided to participate in the electoral campaign independently, evidently not without advice from the region's administration, so as to disperse the patriotic vote See Table 6.1).

This tendency towards strengthening the role of blocs and increasing genuine competition became much stronger in the regional elections that began in the autumn of 2004. It is clear that an analysis of the results of the

Table 6.1 Elections to the legislative assemblies of members of the RF on 7 December 2003 and 14 March 2004

Date of election	Legislative body for which deputies were elected	Threshold (%)	Lists on the voting paper	Lists that crossed the threshold
7 December 2003	People's Assembly of the Republic of Ingushetiya	5	5	5
	People's Assembly and Parliament of the Kabardino-Balkar Republic	5	6	3
	People's Khural of the Republic of Kalmykiya	10	10	2 (with a 5% threshold it would have been 4)
	State Assembly of the Republic of Mordoviya	5	4	2
	Volgograd Regional Duma	7	6	3 (with a 5% threshold it would have been 4)
	Legislative Assembly of the Vologda Oblast	8	6	4 (with a 5% threshold it would have been 5)
	Legislative Assembly of the Ul'yanovsk Oblast	5	10	4
14 March 2004	People's Assembly of the Karachaevo-Cherkessian Republic	5	7	4
	State Council of the Republic of Tatarstan	7	9	1 (under the law a second list, the KPRF, was allowed to share in the allocation)
	Altai Regional Council of People's Deputies	7	6	4
	Sverdlovsk Regional Duma	5	9	5
	State Duma of the Yaroslavl' Oblast	5	10	6
	Duma of the Ust'-Ordynskii Buryatkii AO	No threshold (only 8 seats allocated)	3	Only 2 lists gained deputies

Source: Compiled by the author.

7 December 2003 and 14 March 2004 elections also had an effect on the course of the campaigns and on the use of the techniques for constructing the pre-election unions of the time. The regional authorities played a much more complicated game: there was not a single region where the governor and his administration unambiguously supported one party list, and almost

everywhere the political and economic groups close to the administration spread their participation into different party lists. At the same time administrative pressure, which had previously been noted in elections to single-member districts and elections for governors, etc., began increasingly to be applied in elections from party lists. While in the 14 March 2004 elections in Sverdlovsk Oblast and the Ust'-Ordynskii Buryatskii AO had been marked by mass barring of the regional opposition from the elections, at the end of 2004 and beginning of 2005 they had been joined by Bryansk, Voronezh and Magadan Oblasts and the Yamalo-Nenets AO. In Tula and Amur Oblasts the blocs that had been kept away from the elections were able to reinstate their registration through the Supreme Court.

The campaigns of this period were technically very complicated (for example, in the Koryak and Yamalo-Nenetskii autonomous okrugs 'open' lists were used), and quite possibly this is largely due to the fact that the main regional political forces were able to concentrate all their main staffing, organizational and technical resources on them, without being distracted by participation in federal campaigns. The increased experience of conducting such elections also played their part, as did the President of Russia's initiative of 13 September 2004 to abolish the direct election of governors, and change the election of deputies to the State Duma to a fully proportional electoral system; this greatly increased the interest of both the public and the politico-economic elites in elections to regional legislative assemblies.

At the same time, the announcement by the Russian President of the abolition of direct elections for governors undoubtedly led to an increase in the attempts mentioned above to strengthen administrative control by the governor over elections to legislative assemblies. The legal process of formulating the president's initiative took place during the autumn of 2004 and the final direct elections for governor took place on 6 February 2005 in the Nenets AO. In other words, from September 2004 to February 2005 governors were still elected by the populace, but it was already known that this was the last time. Thus the governors began gradually to concentrate their efforts more and more on setting up control over the legislative assemblies, which, under the new circumstances, would have to approve the candidates for governor proposed by the President.

Overall, the degree of genuine competition in the elections at the end of 2004 and beginning of 2005 was much higher than in the votes of 7 December 2003 and 14 March 2004 (Table 6.2). On voting day there were eleven lists on the voting paper in Tula and Sakhalin Oblasts, nine in Amur, Arkhangel'sk, Voronezh and Irkutsk Oblasts, eight in Bryansk and Kurgan Oblasts and Khakassiya, seven in the Vladimir and Ryazan' Oblasts and the Nenetskii AO, six in the Kaluga Oblast, five in Chita Oblast and Marii-El, and there were just four in the Yamalo-Nenetskii AO and the sparsely-inhabited Koryak and Taymyr AOs. Consequently at least four parties surmounted the threshold in all these regions, except for the Yamalo-Nenetskii AO. Only one party, United Russia, managed to register its lists in all nineteen

Table 6.2 Elections to the legislative assemblies of members of the RF in the second half of 2004 and first half of 2005

Date of election	Legislative body for which deputies were elected	Threshold (%)	Lists on the voting paper	Lists that crossed the threshold
7 October 2004	Tula Regional Duma	5	11	7
24 October 2004	State Assembly of Marii-El	5	5	5
	Legislative Assembly of the Irkutsk Oblast	5	9	6
24 October 2004	Sakhalin Regional duma	6	11	6
14 November 2004	Chita Regional Duma	5	5	4
	Legislative Assembly of the Kaluga Oblast	5	6	5
28 November 2004	Kurgan Regional Duma	5	8	6
5 December 2004	Bryansk Regional Duma	5	8	5
19 December 2004	Arkhangel'sk Regional Council of Deputies	5	9	6
26 December 2004	Supreme Council of the Republic of Khakassiya	5	8	6
23 January 2005	Duma of the Taymyr (Dolgano-Nenets) AO	7	4	4
6 February 2005	Assembly of Deputies of the Yamalo-Nenetskii AO	7	7	5 (with a 5% threshold it would have been 6)
20 March 2005	Legislative Assembly of the Vladimir Oblast	7	7	6 (with a 5% threshold it would have been 7)
22 May 2005	State Duma of the Yamalo-Nenetskii AO	5	4	3
	Magadan Regional Duma	7	4	4
16 October 2005	Belgorod Regional Duma	5	7	4

Source: Compiled by the author from data published by the Central Electoral Commission

regions where elections took place during this period. The CPRF and LDPR managed to register in eighteen regions. The most active of the other parties were the Russian Party of Pensioners (twelve regions) and the Agrarian Party of Russia (nine regions, and part of electoral blocs in another four). The SPS put forward its own lists in eight regions (it joined electoral blocs in another six), Yabloko in just four (in another region the registration of its list was cancelled and in a further seven it joined electoral blocs; during the period in question four instances were noted in the regions of an SPS–Yabloko bloc).

The situation was complicated for Rodina (formerly the Party of the Russian Regions, which changed its name in February 2004): the lists that this party put forward directly were registered in twelve regions; in one region the party's registration was refused and in another two, the Tula Oblast and Sakhalin, this former bloc which was present in the federal elections of 2003 was represented by regional blocs. In the case of the Sakhalin Oblast this bloc, hypothetically linked to the federal Rodina, was called Our Motherland is Sakhalin and the Kuriles, and was set up by the Party of National Revival, the Agrarian Party and the Eurasian Party – Union of Patriots of Russia. In Tula the 'maternal federal bloc' produced two whole regional blocs: 'Zasechny rubezh – partiya Rodina' (Frontier – Motherland) (set up by the Rodina and For Holy Russia parties and supported by Rogozin) and the Voice of the People – For the Motherland party (set up by the Party of National Revival and the Republican Party, and supported by Glazyev and Baburin); both surmounted the 5 per cent threshold. The former comrades-in-arms from the federal bloc Rodina-2003 almost collided in Bryansk where, in addition to the list of the Rodina party, another bloc was put forward, For a Worthy Life (set up by the DPR and the Party of National Revival), headed by Glazyev, but it was subsequently removed from the elections.

The participation of all other parties, apart from those already mentioned, in regional elections in the period under review was insignificant. The most active of the other parties were the People's Party and the Russian Party of Life, which generally appeared among the founders of regional blocs. Acting on their own, the People's Party only managed to enter the Duma of the Taimyr AO, and the RPL won seats in the Legislative Assembly of Vladimir Oblast. Apart from these only the Social Justice Party managed to get into the Arkhangel'sk Regional Assembly by itself. Most other parties were only able to participate in the formation of blocs two or three times at the most. Parties such as the Party of Russia's Rebirth, the DPR, SDPR and the RPRF turned more and more into purely auxiliary technical elements and their candidates became sparring partners for stronger and more promising candidates and bloc.

A feature of the elections of this period noted by analysts was the worsening of the results of the 'system' parties (those represented in the State Duma), United Russia and the LDPR, while the indicators for the CPRF and

Rodina remained approximately the same. At the same time regional blocs were achieving considerable success (in particular in Amur, Arkhangel'sk, Magadan, Ryazan', Sakhalin and Tula Oblasts, Khakassiya and Taimyr), as did parties with a sufficiently well-known brand and a low negative rating, usually politically left of centre, the Russian Party of Pensioners and the Agrarian Party. The 'traditionally' democratic parties failed, with a few exceptions. These successes were often unexpected for sociologists, so one can presume that the undecided voters shared their votes unevenly at the last moment: they preferred to vote either for well-known, but not 'system', parties or for regional patriotic blocs. Compared to the results of the elections to the State Duma, the vote for United Russia only increased in three regions where the lists for the regional elections were headed by the incumbent governor: the Kaluga and Voronezh Oblasts and the Yamalo-Nenetskii AO.[4]

2 Reforms in the second half of 2005–March 2006: toughening of electoral legislation (the electoral counter-reformation); consequences of the abolition of direct elections for governors

New amendments to the federal law, 'On the Basic Guarantees of Electoral Rights and the Right of Russian Federation Citizens to Participate in Referendums' were adopted in June and July 2005 following the results of the thirty-two regional electoral campaigns between 2003 and the start of 2005. The most important changes were the abolition of electoral blocs, the setting of an upper electoral threshold of 7 per cent, which many regions took as a signal to raise their thresholds from 5 to 7 per cent, and a toughening of the procedure for registering lists and candidates, which increased the legal possibilities for the registering and supervising bodies to influence the composition of the candidates (i.e. strengthened administrative control on the process of the elections and the nomination of candidates).[5]

The setting of extremely large electoral deposits (according to the region's choice it was between 10 per cent and 15 per cent of the maximum size of the electoral fund[6]) combined with the virtual impossibility of registration via a collection of signatures[7] signified the virtual creation of a system of high-income qualifications that limited the right of citizens to be elected. At the same time the parliamentary parties (i.e. parties that had crossed the threshold at the last elections to the State Duma), first and foremost United Russia with its parliamentary majority, had freed themselves when registering both from collecting signatures and from paying deposits. In this way the financial qualifications applied first and foremost to the opposition and to new political projects and non-party citizens. All these measures were multiplied by the general increase in the size of electoral districts, and as at least half the deputies of the legislature had to be elected from party lists, this could only be avoided by increasing the overall number of deputies.

It was also decided that two 'single voting days' would be allowed per year for elections. If previous elections to the legislative assemblies of members of the Federation had taken place between 1 November and 31 March, under these amendments the next elections would be held on the second Sunday in March, and if the previous elections had been between 1 April and 31 October, on the second Sunday in October. In this way elections in 2006 should take place on 12 March and 8 October, and in 2007 on 11 March. Consequently the deputies to the representative body, or the official figure, who had been elected at the previous elections would find that, due to the transfer of election dates to the 'single voting days', the period of their mandate would change. According to expert opinion the introduction of the 'single voting days' had the real aim of maximizing the domination of the 'party of power' in the federal mass media, and principally the electronic mass media. United Russia's official reason for introducing this novelty, allegedly an attempt to save budget finances, seems very doubtful since it is impossible to see what savings there could be for a region in having its elections on the same day as the next region, or another day.

At almost the same time the laws on political parties were also considerably toughened and a new rule was introduced requiring a membership threshold of 50,000 instead of the previous threshold of 10,000. The requirements for a minimum membership of regional branches of parties were also increased at the same time: for parties that had branches in at least half the subject of the Federation the requirements were increased from 100 to 500, and from 50 to 250 for other branches. The law required that parties that were already registered should bring their membership into line with the new requirements by 1 January 2006. If they were unable to do this they were obliged to change themselves into some other legal form of public association, otherwise they would be closed down. Newly created parties and regional branches had to conform immediately to the new requirements.

Another major novelty was connected to the problem of calculating and verifying the size of the party. Previously the law had not required that a list of party members be supplied to the registering body. According to the opinion of experts the majority of parties registered did not actually have the membership required by law. The law adopted in December 2004 obliged parties to supply a regional membership list to the area registering body when setting up a regional branch. This worsened the situation for opposition parties since in a number of regions people might be worried about joining them if their membership should become known to the authorities. This meant that the fate of most parties depended upon how thorough the verification was, i.e. it depended on the authorities' attitude towards them.

One can state that in reality the very traditional policy of carrot and stick was used by the federal centre to tighten control over regional elections. The stick was the above-mentioned new repressive regulations in federal law and the increase in governors' personal dependence on the federal leadership brought about by the loss of their previous status of being fully elected. Steps were also undertaken towards politically discrediting and replacing the leaderships of the parties that had achieved a high level of success in the previous regional elections: the Russian Party of Pensioners, Rodina and the APR. Identical means of pressure were applied six months apart to the RPP and Rodina: mass non-admission to regional elections combined with a campaign to discredit the party leaders. Major problems also arose for anyone who tried to create 'new' democratic parties, such as the Republican Party (whose virtual leader was Ryzhkov) and the Democratic Party (which Kasyanov unsuccessfully tried to lead).

A certain increase (mainly symbolic) in the powers of the regional executive body served as the carrot, accompanied by a promise to allocate funds to so-called 'national projects' and the right for the region itself to decide when the new law on local government would come fully into force (it was control over local government that governors had fought for most stubbornly), as it involved a considerable reallocation of power from the regional to a lower level. Parties 'that had won in regional elections' were given the right to submit a candidate for governor[8] to the President of Russia, and this would be a further stimulus for governors to head the United Russia list and mobilize all the administrative resources in support of the party of power. In this instance votes for parties in regional elections effectively turned into a vote in favour of the regional governor.

Eleven electoral campaigns took place under these conditions at the end of 2005. Elections took place in another eight regions on 12 March 2006, the first of the so-called 'single voting days'. In all, nineteen regional parliaments were elected during this period (see Table 6.3).

The results of the set of measures described above were on the one hand the mass appearance of governors heading the United Russia list and consequently different results for this party compared to the previous elections of 2004-5, and on the other hand the transfer of a proportion of the protest vote from the RPP and Rodina, which were being repressed, to the CPRF, which was clearly rising again: there was also a further increase in the percentage of votes which were cast 'against all' candidates.

At the end of 2005 governors thus headed the 'party of power' lists in five of the twelve regions where there had been elections to legislative assemblies, and after the elections of 12 March 2006 it was five out of eight. Initially this bore fruit. United Russia's results increased in eight cases out of twelve in the elections at the end of 2005, but with the continuation of the 'administrative overstatement' the administrative triumph of November–December 2005 was clearly in recession by the spring of 2006. On the 'single voting day' of 12 March 2006, only four of the eight regions showed a clear increase in the vote for United Russia (the Khanty-Mansiskii AO and Kursk, Orenburg and Nizhnii Novgorod Oblasts) and in another two there was a drop (Kirov Oblast and Adygeya Republic), and in the latter it was almost catastrophic – from 51.3 per cent to 33.7 per cent – and this despite the fact that, in the opinion of the opposition, this was an exaggerated result for United Russia in the region. In the Altai Republic and Kaliningrad Oblast the improvement was purely symbolic, with hardly any change, even though

Table 6.3 Election to legislative assemblies of members of the RF during the second half of 2005 and on 12 March 2006

Date of election	Legislative body for which deputies were elected	Threshold (%)	Lists on the voting paper	Lists that crossed the threshold
30 October 2005	Duma of the Agin Buryat AO	No threshold	3	3
27 November 2005	People's Assembly of the Chechen Republic	5	8	3
4 December 2005	Moscow City Duma	10	9	3 (with a 5% threshold it would have been 4)
	Kostroma Regional Duma	4	8	6
	Legislative Assembly of the Ivanovo oblast	4	8	6
11 December 2005	Legislative Duma of the Khabarovsk krai	5	6	4
	Novosibirsk Regional Council	7	7	4 (with a 5% threshold it would have been 5)
18 December 2005	Tambov Regional Duma	7	11	3 (with a 5% threshold it would have been 5)
	Legislative Assembly of the Tver' oblast	5	8	6
25 December 2005	Legislative Assembly of the Chel'yabinsk oblast	5	7	4
	Duma of the Chukotka autonomous okrug	5	2	2

Table 6.3 (continued)

Date of election	Legislative body for which deputies were elected	Threshold (%)	Lists on the voting paper	Lists that crossed the threshold
12 March 2006	State Council of the Adygei Republic	7	8	4
	State Assembly of the Altai Republic	5	13	6
	Kaliningrad Regional Duma	7	7	5
	Legislative Assembly of the Kirov oblast	6	9	5
	Kursk Regional Duma	7	9	3 (with a 5% threshold it would have been 7)
	Legislative Assembly of the Nizhnii Novgorod oblast	5	6	4
	Legislative Assembly of the Orenburg oblast	5	8	5
	Duma of the Khanty-Mansiskii AO	5	5	4

Source: Compiled by the author from data published by the Central Electoral Commission.

governors came to power who were much more loyal to the federal centre. The greatest drop in the 'party of power's' results occurred in a region where the 'administrative overstatement' was almost at its strongest, Adygeya. Here, the Rodina and Patriots of Russia lists were removed from the elections by deleting candidates from these lists in numbers that exceeded the rules, and attempts were made to remove the lists of the Agrarian Party and the Russian United Industrial Party, which had put forward at the head of its list the leaders of the Union of Slavs of Adygeya. In the districts in the regional centre of the Kaliningrad Oblast, where two favourites – Rodina and the People's Party – were removed from the elections (their regional branches in the Oblast are headed respectively by State Duma deputy Nikitin and the well-known local journalist Rudnikov), more people voted 'against all' than ever before, more than 20 per cent of the electorate (the average for the region is 16.8 per cent), and all the well-known opposition deputies won triumphantly in their districts: I. Rudnikov, Ginzburg and Lopata.

The elections to the Moscow City Duma were undoubtedly the 'apotheosis' of management: Rodina and the RPP were removed from them, and the ruling party's list contained a whole group of prefects, heads of administrations and deputies to the State Duma, as well as the Mayor of Moscow; the threshold was set at 10 per cent and voting 'against all' was abolished; registration via signatures was effectively made impossible for opposition candidates and the deposit required was raised to what was an unprecedented amount for the Russian regions. Moreover, Moscow, with its population of 10 million, was divided into just fifteen single-member electoral districts for the elections to the Moscow City Duma, which thus coincided with the abolished districts for the elections to the State Duma. The actual size of the electoral district was the main restriction on the opposition's ability to be represented, becoming effectively a financial qualification of who had the right to become a deputy, and who did not.

Apart from the mass nomination of governors to the heads of United Russia's party lists, one practice that became virtually universal was the barring, for various reasons, of one party list or another from the elections; previously this had been the exception rather than the rule. Such scandals now became more or less the norm, and the only region where not a single party list was barred from the elections in the spring of 2006 was the Altai Republic (it now holds the record for competition in recent regional elections – thirteen party lists registered). Moreover, taking into account that federal political parties had become the only ones able to put forward party lists, this provided certain opportunities for 'undesirable' lists to be removed from elections on the decision of federal, and not local, governing bodies. The exclusion of the RPP from almost all the regional elections (apart from the Tambov and Ivanovo Oblasts, where it remained on the voting paper) at the end of 2005 can serve as an example, even though it certainly did not hinder the regional authorities everywhere (in particular in the Kostroma

Oblast and the Khabarovsk Krai). As a result, the possibilities of conducting a successful campaign ('successful' means first and foremost appearing on the voting paper on the day of the elections) were greatly reduced for opposition lists.

Apart from Moscow and the Adygeya Republic, Nizhnii Novgorod and Kaliningrad Oblasts (where the Muscovites Shantsev and Boos were appointed governors) also displayed a maximum level of administrative pressure. Out of thirteen lists put forward in the Nizhnii Novgorod Oblast only six appeared on the bulletin. The lists of Rodina and the Party of National Revival, led by Rutskoi, were excluded from the elections in the Kursk Oblast.

As a result, as in the elections at the end of 2004 and beginning of 2005, the number ticking the 'against everyone' box increased considerably in all regions (apart from Moscow, which had abolished voting 'against everyone'). The CPRF improved its results slightly. In roughly half the regions its results either did not change or dropped slightly in comparison to 2003, but in all the other regions they increased, and this was particularly noticeable in Moscow, Chechnya, the Khabarovsk Krai and Kaliningrad, Kirov, Nizhnii Novgorod, Novosibirsk, Tver', Kostroma and Belgorod Oblasts. It is clear that the absence from the voting papers of Rodina in some regions and the RPP in others played a major part in this. The LDPR results fell everywhere, apart from exceptions in Chechnya and Chukotka (there were only two lists in Chukotka, and the increased result in Chechnya, from a minimal 1.26 per cent to a minimal 1.46 per cent, was particularly symbolic). In the autumn of 2005 Rodina hovered around its previous results, and in some places it even lost noticeably (in the spring of 2006 it only remained on the voting papers in the Altai[9]). The RPP effectively missed the autumn 2005 elections, but in the elections on 12 March 2006 won triumphant results in the Nizhnii Novgorod Oblast (17.2 per cent instead of 3.2 per cent) and entered the legislative bodies in the Khanty-Mansiskii AO and Kirov and Kaliningrad Oblasts, but it could not surmount the threshold in other regions. The APR had patchy success in Adygeya, the Altai Republic and Kirov, Kostroma, Novosibirsk, Orenburg and Tambov Oblasts (but often there was a drop in the percentage of votes received when compared to 2003).

The abolition of pre-election blocs clearly made it more difficult for liberal right parties to conduct electoral campaigns, since they could no longer hide behind 'regional patriotic' party names as they had done in Taimyr and in Amur Oblast (where Yabloko members stood in the lists of the 'For Our Own Taimyr' and 'We are for the Development of the Amur Oblast' blocs). Apart from the success of a 'combined' list in Moscow (based on Yabloko) and the Ivanovo Oblast (based on the SPS), and an SPS list involving former supporters of Maskhadov in Chechnya, the liberal right forces had nothing else to boast about. At the same time even the results of the 'combined' lists were worse than the total percentages that these parties gained in 2003.

Among other parties the only ones to enter regional parliaments were the Party of National Revival in Tver' (it was supported by the Mayor of Tver',

Lebedev), the Russian United Industrial Party in Adygeya, Patriots of Russia in Kaliningrad and Orenburg Oblasts, and also the Russian Party of Life in Kostroma (with 4.7 per cent thanks to a low 4 per cent threshold), the Kursk Oblast and the Altai Republic.

Against the background of increased administrative control over the electoral process, the most competitive elections can be considered as those that took place in the Altai Republic and Kostroma and Ivanovo Oblasts (in the latter two a low 4 per cent threshold was set), where the behaviour of the regional administration was basically neutral. Tambov Oblast could also have been added to this group (all eleven lists were registered), but in this region a 7 per cent threshold was set.

Thus the abolition of regional blocs and the obvious problems with Rodina and the RPP resulted in several previously 'second echelon' parties simultaneously moving into the group of leading parties: these included Semigin's Patriots of Russia, formed on the basis of several small parties and some former CPRF members, (at the elections on 12 March 2006 it put forward lists in seven regions, and five were registered), the Russian Party of Life, and also the APR, which was patchily successful in participating in elections. At the same time the set of measures adopted by the federal authorities led to increasing mass personal participation by governors in parliamentary elections. There is justification for supposing that, apart from the reasons mentioned above and the direct encouragement for governors to join United Russia, the participation of governors in elections to legislative assemblies took on in part the character of compensation for the loss of the legitimacy that they had received directly from the electorate: the higher were the results for the list headed by the governor, the stronger was the governor's position in the federal centre.

Continuation of the electoral counter-reformation (summer 2006): elections of 8 October 2006

However, the new rules for the game adopted in June and July 2005 remained unaltered for only a short time: unforeseen problems in regional elections clearly propelled United Russia into introducing a new batch of amendments to the electoral laws in the summer of 2006. They set their helm on a complete lining-up of party structures and a sharp toughening of control over elected regional deputies.

The second part of the electoral counter-reformation was the introduction of a ban on political parties including representatives from other parties in pre-election blocs, i.e. parties were forbidden to form not just blocs, but also inter-party unions based on the list of one of the parties, when the members of one party-cum-ally would join the electoral list of another. As well as this, a rule was brought in that a candidate elected from a particular party was forbidden to join another party during his whole period in office. Breaking this rule would lead to the candidate being deprived of his mandate, even if he was elected for a majority-based district. This meant that the federal legislator put the will of the party bureaucracy above the support that the candidate received directly from his own electorate in his own district. The 'against all' box was removed (regions had had the right to remove it voluntarily since 2005, now its removal was obligatory). Previously the existence of this box had, in the light of the continual scandals about the exclusion of opposition candidates from the elections, allowed public opinion in a particular area to have the elections declared void if the choice of candidates offered to the voters clearly did not please them. If the vote 'against all' was greater than for each separate candidate then new elections should be called. Now this mechanism for protecting the public against excessive pressure from the authorities was abolished.

A law 'On Combating Extremist Activity' was adopted. This law barred from the elections any candidate against whom a verdict of 'guilty' had been brought for carrying out actions that contained just one indication of extremist activity. Under this law 'extremist' could be understood extremely widely, and it could effectively mean any statement by citizens in defence of their rights and any criticism of a governing body such as, for instance, accusing an official of incompetence. Even before this law was adopted there was a precedent in the elections to the Kaliningrad Regional Duma on 12 March 2006, when the People's Party list was excluded from the elections because in its electioneering material the People's Party had called for a fight against police corruption. A case was brought against the People's Party, and on its basis the court decided that saying that there was corruption in the police was an instance of stirring up social discord, since the police are a social group. Even earlier the Rodina list had been excluded from elections to the Moscow City Duma as it had been accused of stirring up national discord through a TV advertisement directed against illegal migrants. When the necessity arose for the authorities to bar any list or candidate from elections the new law greatly simplified the procedure.

The electoral campaign of autumn 2006 began against this background: nine regional parliaments were to be elected on 8 October 2006 (another region, Perm Krai, which had been formed through the amalgamation of Perm Oblast and Komi-Permyatskii AO, would hold its elections on 3 December 2006, a date that had been specifically set for it by federal law) (see Table 6.4).

For the first time in recent regional elections a 7 per cent threshold was set in all the regions where there would be voting. In all regions except for the Sverdlovsk Oblast and Tyva at least 20 per cent of the electorate had to vote if the elections were to be declared valid. In the Sverdlovsk Oblast the minimum turnout was set at 25 per cent. Before the start of the electoral campaign in Tyva in June 2006 it was decided to bring in a minimum turnout of 33 per cent for the elections to be declared valid (this was the proposal of the Chairman of the Government of Tyva, Oorzhak; the deputies had proposed 25 per cent). Previously the minimum turnout had been 43 per cent of the total of voters listed in the electoral register at the close of voting. This very high minimum turnout allowed the authorities to facilitate the disruption of elections when necessary and also to maintain the Great Khural with a minimum quorum; since the elections were being constantly disrupted many deputy mandates had not been taken up, and elections sometimes had to be held repeatedly for one and the same district.

In eight regions the incumbent legislative bodies themselves decided about their own re-election. The legislative governing body in the Primorskii Krai was not able to cope with the task of calling elections and the authority to call them passed to the electoral commission of the Primorskii Krai, and the latter duly took the decision on calling elections. A system of closed party lists was used in all these regions (i.e. the voters could not influence the disposition of candidates in the list). Only the lists for the elections to the Legislative Chamber of the Great Khural of Tyva, the State Council of Chuvashiya, the State Duma of the Astrakhan Oblast and the Lipetsk Regional Council were to be broken down into sub-regional groups linked to specific areas in these regions. However, in the case of Tyva this requirement was optional for the party: the party could refuse to break its list down into such groups. In all the other regions the lists were 'flat', i.e. the candidates followed one after another in strict order of hierarchy.

These regions produced considerable differences in their mechanisms for registering candidates and party lists. The most liberal requirements for registration by collecting signatures were set in the Sverdlovsk Oblast (0.75 per cent of signatures from the electoral register). The equivalent figure was 1 per cent in Astrakhan and Novgorod Oblasts, Primorskii Krai, Kareliya and Chuvashiya; in Lipetsk Oblast and the Jewish Autonomous Oblast, 2 per cent of the voters registered for each electoral district were required. In Tyva the requirements were 1.5 per cent for single-member districts and 2 per cent for party lists.

The most liberal requirements for registering by paying a deposit were set in Kareliya (45,000 roubles for a single-member candidate and 150,000 roubles for a party list), the Sverdlovsk Oblast (200,000 roubles for a party list), the Novgorod Oblast (50,000 roubles for a single-member candidate and 300,000 roubles for a party list) and the Jewish Autonomous Oblast (22,500 roubles for a single-member candidate and 180,000 roubles for a party list). The size of the deposits appeared excessively high in Lipetsk Oblast and Chuvashiya (both set 4.5 million roubles for parties, and Lipetsk Oblast had 1.5 million roubles for a single-member candidate). This meant that to register party lists in Chuvashiya and Lipetsk Oblast the amount required was roughly the equivalent of $170,000, and $140,000 in Tyva. A Lipetsk single-member candidate would need $56,600. This seems all the more strange given that Chuvashiya and Tyva are not counted among the wealthier regions.

As far as party lists are concerned, the greatest number of applications to participate in elections was made in the Primorskii Krai (thirteen) and Sverdlovsk and Astrakhan Oblasts (eleven in each). After the completion of all court cases ten lists were registered and appeared on the voting papers in the Sverdlovsk and Astrakhan Oblasts, and also in the Primorskii Krai; there were nine lists in the Novgorod Oblast and eight in the Lipetsk Oblast. Overall there were fewer enforced exclusions of party lists from elections during the electoral campaign of autumn 2006. In this respect it was considerably different from the preceding electoral campaigns at the start of 2006 and the end of 2005. It is possible that this was because the necessary 'cleaning-up' of the political field had already been carried out in 2005 and the start of 2006. During the electoral campaign at the end of 2005 a total of five out of seventy-five applications submitted to register party lists were turned down at the registration stage (i.e. 6.7 per cent). There were no refusals in five out of the nine regions. Of the five refusals, two involved the Russian Party of Pensioners, and there was one each for the RPL, the Agrarian Party of Russia and Patriots of Russia. Three refusals resulted from checks on signature lists, and one each for breaking the rules when paying electoral deposits and holding pre-election conferences. After registration decisions were taken based both on appeals from participants and on information supplied by the Federal Registration Service (FRS) to cancel the registration of three of the seventy lists registered (4.2 per cent). Thus, if one includes those that were refused registration, the total of lists excluded was eight out of seventy-five that had submitted registration documents (10.7 per cent). In three regions (Astrakhan, Lipetsk and Novgorod Oblasts) no lists were excluded and no registrations were cancelled.

In particular the cancelled registrations included:

In the Republic of Tyva: the list of the Russian Party of Life (on the grounds that, as one candidate had left the list, the number of candidates in the list had fallen below the minimum of sixteen laid down in the electoral law of the Legislative Chamber of the Great Khural).

In the Republic of Kareliya: the RDP Yabloko list (on the basis of information from the FRS about an illegitimate conference of the party's regional branch).

In the Jewish Autonomous Oblast: the list of the Russian Party of Life (on the grounds that more than half the candidates had left the list).

The Russian Party of Life clearly dominated in the overall total of refusals to register or cancelled registrations (one refusal and two cancellations). Thus a tendency appeared when, at the end of 2005, most instances of the exclusion of party lists from elections involved the Russian Party of Pensioners, at the beginning of 2006 it was Rodina, and at the end of 2006, the Russian Party of Life: it was precisely these three parties that had set up the so-called Union of Trust in August 2006 and had declared their intention to create a united party.

As a result of challenges to the cancelled registrations of the three lists mentioned above, the registration of two of them was reinstated (in both cases it was for the RPL; the Supreme Court upheld the cancellation in respect of Yabloko in Kareliya[10]). With regard to the lists that had previously been refused registration by electoral commissions, only the Russian Party of Life in the Sverdlovsk Oblast and Patriots of Russia in the Republic of Tyva were able to gain registration through a court decision.

Thus four lists were registered with the help of court decisions: three instances involved the Russian Party of Life and one involved Patriots of Russia. No other list managed to achieve registration through the courts. The reinstatement of the RPL could be linked to the fact that its leader, Mironov, is the third most important person in the state, the Chairman of the Federation Council. It is especially noteworthy that when the RPL submitted its appeals, representatives of the Prosecutor General's office effectively spoke on its behalf.

The greatest number of scandals was recorded in the Republic of Tyva, where the RPP and Patriots of Russia lists were rejected on the basis of a verification of the lists of signatures; subsequently the Supreme Court of Tyva cancelled the registration of the RPL list. However, the RPL, which is led by the Speaker of the Federation Council, was able to challenge this refusal in the Supreme Court, forcing the authorities in Tyva to register the party's list.

The situation in Tyva was a good example of what could be seen as the main political intrigue of the autumn elections: in July and August, right at their start (when United Russia had already decided on the second part of the electoral counter-reformation), it was announced that three centre–left parties, the Russian Party of Pensioners (RPP), the Russian Party of Life (RPL) and Rodina, intended to unite in a single party. Moreover, their leaders announced this after a meeting with Putin. This was taken by public opinion and the regional elites as clear presidential approval of the new union; consequently this would mean a weakening of United Russia's pretensions to the role of monopoly party. This feeling was further reinforced by successful legal challenges from the RPL against refusals to register its lists. Such success for the party in court cases was unprecedented in recent regional elections.

As a result the regional elites that had not found a place in United Russia, or that were in obvious conflict with governors who had joined United Russia, gained a clear focus point for their consolidation. One can say that the increased pressure on the regional elites from United Russia and the excessive toughening of the rules of the game brought about a reciprocal consolidation of the most outspoken sections of the regional elites around one of the autonomous groups in the President of Russia's entourage. There is no doubt that these intrigues are directly linked to the fight over the presidential succession. The mass response surrounding the creation of the Union of Trust (by October the name of the new party was 'A Just Russia – Motherland, Pensioners, Life') brought the union's member parties additional attention and helped in their success. Putin even allowed the RPL to use his picture in its visual material in the Lipetsk Oblast.

However, the representatives of the centre–left alliance being set up announced the formation of their union at the point when the process of putting forward party lists was already under way in the provinces. As a result they often competed against each other. The RPL did not start putting forward lists in the Chuvash Republic and Astrakhan Oblast, nor did Rodina in Kareliya and Lipetsk Oblast. Thus RPL and Rodina lists were registered in seven regions. Consequently the RPL and Rodina competed against each other in the Novgorod and Sverdlovsk Oblasts, the Republic of Tyva, the Primorskii Krai and the Jewish Autonomous Oblast. Sverdlovsk Oblast is particularly noteworthy, as here the leaders of the RPL and Rodina lists, the State Duma deputies Royzman and Zyablitsev, were clear political competitors.

The Russian Party of Pensioners submitted lists in eight out of the nine regions (i.e. in all, apart from the Novgorod Oblast), and they were registered in six. In all these cases the party was competing either against the RPL or Rodina. The lists of all three parties of the centre–left alliance competed against each other in three regions: the Sverdlovsk Oblast, Primorskii Krai and the Jewish Autonomous Oblast.

The greatest formal activity was displayed by parties that were represented in the State Duma, and this continued the tendency shown in the earlier regional elections that had taken place in 2004–6. Only three parliamentary parties, United Russia, the CPRF and the LDPR, put forward and registered lists in all nine regions.

Patriots of Russia is nominally in second place for its activity in submitting party lists; it submitted and registered lists in eight of the nine regions (including Tyva, where it registered its list following a decision of the Supreme Court).

Among the other parties, the most active was the Party for National Revival: its lists were registered in six regions. Concerning the liberal right parties, Yabloko registered three lists: in the Sverdlovsk Oblast, Kareliya and the Primorskii Krai (in Kareliya the registration of the list was cancelled by the courts). No list was registered for the SPS (they held talks with Yabloko in Kareliya, but the list was never finalized and it was too late to participate independently in the elections). Against this background of the fall of the most famous democratic parties, one may observe the increase in activity by 'non-traditional' democrats: the renewed Democratic Party of Russia (with three lists registered) and the Free Russia Party (two lists registered).

The Agrarian Party of Russia was clearly in decline, as it did not have one list registered. The only region where the party tried to act independently was Primorskii Krai, but its list was not registered there. Branches of the party effectively supported the United Russia lists publicly in the Republic of Tyva, the Chuvash Republic and the Novgorod, Lipetsk and Sverdlovsk Oblasts.

Freedom and People Power, the Republican Party of Russia and the People's Party each had one instance of participation in elections. Lists were submitted, but not registered, by the Conceptual Party Unity, the Russian Ecological Party ('The Greens') and the Russian Communist Workers' Party – the Russian Party of Communists (RKRP). The Party for Regional Development 'Nature and Society' and the People's Patriotic Party of Russia were recorded in only single-member districts in some regions.

With regard to success at the elections, only one party entered the parliaments in all nine regions, and this was United Russia; the CPRF crossed the 7 per cent threshold in eight of the nine regions (everywhere apart from Tyva). The RPP entered the legislative assemblies in all six regions where its lists appeared on the voting papers. The RPL had four victories, and Rodina, Freedom and People's Power and Free Russia each had one victory. The LDPR only managed to get seats in regional parliaments in three regions, and this was the party's worst result in recent years. If one takes into account the fact that a number of organizations lost their status as political parties on 1 January 2006 and also the forthcoming amalgamation of the RPL, RPP and Rodina, the makeup of candidates for the next regional elections could be very different. According to information from the FRS, the following parties are likely to lose their status: Freedom and People's Power, RKRP, KP Yedineniye, Development of Enterprise, and the Popular Patriotic Party. A question hangs over the future of the Republican Party.

United Russia's campaign was run in the same inert style of 2005–6; despite a certain disorientation brought on by the appearance of the centre–left alliance, the regional elites proved unable to reorganize themselves quickly enough. At the same time the senior figures of United Russia tried to retain their control over its regional branches as much as possible. To an even greater extent than before the party used the technique of pre-election 'helping hands' (candidates who would stand in the party list with the purpose of attracting extra voters, but who did not intend to be elected as deputies). On this occasion governors headed its lists in eight out of the nine regions. Thus the party's use of this technique affected 41.7 per cent of the regions in autumn 2005, on 12 March 2006 it affected 62.5 per cent and on 8 October 2006 it now affected 89 per cent of the regions. Mayors of cities (predominantly in regional centres), deputies to the State Duma, directors of very large enterprises, etc., also figured extensively in United Russia's lists, in addition to governors. Other parties also used the technique of 'helping hands', but to a much lesser extent than United Russia.

The key players in forming United Russia's lists for regional elections were undoubtedly governors and their teams. One of the leaders of the party, Volodin, formulated an 'ideal pattern' for how to head a party list: the governor, the mayor of the regional centre and the speaker of the legislative assembly. All the regional party lists tried to get as close as possible to this pattern. A strategy was generally selected of minimizing turnout at elections (this was obviously provoked by both the removal of the 'against all' box and the reduction in the overall total of parties and candidates), which would increase the part played by voters who depended on the administration.

Table 6.4 Elections to legislative assemblies of members of the RF on 8 October 2006

Legislative body for which deputies were elected	Threshold (%)	Lists on the voting paper	Lists that crossed the threshold
Legislative Assembly of the Republic of Kareliya	7	7	5
Legislative Chamber of the Great Khural of the Republic of Tyva	7	6	2 (with a 5% threshold it would have been 3)
State Council of the Chuvash Republic	7	5	3 (with a 5% threshold it would have been 5)
Legislative Assembly of the Primorskii kray	7	10	4 (with a 5% threshold it would have been 5)
State Duma of the Astrakhan oblast	7	10	4 (with a 5% threshold it would have been 5)
Council of People's Deputies of the Lipetsk oblast	7	8	4
Novgorod Regional Duma	7	9	4 (with a 5% threshold it would have been 6)
Regional Duma of the Legislative Assembly of the Sverdlovsk oblast (rotation of half the membership, 14 out of 28 deputies)	7	10	4 (with a 5% threshold it would have been 5)
Legislative Assembly of the Jewish autonomous oblast	7	6	3

Source: Compiled by the author from data published by the Central Electoral Commission.

*The second chamber of the parliament of Tyva, the Chamber of Representatives, is elected only through majority-based districts and is effectively a decorative body with no real power.

On the other hand, the increased significance of heading the ruling party's list led to the encouragement of competitors for the current governors inside the regional branches of United Russia; heading the ruling party's list or being second on it had for them the same status as that of 'crown prince'. Combined with the interference of the party's federal leadership (every party list had to be agreed by the General Council of the party), the result was that a number of United Russia party lists were made up of groups that were actually in competition. Because of this, supporters of the Governor of Astrakhan, Zhilkin, and the Mayor of Astrakhan, Bozhenov, had to join the general list, as the two officials were competing with each other for power. The administration of the Lipetsk Oblast was forced to hand over a number of places on its list to the Novolipetsk Metallurgical Combine, and the administration of the Governor of Sverdlovsk, Rossel, had to give places to the supporters of the Mayor of Yekaterinburg, Chernetsky. In Kareliya the leadership of the region was effectively forced to support the candidacy of the incumbent mayor, Maslyakov, in the elections for the mayor of Petrozavodsk. The secretaries of the Primorskii and Tyva regional branches of United Russia, Kurilov and Kara-ool, tried to promote their own candidates on the party's lists.

In some regions, in particular Primorskii Krai and Kareliya, the General Council of the party had to make radical alterations to the makeup of the lists put forward by regional organizations, so as to avoid excessive predominance by the representatives of a single group.

As the election results showed, automatic reliance on the ruling authority did not prove to be correct in every region. The presence of the heads of Tyva and Kareliya, Oorzhak and Katanandov, neither of them very popular, at the tops of the lists led to the fact that in Tyva United Russia lost almost 20 per cent of its vote in comparison to 2003, and in Kareliya its results hardly changed, despite the reduction in political competition and the abolition of voting 'against all'. Overall the ruling party's vote rose only slightly in the Sverdlovsk and Novgorod Oblasts. The greatest increase in the vote for United Russia occurred in Lipetsk Oblast and Primorskii Krai; however, in the latter case there are serious doubts as to the correctness of the voting procedure and the vote count. The party's increased vote in Chuvashiya and the Jewish Autonomous Oblast is justifiable if one takes into account the almost total control of the regional administrations over the political process in the regions. When compared to the results of the 12 March 2006 elections, the overall tendency of United Russia to dominate has clearly weakened, despite the increased involvement of senior figures in the elections and a decreased turnout of voters.

The situation with voting for the CPRF varies greatly in the regions: from maintaining its previous position or even increasing slightly (explicable if one takes into account the drop in competition between the parties) in Kareliya, Chuvashiya, Novgorod Oblast and the Jewish Autonomous Oblast, to a considerable drop in the Astrakhan and Lipetsk Oblasts and a smaller drop in Tyva and Primorskii Krai. It seems that the party's results in a specific region depend directly upon the personal makeup of the specific regional list, how actively the electoral campaign is conducted and also upon the real degree of competition in the protest niche. Above all the party lost votes in places where there were other colourful protest forces (in particular Rodina headed by Shein in Astrakhan and the RPL in Tyva), and it gained votes in places where new figures appeared in its list (in particular Yefimov in Novgorod Oblast). Thus, despite a certain level of basic support from its traditional voters, the appearance of a new centre–left alliance (A Just Russia) has clearly faced the CPRF with the problem of carrying out a major renewal and strengthening of its regional structures. As a rule the party's internal activists dominate its lists, and bringing in people 'from outside' is usually the exception rather than the rule.

The results for the populist and nationalistic LDPR proved to be worse throughout the whole period of regional elections under the mixed system: its vote dropped in every region, except Chuvashiya, irrespective of whether its leader, Zhirinovsky, visited the region during the electoral campaign. Of the three regions where the party received more than 7 per cent of the vote (Kareliya, Novgorod Oblast and Chuvashiya), it only just scraped across the threshold in the Novgorod Oblast. At one point during the count in Astrakhan Oblast the LDPR crossed the 7 per cent threshold, only to fall back below it again. Even with a 5 per cent threshold the LDPR would still not have managed to enter the parliaments in the Jewish AO, Tyva and Lipetsk Oblast. Of particular concern to the party leadership would have been the fall in its share of the vote in the Far Eastern and north Russian regions that had previously constituted the electoral base of the LDPR: Kareliya, Primorskii Krai and the Jewish Autonomous Oblast.

In a number of regions the leadership of the regional organization was changed immediately before the elections (Novgorod Oblast) or it lost a number of former leaders (Sverdlovsk Oblast). As a rule the party's candidates are from small and medium regional businesses, and in the absence of external investors they rely on party functionaries from the regional branches. It would seem that the key issue for the survival of the party is to position itself carefully in relation to the 'party of power', and not just to fight against any other opposition, and also to lower the threshold to 5 per cent.

In comparison with the results for the PRR–RPL bloc in 2003, the Russian Party of Life improved its vote everywhere, and moreover usually several-fold, if not tenfold or more. In Kareliya, Tyva and the Lipetsk Oblast the party came second to United Russia. Overall the party entered regional parliaments in four out of the seven regions, and its result was below 5 per cent in only two regions (the Jewish Autonomous Oblast and Primorskii Krai), although not substantially. This result reflected the significant financial backing it had received for major financing for its regional campaigns, together with federal PR support (linked to the establishment of the Union of Trust) and the high-quality makeup of the regional lists, something that had not been in evidence previously: the leader of the opposition of the parliament in Tyva, the former regional head, Stepanov, in Kareliya, and the charismatic regional politicians Kostyukhin in the Novgorod Oblast and Royzman in Sverdlovsk Oblast. As a rule all the regional lists of the RPL consisted of groups from the regional elite that were in conflict with an 'establishment' group made up of the entourage of a particular governor or mayor. This tendency to turn the RPL into an emergency landing strip for regional elites that are in conflict with United Russia will clearly increase in the near future.

Together with United Russia, the Russian Party of Pensioners was the most effective participant in the elections on 8 October: the party cleared the 7 per cent threshold in all the regions where its lists were registered. Its worst relative result was 9.13 per cent in Primorskii Krai and the best was 18.75 per cent in Sverdlovsk Oblast. The party's lists were not registered in Tyva and Chuvashiya. Generally the party's regional organizations and lists were farmed out to representatives of regional commerce who were new people in regional politics (and therefore not compromised), but there were cases in which genuine professional politicians with high personal ratings headed their lists (e.g. Guzhvin in the Astrakhan Oblast; earlier on, Batin in Kostroma; Bochkarev in the elections to the Nizhnii Novgorod City Duma). In a number of instances these businessmen were in conflict with the local authorities (Konkov in Yekaterinburg, for instance), and sometimes the party tried to build a partner relationship with the regional authorities (Tyva, Kareliya, and earlier on, the Kaliningrad Oblast).

The elections showed once again that since the departure of Rogozin from the position of party leader, Rodina had been going through a profound crisis, and almost everywhere its results were considerably worse than the vote that the Rodina bloc received in the federal elections of 2003. The only region where the party managed to achieve a significant result on 8 October 2006 was Astrakhan Oblast, where its list was headed by Oleg Shein, a charismatic regional politician and one of the region's deputies to the State Duma (he did not appear on the bloc's list in 2003; he supported it, but stood in a single-member district). Votes that went to Rodina in Astrakhan were really votes for Shein personally and his team, rather than for the regional branch of Rodina. The leadership of the RPL, headed by Mironov, also provided support for Shein's list. It appeared that party's regional structures were starting 'pre-merger' preparations and the party was gradually ceasing to be a significant independent force.

The second round of the mass participation by Patriots of Russia in regional elections was much less successful than the elections of 12 March 2006 (when the party entered two regional legislative assemblies). It did not enter a single regional parliament, even though the party's results in Chuvashiya and the Novgorod Oblast seemed perfectly decent, more than 5 per cent of the vote. Individual successes were recorded in single-member districts. The basis of the party lists consisted of former CPRF activists (Kareliya and the Sverdlovsk Oblast), trade union activists (the trade union Sotsprof in Lipetsk Oblast) and small and medium businesses (Veliky

Novgorod). The reasons for its lack of success may have been its tendency to 'flirt' with the authorities combined with the fact that other centre–left parties had better-quality campaigns – it was unclear to the electorate whether or not this was an opposition party.

The results for the liberal right parties, RDP Yabloko, SPS and the Republican Party, in the autumn elections were disastrous. The SPS did not register a single list and Yabloko was excluded from the elections in the one region where it had a chance of success, Kareliya. Moreover, the result gained by Yabloko was considerably worse than both the combined results for the liberal right parties in 2003 and the vote for Yabloko by itself. The list of the Republican Party also failed in Astrakhan Oblast (1.07 per cent), where there was no list either from the SPS or from Yabloko. The mistake of the RPRF in Astrakhan was to field an insufficiently competitive party list headed by Adrov, President Yeltsin's former adviser in the region, who had left regional politics, and the region itself, a long time before.

The Party of National Revival, one of the founders of the Rodina bloc but now outside it (its leader is Sergey Baburin), is at present simply trying to acquire some sort of base in the regions. This would explain why in every region the party list was headed by the party chairman, Baburin, who is not well known to the regional voter. The party has no real specifically regional political position. The party registered everywhere by paying deposits, and was not in a position to retain them anywhere (its best result was a total of 1.58 per cent in Kareliya).

The Democratic Party of Russia's campaign had the clear aim of reminding the electorate of the party's existence and taking advantage of the actual fact that it stood in elections, as this is important for retaining the party's legal status. The party collected signatures everywhere, but everywhere it received fewer votes than it had received signatures.

As a totally new party project, Free Russia is trying to rely on youth and a completely eclectic pre-election campaign, aimed at winning the niche of 'old liberal right' parties. The party can only achieve success in small regions with a low turnout, and by concentrating all its technical resources in one specific region. It seems that most of the votes for Free Russia that the leader of the party, Ryavkin, gained in his own region, Sverdlovsk Oblast (3.2 per cent), were votes for him personally. In Novgorod Oblast (where the party gained a sensational 11.03 per cent), as far as is known, party activists mobilized from the whole country were at work and a 'multi-level marketing' system was implemented. At present Free Russia is seen as a base for the creation of a new 'Kremlin project of the right'. On 8 October no other party participated in elections in more than one region.

Conclusion

On the one hand, regional political life has changed considerably in its formal characteristics during this period. The overall dependence of both governors and regional elites on the federal centre has increased. This led to the fact that, as a result of clear federal interference, regional political regimes in regions that had previously had a reputation for being very authoritarian (Tatarstan, Bashkortostan, Kalmykia, Adygeya, Tyva, etc.) were now forced to liberalize themselves to a certain extent. An opposition, even if not always very significant, appeared in the previously monolithic legislative assemblies of these regions. On the other hand, many regions that had previously possessed developed democratic systems, their own established regional parties and interest groups, etc. (Nizhnii Novgorod and Sverdlovsk Oblasts, Kareliya, the Primorskii Krai, and others) lost their democratic nature because of the same pressure from the federal centre, and moved towards strengthening authoritarian tendencies; their autonomous regional groups were forced to move into the background or to pass themselves off as federal groups. The domination of governors increased and the independence of other players was weakened. In other words the level of authoritarian rule in the Russian regions largely averaged itself out.

On the other hand the variety of interests in the Russian regions and the squabbles among the regional elites never disappeared. If necessary they simply mutated and vanished from public politics behind the scenes. In the same way, genuine conflicts, contradictions and problems moved from the visible into the invisible, not just for many outside observers, but for the federal centre itself. By formally standardizing regional political life, leading it to ostentatious unity rituals and depriving it of many of its channels of self-expression, the federal centre had at the same time deprived itself of objective information about what was happening in the regions.

It is obvious that formal domination by the 'party of power' does not deal with the real problems that exist in society: the regional groupings and clans that de facto still exist simply vanish into the background and continue their fight out of sight inside the officially 'united' United Russia. The official unity of brands and the obvious respect for rank in the federal centre have created a situation where in reality structures with differing values and interests are hiding behind one and the same name in different regions. Imitating unity through an illusion of controllability and good reports cannot replace the country's variety. By depriving society of open political competition, federal power has simultaneously deprived itself of objective information about what is actually happening in the country, and no 'national projects' will make up for this. At one time the CPSU was also the only party in the country (and much more united than United Russia), but this did not prevent the USSR that it ruled from falling apart into completely separate countries with political regimes that are at times at opposite ends of the spectrum. All this artificial controllability is in danger of being swept away by the collapse of this imitation system, and it will then become clear that there are no 'reserve' institutions, institutions that society trusts. Of course, this will not happen immediately, but by turning elections into a mockery, minimizing vertical mobility and destroying the genuine competitive selection of officials, the authorities are inevitably lowering their own professional level and their adequacy. This means that the collapse of such an unreal system, closed in upon itself and isolated from society's main concerns, may be just a matter of time.

Notes

1 The Conference unites all the states of Western and Eastern Europe and the USA and Canada. This European regional organization started work in Helsinki on 3 July 1973. At the end of 1994 the Conference was transformed in to the Organization for Security and Cooperation in Europe (OSCE).
2 B. G. Peters, *Politicheskiye instituty vchera i segodnya: Politicheskaya nauka novye napravleniya*, Moscow, 1999, p. 223; Russian translation of *A New Handbook of Political Science*, Oxford University Press, 1996.
3 The Russian Party of Peace was in second place after United Russia in Ingushetiya.
4 A. V. Kynev, 'V ozhidanii novovo elektoral'novo predlozheniya. Vybory regional'nykh zakonodatel'nykh sobraniy kontsa 2004–nachala 2005 g', *Polis*, No. 3, 2005.
5 A. V. Kynev, 'Vybory Moskovskoy Gorodskoy Dumy 4 dekabrya 2005: apofeoz imitatsionnykh vyborov', http://www.igpi.ru/info/people/kynev/kynev-moskovskie_vybory_2005.htm
6 For example, in Moscow the deposit to stand for the Moscow City Duma was 1,350,000 roubles (about $50,000) for candidates in single-member districts and 15 million roubles (about $550,000) for a political party list.
7 The permissible amount of rejections was reduced from 25 per cent to 10 per cent, while Russian legislation does not distinguish between unreliable, i.e. forged, signatures and so-called 'invalid' signatures: signatures of genuine voters which include an error such as the omission of the last letter of the street name of their address. In addition a requirement was brought in for the lists of signature collectors to be legally authenticated. Since the 'technical rejection' of signatures is almost always at a level of at least 20 per cent (the collection of signatures among the least-educated section of the elderly population – and consequently those most likely to make mistakes – always presents special problems) registration by presenting signatures was thus possible only when the electoral commission had an obviously benevolent attitude towards the candidate or the party list.
8 Without doubt this rule was completely 'virtual' since the fact that the party could submit a candidate to the President of Russia did not put the President under any obligation. A number of instances arose in 2005-6 when regional branches of United Russia fought actively against the reappointment of a number of incumbent governors (in particular in the Kostroma and Amur Oblasts, and the Komi Republic). When the President nominated the former incumbents the regional 'United Russians' gave way obediently and approved all the President's nominations.
9 Here the party had very strong personalities on its list (in particular the incumbent State Assembly deputies Bezruchenkov and Shefer), thanks to which it won 10.5 per cent instead on 3.68 per cent.
10 It is interesting to note that in an identical situation in another region, the Sverdlovsk Oblast, the regional court decided to reject the case against Yabloko.

7 Russian political parties and regional political processes

The problem of effective representation

Petr Panov

Politics in the contemporary era, in contrast to former traditional 'dynastic states' and 'empires', is based to a large extent on democratic discourse. Even under authoritarian regimes ruling elites, while attempting to remove opposition from the political arena, try to reinforce their legitimacy by convincing the population (the masses) that they truly represent the interests of the people. In competitive regimes this issue is even more pressing because power is sought by various political forces, each of which tries to make itself look appealing to the masses. It is only when the masses perceive the 'political class' as their own representatives that a legitimate political order arises and the effectiveness of political representation can be discussed as an issue.

It is our understanding that this problem is one of the key issues in modern Russia. Under Soviet authoritarianism the leaders used to inculcate amongst the masses the idea that communism is the embodiment of popular expectations and aspirations, and the regime remained durable as long as people continued to believe that the Communist Party did express their will. The disillusionment that was mounting in the 1970s and 1980s became one of the precursors of Perestroika. In post-Soviet Russia a radical redistribution of resources has taken place: instead of a unitary political actor (the Communist Party) a multitude of actors have appeared. At the same time democratic political procedures have been introduced. These developments preconditioned the transition to a competitive type of political process but were hardly sufficient enough to solve the problem of the 'effectiveness of political representation'.

Political representation is an extremely complex and multi-faceted phenomenon. In different combinations its various dimensions bring about a different outcome in terms of its effectiveness. The aim of this chapter is to determine which characteristics of representation dominate in modern Russia, to explain why, and to analyse the consequences of our findings from the viewpoint of their effectiveness. At the same time we focus on the regional level of Russian politics, which has been far less researched than the national level.[1]

The chapter is structured in the following way: at the beginning several theoretical models of representation are analysed (I take as the basis such criteria as universalism versus particularism; party-based representation versus non-party representation). Then through the prism of these models the Russian political process is analyzed. From the perspective of rational choice theory, I offer an explanation for the growth in the importance of political parties in Russian regions in the 2000s. I then present a case study of Perm Oblast which helps trace the interrelationship between universalist and particularist elements in the functioning of political parties. In the conclusion I summarise my findings and present certain observations regarding future political developments.

Models of representation under political competition

Representation is one of the most important and controversial concepts in modern political theory. It has a long history and numerous connotations. Without attempting to review the whole volume of discussion, I will try to look into two aspects of this concept. First, what sorts of interests are to be represented? Second, what are the mechanisms of representation?

Theoretically, we can distinguish individual (personal), group and public interests.[2] Strictly speaking, it is public interests that are articulated and realized through political activity. The political community (1) determines the scope of issues that are of public significance – 'agenda setting' and, (2) works out solutions to such issues. All other issues and kinds of activity (both personal and group-related) can be considered as 'personal', or particularist.

The crux of the matter, however, is that the political community is divided (segmented) by its nature, and the public sphere is the subject of permanent conflict. Separate segments differ in the ways they determine which problems are to be considered public. There are different approaches as to how such problems are to be solved. Besides, private and public interests interpenetrate each other. On the one hand, actors' interpretations of public interest depend on their private preferences. In other words, each political actor decides if a given problem is public or not and what solution should be adopted on the basis of their social experience and subjective perception of reality. At the same time, an actor's motivation (the meaning they attribute to their actions) can be public, but those are public motivations of a single (private) actor. On the other hand, entirely private preferences can be dressed up in public clothes, and adopting public decisions results from purely private interests.

Hence, two 'pure' types of representation of interests can be distinguished. The first one is representation based primarily on private interests. Here, private interests are pushed through onto the public agenda and transformed into public decisions. Such a type of representation is close to interest group theory,[3] as well as an aggregate (pluralist) concept of democracy.[4] At its core, it is the belief that the 'public interest' can only be revealed by adding up 'private' understandings as to what the public authorities should do.

From the point of view of the effectiveness of representation, this type has both strong and weak points. One of the problems with this type is majoritarianism ('the victor wins all'), when the interests of few (or only one) influential actors can be represented in bodies of power. Such actors extend control over the public sphere and dictate their own interpretation of the public interest to society. Another problem is that there is always a probability of ending up in a political deadlock, when several influential actors with roughly equal resources enter into conflict, and neither is able to achieve victory by way of 'aggregating interests'.

Hence, the political community requires additional institutional structures to eliminate these weaknesses. Goodin, in particular, considers two possibilities.[5] The first one is a system of the division of powers, including checks and balances mechanisms, which protects the political sphere from being monopolized because neither political group controls all branches of power. The second one is institutionalizing representation and providing guarantees to various interest groups while making decisions (proportional representation, the right of veto, etc.). These options are consistent with Lijphart's well-known Westminster and Consensual patterns of democracy.[6]

It is quite clear that yet another crucial precondition for the effectiveness of this type of representation lies in a high level of development of civic associations, i.e. strong self-organized and self-governed groups representing a whole range of voices, not only financial or business interests.[7]

Such structures can help a political community achieve high efficiency and representation even though certain political actors are predominantly driven by private interests. In other words, this type of representation without imposing strict requirements as to the actors' motives and intentions sets tough constraints on political institutions.

It should be emphasized that such an institutional context gives rise to a situation of interdependency, and making public decisions becomes not so much a process of aggregating private interests regarding a particular issue, as negotiating (bargaining) the positions of various actors. As rightly noted by Sened, this is a sign of a true democratic process.[8]

The second type of representation is based primarily on public interests. This means that political discussions primarily focus on issues with public repercussions. As was noted above, the actors' perception of public issues is inevitably influenced by their particularist interests, but in this case what is important is that actors represent their positions on a wide range of issues that are definitely part of the public domain. This type of representation clearly corresponds with the communitarian tradition in the history of political thought, and the deliberative concept of democracy.[9]

It is common knowledge that the first political communities – the Greek *polis* and the Roman *res publica* – were based on the concept of citizenship, involving citizens in public activity, and politics was perceived as solving problems of public significance (common good), which, according to Arendt, were not even related to satisfying material needs.[10] It is not by accident that Aristotle drew a clear demarcation line not only between *polis* and *oikos* (household), but also between *polis* and *ethnos* – communities he did not consider as political, since the population of an *ethnos* was incapable of participating in decision-making regarding the common good.

Presently, communitarianism is to a large extent a reaction to a tendency towards individualization, which is characteristic of contemporary society. It points to negative consequences of people's withdrawal from the political sphere, diminishing trust, social capital, solidarity, etc.[11] This type of representation looks as if it is normative and prescriptive. It can, nonetheless, be a feasible practice, provided that public issues are more the focus of political competition than private interests. This provides an incentive for political actors to work out their positions vis-à-vis the public agenda. So far, representation practices in European states are rather close to this very type, whereas the American political tradition leans towards the first model.

The opposition between the public and the private is closely connected with the issue of universalism versus particularism. As Delanty notes, the latter is one of the fundamental contradictions of a political community. On the one hand, the polis was originally considered as a certain universal, somewhat similar to the cosmos. On the other hand, the actually existing polices were local and exclusive because they were based upon the principle of rigid distinction between 'self' and 'other'. 'The ambivalence in the meaning of "community" ... has always been central to the idea of a community.'[12] Overall, universalism and particularism should be considered as more or less clearly marked tendencies relative to each other rather than certain absolutes, 'a stable state of a system'. An 'absolute political universal' is only possible as an idea (Christian universalism, Communist society, totalitarianism, etc.). So far, as humanity is divided into different political entities, universalism in any cosmo-political sense is unrealistic. On the other hand, 'absolute political particularism' is hardly possible either, as politics is a collective activity by nature. As was noted above, politicians try to dress even purely private (in their original subjective sense) interests into public clothes. Hence, there is a continuum between two 'ideal' poles – 'universalism' and 'particularism', and actual practices of political representation are somewhere within this continuum but never taking extreme forms.

As a rule, the first type of representation is characterized by actors focusing on representing themselves as defenders of interests of particular groups (segments) of the political community – local communities, professional, ethnic, religious, etc. Political competition under the conditions of the second type of representation is, on the contrary, to a larger extent based on 'public discourse' – national interests, universal welfare, 'political agendas' (reforms, programmes) aimed at the political community as a whole.

Let us now consider the second issue – the mechanisms of political representation. Undoubtedly, one of the main instruments of representation are organized interest groups, which usually do not attempt to bring bodies of public authority under their direct control but prefer to act through various officials and public politicians. Among those are members of parliament (deputies) who are engaged in political representation and play a special role. They are the target category of influence.

Traditionally, two main mechanisms are distinguished in the activity of members of parliament – 'party' and 'non-party' ones. The latter implies that each deputy is viewed as an 'independent representative'; in the former case it is a party faction in parliament that is a 'unit of representation'. Taken in conjunction with the two types of representation, these mechanisms produce four models:

1 Non-party deputies primarily represent universal interests.
2 Party deputies primarily represent universal interests.
3 Non-party deputies primarily represent particularist interests.
4 Party deputies primarily represent particularist interests.

1. It is common knowledge that it is the first model that was supported by many prominent political thinkers. In particular, the Founding Fathers of the USA were strongly against 'party factionalism'.[13] There was, however, one concern whether 'independent' deputies were capable of working out a substantiated position on all issues of the public agenda. Another question was how they would coordinate their positions in the process of decision-making. Last but not least, there was a question of how voters could make an informed choice between 'independent' candidates competing in elections. In terms of rational choice theory, such elections would be accompanied by huge transaction costs for the population, since the electorate would have to study and compare the positions of all candidates on all the issues on the agenda. 'Independent' deputies themselves would incur losses that were smaller while working out and making decisions. Parliamentary debate would cause enormous time losses while identifying and comparing stances of all deputies, let alone passing a law. In practice, this model is a utopia.

2. The model of representation based primarily on universal interests can be operational only through political parties. The statement that parties are a necessary institution for articulation, aggregation and representation of political interests is one of the key concepts in modern political theory.[14] While interest groups represent particularist interests, parties formulate positions (opinions) on a wide range of public issues. Parties are capable of performing this function because they are much more than mere temporary coalitions of political actors whose views of certain issues happen to coincide. On the contrary, they are based on common political values and ideological orientation of a primarily universalist character. It is this unity that allows party members to overcome differences on certain issues, making parties relatively robust and institutionalized entities. Besides, the presence of such entities on the political arena makes informed voting much easier because there is no need for the electorate to know the positions of each candidate on all issues on the agenda but rather the platform of the party they belong to. In other words, a 'roadmap' providing a kind of framework

for parties and ideologies (the 'left-right' continuum, for example) plays a crucial role in the process of communication between political elites and the masses. Nonetheless, such a model is only effective on condition that deputies stick to their party programme and party discipline.

3. Just as the 'party' mechanism of representation correlates with the universalist type, so the particularist type is to a great extent associated with non-party representation. In the contemporary world it is rather hard to come across examples of this model functioning in its pure form. It is customarily believed that the US Congress is a reasonable approximation. American congressmen and women are relatively independent of their party leaders, though they have tenser links with their constituencies, especially with influential interest groups operating in those constituencies. Hence, a huge number of interests are represented in parliament and virtually none of the groups of legislators has a majority. Trying to answer the question of how decisions are made under such conditions, American researchers have put forward several theories. Buchanan and Tullock focus on 'vote exchange' ('log-rolling').[15] Proponents of neo-institutionalism have demonstrated the significance of institutional rules, such as the discretional powers of the committees, the seniority system, etc.[16] Therefore, it is quite clear that this given model can only be effective on condition that there are certain additional formal and informal institutional structures in place.[17] Utilizing those structures, non-party legislators are capable of building relatively stable coalitions around certain issues.

4. The fourth model of representation at first glance is a hybrid of the second and third models. It is, however, a perfectly independent model in its own right. In certain cases, guided by particularist interests, politicians can find it useful to form not only a temporary coalition on a certain issue, but also a more durable organization. Apart from purely rational calculations, this can be facilitated by certain institutional rules (for instance, electoral systems). Such kinds of parties, however, do not exactly conform to the classic definition of a political party. They are much closer to 'cartel parties',[18] which can be seen as tools whereby political leaders exchange resources necessary for competing at elections and distributing posts within the state hierarchy, rather than associations of citizens sharing common political values and ideas.

The model of representation of primarily particularist interests, used as a mechanism by a cartel-type party, appears to be less effective than non-party representation. In the latter case each actor is connected with a certain specific interest group (or groups), which offer(s) representation to a wide circle of interests. Moreover, political competition works as an incentive for politicians to expand this circle, and a certain semblance of democracy in Schumpeter's understanding appears.[19] The creation of 'cartels' (even if there are more than one), on the contrary, reduces the degree of competition. Extending Schumpeter's analogy between politics and economics, this situation can be characterized as 'imperfect competition' – 'oligopoly'. As a result, the incentive to expand the circle of represented interests is significantly diminished. It should be noted that the very process of formation of party cartels has a certain bearing. When classic (mass) parties are transformed into a cartel, the cartel retains the features intrinsic to the former parties for a long time. If a cartel springs up from scratch, such an option is much less desirable in terms of representation effectiveness.

From non-party to party representation: regional policy in transition

The Russian Federation consists of eighty-five subjects[20] which differ substantially in terms of their economic potential and political characteristics. Moreover, the weakness of the Centre in the 1990s induced decentralization and significant diversification of regional political processes, including the set-up of regional political institutions. Prior to 1993 the principal representative bodies of authority in the regions were regional councils, which were leftovers from a previous political system. After the political crisis of 1993 they were dissolved, and regional legislatures started to be formed instead.[21] At first, their powers and structure differed greatly, but since 1999 there has been significant unification, as the new federal law set the main organizational principles for bodies of state authority in federal subjects.

Among the peculiarities of the Russian electoral system is the fact that elections to regional assemblies take place at different times. Since 1994 there have been three complete and one incomplete election cycles.[22] The first cycle (1994–5), or the so-called 'constituent elections', was rather irregular and is hardly a good illustration for studying representation.[23] Therefore, in this chapter I refer to the results of the second (1996–8), third (2000–2) and fourth (uncompleted, 2003–7) cycles. The electoral statistics are presented in the Appendix.

Up until 1991, political struggle on both the federal and regional levels took place within the framework of a one-party system headed by the Communist Party. Thus, the first 'alternative' regional legislature elections of 1990 were characterized by mainly 'intra-party' competition (where it actually took place). It was only after the CPSU was dissolved in 1991 that the party formation process gained momentum. However, despite the appearance in the 1990s of a great number of parties, their input in regional political processes was insignificant. The share of party deputies in the regional assemblies is represented in Tables 7.1 and 7.2 (for illustrative purposes I divided the regions into 4 groups). A glance at these numbers will suffice to realize that the parties had little success in regional legislature elections. In the 'second cycle' legislatures, in particular, the share of party deputies rose above 40 per cent of the total number of representatives in only 16 assemblies, whereas 17 regional parliaments were solely comprised of 'non-party' deputies. The 'third cycle' was characterized by an even lower percentage of party representatives. The number of regions in the first group went down to 11, and in the second – to 15.

The collapse of Russian communism brought about a certain vacuum of political values, ideas, aspirations, and under these conditions the actors' choice of political strategies was primarily dictated by rational and purpose-orientated motivations. Therefore, I consider it appropriate to apply rational choice theory to explain the weakness of political parties on the regional level. Stemming from this, it can be hypothesized that a rational politician, who strives to become a regional parliament deputy, may choose between a 'party' and 'non-party' strategy. Estimating the anticipated benefits and costs (losses) of each of these, rational actors will choose the most beneficial option.

The main advantage of the 'party' strategy is access to party resources – image-building, organizational (apparatus, activists), financial, information (party press), etc. A party, however, offers resources to a politician only in return for something, such as their membership and certain subsequent commitments (financial support, obeying party discipline, supporting the party's political course, lobbying for certain decisions, etc.). All these are 'costs' for a 'rational' politician. The 'non-party' strategy presupposes that a politician has no access to party resources, but at the same time incurs no associated costs. Hence, the rational choice of an actor depended on the correlation between (1) party and non-party resources; (2) resources and costs.

In the 1990s Russian political parties could not boast an abundance of political resources. Lack of funds, few activists and other weaknesses were typical characteristics of regional party organizations. Neither did the parties have any institutional election preferences. An overwhelming majority of federal subjects used a plural election formula and single-member constituencies.[24] Starting from the works by Duverger,[25] it is widely believed that such a system does not facilitate the development of political parties.[26] Thus, it is not surprising that most regional politicians favoured the 'non-party' strategy. As a rule, they relied on the support of business groups or on personal resources. Theoretically, politicians could also utilize the resources of civic (non-for-profit) organizations, but the latter were just as weak as parties. Besides, there was one other political force in the regions that was capable of providing the necessary resources to politicians – the executive authority, the governors (usually free from party affiliation) who were very interested in the formation of an obedient regional legislature. Thus in reality a politician without one's own resources had only two options: represent the interests of either a business group or the governor. The parties, therefore, found themselves in a vicious circle: they had no resources because influential actors were reluctant to join them, which came about in the first place because parties had no resources to attract such figures.

In total, regional legislatures reflected the makeup of the respective regional elites. This characteristic differed immensely from region to region. Aggregating a great deal of research on comparing regional political processes,[27] the following types of regional elites can be distinguished:

Table 7.1 The share of party deputies in 'second cycle' regional legislatures (in per cent

Kemerovo Oblast	97.1
Volgograd Oblast	87.5
Krasnoyarsk Krai	83.3
Krasnodar Krai	82.0
Sverdlovsk Oblast	69.4
Koryak AO	66.6
Novosibirsk Oblast	55.1
Bryansk Oblast	52.0
St. Petersburg	52.0
Adygeya	51.0
Ryazan Oblast	50.0
Kamchatka Oblast	48.7
Kaluga Oblast	45.0
Altai Krai	44.0
Belgorod Oblast	40.0
Stavropol Krai	40.0
No. of regions	**16**
Penza Oblast	37.8
Smolensk Oblast	36.7
Kaliningrad Oblast	34.4
Omsk Oblast	33.0
Khabarovsk Krai	32.0
Kirov Oblast	31.5
Rostov Oblast	31.1
Altai	29.0
Astrakhan Oblast	27.6
Voronezh Oblast	26.7
Ust'-Ordynskii Buryatskii AO	26.3
Moscow	25.0
Kareliya	24.6
Orel Oblast	24.0
Tula Oblast	22.9
Mordoviya	22.7
Irkutsk Oblast	22.0
Tyva	21.9
Orenburg Oblast	21.3
Karachaevo-Cherkessiya	20.5
Ivanovo Oblast	20.0
Jewish AO	20.0
Murmansk Oblast	20.0
Tambov Oblast	20.0
Ul'yanovsk Oblast	20.0
No. of regions	**25**
North Osetiya-Alaniya	18.7
Chuvashiya	18.4
Pskov Oblast	18.2
Lipetsk Oblast	15.6
Moscow Oblast	14.0

Table 7.1 (continued)

Kemerovo Oblast	97.1
Vladimir Oblast	13.5
Aginsk Buryat AO	13.0
Kursk Oblast	13.0
Samara Oblast	12.0
Saratov Oblast	12.0
Sakhalin Oblast	11.0
Marii El	10.4
Yakutiya	10.0
Yaroslavl Oblast	10.0
Yamalo-Nenets AO	9.5
Taimyr AO	9.0
Tver′ Oblast	9.0
Leningrad Oblast	8.0
Tomsk Oblast	7.0
Tatarstan	6.2
Magadan Oblast	5.8
Perm Oblast	5.6
Khakasiya	5.3
No. of regions	**23**
Nizhni Novgorod Oblast	4.4
Tyumen Oblast	4.0
Vologda Oblast	3.3
Kurgan Oblast	3.0
Arkhangel′sk Oblast	2.6
Dagestan	.8
Amur Oblast	.0
Bashkortostan	.0
Buryatiya	.0
Chelyabinsk Oblast	.0
Chita Oblast	.0
Chukotka AO	.0
Yevenk AO	.0
Ingushetiya	.0
Kalmykiya	.0
Khanty-Mansiskii AO	.0
Komi-Permyak AO	.0
Komi Republic	.0
Kostroma Oblast	.0
Nenets AO	.0
Novgorod Oblast	.0
Primorskii Krai	.0
Udmurtiya	.0
Kabardino-Balkariya	.0
No. of regions	**23**

Source: Compiled by the author.

Table 7.2 The share of party deputies in 'third cycle' regional legislatures (per cent)

Kemerovo Oblast	100.0
Volgograd Oblast	87.5
Krasnoyarsk Krai	85.7
Bashkortostan	81.7
Sverdlovsk Oblast	67.3
Tuva	63.4
Udmurtiya	51.0
Koryak AO	50.0
Pskov Oblast	48.5
St.Petersburg	46.0
Novosibirsk Oblast	44.9
Kamchatka Oblast	43.5
No. of regions	**11**
Ryazan Oblast	38.9
Bryansk Oblast	36.0
Altai Krai	34.0
Tver Oblast	30.3
Altai	29.0
Saratov Oblast	28.6
Voronezh Oblast	26.7
Kaliningrad Oblast	25.0
Krasnodar Krai	24.3
Vladimir Oblast	24.3
Tula Oblast	22.9
Tambov Oblast	22.0
Karachaevo-Cherkessiya	21.9
Chita Oblast	20.5
Penza Oblast	20.0
No. of regions	**15**
Amur Oblast	19.4
Sakha	18.6
Adygeya	18.5
Kirov Oblast	16.7
Omsk Oblast	16.7
Smolensk Oblast	16.7
Samara Oblast	16.0
Tyumen Oblast	16.0
Ulyanovsk Oblast	16.0
Moscow	14.3
Moscow Oblast	14.0
Komi Republic	13.3
North Osetiya -Alaniya	13.3
Rostov Oblast	13.3
Arkhangel'sk Oblast	12.8
Primorskii Krai	12.8
Kaluga Oblast	12.5
Khabarovsk Krai	12.0
Leningrad Oblast	12.0
Mordoviya	12.0

Table 7.2 (continued)

Kemerovo Oblast	100.0
Ivanovo Oblast	11.4
Sakhalin Oblast	11.0
Marii El	10.4
Astrakhan Oblast	10.3
Chuvashiya	9.6
Orel Oblast	8.0
Stavropol Krai	8.0
Novgorod Oblast	7.7
Perm Oblast	7.5
Kabardino-Balkariya	6.9
Aginsk Buryat AO	6.7
Khakasiya	6.7
Komi-Permyak AO	6.7
Nizhni Novgorod Oblast	6.7
Ust-Ordynskii Buryatskii AO	6.7
Orenburg Oblast	6.4
No. of regions	**37**
Tomsk Oblast	4.8
Yamalo-Nenets AO	4.8
Kursk Oblast	4.4
Yaroslavl' Murmansk Oblast	4.0
Vologda Oblast	3.3
Buryatiya	3.1
Belgorod Oblast	2.9
Lipetsk Oblast	2.7
Dagestan	2.5
Kareliya	2.5
Chelyabinsk Oblast	2.2
Tatarstan	1.5
Chukotka AO	.0
Yevenk AO	.0
Ingushetiya	.0
Irkutsk Oblast	.0
Jewish AO	.0
Kalmykiya	.0
Khanty-Mansiisk AO	.0
Kostroma Oblast	.0
Kurgan Oblast	.0
Magadan Oblast	.0
Nenets AO	.0
Taimyr AO	.0
No. of regions	**25**

Source: Compiled by the author.

1 'Autocracy' (a virtually homogeneous elite, the dominant actor is the governor or a business group exercising full control over regional politics);
2 'Soft autocracy' (there is a weak opposition group or groups);
3 'Elites settlement' (the regional elite is heterogeneous, but the leader, governor, is powerful enough to reconcile conflicts and secure consolidation of elite groups);
4 'Fragmented elite' (the regional elite is split, hence political instability and acute struggle between elite groups);
5 'Polarized elite' (elite groups are integrated into two opposing camps).

Consequently, the regional legislatures were not amorphous packs of 'independent' deputies. On the contrary, they were structured into informal groups[28] reflecting the makeup of regional elites, which provided the deputies with a means of coordination. Formally 'independent' deputies would represent the interests of one or another elite group. On occasion the governor or some influential clique would publicly declare an informal 'list of candidates' they supported at regional legislature elections. Therefore, the process of institutionalization of the political structure in most regional assemblies was largely precipitated by financial and economic interests rather than by political or ideological orientation. In 'autocratic assemblies', for example, deputies' 'independence' made no difference, as almost all of them were in fact members of informal groups – clienteles of the dominant regional actor. In regions with a 'fragmented elite' there were several such clienteles.[29]

The picture painted above was typical of the Russian regional politics in the 1990s. At the same time, there were a few deviant cases when political parties did play a significant role. It should be pointed out that in itself a deputy's membership in a party was not equivalent to the party mechanism of representation. In the majority of cases party deputies secured election victories without much recourse to party resources, so they were not burdened by any obligations.[30] Therefore, speaking about deviant cases I do not refer to the membership of deputies in parties but rather to the small number of regions where political parties were actually structuring the composition and activity of regional parliaments. There were several reasons for the formation of these deviant cases:[31]

First, the Communist Party, re-established in 1993, was rather strong in some regions (the so-called 'Red Belt'). For instance, Volgograd, Bryansk, Kamchatka oblasts and the Koryak Autonomous Okrug can be regarded as regions where Communist Party representation was fairly active, as the regional Communist Party branches steered the political process and controlled their own deputies. In these regions a significant percentage of the electorate were more interested in the party affiliation of a candidate than in the candidate's personal qualities.

A second factor is related to the peculiarities of the regional electoral systems. Prior to 2003 subjects of the Federation had a right to set up their own electoral institutions, and some of them adopted a proportional representation system. For example, the elections to the Sverdlovsk Oblast Duma (the lower house of the regional legislature) were based on party lists alone. The Krasnoyarsk Krai Legislature was formed on the basis of a mixed system, and almost half of the deputies (20 out of 42) were elected on the principle of proportionate representation. In Pskov Oblast one third of the regional assembly deputies (11 out of 33) were elected in a similar fashion.[32] A mixed electoral system is known to increase the influence of political parties due not only to the so-called 'mechanical effect', when those deputies elected on the basis of proportionality tend to have party affiliations, but also to the 'contamination effect'.[33] Hence, there is nothing unexpected about the spreading of party representation in those regions.

Third, the deviations took place in certain 'autocratic' regions. There, the dominant actor, exercising control over the regional elite, was capable of establishing a new party or was able to bolster the powers of existing ones (Aman Tuleev in Kemerovo Oblast, Nikolai Kondratenko in Krasnodar Krai, etc.). Under such circumstances party affiliation among regional legislature deputies was very unstable. For example, in the Udmurt Republic and the Republic of Bashkortostan it rose from 0 per cent in the first cycle to 51 per cent and 81 per cent in the third cycle, respectively.

It should be noted that most deviations (except for the first group) relate not to national, but to the so-called 'regional' political parties which represented the interests of various elite groups within the regions.[34] The development of such regional parties was prolific during the Yeltsin period.

Therefore, despite a number of deviations a typical regional assembly in the Russia of the 1990s was comprised of the most influential business groups and the governor. Hence, the following conclusion can be drawn: political representation in an overwhelming number of Russian regions was closest to the 'non-party deputies representing predominantly particularist interests' model. As was pointed out above, the effectiveness of this model to a large extent depends on the development of civic associations and additional institutional structures, which were poorly developed in Russia.

In early 2000s the situation began to change. This was largely due to the policy of recentralization carried out by the federal Centre. The implementation of this policy was to be given to the 'party of power' – 'United Russia' – which was charged with the task of capturing control over the regional assemblies. To assist it in this task, a number of institutional reforms were carried out to strengthen its development in the regions. In 2001 the Federal Law on Political Parties was enacted, introducing tougher requirements regarding the creation and operation of political parties and effectively abolishing 'regional' parties. Electoral legislation was updated in 2002. According to the new rules, at least half of all regional assembly deputies had to be elected on the basis of proportional representation.[35]

The rational actor model is useful in revealing how the preferences of regional politicians have changed in relation to these new developments. Regional party branches have now been given a powerful political resource:

half the seats in the regional legislature are allocated to them. Consequently, a 'party strategy' has become much more appealing for the rational actor, which will vary depending on the electoral potential of a given party. On the other hand, all the benefits are accompanied by costs that include an input into party formation and regional party activity. If there is a regional branch of a party, the rational politician has to bring it under their control or at least take one of the key positions in its leadership to secure a winning seat on the party list. If a given party has no regional branch, it needs to be created, for which the support of the central party leadership must be enlisted, the required number of members recruited, and their registration completed, etc.

The correlation between costs and benefits is not easy to calculate. There are approximately 40-50 political parties officially registered in Russia, and almost none of them have strong branches in all federal subject. Therefore, the rational politician faces the question of which party to choose for 'investment'. It is not difficult to establish control over a weak regional branch, but it will require a great deal of 'investments' in order to 'offset the costs' (the party needs to win seats in the regional assembly). Participating in the development of a strong (well-publicized) regional branch could be less costly but more competitive.

In addition, the rational politician has to take into account the aspirations, preferences and probable actions of other actors. Here, the calculations are largely dependent upon the makeup of the regional political elite. Under 'autocracy' the dominant actor has nothing to worry about: they can choose any party and none of the regional politicians will be capable of putting up any opposition. In competitive regions the situation is drastically different. Here, a whole group of political actors are strongly motivated to opt for a 'party strategy'. Hence, the risks are higher as well, as the struggle for attractive regional party branches is fraught with unpredictable consequences.

Last but not least, while assessing possible alternatives and choosing their strategy the rational politician must take into account the central party leadership. As a rule, influential regional actors (the governor or a successful entrepreneur) are reluctant to sacrifice their independence. In practice, however, the central leadership of many parties does not aim at totalistic control; party discipline can often be compromised if it results in greater recruitment to the party from regional elites.

The choice in favour of a 'party strategy' is, therefore, not that obvious. Nevertheless, the institutional and political changes at the beginning of the 2000s have clearly stimulated the development of political parties in the regions. Many influential politicians, who earlier preferred to keep away from parties, have begun to play a more active role in party formation. The fourth regional legislature election cycle demonstrates a steady growth of party affiliation among deputies. Since December 2003 new electoral rules have been implemented in seventy-five subjects of the Russian Federation.[36] Only ten 'new generation' legislatures have more than a quarter of non-party deputies. In the other sixty-five regional assemblies, on the contrary, over half the deputies elected in single-member constituencies belong to a party. Party membership is on the rise even in those regions where elections have not yet taken place (the fourth cycle is not completed).

More importantly, party factions are becoming the main 'unit of representation'. It is parties, not non-party 'deputy groups', that are starting to coordinate the activity of the deputies. In particular, this is expressed in public statements on political positions and preferences aired by the factions on behalf of their members. In these circumstances casting votes at elections becomes more party-oriented than before. In conclusion, it can now be stated that the policies of parties are now an important factor in regional politics.

It is not unexpected, then, that it is United Russia that has become the most successful party in the regions – it secured over half the seats in forty subjects of the Federation. Even although its deputies make up less than a third of the assemblies in fifteen regions, the 'party in power' has been able to exercise a major influence through the formation of large legislative factions in these assemblies (with the exception of Volgograd Oblast and Koryak Autonomous Okrug).

Nevertheless, the Centre's efforts to make United Russia forge strong roots in the regions has inevitably made other political parties more active. There are, however, significant cross-regional differences. The development level of various parties can be measured with an Effective Number of Parties in Parliament Index (ENP).[37] The index values for the fourth cycle are given in Table 7.3.[38]

The table shows that approximately one quarter of the regions demonstrate a relative high level of party competition (ENP > 3). There is nothing unexpected in the fact that from the viewpoint of elite configuration almost all these regions belong to the 'elites settlement' or 'fragmented elite' type. Political figures have an especially strong incentive to invest resources in regional branches of various parties (not only in United Russia) in those regions where there is more than one influential political actor. As a rule, the more diversified the political resources in a region, the more competitive the political process and the better developed the regional branches of various political parties.

At the same time there is a group of twelve regions where party competition is almost non-existent (ENP < 1.5). Among them there are both economically poor and rich regions, 'oblasts' and 'ethnic republics' and 'national autonomies' (autonomous okrugs/oblast). This shows that the level of development of political parties at the regional level can be explained neither by the level of socio-economic development nor by the status of the subject of the Federation. The key determining factor is the configuration of the regional elite. Most regions in this group are 'autocracies' (either 'harsh' or 'soft'). This suggests that an active party formation promotes, rather than restricts, the diversification of regional politics. Regions displaying authoritarian tendencies are becoming even more authoritarian, while competitive regions are turning even more competitive.

Table 7.3 Effective number of parties in 'new generation' regional legislatures

ENP>3	
Amur Oblast	5.00
Ryazan' Oblast	5.00
Tula Oblast	5.00
Yaroslavl' Oblast	5.00
Altai	4.76
Ingushetiya	4.38
Vladimir Oblast	4.38
Khakasiya	4.00
Sakhalin Oblast	3.85
Kaluga Oblast	3.70
Arkhangel'sk Oblast	3.57
Nenets AO	3.45
Kurgan Oblast	3.33
Altai Krai	3.23
Kostroma Oblast	3.23
Novosibirsk Oblast	3.23
St Petersburg	3.13
Stavropol Krai	3.03
No. of regions	**18**

ENP>2<3	
Bryansk Oblast	2.94
Chita Oblast	2.94
Irkutsk Oblast	2.94
Magadan Oblast	2.86
Tver' Oblast	2.86
Adygeya	2.78
Kaliningrad Oblast	2.78
Leningrad Oblast	2.63
Volgograd Oblast	2.56
Voronezh Oblast	2.56
Kirov Oblast	2.50
Krasnoyarsk Krai	2.50
Koryak AO	2.38
Orel Oblast	2.38
Samara Oblast	2.38
Astrakhan Oblast	2.33
Perm Krai	2.33
Tambov Oblast	2.33
Ulyanovsk Oblast	2.32
Daghestan	2.27
Ivanovo Oblast	2.27
Taimyr AO	2.22
Kareliya	2.17
Marii El	2.13
Murmansk Oblast	2.13
Novgorod Oblast	2.13
Pskov Oblast	2.13

Table 7.3 (continued)

ENP>2<3	
Vologda Oblast	2.08
Nizhni Novgorod Oblast	2.04
Komi Republic	2.00
Tyva	2.00
Ust'-Ordynskii Buryatskii AO	2.00
No. of regions	**32**

ENP >1.5 <2	
Chelyabinsk Oblast	1.96
Moscow Oblast	1.96
Orenburg Oblast	1.96
Khabarovsk Krai	1.82
Tomsk Oblast	1.82
Belgorod Oblast	1.79
Primorskii Krai	1.79
Kursk Oblast	1.75
Jewish AO	1.72
Karachaevo-Cherkessiya	1.69
Lipetsk Oblast	1.69
Sverdlovsk Oblast	1.67
No. of regions	**12**

ENP<1.5	
Chuvashiya	1.50
Moscow	1.50
Khanty-Mansiisk AO	1.49
Yamalo-Nenets AO	1.47
Aginsk Buryat AO	1.45
Kabardino-Balkariya	1.32
Omsk Oblast	1.30
Kalmykiya	1.28
Tyumen Oblast	1.28
Chukotka AO	1.19
Mordoviya	1.15
Tatarstan	1.10
No. of regions	**12**

Source: Compiled by the author.

Surprisingly, the low ENP group also included several regions that, according to all estimates, have a high level of political competition – Sverdlovsk, Chelyabinsk and Kursk oblasts. How can this be explained? First, during an election campaign an extraordinary event may happen, for example some parties may be struck off the ballot, as happened in Kursk Oblast.[39] This automatically causes the ENP to fall. Another, perhaps a slightly more important reason is that political competition can become internalized within the ranks of United Russia. Besides, an opposite scenario is equally possible, when several parties are under the control of one political actor. Therefore, the ENP can only be used to reveal general tendencies and is insufficient as an indicator for characterizing the level of party development in a given region.

Thus, we can draw the conclusion that since the beginning of the 2000s the practice of political representation in Russian regions has markedly changed – there has been a transition from a non-party to a party-focused mechanism of representation. The remaining question to be answered is whether the type of representation has changed. So far it has been our assumption that political figures join a party and participate in party life primarily out of rational (pragmatic) and purpose-orientated considerations. They strive to strengthen their political positions and make a certain gain, which makes it quite obvious that regional branches of political parties must represent predominantly particularist, rather than universalist interests. This thesis, however, cannot be tested by using quantitative methods (electoral statistics, as we have demonstrated, have some limitations). Therefore, we need to add a qualitative dimension through the examination of a detailed case-study of party development in one region.

Political parties and representation in Perm Oblast[40]

Perm Oblast is a typical Russian industrial region situated to the west of the Urals in the Kama river basin which had a population of over 2.8 million in 2002. Seventy-five per cent of the population of Perm live in urban areas. The region is rich in mineral resources (especially crude oil and potassium) and forestry. The regional centre, Perm, is a large industrial city with many chemical and engineering plants, most of which were built over the period 1930-50. The per capita Gross Regional Product is USD 8,465 (2002), which is somewhat higher than the national average (USD 7,278). In terms of this and other key economic indicators Perm Oblast is in the top twenty Russian regions.

The economic transformation of the 1990s made a crucial impact on the regional political process. Privatization led to the formation of several large business groups, among the most influential of which are the oil (the oil giant LUKOIL is a regional monopolist) and potassium groups (Dmitry Rybolovlev, the owner of Uralkalii is the richest man in the region). Apart from those, other strong business groups have been formed in various industries, for example, EKS created by Yury Trutnev. A high degree of industrial diversification of the regional economy also induced a sharper diversification of political resources.

The fact that in the 1990s the highest-ranking regional officials did not originally come from the business environment was of no less importance. The first head of the regional administration (1992–5), Boris Kuznetsov, had no personal political ambitions and was usually content to follow the federal line. His successor, Gennady Igumnov (1995–2000) was a much more colourful political figure but he lacked his own financial and economic resources. Thus, on the one hand, regional power was not 'hijacked' by a single business group (as was the case in some regions with a mono-structured regional economy). On the other hand, the regional administration did not have direct control over the regional economy (unlike Tatarstan and Bashkortostan, for instance). The situation changed when in 2000 Igumnov lost the gubernatorial election to Trutnev, who had been serving as mayor of Perm. By that time, however, most of the region's economic resources had been distributed, and that made Trutnev take account of the interests of a diverse set of other powerful elites in the Oblast.

As a whole, Perm Oblast belongs to the category of regions with hetero-geneous but non-fragmented political elites. For a number of reasons these elite groups were induced to engage in cooperative activities rather than to competition and conflict.[41] In these conditions the regional administration played an active role as a mediator (or broker) of intra-elite interests. The regional assembly (the Perm Oblast legislature), formed in 1994, became a ground for coordinating and negotiating interests between the various groups. As a rule, deputies tried to find a compromise, and decision-making was based on compromise and cooperation. Acute conflicts were rare and gradually something approaching an 'elites settlement' was formed.

From the viewpoint of interest representation Perm Oblast is quite a typi-cal region. The regional legislature consisted of forty deputies who are elec-ted in single-member constituencies predominantly on a non-party basis. In the second electoral cycle (the 1997 election) only two deputies belonged to a political party. Four years later, in the 2001 election the number of party-affiliated deputies hardly changed (only three legislators had party member-ship). Nevertheless, several informal groups, reflecting the makeup of the regional elite, were formed in the legislature. Some of them took the form of 'deputies' groups'. In 1997–2001 the most influential among those were the 'Industrialists of Prikamye' (supporters of Igumnov) and the 'Dialogue' group (those supporting Trutnev).

By the beginning of the 2000s the situation had started to change. In line with national tendencies the role of political parties became more prominent. Influential politicians started to join parties and participate in party life. In 2001 a United Russia faction was created in the regional legislature, com-prising nearly half the deputies, mostly from the Industrialists of Prikamye group. The second party faction, the Union of Right Forces (SPS), was formed by five legislators. In addition, four more deputies declared their affiliation with other parties (Yabloko, the People's Party, CPRF and Liberal Russia). The operational practices of the Perm legislature reveal, however, that the deputies' party affiliations do not necessarily create a party-based mechanism of representation. Up until 2003 party discipline was weak and legislators identified themselves as independent deputies rather than party representatives. It is highly indicative that membership of one party faction did not preclude deputies from joining other factions at the same time.

The years 2003-4 became a turning point. It became clear that in line with the newly adopted electoral legislation that future regional assembly election would be based on a mixed electoral system. Discussions around the drawing up of the 'Regional Legislature Election Law' revealed a marked conflict of interests. Some (mainly non-party) deputies insisted on doubling the number of seats in the regional legislature. This would allow the retention in the assembly of all the single-mandate seats, and give a powerful boost to the incumbents' prospects for re-election. The regional administration, on the contrary, wanted to retain the same number of seats (40): the smaller the legislature the easier it would be for the executive power to bargain with the deputies, since such political bargaining was common practice in the interrelations between branches of power in the region. The debate resulted in a compromise. It was decided that the legislature would consist of 60 seats: 30 from single-member constituencies and 30 from proportional representation/party lists. The issue of the electoral threshold spurred no less vigorous debate. While strong parties were interested in a higher threshold, the smaller ones, on the contrary, insisted on a lower one. As a result, a 7 per cent threshold was agreed.[42]

The new electoral system significantly speeded up the process of setting up regional branches of political parties. There are presently over 25 of them. The most influential among them is undoubtedly the regional branch of the 'party in power', United Russia. The latter is known to have been created in 2001 as a result of a merger between Unity and Fatherland-All Russia (OVR). Unity was originally created as an official 'party in power' for mobilizing the electorate to support the Kremlin in the 1999 State Duma elections. OVR was a bloc of influential regional leaders (Tatarstan, Moscow, St. Petersburg, etc.), and in 1999 was the principal opponent to Unity. In reality, however, both parties were Kremlin-backed 'parties of power'. Their temporary, though no less fierce, confrontation was caused by an exacerbation of the power struggle within the ruling elite which erupted in the period 1998-9, on the eve of President Yeltsin's resignation. Therefore, there was nothing unexpected in the fact that after the Duma elections in 1999, Unity and OVR consolidated their power in the State Duma and created a united 'party of power' ('United Russia').

It looked as if originally the founders of Unity and OVR were more interested in regional politicians than the latter were in them. Both parties made use of administrative resources and personal connections to recruit members and open regional branches. Therefore, the process of party formation to a larger extent was based on political bargaining and an exchange of resources between political actors (for example, a certain contribution to party funds was exchanged for business preferences), rather than on common political values. It was not by accident that most leaders of those parties were high-ranking civil servants or directors of large enterprises. Thinking strategically, Perm's most influential regional actors sent their representatives to the governing bodies of both parties. For example, Vladimir Nelyubin joined the ranks of Unity from the Trutnev group (Trutnev decided to distance himself from the parties), and Nikolay Yashin from OVR. The latter was elected Chairman of the party's regional branch. The regional branch of Unity was headed by Vladimir Rybakin, a regional deputy and Director General of Uralsvyazinform, a company holding a monopoly in the regional telecommunications sector. Besides, he was known as a supporter of Governor Igumnov. Therefore, the balance between the elites within the regional governing bodies varied and the merging of the parties (which took place after Trutnev's victory in the gubernatorial election) was a complicated endeavour. Each elite group had invested considerable resources in the separate party formations and they were eager to retain positions in the leadership of the new united party. Rybakin managed to keep the status of leader, but representatives of other elite groups (the regional administration, the 'oil group', the 'gas group', etc.) were also included in the regional leadership.

After the 2003 State Duma election United Russia became the most attractive party for political actors.[43] This exacerbated the power struggle within the regional branch of the party. New politicians started joining the party's ranks and entered into competition with the former leaders. In addition, in 2004 Trutnev was appointed Federal Minister for Natural Resources. His successor (and an old business partner) Oleg Chirkunov turned out to be a much less flexible and less popular politician.[44] This destabilized the situation in the regional political elite, and the 'elites settlement' started to crumble.

The balance of political forces within the regional branch of United Russia is highly complex. The strategy of the leadership is quite contradictory. On the one hand, it makes attempts to involve new influential actors in the party in order to increase its electoral appeal. On the other hand, the more heavyweight actors that are involved in a party, the more amorphous and competitive becomes its regional branch. This was most clearly demonstrated in 2006 when elections were held for the Mayor of Perm City and City Duma, and also for the Perm Regional Assembly.

Even although the March 2006 election for the Mayor of Perm was fiercely competitive, United Russia failed to put forward a common candidate. Officially the regional party council supported Igor Shubin, governor Chirkunov's protégé. However, another member of the party, State Duma deputy Pavel Anokhin, entered the race. Anokhin had been in a long-standing and acute conflict with the regional branch of United Russia, and it is noteworthy that the central party leadership refused to get involved. This testimony provides little evidence for the existence of a 'party vertical'.[45]

Moreover, United Russia failed to work out a common position regarding the list of candidates for seats in the city Duma. The Perm Duma consists of thirty-six deputies who were elected in single-member constituencies. On behalf of the party Shubin produced a list of candidates, but at the same time a 'tandem' of the Perm city branch leaders, Andrey Agishev (a successful entrepreneur and director of a large natural gas company) and

Vladimir Nelyubin, put together a group of candidates under the name United Perm. Even though United Perm was endorsed at the city party conference, in reality the United Russia had two lists of candidates which did not fully coincide. As a result, in some constituencies candidates from United Russia were competing against those from United Perm.

Intra-party struggle continued throughout the December 2006 electoral campaign for the Perm Regional Assembly. The Regional branch of United Russia had difficulties in drawing up its party list. One of the regional party leaders, Yurii Medvedev, a Deputy to the State Duma, noted that some influential figures in the party were unhappy with the selection criteria, 'which were based on accommodating members of different elite groups rather than on a candidate's devotion to the ideals of the party'.[46] Nevertheless, it was impossible to satisfy all elite groups and to provide all of them with win seats. Additionally, the intervention of the Central party leadership in the process complicated the issue. The Centre demanded that the Governor had to head the party list. Also it insisted on improving the representation of youth, and female candidates. In the end, a compromise was reached, although some influential party members still took offence. In particular, Agishev entered the election in one of the single-member constituencies and he defeated the official candidate of United Russia.

In total, United Russia won 34.6 per cent of the votes. On the one hand, it was much less than the central leadership had predicted. On the other hand, the party fared very well in the single-member constituency elections. Of the twenty-four candidates nominated by United Russia, officially seventeen were victorious.[47] However, when we add the members from the single-constituencies, United Russia won an absolute majority in the Regional Assembly.

Up until recently the regional branches of two other large Russian political parties – the Communists (CPRF) and the Liberal Democrats (LDPR) – could hardly be considered as influential regional actors. In spite of their winning substantial shares of votes in federal elections,[48] the regional party organizations did not attract much of the regional elite's attention. Both parties were in need of charismatic leaders and financial resources, and therefore they were totally dependent on their central leaders. More recently both parties have received a significant electoral resource which has boosted their attractiveness in the eyes of regional elite groups. The fate of the Liberal Democrats is already sealed. The former leader of their regional branch, Oleg Plotnikov, was promoted to the central party apparatus, and his successor, Andrei Alikin, is known to be a protégé of 'Uralkalii'. At the same time this elite group is not in opposition to United Russia. Moreover representatives of 'Uralkalii' even managed to receive some seats in United Russia's list of candidates. In the December 2006 election the Liberal Democrats received 13.8 per cent of the votes, which translated into 5 seats.

In contrast to the 'cynical' ploys of the LDPR, the CPRF is keen to promote the impression of an ideologically driven party. Even though there are elite groups which would like to gain control over the regional Communists, they are apprehensive of becoming associated with Communist ideas. Therefore they aspire not to capture the regional party branch as a whole but to gain some party list seats in exchange for their financial support. Besides, the regional branch of the CPRF has partially fallen under the control of a group of political technologists which is closely associated with the regional administration. In December 2006 the CPRF won 8.6 per cent of the votes and three seats.

One of the peculiarities of regional politics in Perm is the prominent role of liberally orientated parties, such as the Union of Right Forces (SPS) and Yabloko. Even in 2003, when these parties failed to secure victory in the State Duma elections, in Perm Oblast their performance was not so poor: they won 8.6 per cent and 5.50 per cent of the votes respectively. The regional branch of SPS was created in 1999 mostly on the basis of the regional organization of 'Democratic Choice of Russia' (former Prime Minister Yegor Gaydar's party), which was quite influential in the region. It was headed by State Duma deputy Victor Pokhmelkin, the only Perm politician who has won all Duma elections (since 1993). Pokhmelkin wielded considerable influence in the Igumnov administration. His scandalous alliance with Boris Berezovsky (creating the political movement 'Liberal Russia'), and his walkout from SPS in 2002, sparked an acute crisis in its regional branches. There were a number of influential political figures, young and successful entrepreneurs in SPS's ranks, who managed to overcome the crisis. In 2005, however, the party entered another period of turmoil, as Nikita Belych was elected federal party leader. His statements in opposition to the policies of President Putin split the regional branches, and some members led by the new leader Alexey Chernov, who were more inclined to cooperate with Putin, left the party.

As far as the Perm branch of Yabloko is concerned, it was a lack of financial resources that appeared to have made it offer the leadership to Valery Chuprakov, a successful industrialist and a former member of United Russia. Churpakov might have been cherishing a hope to gain more political weight, as he was planning to run for the post of mayor of Perm. After his defeat he left Yabloko and joined United Russia once again. One specific feature of the regional Yabloko is that it has brought together several charismatic – far from wealthy but nonetheless popular – personalities, who are resisting the particularist aspirations of Churpakov and other entrepreneurs.

In the December 2006 elections for the Regional Assembly, SPS and Yabloko agreed to find ways to work together in order to overcome the 7 per cent electoral threshold. In particular, Yabloko agreed not to propose its own party list. The two parties also agreed not to field candidates against each other in the single-member constituencies. As a result, 16.35 per cent of the electorate voted for SPS and the party received six seats in the regional legislature.

During 2004-6, when there was a weakening of the powers of the regional administration and a reconfiguration of the regional elite, a number of new and influential actors entered the Perm political arena. Viewed as 'outsiders' by the previous 'elites settlement', they tried to make the most of the available opportunities. Among those one should single out the group led by Vladimir Plotnikov, a successful entrepreneur with a criminal past. Despite Chirkunov's active resistance (at times rather crude), in December 2004 he managed to win a by-election and secure a seat in the regional legislature. Later, after joining with Pokhmelkin's supporters he formed a faction in the regional parliament consisting of four deputies. Prior to that Plotnikov had established control over the regional branch of the People's Party. It was Plotnikov who was Shubin's principal rival in the Perm mayoral elections, although he was disqualified under the trumped up charges of infringing electoral legislation.[49] However, he was still able to put forward his own informal list of candidates for the Perm city assembly, but only three of them eventually won seats. Nevertheless, Plotnikov's group remained a significant counteracting force to Chirkunov. Taking into account that the People's Party and Liberal Russia (under Pokhmelkin's control) had virtually no chance of reaching the 7 per cent threshold, Plotnikov was in need of a party with a more significant electoral potential. In 2006 he tried to take control of the regional branches of Yabloko (after Churpakov had exited), the Democratic Party, and even the CPRF, but he has not been successful.

One of the most important recent events in Russian political life was the creation of the party 'A Just Russia' which was formed through a Kremlin-inspired merger of 'Rodina', the 'Russian Party of Life' and the 'Russian Pensioners' Party'. In Perm region the strongest among these was the latter. In the 2003 elections for the State Duma, the Pensioners' Party won over 5 per cent of the votes in the region. The struggle for control over the party's regional branch between several influential elites ended in the victory of the regional natural gas supplier ('Permregiongaz'). It is noteworthy that two most recent successive managing directors of the company, Shubin (former) and Agishev (current), are active members of United Russia. This convincingly shows that, in order to minimize risks, those political actors who have meaningful resources invest them in a variety of party projects.

In spite of its success in the 2003 State Duma election (5.79 per cent of regional voters) Rodina did not manage to form a strong regional branch in Perm. This can be explained by the party's split at the national level. Additionally, regional party leader Valentina Sevostyanova, a deputy of the State Duma, lacked financial resources. Therefore the regional branch was activated only on the eve of December 2006 election.

As the Russian Party of Life headed by Sergei Mironov became stronger, some elite groups entered the struggle to control its regional branch. The most active were three well-known regional politicians (regional assembly deputy Konstantin Okunev, former Vice-Governor of Perm Yuriy Belousov, and Federation Council member Vladimir Solomonov) who undoubtedly also represented different business groups. The central party leadership remained undecided over which of these groups and leaders to back, and the situation remained unresolved until the party was assimilated into the new coalition, 'A Just Russia'.

As a result, the regional branches of all three of the coalition partners which made up A Just Russia, which were meant to be united, were in reality under the control of different elite groups. That is why their merger was such a difficult enterprise. The December 2006 election slowed down the process since it was held before the unified party congress and before A Just Russia had gained the right to participate in elections. At the same time the election intensified the contradictions between the three partners. The Russian Party of Life refused to take part in the election, but the two other 'partners' decided to enter it on their own. During the election campaign the conflict became so sharp that Sevostyanova declared that unification was impossible and the central leadership of A Just Russia even tried to withdraw Rodina from the election.[50] As a result in December 2006 the Russian Pensioners' Party got fewer votes than was expected (11.65 per cent, and four seats in assembly) and Rodina did not manage to overcome the electoral threshold at all (3.19 per cent).

In addition to the parties discussed above there are a number of other regional branches of parties with good electoral prospects. The Agrarian Party commands considerable electoral resources. In the December 2006 election it just failed to clear the 7 per cent electoral threshold, winning 6.34 per cent of the votes.[51] The 'Patriots of Russia' party won 2.44 per cent of the votes, but the party has suffered from a lack of popular leaders.

Since party formation is a costly endeavour, it can be regarded as a business in its 'purest form'. Under the new rules of the game created by the recent changes to the electoral rules, those parties that were created by political technologists 'for sale' have suddenly developed a certain appeal. One such party, Free Russia, has attracted the patronage of governor Chirkunov. Several politicians joined its regional branch, and in April 2006 it formed a faction in the regional legislature. Free Russia is known in the country as a 'killer party', which has occasionally been used in elections to steal votes from other parties. Nevertheless, a short time later Chirkunov rejected this project.

Thus, the Perm case study illustrates that the key political actors in the region have begun to actively utilize regional branches of political parties, primarily as instruments for building up their political resources. Hence, particularist interests in party activity clearly dominate over universalist. The less important values and ideas are for a party, the more autonomous are its regional organizations. This gives regional actors additional incentives to participate in party formation. Here, three main strategies can be identified. Some actors are trying to play on United Russia's field, which causes splits and conflicts within the regional branch of the 'party in power'. Others are seeking to extend their control over the existing regional branches with a significant electoral potential. A third kind of actors are getting involved with marginal regional organizations and have to invest significant resources in order to increase their attractiveness.

In addition, the heterogeneity of the regional elites, coupled with an exacerbation of political struggle in the run-up to the 2006 regional elections, and a high degree of uncertainty as regards the current political process – are encouraging those who have access to resources to invest them simultaneously in a number of different parties. Investments do not only come in the form of funds for party building but also in the influence entrepreneurs can wield when it comes to providing the regional branch with members (by coercing employees of the companies owned or controlled by the politician to join the party). Such a power is of no little significance in light of the new and tougher legislation recently adopted on party membership.[52] In any case parties are mainly regarded as instruments for promoting particularist interests of political actors. At the same time, realizing the growing importance of political parties, regional authorities have begun to more actively influence and engage in the process of party formation.

Conclusion

A transition from a non-party mechanism of representation to a party-based one was underway in the Russian regions in the 2000s. It was largely caused by changes in the institutional context introduced by the Federal Centre. The new electoral system has transformed regional actors' preferences. It is pragmatic, purpose-driven and rationalistic considerations (desire to push certain private interests through into the public sphere) that impel regional politicians to actively participate in party formation. Therefore, regional political representation practices are moving closer towards the 'party deputies predominantly representing particularist interests' model.

Russian political parties are obviously much more than mere coalitions of actors on single issues; they are built on a different foundation from 'classical mass parties' which are traditionally centred on universal political values and ideologies. It is particularist interests that are dominant in Russian political parties, and this spurs the latter to develop rather complex mechanisms of intra-party interaction that can be referred to as 'a system of personalized exchanges' – a system of political bargaining between influential actors to coordinate and reconcile particularist interests. By joining a party and interacting with partners, a political actor expects certain guarantees regarding their (either personal or collective) interests, and they are ready to invest their own resources in the party as long as such guarantees are in place.

We can say with a strong degree of conviction that maintaining the balance of interests between various actors is an extremely difficult task. Constant reconfiguration and resynchronization of actors makes it critical to hold permanent talks, to negotiate and renegotiate respective contracts. This makes political parties insufficiently institutionalized entities.

The 'system of personalized exchanges' determines both horizontal and vertical functioning of parties. At the regional (horizontal) level inter-party and intra-party interaction depends on the correlation of resources and interests of party leaders. In 'autocratic' regions the dominant actor usually controls the regional branch of United Russia, and all other parties are marginalized. In 'competitive' regions the situation is different. In principle, a 'pure' model is possible, when the party configuration accurately reflects the makeup of the regional elite, but in reality there are two ways in which political practice can deviate from such a model. On the one hand, contradictions between elite groups can become internalized within parties, which can cause splits within party organizations. On the other hand, influential actors can extend their control over several regional party organizations at one time.

As far as the 'vertical' dimension is concerned, the more influential (resource-contributing) actors are involved in a regional branch of a party, the weaker is the ability of the central party leadership to maintain control. The degree of subordination varies significantly from region to region and from party to party. It primarily depends on the correlation of resources between the centre and its regional branch, but since parties are based on mutually beneficial exchanges of resources rather than on common political preferences, weak subordination does not constitute a threat to them as long as the 'system of personalized exchanges' remains in place.

The existing model of representation turns out to be even less effective than the previous one based on the 'non-party' mechanism, because the circle of interests being represented is much narrower. More and more often election campaigns turn into competitions of political technologies, including the so-called 'black technologies'; public disillusionment is growing, which is reflected in a rise in absenteeism. This means that most of the parties in Russia lack popular legitimacy. A study of federal and regional elections clearly demonstrates that there is a high demand in society for more universal and value-orientated parties.

Appendix 7.1 Regional legislature elections results

	First cycle elections		Second cycle elections		Third cycle elections				
	No. of seats	Share of party deputies	No. of seats	Share of party deputies	No. of seats	Share of party deputies	ENP	United Russia's share of votes	United Russia's share of seats
Adygeya	45	51.0	54	18.5	54	55.6	2.78	33.74	42.59
Aginsk Buryat AO	15	13.0	15	6.7	18	88.9	1.45	67.30	77.78
Altai	41	29.0	41	29.0	41	57.8	4.76	27.20	31.71
Altai Krai	50	44.0	50	34.0	68	52.9	3.23	24.43	32.35
Amur Oblast	30	.0	36	19.4	36	58.8	5.00	16.26	19.44
Arkhangelsk Oblast	39	2.6	39	12.8	62	67.4	3.57	23.63	40.32
Astrakhan Oblast	29	27.6	29	10.3	58	81.5	2.33	38.73	57.14
Bashkortostan	174	.0	120	81.7	.0	.0	.0	.0	.0

	First cycle elections		Second cycle elections		Third cycle elections				
	No. of seats	Share of party deputies	No. of seats	Share of party deputies	No. of seats	Share of party deputies	ENP	United Russia's share of votes	United Russia's share of seats
Belgorod Oblast	35	40.0	35	2.9	35	47.0	1.79	52.78	54.29
Bryansk Oblast	50	52.0	50	36.0	60	30.8	2.94	34.19	31.67
Buryatiya	65	.0	65	3.1	.0	.0	.0	.0	.0
Chelyabinsk Oblast	41	.0	45	2.2	60	83.3	1.96	51.98	65.00
Chita Oblast	39	.0	39	20.5	42	52.4	2.94	35.61	38.10
Chukotka AO	13	.0	13	.0	12	83.3	1.19	69.21	83.33
Chuvashiya	87	18.4	73	9.6	44	77.3	1.50	51.89	70.45
Daghestan	121	.8	121	2.5	72	.0	2.27	63.67	65.28
Yevenk AO	23	.0	23	.0	.0	.0	.0	.0	.0
Ingushetiya	27	.0	21	.0	34	17.6	4.38	36.31	20.59
Irkutsk Oblast	45	22.0	45	.0	45	55.0	2.94	30.19	42.22
Ivanovo Oblast	35	20.0	35	11.4	48	87.5	2.27	32.10	60.42
Jewish AO	15	20.0	15	.0	16	87.5	1.72	55.32	68.75
Kabardino-Balkariya	.0	.0	72	6.9	110	72.7	1.32	72.50	74.55
Kaliningrad Oblast	32	34.4	32	25.0	40	63.4	2.78	34.12	45.00
Kalmykiya	27	.0	27	.0	27	66.7	1.28	41.74	74.07
Kaluga Oblast	40	45.0	40	12.5	40	58.8	3.70	40.03	35.00
Kamchatka Oblast	39	48.7	39	43.5	.0	.0	.0	.0	.0
Karachaevo-Cherkessiya	73	20.5	73	21.9	73	66.7	1.69	55.69	63.01
Kareliya	61	24.6	57	2.5	50	64.0	2.17	38.92	54.00
Kemerovo Oblast	35	97.1	35	100.0	.0	.0	.0	.0	.0
Khabarovsk Krai	25	32.0	25	12.0	26	92.3	1.82	40.99	69.23
Khakasiya	75	5.3	75	6.7	75	69.4	4.00	23.17	32.00
Khanty-Mansiisk AO	23	.0	25	.0	28	85.7	1.49	54.63	75.00
Kirov Oblast	54	31.5	54	16.7	54	85.2	2.50	28.54	55.56
Komi-Permyak AO	15	.0	15	6.7	.0	.	.	.	.
Komi Republic	50	.0	30	13.3	30	86.7	2.00	36.18	63.33
Koryak AO	12	66.6	12	50.0	12	60.0	2.38	22.68	16.67
Kostroma Oblast	21	.0	21	.0	36	58.8	3.23	22.99	38.89
Krasnodar Krai	50	82.0	70	24.3	.0	.0	.0	.0	.0
Krasnoyarsk Krai	42	83.3	42	85.7	52	88.5	2.50	42.52	55.77
Kurgan Oblast	33	3.0	33	.0	34	58.8	3.33	25.74	38.24
Kursk Oblast	45	13.0	45	4.4	45	84.2	1.75	37.36	69.05
Leningrad Oblast	50	8.0	50	12.0	50	68.0	2.63	35.24	46.00
Lipetsk Oblast	38	15.6	38	2.7	56	92.9	1.69	50.65	72.22
Magadan Oblast	17	5.8	17	.0	25	30.0	2.86	28.76	32.00
Marii El	67	10.4	67	10.4	52	76.9	2.13	32.28	57.69
Mordoviya	75	22.7	75	12.0	28	87.5	1.15	76.23	87.50
Moscow	35	25.0	35	14.3	35	100.0	1.50	47.25	80.00
Moscow Oblast	50	14.0	50	14.0	50	.0	1.96	49.57	66.00
Murmansk Oblast	25	20.0	25	4.0	32	81.3	2.13	42.19	59.38
Nenets AO	15	.0	15	.0	20	75.0	3.45	24.01	35.00
Nizhni Novgorod Oblast	45	4.4	45	6.7	50	96.0	2.04	43.91	66.00
North Osetiya-Alaniya	75	18.7	75	13.3	.0	.0	.0	.0	.0
Novgorod Oblast	26	.0	26	7.7	26	91.7	2.13	43.75	61.54
Novosibirsk Oblast	49	55.1	49	44.9	98	55.1	3.23	33.12	34.69
Omsk Oblast	30	33.0	30	16.7	44	100.0	1.30	55.65	86.36
Orenburg Oblast	47	21.3	47	6.4	47	91.3	1.96	40.44	63.83

	First cycle elections		Second cycle elections		Third cycle elections				
	No. of seats	Share of party deputies	No. of seats	Share of party deputies	No. of seats	Share of party deputies	ENP	United Russia's share of votes	United Russia's share of seats
Orel Oblast	50	24.0	50	8.0	50	80.0	2.38	39.02	52.00
Penza Oblast	45	37.8	45	20.0	.0	.0	.0	.0	.0
Perm Oblast (Krai)	40	5.6	40	7.5	60	58.6	2.33	34.58	49.15
Primorskii Krai	39	.0	39	12.8	40	50.0	1.79	48.27	55.00
Pskov Oblast	22	18.2	33	48.5	44	95.5	2.13	45.42	65.90
Rostov Oblast	45	31.1	45	13.3	.0	.0	.0	.0	.0
Ryazan Oblast	26	50.0	36	38.9	36	66.7	5.00	22.19	30.56
Sakhalin Oblast	27	11.0	27	11.0	28	21.4	3.85	17.74	17.86
Samara Oblast	25	12.0	25	16.0	50	68.0	2.38	33.54	52.00
Saratov Oblast	35	12.0	35	28.6	.0	.0	.0	.0	.0
Smolensk Oblast	30	36.7	48	16.7	.0	.0	.0	.0	.0
St. Petersburg	50	52.0	50	46.0	50	.0	3.13	37.37	46.00
Stavropol Krai	25	40.0	25	8.0	50	48.0	3.03	23.87	30.00
Sverdlovsk Oblast	49	69.4	49	67.3	49	52.4	1.67	38.24	38.78
Taimyr AO	11	9.0	11	.0	14	80.0	2.22	31.16	50.00
Tambov Oblast	50	20.0	50	22.0	50	84.0	2.33	40.49	56.00
Tatarstan	130	6.2	130	1.5	100	78.0	1.10	69.20	85.00
Tomsk Oblast	42	7.0	42	4.8	42	76.2	1.82	46.79	64.29
Tula Oblast	48	22.9	48	22.9	48	45.8	5.00	22.31	25.00
Tyva	32	21.9	22	63.4	32	81.8	2.00	46.38	48.15
Tver Oblast	33	9.0	33	30.3	33	69.8	2.86	33.23	45.45
Tyumen Oblast	25	4.0	25	16.0	34	100.0	1.28	65.89	88.24
Udmurtiya	100	.0	100	51.0	.0	.0	.0	.0	.0
Ulyanovsk Oblast	25	20.0	25	16.0	30	53.3	2.32	27.38	46.67
Ust-Ordynskii Buryatskii AO	19	26.3	15	6.7	18	77.8	2.00	58.81	55.56
Vladimir Oblast	37	13.5	37	24.3	38	66.7	4.38	20.53	28.95
Volgograd Oblast	32	87.5	32	87.5	38	43.8	2.56	36.69	31.58
Vologda Oblast	30	3.3	30	3.3	34	82.4	2.08	41.90	61.76
Voronezh Oblast	45	26.7	45	26.7	56	54.2	2.56	29.12	42.86
Sakha	70	10.0	70	18.6	.0	.0	.0	.0	.0
Yamalo-Nenets AO	21	9.5	21	4.8	22	55.6	1.47	60.69	59.09
Yaroslavl Oblast	50	10.0	50	4.0	50	40.9	5.00	25.98	24.00

Source: Official data from the Central Election Commission of the Russian Federation, http://www.cikrf.ru; data collected by Alexander Kynev (Russian Institute of Humanitarian and Political Studies), http://www.democracy.ru

Notes:
The share of party deputies in the forth cycle is calculated only for the deputies who were elected on the basis of majoritarian principle.
The Chechen Republic was not taken into account.
In regions with two-house legislatures (Sverdlovsk Oblast, Bashkortostan, Yakutiya, Kabardino-Balkariya, Adygeya, Kareliya, Tyva) aggregate data was used.
Elections in Volgograd, Vologda and Sverdlovsk Oblasts are based on the rotation principle when only half the regional assembly deputies stand for re-election at any one time.
For Vologda Oblast I summed up the 1996 and 1998 rotations and put them down as the second cycle; the 1999 and 2002 rotations were aggregated and put down as the third cycle. In the fourth cycle in 2003 only half the deputies were elected on the proportionate principle, while the other half are still serving as their terms have not expired yet. Therefore, I use date here for the 2007 election.

For Volgograd Oblast I put the results of the second cycle elections down as the third cycle because the latter was virtually non-existent (the region had abandoned the rotation principle, and after the mandate of half the deputies had expired their seats remained vacant until the fourth cycle elections).

The Sverdlovsk Oblast legislature consists of two houses the Duma (28 deputies) and the House of Representatives (21). Half the deputies in the lower house (the Duma) stand for re-election every two years according to the proportional system, so there have been seven elections. I regarded the 1996 and 1998 elections (aggregately) as the second cycle; the 2000 and 2002 elections as the third cycle and, the 2004 and 2006 election as the forth cycle. For the fourth cycle the ENP was calculated on the basis of the 2004 election. Prior to 2000 the upper house was biannually elected on the basis of a pluralist system, and after 2000 – every four years. I regarded the 1998 election results as the second cycle and the 2000 results as third.

In Kemerovo Oblast regional legislature the deputies' term in office was three years, so by 2003 there had been four, not three elections. I regarded the 1999 elections as the second cycle and the 2003 as the third.

Nine regions (Ulyanovsk Oblast, Adygeya, Ingushetiya, Kabardino-Balkariya, Kalmykiya, Karachaevo-Cherkessiya, Mordoviya, Tatarstan, Taimyr AO) had one election fewer than the other regions because unlike other federal subjects the first regional legislature there served full (4–5 years) terms, not shortened terms. Therefore, the results of the first elections in those regions were put down as second cycle, and the second elections – as third.

Five regions (Bashkortostan, Dagestan, Komi Republic, North Osetiya-Alaniya and Udmurtiya) due to a number of reasons had a 'shifted cycle', so second cycle elections took place in 1999 (not in 1996–8) and third cycle elections were carried out in 2003 (not in 2000–2).

Notes

1 See, for example, R. Moser, *Unexpected Outcomes: Electoral Systems, Political Parties, and Representation in Russia*, Pittsburg, PA: University of Pittsburg Press, 2001.

2 J. Buchanan and G. Tullock, *The Calculus of Consent*, Ann Arbor, MI: University of Michigan Press, 1962.

3 A. Bentley, *The Process of Government*, Cambridge, MA: Belknap Press, 1967.

4 R. Dahl, *Who Governs?*, New Haven, CT: Yale University Press, 1961.

5 R. Goodin, 'Institutionalizing the public interests: the defense of deadlock and beyond', *American Political Science Review*, Vol. 90, No. 2, 1996, pp. 331–43.

6 A. Lijphart, *Patterns of Democracy: Government Forms and Performance in Thirty-Six Countries*, New Haven, CT: Yale University Press, 1999.

7 R. Putnam, *Making Democracy Work: Civic Traditions in Modern Italy*, Princeton, NJ: Princeton University Press, 1993.

8 G. Doron and I. Sened, *Political Bargaining: Theory, Practice and Process*, London: Sage Publications, 2001, pp. 14–15.

9 J. Habermas, *The Inclusion of Other: Studies of Political Theory*, Cambridge, MA: MIT Press, 1998.

10 H. Arendt, *The Human Condition*, Chicago, IL: University of Chicago Press, 1958.

11 R. Sennett, *The Fall of Public Man,* New York: Knopf, 1976; R. Putnam, *Bowling Alone*, New York: Simon and Schuster, 1999.

12 G. Delanty, *Community*, London, Routledge, 2003, p. 12.

13 *The Federalist*, Middletown, CT: Wesleyan University Press, 1961.

14 M. Duverger, *Political Parties: Their Organization and Activities in the Modern State*, London: Methuen, 1954; K. Janda, *Political Parties: A Cross-National Survey*, New York: Free Press, 1988.

15 J. Buchanan and G. Tullock, *The Calculus of Consent*, Ann Arbor, MI: University of Michigan Press, 1962.

16 K. Shepsle and B. Weingast (eds), *Positive Theories of Congressional Institutions*, Ann Arbor, MI: University of Michigan Press, 1995.

17 It is worth noting that some American researchers disagree with the view that congressmen can be regarded as independent actors. G. Cox and M. McCubbins, on the contrary, argue that it is the party system that plays a decisive role in the functioning of the US Congress, see G. Cox and M. McCubbins, *Legislative Leviathan: Party Government in the House*, Berkeley, CA: University of California Press, 1993.

18 R. Katz and P. Mair, 'Changing models of party organization and party democracy: the emergence of the cartel party', *Party Politics*, Vol. 1, No. 1, 1995, pp. 5–28.

19 J. Schumpeter, *Capitalism, Socialism, and Democracy*, London: Allen and Unwin, 1943.

20 Since the completion of this research the number of federal subjects has fallen to 83.

21 Regional legislatures are also referred to as legislative assemblies or dumas, and in a number of regions the old term 'council' has been retained.

22 Deviations from the 'normal cycles' in some regions are described in the Appendix.

23 Furthermore, final and comprehensive election results are unavailable in some regions.

24 G. Golosov, 'Electoral systems and party formation in Russia: a cross-regional analysis', *Comparative Political Studies*, Vol. 36, No. 8, 2003, pp. 912–35.

25 M. Duverger, *Political Parties: Their Organization and Activities in the Modern State*, London: Methuen, 1954.

26 A. Lijphart (ed.), *Electoral Systems and Party Systems: A Study of Twenty-Seven Democracies, 1945–1990*, Oxford: Oxford University Press, 1994; R. Taagepera and M. Shugart, *Seats and Votes: The Effects and Determinants of Electoral Systems*, New Haven, CT: Yale University Press, 1989.

27 See, for example, V. Gel'man, S. Ryzhenkov and M. Brie, *Making and Breaking Democratic Transitions: The Comparative Politics of Russia's Regions*, Lanham, MD: Rowman and Littlefield, 2003.

28 At times such groups were formalized into so-called 'deputy groups' which are essentially 'non-party factions'.

29 A. Steen and V. Gel'man (eds), *Elites and Democratic Development in Russia*, London and New York: Routledge, 2003.

30 Quite often politicians running for political office will seek to conceal their party affiliation, and will run as 'independent' candidates.

31 In some cases such as St Petersburg, Altai Krai and Novosibirsk Oblast there are other factors at work which explain the high party saturation of their legislatures.

32 A number of regions have a much smaller number of deputies elected by PR. In Kaliningrad Oblast only 5 of the 32 deputies were elected in this way. Koryak and Ust-Ordynskii Buryatskii autonomous okrugs used the mixed system only in the second cycle of elections (4 out of 12, and 4 out of 19 respectively, were elected on the basis of proportionality). In addition, three regions (Saratov Oblast, Republic of Tyva and Republic of Marii El) used PR in the first round of elections but subsequently abandoned it.

33 E. S. Herron and M. Nishikawa, 'Contamination effects and the number of parties in mixed-superposition electoral systems', *Electoral Studies*, Vol. 20, No. 1, 2001, pp. 63–86.

34 G. Golosov, *Political Parties in the Regions of Russia: Democracy Unclaimed*, Boulder, CO: Lynne Reinner, 2004.

35 The underdevelopment of political parties in most regional assemblies in 2002–3 was the reason why a minimum share (50 per cent) of deputies elected on the basis of PR was introduced in majority of regions. Three regions – Daghestan, Moscow Oblast and St Petersburg – chose a completely proportional system.

36 Including Chechnya, which is not included in our analysis. Besides, in Sverdlovsk and Vologda oblasts elections were held twice.

37 M. Laakso and R. Taagepera, 'Effective number of parties: a measure with application to West Europe', *Comparative Political Studies*, Vol. 12, No. 3, 1979.
38 While calculating the ENP index I did not take into account non-party deputies because their number had drastically diminished and did not distort the overall picture.
39 Regretfully, excluding opponents from the ballot under the pretext that they violated electoral legislation is common practice in Russian regions.
40 This section is mostly based on the empirical data gathered in participant observations and expert reports.
41 One of the main reasons for this was the fact that the interests of the most influential groups did not directly overlap. Each of them were in control of their own sphere.
42 In actual fact, these rules were applied in 2006 to the Perm Krai Legislature elections, not the oblast legislature elections, as in 2005 Perm Oblast and Komi-Permyak Autonomous Okrug were merged to form a new subject of the Federation – Perm Krai.
43 In Perm Oblast United Russia won 30.72 per cent of the ballot, which was comparable with the votes cast for Unity and OVR together in 1999 (19.82 per cent and 10.03 per cent respectively).
44 In addition, because of the ongoing merger he could not become a fully-fledged Governor for legal reasons, having to make do with the status of 'acting' Governor for eighteen months. It was only once all the legalities regarding the formation of a new federal subject, Perm Krai, had been completed in December 2005, that full gubernatorial powers were bestowed upon him (according to the new laws, he was nominated by President Putin for the position of governor to the legislatures of Perm oblast and Komi-Permyak autonomous okrug and he received endorsement by both assemblies).
45 A lack of coordination between the central leadership and regional branches of United Russia has often been observed. For example, an acute collision of interests came about in the elections for the Belgorod Regional Assembly in 2005. The regional branch of United Russia actively campaigned against candidates unofficially supported by the mayor of Moscow, Yury Luzhkov, who is one of the most influential leaders of United Russia. The conflict had been fuelled by overlapping financial and economic interests.
46 'Permskim edinorossam ne chvataet mesta v predviybornych spiskach?', Noviy Kompan' on Website, http://www.nk.perm.ru/news.php?news_id = 5236, accessed 17 August 2006.
47 It is worth noting that in an overwhelming majority of the winning single-member constituencies United Russia candidates had no serious rivals. In some cases it was explained by the great private resources of the candidates. In other cases political bargaining and pressure cleared the constituencies of opponents.
48 Respectively 11.08 per cent and 14.75 per cent in 1995; 14.15 per cent and 7.51 per cent in 1999; 7.62 per cent and 12.91 per cent in 2003.
49 Plotnikov was accused of 'bribing' voters, which had allegedly taken place in the form of promises of improving the welfare of pensioners. Other candidates have also resorted to the same false promises in their election campaigns.
50 The conflict between these three parties in the process of unification has taken place in many regions. Some parties' branches do not like to be seen as one of the 'party of power' as is the case with 'A Just Russia' (the St Petersburg branch of Rodina joined the Patriots of Russia instead of a Just Russia). Others on the contrary do not like to be the second 'party of power' (the Tatarstan branch of the Russian Pensioners' Party cooperated with United Russia instead of a A Just Russia).

51 In 2003 the State Duma election the party also had fairly good result in Perm region – 4.38 per cent.
52 After amendments were introduced to the Federal Law in 2004, to be officially recognized a political party must have no less than 500 members (formerly 100) in over half of the subjects of the Federation.

8   The representation of business elites in regional politics

Étatism, elitism, and clientelism

Rostislav Turovskii

Business and politics are closely connected. Many members of the business elite are members of influential interest groups. In democratic polyarchies, western students of political science have noted the disproportionate influence of large economic corporations in the political process.[1] The role of economic corporations with their resources and political interests is one of the reasons for a deformation of polyarchies, in which the dispersion of power is far from even.

Russia is clearly not a western-type polyarchy. The concentration of power in the hands of certain influence groups is much higher than in the West, and politically active business structures usually compete with high-ranking state officials for influence or enter into clientelistic relations with them. The Russian situation should be analysed from the standpoint of elitism, rather than competitive polyarchy because of this massive concentration of power in the hands of power and business elites. Members of these economic and political elites are closely intertwined and at the same time split into rivalling groups.

Unequal access to power has been characteristic of Russia at every stage of its history. The post-Soviet period is no exception, epitomized as it is by a sharp increase in socio-economic inequalities and new and deeper forms of social inequality brought about in the transition from communism to capitalism. When public interest in politics is low, personal involvement is insignificant and party politics and interest group activity is badly organized, politics becomes a playground for small groups well endowed with financial resources and roots in the business environment, or those enjoying patrimonial–clientelistic relations with the business environment.

The universal rationality model, or 'rational choice theory', seems to be the most obvious analytic paradigm to employ when studying the political activity of business structures and individual entrepreneurs. This stems from another principle widely regarded as self-evident, namely that an entrepreneur is by definition a rational actor in the economic realm and that such rational behaviour will be transferred to the political realm. In our case gain means not only a growth of political influence, but also an expansion of the firms of those entrepreneurs who engage in politics. The political market, as referred to by Schumpeter,[2] can be viewed as analogous to the economic market, even as its extension, if groups with specific economic interests enter the political market.

The application of rational choice theory to the study of business elites entering politics has serious limitations. First of all, business interests connected with certain branches of the economy, types of ownership and enterprise, etc., must be considered in view of the authority of specific political institutions. Seeking a measure of control over political administrations may be considered optimal and rational behaviour on the part of businesses. Such control can be exercised indirectly through lobbying or through the direct infiltration of business representatives in legislative or executive bodies of state power.

Whilst studying the above-mentioned links, it is important to consider the specific economic model and political regime. The Russian model is often referred to as a form of state-bureaucratic capitalism, in which the bureaucracy performs a number of regulatory functions and possesses massive capabilities for influencing or pressurizing businesses. At the same time the existence of a widespread shadow economy, and a tolerant attitude towards it on the part of the bureaucracy, creates infinite possibilities for manipulating legislation in order to put pressure on some businesses whilst stimulating the growth of others. The following areas can be identified in which the interests of both businesses and political structures intersect:

- Regulating functions of state and municipal administrations, in particular licensing various economic activities, including the exploitation of mineral resources.
- Aspects of economic reforms such as the privatization of state and municipal property or the leasing of state and municipal assets (including land, forests, real estate, etc.).
  The activity of the state as an economic actor, including public and municipal procurement. Partnerships between private business and the state, such as the co-financing of joint projects, are now widespread.
- Threats of state sanctions which constitute a permanent threat to business. The imposition of such sanctions is used by the state, often in an underhand way, to secure the loyalty of businesses.
- Lobbying for state support for economic projects, both direct (through representatives of business structures in the authorities) and indirect (through professional lobbyists working with various clients).

In this study we analyse the relationships between business elites and regional authorities in Russia. The rationale governing the political behaviour of business elites can be described as a 'rule of conformity'. This rule defines the correlation between the interests of businesses in power, and the delimitation of competencies between various levels of power. In other words, a business is interested in extending control over that level of power, which is responsible for taking decisions vital for that business.

At the same time one must take into account the important changes in the nature of business interests when economic elites successfully gain access to political power. They immediately stop being purely business interests. From the perspective of rational choice theory, new incentives emerge, namely the retention of power, which, in turn, leads to demands to integrate into the existing political system on the most beneficial terms. In the long run, such political behaviour provides an opportunity for successfully solving economic issues. In Russia, where competition on the political – as well as any other – market is suppressed and heavily regulated, it is in the interests of businessmen to become loyal actors. Political opposition would bring unacceptable economic risks. Loyalty to the relevant powers – to the president, regional governors or city mayors – a majority of whom operate within monocentric regimes where there is no viable opposition – is the most rational and common pattern of business–state relations. Moreover, one must not forget the 'rule of conformity', since political loyalty is rational and necessary in relations with those bodies of power that are meaningful for that given business. Amongst the most common types of entrepreneurial political behaviour is membership of United Russia, and participation in elections to regional legislatures on the United Russia party list. Entrepreneurs may also act as party sponsors.

On the other hand, rational choice theory is incapable of providing an explanation for all aspects of business–power relations in modern Russia. Business in Russia is socially active and interested in gaining access to administrative resources, and in cooperation with bureaucracies, taking power under its control. Representatives of business, however, are an insignificant minority among governors and mayors. A more nuanced theory is required, and neo-institutionalism, which in particular 'brings the state back in',[3] is the most relevant. While applying the neo-institutionalist paradigm we proceed from the belief that the relationship between rationality and political behaviour is empirical in character.[4] Some Russian businessmen go into politics; others (they are an overwhelming majority) do not. It would be inaccurate to consider the former as winners and the latter as losers. The rationality of the political behaviour of businessmen is conditioned by the dominant political culture, institutional context and current political situation (alignment of forces). The non-interference of businessmen in politics often turns out to be a more rational model of behaviour. This does not allow businesses to reap super-profits, but at the same time it is a safeguard against political risks that could destroy a business if the political situation changed. In Russia the need for adapting business structures' political behaviour to bureaucratic interests and the institutional context is extremely high because of the strong bureaucratic tradition that dates back to the times of the Russian Empire, and which even after the disintegration of the Soviet Union still remains largely intact.

Let us consider the influence of political culture on the behaviour of business elites in politics. Business people are by definition representative of a more active political culture than society in general. It is also possible to assume that in Russia entrepreneurs will have high levels of political participation, a high personal interest in politics and a low level of trust in the authorities. If this assumption is accurate, then political culture has to provide incentives for their political participation and determine its nature and intensity. Though from an empirical point of view it is impossible to speak about universal participation of the business elite in politics, each individual political decision is the result of a choice conditioned by personal preference. The political culture of Russian business could become a separate subject for research, as at present it is scarce and fragmented (especially when it comes to regional businesses). One must note that social activity does not automatically transform into political activity, which is a vivid characteristic of socially mobile strata of Russian society. This is also evident from the seemingly paradoxically high level of participation in elections among the older voters and much lower figures for the younger people and business elites.

The dominant political culture in Russia is characterized by a medium level of political interest; loyalty to the authorities in the 2000s has been growing in intensity (in the 1990s, according to our estimates, Russian political culture could have been characterized as 'autonomous', but at present it may have been transformed into 'subject'[5]). Even although some entrepreneurs in Russia are politically active, they cannot fail to take into account the dominance of the wider national political culture and play by its rules. These rules, in particular, presuppose that displaying high levels of political participation, independence and initiative may be punished (as illustrated by the YUKOS case).

From the viewpoint of business, political activity can alleviate some political risks by giving entrepreneurs greater access to the political decision-making process and providing greater opportunities to forecast the development of the business environment (the process of decision-making in Russia has never been – and still is not – transparent or public). This is one optimal path involving maximum political participation without becoming oppositional. There is another approach epitomized by the phrase 'more haste, less speed'. Political participation under the conditions of non-free competition creates other risks related to the struggle for positions of power – the rise of enemies, the need to enter into clientelistic relations with some officials and sharp competition with others.

It is hardly surprising that in such a situation each entrepreneur faces the problem of personal choice. The passive (or adaptational) model of political behaviour presupposes a constant adaptation to the changing model of the relations between business and power. In this case business in politics only exists at the level of non-associated interest groups. The active model of political behaviour has various forms:

- Membership in business associations: 'The Russian Union of Industrialists and Entrepreneurs', regional unions of industrialists and entrepreneurs, 'Business Russia, 'OPORa of Russia' (an association of small and medium enterprises), and a network of chambers of trade and commerce. In practice, in such associations the political interests of business are aggregated rather poorly. This can be partially explained by the individualism and competitiveness of the business environment, where actors pursue their personal gains. As most recent Russian experience shows, the pressure from a stronger state has led not to consolidation of business, but to a search for individual expansion and survival strategies while maintaining political loyalty. Under Putin we have witnessed a growing dependency of large business on the state. This stems from the corrupt nature of big business, which often conducts illegal or semi-legal commercial operations. We have also witnessed the government's use of the power ministries and the judiciary for political purposes. As a result, the aggregation of political interests does not always take place within the framework of business associations, but rather is conducted through non-institutionlized forums based upon family and friendship ties, common economic interests and joint projects. The following relations are common:

- Lobbying business interests in bodies of authority. The sphere of government relations is becoming increasingly popular in Russian companies, though one has to admit that there are few of them whose work in this area is very effective. Russian lobbyism is still at its early stages of development where it operates in corrupt forms. Its development (in any form) is conditioned by a number of factors, among which are the officials' competency and their understanding of business interests, as well as their actual capabilities (which are often overestimated by business people because they have no clear understanding of decision-making mechanisms, scope of authority, budgetary limitations and conflicts within power structures). Another important factor is that bureaucrats' own strategies that vary and are not always *a priori* obvious. They could have an interest either in cooperation with business or in administrative control over business, i.e. readiness to play the role of client of a business group, or a desire to become an influential patron. It is possible that some bureaucratic groups may become amalgamated with certain business groups to the detriment of others, or that they perform a careful balancing act and try to maintain relations with several business groups.

- Direct entry of representatives of business in power structures. This results from the weakness of business associations and the low effectiveness of indirect lobbying. The most widespread form is entrepreneurs running for elected regional and municipal offices. This form is particularly convenient because the majority of the deputies in the regions work on a part-time basis, combining public service with their main occupation. As regards full-time work in executive bodies of power, this would require a complete transition from business to politics. This is one of the reasons why taking up a position in executive bodies is hardly a rational model of political behaviour for business executives. Amongst civil servants there are far more former managers of small businesses than there are representatives of larger companies. Industrialists from big business prefer to create networks of their 'people' in the regional and local administrations.

One can often come across the chain reaction principle in politics. It comes into play when competition springs up between different business groups not only over economic niches, but also over the struggle for political influence. The economic interests of business groups may not collide, but their competition on the political field is determined by their struggle over gaining priority in the decision-making process and the distribution of state resources. In this case the activity of one business group may automatically cause the others to come out of 'hibernation', thus starting a chain reaction. In other words, one can speak about 'a vortex of political participation', sucking in more and more business actors.

The influence of the institutional context is also very important for political activity in business. The level of such political activity depends on the transformation of the political regime and institutions, as well as on the focus of this activity on the various bodies of authority or other political institutions. In the more competitive and polycentric political and economic environment of the 1990s business played a more active and independent role. It took more independent decisions, including promoting its own candidates in elections at various levels, often achieving impressive results. Under monocentrism, characteristic of the Putin political regime, authoritarianism and bureaucratic regulation have intensified, forcing business structures to demonstrate political loyalty and informally consult the authorities about their interests and political actions.[6] Business has returned to the tactics of forming alliances with the bureaucracy, which has once again started to feel that it is a powerful force. As a result of this, the bureaucracy's interest in appointing business leaders to decision-making positions has diminished. The bureaucracy now strives to patronize business from its position of power. Thus, for example, one of the consequences of Putin's abolition of gubernatorial elections was the strengthening of business interest in winning seats in municipal and regional legislatures.

The organization of interaction between business and power in Russia can be described in the terms of corporatism, étatism and political management networks. Russian corporatism has been the subject of many studies.[7] However, some specific features of its development should be clarified. Russian corporatism is characterized by a high degree of étatism, i.e. étatism displaces classic corporatism observed in some western countries. The state in Russia plays an active role instead of the 'simple' and 'democratic' representation of public interests, and the bureaucracy is indeed a corporation with its own interests which are strictly adhered to.[8]

At the same time, the Russian government is not involved in classic corporatist tripartite negotiations. There is interaction between power and business in which the bureaucracy utilizes power resources to establish its superiority. Russian corporatism does presuppose the creation of consultative forums for business leaders within political administrations, including the offices of regional governors. However, the influence of such forums has proved to be insignificant, their decisions are the result not of open debates but behind-the-scenes deals. The role of the third party, the trade unions, in the power–business dialogue is virtually non-existent. It is more accurate, therefore, to speak about an etatistic-clientelistic model of interaction between the authorities and business in Russia.

The political-management networks model is more relevant than the classic corporatist model. A network includes actors, interests, power interaction and collective actions.[9] Informal network structures, uniting power and business, are typical of Russia. Their influence is much stronger than the consultative bodies discussed above. It is in the framework of such networks that a significant, if not overwhelming number of decisions are made.

Étatism assigns the state a leading role while 'not allowing' business to 'privatize' the state, holding it at a certain distance and interacting with it by means of clientelistic and networking relations. The more recent penetration of business elites in power structures following the abolition of gubernatorial elections in 2005 is a break with past practice and should be viewed as exception rather than as a rule. These processes, however, are also connected with the specificity of elite formation, hence more attention needs to be devoted to analysing the specificity of Russian elites.

Elitism offers a different set of coordinates from which to study the infiltration of business elites into political bodies. For representatives of the business elite, infiltrating the state in conditions of Russian étatism is important for maintaining and reinforcing their elite status. They often count on expanding their political status whilst preserving their business positions. Sometimes business people make up for a loss in business status by going into politics, thereby retaining their membership in the elite.

Russian elitism in the present historical period has its own peculiarities. As regards the relationship between democracy and elitism there is an obvious shift towards the latter. At the same time one cannot speak about competitive elitism in Schumpeter's understanding of the term,[10] or pluralism of elites, as defined by Dahl.[11] In Russia one can witness the development (or preservation) of authoritarian elitism.

Moreover, in Russia we have elitism, but the incomplete formation of elites. It is not the first time in Russian history that the elite, the ruling class, has undergone major changes in its formation. After the 2000 presidential election, when a new president was sworn in, this process entered a new stage: new influence groups, earlier connected with Putin or having secured his support, started to exert pressure on the old ones. Among the new, post-Soviet elites there is a fierce struggle for a 'place under the sun'. It is, however, inaccurate to talk about a conflict of political generations, about a struggle between the old Soviet nomenklatura and the new post-communist business elites. The struggle is between mixed elite groups that have sprung up sporadically in the process of privatization bringing together members of the top business and bureaucratic elites.

The formation of the post-Soviet elite has been directly linked to economic reform and particularly privatization and liberalization of the economy. The desire of the politically active part of the business elites to shape the power elite, or at least influence its activity, is rather natural. From the point of view of the business elite, the key task of political authorities is to represent the social interests of the business circles: namely, the accumulation of capital from privatization programmes, and the establishment of strategic positions at all levels of the economy which will ensure the stability and the prosperity of the businesses.

Finally, there are some aspects in the relations between business and power that are connected with neither rational behaviour nor the institutionalized context. Lasswell's behaviourist model which focuses on decision making at the micro-level and the importance of psychological factors is particularly useful.[12] In this approach it is argued that the behaviour of the business elite can be explained using psychological concepts. For instance the active involvement of entrepreneurs in politics can be explained by the increasing popularity of political activity as a model of behaviour for entrepreneurs. Such behaviour patterns are emulated by other entrepreneurs and simultaneously become the means of reaffirming their elite status (for example, through election to regional legislatures, even though the institutional influence of such assemblies is weak).

Businessmen-governors in Russia

Our research focused on fifteen federal subjects where power is in the hands of former businessmen of various origins, including those coming from state-owned companies. The number of regions where businessmen or CEOs from large companies have come to power is modest and hardly exceeds 20 per cent of all federal subjects. This is a clear indication of the fact that Russian elitism does not facilitate the infiltration of representatives of business into power, and furthermore that regional bureaucracies, formed in the 1990s or even in the Soviet period, have been renewed very slowly and mostly from within their own ranks, rather than recruiting from business. Before their abolition, gubernatorial elections were an important means of renewing the elites, but in practice it was not often that business managers were able to secure a victory over candidates with a more 'traditional' background in politics.

It is interesting to note that very few of the regions headed by a members of the business elite are economically developed. One would expect people with business connections to come to power in rich regions where the political environment is more competitive, but in our case studies this is not the case. Among such regions are Krasnoyarsk Krai, where Khloponin, a representative of one of the leading Russian business groups (Interros, including Norilsk Nikel), won the gubernatorial seat in 2002, and Perm Krai (formerly Perm Oblast), where in 2004 local businessman Chirkunov replaced his business partner, Trutnev, who won the 2000 election. But usually in wealthy and polycentric regions the elites need a governor with no direct links to any particular business who can play the role of arbiter. Regional authorities headed by arbiters often turn out to be more robust; by establishing links with various groups they are more successful in resisting attempts by powerful groups to take power under their control. In Krasnoyarsk Krai and Perm Oblast the diminishing credibility and/or instability of the previous administration paved the way for a more radical change of elites to the advantage of some business groups. But such examples are rare.

Paradoxical, businessmen are more liable to come to power in poor and underdeveloped regions which depend for their survival on financial aid. In Kalmykiya the transfer of power into the hands of the young businessman Ilyumzhinov happened as early as 1993, which was the first case ever in Russian history.[13] Among regions in the central part of Russia, the least developed are Pskov and Bryansk oblasts. In these regions in 2004 representatives of business elites (Kuznetsov and Denin) came to power. The economic situation in Tver' Oblast was hardly any better, but nonetheless Zelenin, a well-known Moscow entrepreneur, was elected as Governor in 2004.

Special attention should be given to the northern autonomous okrugs where the number of governors coming from business groups is especially high. The remote Koryak, Chukotka, Evenkia and Taimyr autonomous okrugs lie in extremely inhospitable natural and climatic zones, and lack such a strong resource base as Khanty-Mansiysk and Yamalo-Nenets autonomous okrugs, the leading producers of oil and natural gas in Russia. Each of the above-mentioned districts has promising deposits of natural resources, but their exploitation requires huge investments. In such regions the population is scarce and the territory is vast. In other words, they are hardly an asset for a businessman. Nonetheless, businessmen have been winning elected offices in these regions as well. One of the most powerful Russian oligarchs, Abramovich, won the 2000 gubernatorial election in Chukotka; in 2001 Khloponin became governor of Taimyr (he was later elected governor of Krasnoyarsk Krai, whereas in Taimyr a representative of the same business group, Budargin, took over as Governor); later the YUKOS manager Zolotarev won in Evenkia. Finally, in 2005 Kozhemyako, a prominent fishing tycoon from Primorskiy Krai, became Governor of the Koryak Autonomous Okrug.

The remaining examples are taken from relatively large but averagely developed regions. In Primorskiy Krai the 2001 gubernatorial election brought to power Dar'kin, who had business interests in fishing and agriculture. Primorskiy Krai, Russia's gateway to the Asia-Pacific area, has considerable economic development potential, but its economy is currently rather weak, and the region is one of the country's largest recipients of federal aid. Following the 2005 presidential initiatives, former directors of state-owned enterprises came to power by presidential nomination in three regions: Tishanin in Irkutsk Oblast (from Russian Railways), Ipatov in Saratov Oblast (from Rosenergoatom) and Dudka in Tula Oblast (from a large military-industrial complex enterprise).

Thus, the change of power elites in regions in favour of the business elite has, to a large extent, been going along the line of least resistance from the state. It has occurred in regions where there were no stable ruling bureaucratic groups or where the latter has become delegitimatized in the eyes of the electorate. A difficult and volatile socio-economic situation could have become one of the delegitimatizing factors for the previous elites. However, the case of a businessman coming to power in a poorer region is only valid because power is easier to get in such a region. At the same time, another question arises – how rational is it for a businessman to secure power in such an unattractive region?

Most of the governors' biographies show that they are outsiders, and that they made their careers outside the regions which they head. There are far fewer cases of top regional officials coming from within the same region. For example, Dudka, who was born and lived all his life in Tula, made his career at his factory and was nominated for governor. The Primorkiy Krai Governor Dar'kin is also a local resident who made his career in his native region. The Governor of Perm Krai, Chirkunov is also of local origin (born in Murmansk Oblast but moved to Perm in his childhood), as is the governor of Bryansk Oblast, Denin (born in Bryansk Oblast). The Governor of Saratov Oblast, Ipatov, was born in Sverdlovsk Oblast, but made his career in Saratov Oblast, where he became director of the Balakovskaya Nuclear Power Station back in 1989 and remained in this position almost until his nomination for governor.

There are also cases of someone from a region making a career in Moscow and then coming back to their native region as governor, using their superiority in terms of resources and influence (the come-back model). This was the first example of electing a businessman, Ilyumzhinov, for the office of president of Kalmykia in 1993. Ilyumzhinov graduated from university and then went into business in Moscow and returned to Kalmykia only because of the election. There is a similar example in another economically underdeveloped southern republic, Kabardino-Balkaria, where Putin appointed Kanokov as president in 2005. The latter had for many years been a successful businessman in Moscow. He also became a State Duma deputy on the LDPR party's list (later he joined United Russia).

Examples of entrepreneurs or company CEOs with no connection with a region being elected or appointed as governors are of particular interest. One example is Zolotarev, a native of Krasnodar Krai, who made his career in the Moscow business groups Menatep and YUKOS led by Khodorkovsky and was sent by his company to run for governor in Evenkia. Another example is Tver's Governor Zelenin, who had made his career in Moscow and had no interest in Tver Oblast prior to his election.

In other cases outsider entrepreneurs gradually integrate into the local environment (the gradual integration model). For example, Abramovich at the end of 1990 had business interests in Chukotka, and he became a leading figure in the region after his election to the State Duma in 1999 from a single-member constituency in the region, and subsequently as governor in 2000. The nominations of Khloponin and Budargin as governors of Krasnoyarsk Krai and Taimyr are the result of the expansion of the Moscow-based group Interros and its purchase of Norilsk Nikel, a company vital for both regions. Khloponin started his career in Moscow and came to Norilsk as director of Norilsk Nikel, from where he moved to become governor.[14] Primorskiy Krai is the native region of not only the Governor Dar'kin, but also of Kozhemyako. The latter, having control over one of the largest fishing companies in Russia, expanded his business into Kamchatka Oblast and Koryak Autonomous Okrug where he managed to secure a place in the fishing business. Kozhemyako was appointed governor of Koryak Autonomous Okrug.

Examples of gradual integration of outsider entrepreneurs into a regional economy and their subsequent nomination for governor can be found in other regions as well. The Pskov Governor, Kuznetsov, for many years had been a businessman in Moscow and a Duma deputy elected on the Liberal Democratic Party of Russia (LDPR) party list. He became interested in Pskov Oblast only after another LDPR member, Mikhailov, was elected governor in 1996 and opened up the region for affiliated businesses. This allowed Kuznetsov to acquire assets in the region and then, after a conflict with the serving governor, to take part in a number of election campaigns and, finally, win the office of governor in 2004.

The model of gradual integration in a region can be illustrated by the example of Irkutsk Oblast. Tishanin was born in the Urals, in Chelyabinsk Oblast, where he worked until 2001 (when he gained the position of deputy director of Southern Urals Railways). In 2001 he was transferred to Chita Oblast, in Siberia, where he worked at the Transbaikalia Railways. Tishanin moved to Irkutsk only in 2004 to become head of the Eastern Siberian Railways. In 2005 Putin appointed him governor of Irkutsk Oblast.

Thus, while in most cases it is representatives of the business elite from Moscow or other regions who are nominated for gubernatorial positions, in a 'softer' version it is a region's natives who have made it in the capital. The superiority of such business elites over local elites creates a wide spectrum of attitudes to the new governor – from overly elevated hopes and expectations to blunt aversion to the outsider. Fostering local entrepreneurs directly in a region so that they can capture the office of governor, on the other hand, is a rare phenomenon. Regional-level businessmen are too weak to secure power in rich regions, and in poor regions it is the 'outsiders' who are more successful.

A wide variety of businessmen-governors of various status and origin have appeared in Russia. Among large industrialists, the so-called 'oligarchs', the only example is Abramovich in Chukotka, which is an exception rather than a rule. Moreover, Abramovich's career as governor is close to the end as he tries to get Putin's approval and resign. The majority of businessmen-governors are representatives of medium-sized businesses, both from the capital and from the regions. For them the position of governor approximates with their status in the Russian elite. Former CEOs of large companies are another type of governor. Finally, chief executives of large state-owned companies form a separate category. The appearance of such managers is a consequence of the strengthening in the early 2000s of the political influence of state-owned companies, which have direct access to the head of state.

Changes in regional elites

The election/appointment of businessmen to governorships usually leads to a circulation and rejuvenation of the regional elites. Thus, for example, when Ilyumzhinov, Khloponin, Abramovich, Dar'kin, Kuznetsov and Tishanin came to power, they were barely 40 years of age (Ilyumzhinov just turned 31). At that time only Ipatov was over 50, but he represented a different type – an experienced manager who had made his career during the communist era. Just over half the businessmen-governors were age 40–50 by the time they came to power, which for Russian regional leaders is considered to be young. Such a renewal of the regional elite often stimulates radical changes in the political life of the region.

A detailed analysis of how governors have come to power shows that their initial level of electoral support was rather low. Of the fifteen governors in our study, nine were elected and six were appointed by the president. The only case when a businessman received an absolute endorsement by the electorate was Abramovich who won 90.6 per cent of the votes. Abramovich, however, was considered to be the only serious candidate in that election. The former Governor, Nazarov, a representative of the local elite, withdrew from the race and gave his support to Abramovich.

In other regions electoral competition was much fiercer. Only Ilyumzhinov and Zolotarev managed to secure 50 per cent of the vote in the first round. They were competing in poor and disadvantaged regions where the former elites had lost influence and popularity. In Evenkiya the former governor Bokovikov, following the 'Chukotka model', did not stand for office and supported Zolotarev. However, there appeared competition of a different type – between oil companies, because his competitor Vasilyev (from Krasnoyarsk, i.e. an outsider for Evenkia) was supported by the oil company Slavneft (Zolotarev secured 51.1 per cent of the vote, whereas Vasilyev got 35.3 per cent). Ilyumzhinov came to power amidst a sharp conflict between warring nomenklatura clans in Kalmykia, which led to a disruption of the 1991 presidential elections (neither of the two main candidates won over 50 per cent of the votes, which according to local legislation required a new election to be called). The main competitors were influential kalmyks who had established themselves in Moscow: entrepreneur Ilyumzhinov (who won 63 per cent of the votes) and the army general Ochirov (21 per cent). Later on, the support for Ilyumzhinov was 'artificially' raised to an even higher level (in the 1995 single-candidate election, when he secured 85.1 per cent of the vote), and then started to decline (in 2002 Ilyumzhinov failed to win the first round, winning only 47.3 per cent, but he won the second round with 57.2 per cent).

Khloponin's victory in Taimyr became possible in the first round of elections, although his competitor was Governor Nedelin, who had been the region's leader since Soviet times. The influence of Norilsk Nikel in Taimyr, where this company is the largest in the regional economy, and Khloponin's appealing image played a positive role in his victory. The director general of Norilsk Nikel won 62.8 per cent in the 2001 election, whereas Nedelin received only 32.4 per cent. At the same time, much more effort was required for Khloponin's success in Krasnoyarsk Krai. In the northern part of the region, where Khloponin's popularity was at its highest, the population is low. Also in Krasnoyarsk Krai regional patriotic sentiment, characteristic of Siberia, is widespread. In the first round of the 2002 elections Khloponin came second with 25.2 per cent of the vote, and it was only in the second round that he was able to gain victory with 48 per cent, against the 42 per cent received by his opponent, Uss, who was the speaker of the regional legislature. A lack of unity among the elite in Krasnoyarsk, which had never had stable gubernatorial power, was an important factor in Khloponin's success. Veprev, an agricultural manager who was appointed governor in 1991, was replaced after his retirement in 1993 by economist Zubov. In 1998 he lost to the influential Moscow politician, General Lebed, who was third in the 1996 presidential election. This was the first time that a politician with no local roots had been elected governor of a Russian region. Under Lebed, Krasnoyarsk Krai was torn apart by conflicts, and after his death in a helicopter crash in 2002, there were no local leaders with enough popularity to win power. Since the Krasnoyarsk elite was in a state of disintegration, Khloponin with his financial resources and attractive image was able to win the election. After that, the election in Taimyr was easily won by Budargin who also had links with Norilsk Nikel, and who prior to the gubernatorial elections had served as mayor of Norilsk.

The disintegration of the local elite and the discrediting of a corrupt governor created favourable conditions for Zelenin's victory in Tver Oblast. Governor Platov could not even scrape through the first round, and the election turned into a struggle between two Moscow candidates. Zelenin's main rival, Zubov, was a police general who had connections with the large business group, 'AFK Sistema'. Zelenin won by securing 43 per cent of the vote in the first round and 57.4 per cent in the second. He was supported by Putin's 'party of power', United Russia.

It should be noted that entrepreneurs of lesser significance have had a much harder time. Their initial level of support was very low because of a lack of popularity among the electorate and the much more modest resources available to them. Kuznetsov was initially connected with a large business group; he was a founder of MDM-Bank, currently one of the biggest in Russia. Later, however, he split with his partners and went his own way in Pskov Oblast. When the regional elites were in a state of disintegration, Kuznetsov became one of many opponents of the failing governor Mikhailov. In 2000 Kuznetsov was third in the election for governor. In 2004 in the first round he did not win many votes, only 18.4 per cent, but this result allowed him to enter the second round and, playing on widespread popular discontent was able to beat the incumbent Mikhailov, who was supported by United Russia. It is hardly surprising that he has very difficult relations with the Kremlin.

In the 2001 gubernatorial elections in Primorskiy Krai, Dar'kin did not enjoy much support either. In this region the circulation of elites was precipitated by the absence of a strong regional leader, but whereas in Tver and Pskov Oblasts the situation could be explained by the low credibility and poor managerial competence of the serving governors, in Primorskiy Krai the turmoil was created by the removal to the federal government of a strong governor, Nazdratenko. This led to several candidates being put forward, one of whom was the entrepreneur Dar'kin. The Kremlin supported another candidate, Apanasenko, who, however, had no support from the local elites, and who worked in neighbouring Khabarovsk (i.e. was not perceived as a 'native'). As a result, only two candidates entered the second round, Dar'kin (receiving only 23.9 per cent of the vote) and the well-known local populist politician and former Vladivostok mayor Cherepkov, who, however, was barred from participating in the second round. This allowed Apanasenko to continue the race in the second round, but he lost to Dar'kin nonetheless. The latter secured 40.2 per cent in the second round, but after an intense struggle managed to win the gubernatorial seat.

The Governor of Bryansk Oblast Denin was no popular figure. Earlier, he was unsuccessful in the 1999 State Duma elections, when he was the runner-up in a single-member constituency, and in 2000 he came second in the election for governor with a poor 21.15 per cent of the votes. Only in 2003, when Denin joined United Russia and enlisted its support, did he win a Duma seat, after which he entered the 2004 gubernatorial race. His chances for success were largely boosted by the fact that the serving communist governor Lodkin was barred from running for the office, as the centre did not want to see him re-elected. In these circumstances Denin became the favourite. Failing to beat his opponents in the first round when he received 44.75 per cent of the votes, he was victorious in the second round winning an overwhelming majority of the votes (77.8 per cent).

In the remaining case studies governors never had to pass an electoral test, as they were appointed by the president in 2005. At the same time the results of sociological studies show that the level of public support for many of them is low.

Overall, the analysis of elections and appointments shows that when businessmen or CEOs of large companies come to power in a region, it is primarily a consequence of the current alignment of forces within the elites (and subsequently the cause of a significant realignment of such forces). Representatives of business elites take up the empty niches formed after the break-up of local elites, or if a governor is discredited or moves on to work in another position elsewhere. This 'empty niche' rule applies to both gubernatorial elections and appointments. Kozhemyako was appointed after the president stripped the elected governor Loginov from his post (under Loginov the region had fallen into political and economic crisis). In an attempt to defuse conflicts within local elites in Irkutsk and Tula oblasts the centre decided to conduct an experiment and introduce a 'third party' which was not involved in those conflicts (in both cases, directors of large state-owned companies – a new recruitment reserve of the federal government in the 2000s). In Tula Oblast the centre was not happy with the then governor, Starodubtsev, who was a member of the Communist Party. In Irkutsk Oblast, the Governor Govorin had a solid power base but he had put himself in conflict with a number of opposing elite groups which were able to field their own candidates. The appointment of Kanokov in Kabardino-Balkaria took place after the incument President of the Republic, Kokov, had resigned on grounds of ill health (and died soon after) and under whom there had been a decline of the socio-economic situation in the region.[15] The reverse side of the 'empty niche' rule gives rise to a fairly random choice of regions, which are rarely among the economically developed and are, therefore, of little interest to business.

The analysis of the renewal of regional elites prompted when businessmen and entrepreneurs enter their ranks can be extended by studying the composition of the new teams. Changes in the membership of executive bodies of power can be quite radical. Usually, only a small number of the deputy governors retain their offices, and only those who are experienced specialists able to work with the new team. For example, in the Evenk AO one of the two first deputy governors is Bokova, who was in charge of economy and finance under the previous administration. In Pskov Oblast, the Deputy Governor for Social Issues, Demyanenko previously worked under the governors Tumanov and Mikhailov. In the Khloponin administration one of the first deputy governors is Kuzubov, who held various positions under Zubov and Lebed. In the Koryak AO Kozhemyako appointed as one of his deputies the former Governor Bronevich.

Relying on professional bureaucrats for support is widespread in Russian practice because it helps to make the transition of power more evolutionary, avoid unnecessary conflicts and retain relative political stability. An incoming governor usually adopts coalition policies vis-à-vis influential local groups. Even Zelenin, who in Tver Oblast relies on the team he had brought from Moscow, appointed an experienced local politician, Krasnov as Deputy Governor. Krasnov had previously been second in command under the previous Governor, Platov.

However, the majority of deputy governors have been brought in from the outside. Such appointments may offend local elites but there is general agreement that a governor should have *carte blanche* in forming his own team. In the long run, the most important assessment criterion is the competence of the new appointees. When Abramovich was elected governor of Chukotka, a new team was formed whose core consisted of Muscovites. Gorodilov, former vice-president of Sibneft, born in Noyabrsk, an oil producing town in Yamalo-Nenets AO, where Sibneft had most of its oil producing assets, became Abramovich's first deputy. He played a crucial role when the Governor was on one of his frequent trips outside the region.[16] A team comprised predominantly of Muscovites was formed by Tver Governor Zelenin, who, like Abramovich, has no local roots. Zelenin's first deputy Bershadskii used to work in the same business structures as Zelenin.[17]

When Khloponin came to power in Krasnoyarsk Krai, a large group of officials from Norilsk were given posts in the regional administration. The key positions are held by First Deputy Governor Kuznetsov, who used to be Khloponin's first deputy at Norilsk Nikel and in Taymyr Autonomous Okrug. Among those with a Norilsk origin are Sokol (chief of staff, former director of Norilskgazprom[18]), Gnezdilov (oversees natural resources and forestry; formerly employed by Norilskgazprom), Bobrov (industrial policy, former manager at Norilsk Nikel), Novak (in charge of finance; worked at Norilsk Nikel and in Norilsk city administration). Overall, Khloponin's administration consists of micro-groups of various origins, primarily from Norilsk and Krasnoyarsk City (those who used to work in Krasnoyarsk City Administration[19]), as well as those from various towns and rural areas of Krasnoyarsk Krai and officials working under the previous administration (for example, Kuzubov mentioned above). Such an administration is an example of a relatively balanced approach to team formation, when officials are recruited from various influential groups, whose members previously worked with the governor or were part of a newly formed alliance.

While analysing the composition of new regional administrations, one should take into account the vast differences in the previous status of new governors in the business elite. Arguably, only Khloponin and Abramovich represented really large financial-industrial groups (FIG) with their own recruitment reserve. In the rest of the cases, incoming governors formed their teams from their former subordinates and personal acquaintances who often had no experience of public service. Often a governor's own business became the recruitment ground; for example Roliz in Primorskiy Krai, and the Snezhka poultry factory in Bryansk Oblast. In Irkutsk Oblast many officials are originally from Chelyabinsk Oblast, i.e. the native region of Governor Tishanin. For example, Paranichev (who had previously worked in Chelyabinsk City Administration), was appointed First Deputy Governor.

As governors are now appointed, the federal officials involved in this process often integrate representatives of their own groups in new administrations. For instance, Yarin, who had worked in the office of Kozak, the Presidential Plenipotentiary Representative in the Southern Federal District (also in administrations in Vladimir and Ryazan oblasts and the Chechen Republic), became Prime-Minister in Kabardino-Balkariya.

Change of rule in regions makes the structure of the regional elite more complex and often sparks internal conflicts. In most cases, influential groups emerged that were hostile to the governor. For instance, in Irkutsk Oblast, Governor Tishanin, having defeated influential local politicians in his bid for the governorship, and having substituted the whole regional administration, soon found himself in conflict with the two largest centres of power – the regional legislature and the Irkutsk City Administration. Conflict between the regional governor and the mayor of the capital city is also evident in Pskov Oblast and relations between the governor of Primorskiy Krai and the mayor of the regional capital have been deteriorating. A common problem seems to be that 'businessmen-governors', as a rule, have limited political experience and poor connections with the regional elites. In the end, they fail to become consolidators of local elites, which in Russian conditions is one of the most important informal functions of a political leader. At best, thanks to the monocentrism of regional political regimes, observed nationwide, a governor often has to seek outward loyalty from other groups, which makes his power base very volatile.

As the analysis of businessmen-governors' political regimes shows, the regions are hardly moving towards democracy. Russian business is liberal only as far as the economy and the freedom of entrepreneurship are concerned. In politics, however, it often demonstrates strong authoritarian tendencies. Kalmykiya is a vivid example, where a young president, a businessman by origin, has established one of the harshest authoritarian regimes in Russia. The political regimes in Krasnoyarsk and Perm, however, look rather liberal, at least by Russian standards. At least in these two regions administrative resources are not concentrated in the hands of the governor and have not been employed to destroy the opposition. In these cases the governors' policies are more flexible and are based on compromise, and power is somewhat dispersed. These, however, are exceptions. Due to the particularities of the Russian period of the 'primitive accumulation of capital', entrepreneurs were matured in conditions of fierce and uncompromising competition, and such an experience could not but fail to leave a lasting imprint on their leadership styles. This is why it would be naïve to make a link between the current renewal of regional elites with a strengthening of democratic tendencies. Some new governors have illegal business dealings and maintain links with criminal cartels. The entry of businessmen into positions of political power has not led to a qualitative improvement in the openess and democratic credentials of the elites, and this is one of the key problems of political development in modern Russia.

Businessmen-governors and economic interests

The connection between the new governors' policies and the pursuit of their own personal and corporative gains in business following their accession to power in the region deserves special attention.

If one links business interests with regional competencies, or in other words searches for an economic rationale driving businessmen to run for gubernatorial offices, it becomes clear that the largest businesses currently have no interest in bringing governors under their total control. Large business in Russia deals with raw materials, and for the last few years decisions regarding the exploitation of natural resources (oil, natural gas, metal ores) have been under the competency of the centre. Similarly, today a governor is unable to create a 'most-favoured company regime' for a certain business, helping them to get grants for exploiting oil deposits, as was the case in the 1990s. Formerly, if YUKOS' protégé Zolotarev had become Governor of Evenkiya, this would have allowed it to strengthen its position in the region. Under new conditions this would be impossible without the agreement of the federal centre.

Other regional competencies useful for businesses were connected with the possibility of creating tax havens. Here we mean the right to abolish the regional component of the profit tax. Kalmykiya became the first large example of such a tax haven, which led to the registration of numerous companies from outside the Republic. At the same time Ilyumzhinov established informal relations with the leading business groups. In particular, this tax haven was used by MDM-Bank, LUKOIL and others. The practice of tax breaks played an important role in Chukotka, where after Abramovich came to power, subsidiaries of his oil company, Sibneft-Chukotka, Sibneft-Trading and Slavneft-Trading were registered. According to some estimates, by registering in Chukotka, Abramovich's group saved around one billion US dollars each year.

However, the right of regions to administer taxation have been drastically curbed (now a region can only cut its profits tax rate by a mere 4 per cent, and is not permitted to abolish it completely). For businesses even this, of course, is quite important. It is interesting to note that the Governor of Perm Krai Chirkunov, who came to politics from the business community, cut the regional profits tax rate for all companies in the region by 4 per cent. His decision could be viewed as an example of liberal economic policy, but not as the full introduction of a tax haven regime. Up until very recently, big business in Russia was primarily interested in the latter. It is hardly surprising then, that after regional taxation power was reduced, Abramovich's interest in the position of governor dropped sharply.

Alongside direct commercial benefits, another incentive for large businesses to take part in the political process is as an insurance against political risks. Putting one's 'own man' in a governor's seat helps create a more favourable business environment, which can be useful, though not vital, for a company. This also helps to explain the election of Khloponin as Governor of Taymyr, which coincided with the restructuring of Norilsk Nikel's assets and the registration of the company in Taymyr. Moreover, because Krasnoyarsk Krai is the main region of Norilsk Nikel's operations and Taymyr is its integral part, it was later decided to move Khloponin to the office of governor of the Krasnoyarsk Krai.

The decisions of large businesses to promote their own candidates to gubernatorial posts were rooted in the political situation in the 1990s, which was partially retained at the beginning of the 2000s, immediately after Putin came to power. The cases under our consideration are the 'first wave' of promotion of entrepreneurs to governors' offices, which reached its peak in 2000–2. At that time the 'power vertical' was not as rigid as at present, and business retained some autonomy from the bureaucrats.[20] The fact that governors were elected allowed them to work with the electorate independently of the federal centre and even to present the centre with a *fait accompli* when representatives of a FIG gained power. The scope of their authority allowed such governors to bring real commercial benefit to their patron FIGs. This situation, however, changed very quickly due to the more active stance of the centre which was alarmed by FIGs' desire to create political footholds in the regions.

Yet at present, one can speak only of marginal benefits for those FIGs which have a representative in a governor's office. FIGs may enter into joint projects, be granted privileged negotiations over the budget process and regional socio-economic programmes, and gain access to valuable information held by the regional administration. Such companies can also use governors as their lobbyists at the federal level, for instance, through their membership of the State Council which is chaired by the President. Khloponin, for example, is known to be a successful lobbyist.

In this situation one can assume that it is small and medium businesses (which are affected by regional authorities to the greatest extent) that should be the ones most interested in gubernatorial positions. However, the influence of such business is usually too weak to promote its representatives into gubernatorial posts. At the same time there are serious institutional limitations prohibiting small businesses from reaping commercial profits.

The major restriction is federal policies. Putin's centralization reforms have made the governors more dependent on the Kremlin. Especially after abolishing gubernatorial elections and the introduction of the appointment system, a governor is primarily perceived as a conductor of federal interests, as an ordinary bureaucrat operating within the limits of a prescribed mandate. Abusing one's authority too blatantly by expanding one's own business can have negative repercussions on a governor's relations with the centre. The Kremlin tolerates it as long as it does not cause public scandals or conflicts with other power groups. However, understanding the changing rules of the game and new institutional constraints (the presidential appointment of governors, more rigid and better organized federal control via the presidential plenipotentiaries and power ministries), a governor needs to act cautiously. Besides, as public servants, they are prohibited by law to be involved in commercial activity; otherwise they might risk ruining their career.

One result of these centralizing policies is a slow down in the growth of the new business groups which were created by the governors. Or if there is any expansion, it is being concealed, as are governors' connections with such expansion. A governor with business roots has been turned into an 'ordinary' governor, i.e. a political figure operating within the framework of Putin's system of centre-regional relations. First and foremost, there is 'loyalty to the biggest boss', i.e. to the President, upon whom all governors depend. This rule, in its turn, leads to another, the 'rule of caution', which discourages a governor from acting in support of his patron company.

A governor, striving to strengthen his political position, seeks to show his support of other business groups, even those which were previously treated as enemies. For example, Khloponin in Krasnoyarsk Krai tries to adopt policies which are beneficial for all business groups operating in the region, and not only for Norilsk Nikel. He has established relations with Deripaska's Basic Element Group, even though they were his opponents in the race for governor. One of the main lobbyist projects in Krasnoyarsk Krai is the Lower Angara Development Programme, which was approved by the federal government in 2006 and financed through the Investment fund. This programme is largely in the interests of Basic Element. Thus, Deripaska's group has not been negatively affected by the fact that a protégé of Interros came to power in the region.

The example of Krasnoyarsk Krai shows that the policies of Russian governors are too flexible to be analysed from the viewpoint of the interest of only one particular business group. Having obtained a political status, a businessman enters a completely new institutional environment. With the main task ahead of him – retaining power in the region, a governor takes orders from the federal centre, pledges political allegiance to the President. Operating within a highly centralized power structure where there are sharp resource inequalities between the centre and the regions, and widespread authoritarian practices, autonomy from the centre is impossible for most governors.

Previously, a governor could be guided by public opinion, since he was preparing grounds for his re-election. And often the centre had to reconcile itself with the popularity of some 'independent' governors. Now however, public opinion is less important. A governor is also interested in neutralizing his political rivals by improving relations with them and thereby minimizing their opposition. Since most governors in our sampling have not served long, it is even more vital for them to fit into the existing system of relations which they are unable to change.

The 'second wave' of former entrepreneurs who have made it into the Russian regional power is connected with gubernatorial appointments.

Nominating former directors and CEOs of large state-owned companies, such as Tishanin, Dudka and Ipatov, has become a clearly defined tendency. These appointments, however, reveal another tendency. Back in the Soviet times the concept of 'nomenklatura' comprised not only party officials and high-ranking civil servants, but also the 'directorial corps'. Certain members of the elite could move from positions in the economy to state structures and vice versa. A similar circulation of elites is being applied today, when certain forms of social organization typical of the Soviet period are being restored. State-owned companies are influence groups (or coalitions of influence groups), which are headed by people with access to the presidential inner circle. The most vivid examples are Gazprom, Rosneft, Russian Railways and Rosoboronexport. These companies have turned into influential political actors capable, among other things, of promoting their protégés into gubernatorial positions.

The rationale of such nominations lies not in the desire to carry out economic expansion in the regions using the governor's support. Such companies command powerful federal administrative resources that would compel any governor to take their interests into account. It is more likely that the heads of such companies are creating their own clientelistic networks in the regions with the object of increasing their political influence in the run-up to the 2007–8 federal elections and the upcoming struggle for power.

For the first wave of governors the primary motivation of seeking regional power is gradually being lost. In 2000, when the country saw a transition of power from one president to another, Abramovich, who had played a key role in Yeltsin's inner circle, decided to go into politics to secure his position. The office of governor, even in such an underdeveloped and remote region as Chukotka, turned out rather convenient for Abramovich and was used for attaining business objectives. This was despite the fact that, according to some sources in Abramovich's administration, over 1.5 billion US dollars were spent by Abramovich on the region's development, which is 1.5 times more than he saved by tax breaks.[21] Clearly, for Abramovich being Chukotka's governor was much more important than economic gain. His integration into the new political elite and his image of a successful and caring regional leader was certainly worth the losses. However, gradually his interest in such work declined. Following the sale of his main asset, Sibneft, to Gazprom, there was even less sense for him to remain in the position. It was not so much because the tax haven system was no longer available, but because the largest tax payers brought by Abramovich had left the region. The company Gazprom Neft, created on the basis of Sibneft, was registered in St Petersburg and did not need to register its subsidiaries in Chukotka. This meant that Chukotka, whose economy under Abramovich used to be termed 'virtual', has again become impoverished and totally dependent on federal financial aid.[22]

At the same time, serving as a governor offers new incentives in the form of belonging to Russia's power elite. In starting a new career, a governor becomes part of the presidential 'nomenklatura' and earns points for the future continuation of his career at the federal level. The first example was Perm governor Trutnev, who was appointed Russian Minister of Natural Resources.[23] After Khloponin's re-election as Krasnoyarsk Krai Governor, his imminent relocation to Moscow to a high-ranking position was often discussed in the media and among the experts.

Nonetheless, the appointment of a businessman as governors has still been possible even after 2005, as was shown by the examples of Kanokov and Kozhemyako. At the moment, however, it is too early to speak about a new tendency. In present conditions it is quite obvious that the Kremlin is not interested in appointing protégés of large private nationwide companies as governors, as the federal centre is trying to weaken their political influence. Medium-level businessmen are no threat to the Kremlin, and so their occasional appointment has been witnessed. Finally, speaking about the genesis of Russian elites, one should note that the old Soviet elites are giving up their positions and are being replaced by a new generation of individuals often with experience of working in business, which in the post-Soviet period has become an important recruitment ground.

Notes

1 C. E. Lindblom, *Politics and Markets: The World's Political-Economic System*, New York: Basic Book, 1977.
2 J. A. Schumpeter, *Capitalism, Socialism and Democracy*, New York: Routledge, 1942.
3 T. Skockpol, 'Bringing the state back in: strategies of analysis in current research', in P. Evans, D. Reuschemeyer and T. Skockpol (eds), *Bringing the State Back In*, Cambridge: CUP, 1985.
4 C. Hay, *Political Analysis. A Critical Introduction*, Houndmills and New York: Macmillan, 2002.
5 Our analysis of the Russian political culture is based on Heunks and Hikspoors' classification: F. Heunks and F. Hikspoors, 'Political Culture 1960-1990', in R. De Moor (ed.), *Values in Western Societies*, Tilburg: Tilburg University Press, 1995) and the empirical data provided in the World Values Survey, http://www.worldva luessurvey.com
6 A. Yu. Zudin, 'Putin's regime: contours of a new political system', *Obshchestvennye Nauki i Sovremennost*, No. 2, 2003, pp. 67–83.
7 S. P. Peregudov, N. Y. Lapina and I. S. Semenenko, *Interest Groups and the Russian State*, Moscow: editorial URSS, 1999; S. P. Peregudov, *Corporations, Society and the State: Evolution of Relations*, Moscow: Nauka, 2003.
8 M. Weber, *Economy and Society*, New York: Bedminister Press, 1968; F. Schmitter, 'Neocorporativism', *Polis*, No. 2, 1997.
9 D. Knoke, *Political Networks: The Structural Perspective*, New York: CUP, 1990.
10 Schumpeter 1942, op. cit.
11 R. A. Dahl, *On Democracy*, New Haven, CT and London: Yale University Press, 1998).
12 H. Lasswell, *Power and Personality*, New York: W.W. Norton, 1948.
13 A. Magomedov, 'Kalmykia Corporation – an expression of ruling elite ideology', *Mirovaya Economika i Mezhdunarodnye Otnosheniya*, 1995, No. 12.

14 Budargin exemplifies a manager of local origin. He was born in Kamchatka but educated in Norilsk where he began working at Norilsk Nikel even before moving to work for Interros. Being with Interros, he rose up in his career and became mayor and later governor.
15 Chirkunov's appointment was prompted by different circumstances. He succeeded another former entrepreneur, Trutnev, who won the gubernatorial elections in 2000 and in 2004 was invited to join the federal government.
16 Gorodilov's father was director of the oil producing company Noyabrskneftegaz, which was later taken over by Sibneft.
17 Some of Zelenin's team followed a path of gradual integration into the local elite. At first, they worked in Tver city administration, after the local politician Lebedev, supported by Zelenin's group, had lost the mayoral election. When Zelenin won the race for governor, those officials, and in particular Bershadskiy, were invited to work in the Oblast administration.
18 An independent company, not part of Gazprom.
19 Krasnoyarsk mayor Pimashkov stood for governor and supported Khloponin in the second round.
20 N.V. Zubarevich, 'Came, saw, conquered? (large business and regional power)', *Pro et Contra*, Vol. 7, No. 1, 2002, pp. 107–19.
21 Indeed, charity foundations and socially orientated target programmes were functioning in the region, even though it is not quite clear how their funds were spent and whether all the money was spent on charity.
22 It should be noted that the active exploitation of the region's own mineral resources was never started under Abramovich. Gold mining was Chukotka's main hope, but by 2005 it fell to its all-time low (less than 4 tons per year, as compared with 35 tons in the 1970s).
23 Prior to that, Trutnev was one of the largest businessmen (he worked in the trade sector) in Perm city, in 1996 he was elected mayor, and in 2000 governor.

9 The struggle for power in the Urals

Elena Denezhkina and Adrian Campbell

Introduction

The aim of this chapter is to analyse the evolution of the conflict between the Governor of Sverdlovsk Oblast (region) and the Mayor of the regional capital, Ekaterinburg (formerly Sverdlovsk) over the period from the early 1990s up to 2007. The chapter draws on research which was conducted over a long period and through different means. Initial visits were made in 1993–5 to analyse the development of federal–regional and regional–local relations. There followed a period of intense participant observation in 2000–3 during which the authors were directly involved in the development and implementation of a strategic plan for the city of Ekaterinburg[1] (which for a brief period in the spring of 2003 was the main focus of political conflict), followed by documentary research of local media and a follow-up visit in 2007. Due to the nature of the subject matter and the fact that most of those involved are still in post in what remains a highly sensitive political environment, we have made relatively little use of direct quotation from interviews or conversations, but have rather let the insight from these inform our reading of printed sources.

Sverdovsk Region and Ekaterinburg

Strategically situated on the Europe–Asia boundary, and with a population of 4.6 million, Sverdlovsk is one of the most populous of Russia's subjects of the Federation. The pattern of industrial development has meant that, after Moscow, St Petersburg and Moscow Region, Sverdlovsk is the most urbanized of Russia's Regions (over 4m urban inhabitants), the majority of the population living either in Ekaterinburg (1.3m) or in the belt of industrial towns which surrounds Ekaterinburg in the south of the region.[3] The concentration of defence high technology research and development facilities meant that Ekaterinburg (a closed city until 1992) possesses a high concentration of what was in soviet times termed the 'scientific technical intelligentsia'. As a result the city became a centre of progressive politics, and closely associated with Boris Yeltsin who was Party First Secretary for the region 1976-85. In the first multi-party elections in 1990, Ekaterinburg (then under its soviet-era name of Sverdlovsk) was one of only three large Russian cities to return a large majority of pro-reform candidates.

For several years the city has enjoyed the highest levels of growth in retail and commerce, (and highest property prices) of all cities outside Moscow and St Petersburg. The city has seen a shift in industrial profile with more profitable enterprises being found in the food, drink and consumer products sectors than in traditional defence sectors (a shift less pronounced in the smaller cities in the regions where industry is primarily heavy and defence-oriented). As a result, by 2000, the city of Ekaterinburg accounted for over 60 per cent of the economy of Sverdlovsk Region and over 80 per cent of its service sector income.

This has an impact on the economic strategies of the city and regional levels. The region has pursued an active but traditional strategy emphasizing support for defence and heavy industry. The city, on the other hand has in recent years been pursuing a consciously post-industrial strategy, on the European model, promoting the city as a centre of business services.

The Urals Republic versus the Centre

Following Boris Yeltsin's election to the executive presidency of the Russian Federation in June 1991, Eduard Rossel was appointed the first governor of Sverdlovsk Oblast (region). Rossel then appointed Arkady Chernetsky to the post of mayor of Ekaterinburg in 1992.

Rossel was one of the most assertive governors from the start. His project for a Urals republic pursued two aims. First, the immediate aim was to 'upgrade' Sverdlovsk to republic status, thereby eliminating the difference between Sverdlovsk as an ethnic Russian region and titular ethnic republics such as Bashkortostan or Tatarstan (which at that stage was seen to enjoy substantial fiscal privileges). This would effectively neutralize the nationality (as opposed to territorial) principle in the regional structure of the federation. The advocates of the Urals Republic considered that having three categories of subject (as in the Federal Treaty) was an attempt by a weak centre to divide and rule, and that the national ethnic principle of regional policy was 'a bomb planted in 1918 that will sooner or later go off, now that the Party is no longer there to exert pressure from above'.[4]

Second, Rossel had, in 1990, established an Association of Economic Cooperation between six regions in the wider Urals area. The aim was now to convert this into a larger territorial unit. The historical precedent was the larger Urals Region that existed before 1933[5] and the proposal presaged the Urals Federal District as created in 2001. The argument pursued by Rossel and his supporters had much in common with that of the SOPS economic planning network that had always opposed the smaller regions that emerged from the Stalin period and sought to restore the larger Gosplan economic planning regions of the 1920s.[6]

As mayor of Ekaterinburg, Chernetsky had been pressing an analogous demand, also based on the precedent of Gosplan, for Ekaterinburg to be made a subject of the federation in its own right, on the basis of its past status as a separate Gosplan entity. This thinking was to inform subsequent campaigns (after 2000) to have Ekaterinburg recognized as a 'Third Capital' as this would open up the possibility of becoming a 'federal city' like Moscow or St Petersburg (i.e. to be a region in its own right).

The prospect of an aggrandized ethnic Russian region raised for some the spectre of secession, and the move was rejected both by parliament and president. On 10 November President Yeltsin (having just suppressed the parliamentary insurrection) dismissed Rossel from the post of governor and replaced him with Aleksei Strakhov (Chernetsky's First Deputy Mayor) who was opposed to the Urals republic. Rossel was once more elected chair of the Oblast Duma and from there successfully lobbied for federal support for a law whereby a the governor of the region should be elected.

'Transformation of the Urals' versus 'Our Home is Russia'

In the election, held in July 1995, the federal authorities attempted to get Strakhov re-elected for Our Home is Russia – the then party of power associated with the then Prime Minister Viktor Chernomyrdin. However Rossel's campaign was far more effective and he won almost 70 per cent of the votes on the second round.[7]

Rossel's campaign was a landmark in the use of PR techniques in Russian elections.[8] This was not new to the Urals, as Boris Yeltsin's move to Moscow from Sverdlovsk had been the result of a systematic campaign of image-making and projection in the early 1980s.[9] The campaign involved the creation a new party '*Preobrazheniye Urala*' (Transformation of the Urals). This was a broad coalition, including groups as diverse as communists, Cossack nationalists and Yabloko social democrats.

An important factor in the success of Rossel's campaign was the support he received from a team headed by Anton Bakov, a young political operator, who had been elected to the Regional Duma under Shakhrai's Unity and Agreement Party (PRES) and who had actively supported the Urals Republic idea in 1993 and who joined Rossel's Transformation of the Urals. Bakov, described by his associates as a 'Napoleon'[10] figure and by journalists as an '*affairiste*', was a metallurgist who had already made a fortune in the aluminium business and was eager to establish himself politically. He saw the campaign very much in terms of preventing Moscow from dictating to the regions and wanted to see this principle extended to stopping the 'neo-colonial' expansion of Moscow banks buying up property in the regions.[11] This defensive position against Moscow business was shared by the criminal gang OPS Uralmash, who took a protectionist view of the region's resources. Rumours of the organization's support for Rossel date from this period.

Strakhov had attempted to build support among local authorities by passing a new regional law that would allow elections for municipal heads. In the event this was ruled out by a court decision, but the passing of the Federal Law on the General Principles of Local Self-Government in the Russian Federation meant that elections for municipal heads would take place in any case.

'Transformation of the Urals' versus 'Our Home, Our City'

Immediately after the victory in the gubernatorial election it was agreed that Rossel's team would support Bakov as an official Transformation of the Urals candidate for mayor against Chernetsky at the first election on 17 December 1995. Chernetsky, for his part, formed his own party 'Our Home, Our City', echoing the federal Our Home is Russia' party. Chernetsky's party colleague, Vladimir Tungusov, ubiquitously referred to as the 'grey cardinal', had supported Strakhov directly through the party. He had considered supporting Strakhov, but had not done so actively as it had soon become clear to all that the latter's campaign was heading for a heavy defeat[12] and that supporting it would only reduce Chernetsky's own chances in the mayoral election a few months later.

The Bakov camp considered Chernetsky a worthy if somewhat traditional opponent but expected Rossel to 'put him in his place'.[13] In the wake of Rossel's victory, Chernetsky appeared isolated – he was seen as having no need for the city council, seeing them as a dilution of mayoral authority, although his high level of professional ability (not universal among mayors in the early 1990s) meant that many councillors still supported him.[14] Nonetheless the poor relations between mayor and at least some councillors opened up a line of attack that would be exploited by Rossel's supporters in this and future elections. When it came to the election on 17 December 1995, Chernetsky beat off Bakov's challenge, the latter winning only 16 per cent on the second round. Bakov showed himself once again to be a gifted political campaigner, but not a credible replacement for Chernetsky, who had built up a base of genuine popularity in the city, projecting an image of dependable professionalism, confirmed by his winning the all-Russian competition 'Russian Mayor-95'.[15] The basis for Chernetsky's success in this and subsequent elections was his ability to combine a liberal/social democrat outlook with the style and experience of a late Soviet-era industrial magnate, and a detailed understanding of how the city's infrastructure actually worked. This ensured that he outlived both the first generation of well-meaning progressive mayors who were out-manoeuvred by vested interests and the old-guard industrial managers who were unable to adapt to electoral politics and the need to interact with the public.

If, in the early years of democratization (1990–3), conflict had been on the *horizontal* level – between executive and representative bodies, from this point the main axis of conflict was *vertical*, between city and region. From this election onwards, the political, economic and social dynamics of the region were to reflect the struggle for supremacy between governor and mayor. While in some respects this was not new – for example the Institute of Philosophy had supported Rossel whilst the Institute of Economics had supported Strakhov[16] – this principle was now to become further embedded in all electoral contests, and the increasingly long and bitter campaigns that preceded them became duels between Rossel and Chernetsky, either directly or through surrogates. This was true not only for the gubernatorial elections of 1999 and 2003, and the mayoral elections of the same years, but also for the elections to the Regional Assembly and the Ekaterinburg City Duma. It became standard practice for the Governor's team to create and support an anti-mayoral bloc of deputies in the City Duma and for the Mayor's team to do the same in the Regional Duma. In addition, Chernetsky was elected a member of the region's second chamber, the legislative assembly, where he chaired the committee on local self-government (he had also been a deputy of the Regional Council in 1994–6). In the 1998 elections for the Regional Duma, Chernetsky's Our Home Our City won over 20 per cent against a mere 9 cent for Rossel's Transformation of the Urals, encouraging Chernetsky to aim for the governorship in 1999.

In the 1999 election Chernetsky, who started from a position of strength after the Regional Duma results of the previous year, was targeted in a sustained PR campaign of unprecedented intensity from the regional media, which succeeded in damaging his campaign. In the meantime the regional media gave an easy ride to and even assisted the other main challenger, Alexander Burkov, who had, together with Anton Bakov, set up the oppositionist movement 'May' which was given to carrying out high-profile provocations, such as occupying buildings, calling officials to public account.[17] As a result, at the first round Chernetsky was pushed into third place. For the second round the regional media turned their fire wholly onto Burkov and the dangers presented by his 'extremist' movement,[18] and Rossel was able to win comfortably.[19]

Chernetsky's media were seen to have been outgunned by that of the Governor in terms of resources, scale, intensity and ruthlessness. Although Chernetsky's own re-election campaign had been successful, his team under Tungusov were obliged to expand their media resources in order to keep pace and by 2003 they were seen to have achieved parity with the regional media, or even attained a relative advantage, with two television stations, Channel 41 and RTK, against the region's OTV channel.

Chernetsky was also active in politics beyond the confines of Sverdlovsk Region. He was leader of the association 'Cities of the Urals' and was a leading figure in the Union of Russian Cities, of which he has been President since 2001. He was also to be a member of the Council of Local and Regional Authority representatives at the Council of Europe and a member of the presidential Council for Local Self-Government established by Putin.[20] Most significantly Chernetsky was elected head of the regional branch of 'Fatherland' (*Otechestvo*), which had been set up the previous year by Yuri Luzhkov, mayor of Moscow. As federal power stabilized under Primakov's premiership and later the Putin premiership and presidency, lobbying of the federal level and competing to demonstrate federal-level approval became increasingly important – hence Rossel and Chernetsky both (separately) meeting with Primakov in Moscow in the run-up to the gubernatorial elections of 1999.

After 2000 it was Rossel who began to appear vulnerable. As the archetypal assertive regional boss he might have been expected to be out of favour with the Putin presidency, especially as Chernetsky was, from 2001, the deputy head of the regional branch of the pro-Putin party United Russia which had emerged from the union of 'Unity' and 'Fatherland'. Chernetsky's ally Porunov was chair of the Regional Duma, supported by the United Russia fraction, controlled by Chernetsky and his team. Rossel's attempt to remove Porunov led to a boycott by his supporters and the Regional Duma ceased to function for much of the period 2001–2. In the meantime Chernetsky had built up good relations with Pyotr Latyshev, the president's representative for the new Urals Federal District, whereas Rossel was outspoken in his criticism of the institution of federal districts.[21] When, on arrival in the city in 2001, Latyshev attempted to place his headquarters in the most imposing building in Ekaterinburg, which happened to be used as a children's centre, and was obliged to back down after well-publicized protests which were supported by the Governor, it was the mayor's administration that found the federal district alternative accommodation.

Hemmed in from above and below, Rossel was not to be marginalized, however. In mid-2001 he succeeded in recruiting the Chernetsky's First Deputy Mayor, Yuri Osintsev, and appointing him as External Affairs Minister in the regional government. Osintsev, who formerly as senior manager at the Uralmash factory, had become well known in the city, was charismatic and regarded as a progressive modernizer. From 2000 Osintsev had been responsible for the setting up the City Strategic Plan (see below).

It was soon apparent that Osintsev was being groomed as the next region-backed challenger for the mayoral election of 2003,[22] especially when Rossel appointed Osintsev as the 'curator' of Ekaterinburg (after winning the 1995 election Rossel had divided the region into sectors, each of which had a curator who in effect had the task of checking on the activities of local authorities). Assigning to Osintsev the role of checking on his former boss was a means of giving him a head start in the election campaign. Osinstev began to cultivate the opposition (i.e. anti-mayor) deputies of the city duma, and was considered to be the initiator of a new fraction, the 'inter-regional' group bringing together enemies and erstwhile allies of Chernetsky. Osintsev's intentions became more explicit in January 2003, when Osintsev caused a sensation by stepping onto the floor of the City Duma at the end of the budget debate and (in front of the assembled media) accusing the city administration of massive fraud.[23]

In the meantime Rossel's lobbying of the federal authorities began to bear fruit. First, he was granted the possibility of running for a third term, and second, as the campaign for the mayoral election campaign commenced, United Russia endorsed Osintsev as their official candidate (although he had not previously been a member of the party), and not Chernetsky, despite the latter being deputy head of their regional organization. Chernetsky as a result was effectively marginalized and snubbed by federal United Russia, as were his allies who had constituted the United Russian fraction on the Oblast Assembly.

However, the problem facing Osintsev's future campaign was that it lacked a major issue to campaign on, beyond Osintsev's personal appeal. The previous year the city had been voted the most flourishing regional capital, winning the 'golden rouble' award for financial-economic regeneration, and had successfully launched the large-scale Urals-Siberia Exhibition in July.

The one area which Osintsev could potentially use in a future mayoral campaign was the Strategic Plan, for which he had been the lead official in its early stages, as First Deputy Mayor for the Economy.[24]

The conflict over the city Strategic Plan

The Strategic Plan was a major theme in the political and administrative life of Ekaterinburg in 2000-3, the most intense period of region–city rivalry. The issue acquired a highly symbolic status as it provided an arena for both cooperation (in the early stages) and conflict (in the later stages) between city and region. The Plan's preparation mobilized a substantial part of the city's elite and civil society at the same time as projecting the city's image to a wider audience at federal level and other large cities in the Federation.[25] The strategy development process was supported by a UK bilateral project, for which the authors of this chapter were responsible.[26]

Work had begun on the Strategic Plan for Ekaterinburg (intended to guide development until 2015) in 1999 not long after the publication of the St Petersburg City Strategy, seen as the first modern city strategic plan in the Russian Federation. Osintsev presided over a group of academics and local consultants who were in favour of moving Ekaterinburg away from its traditional reliance on defence industry and towards a 'twenty-first century' post-industrial commercial future, capitalizing on its location on the Eurasian overland trade route.[27]

> Each of the two main political forces seeking to run the city for the next four years will be presenting the electorate with its own development plan ... the city authorities think that the Urals capital should become a commercial-financial, entertainment and conference centre on the border of Europe and Asia ... Mayor Chernetsky himself states that his plan is based on the experience of the British city of Birmingham which has changed over the last thirty years from being an industrial city to a

financial and entertainment centre dominated by the service sector ...
An alternative development plan for the city is proposed by Sverdlovsk
Regional Administation under the humble title of 'Scheme for the
Distribution of Productive Forces'...oriented primarily to the real sector
of the city's economy ... The struggle between these two conceptions
takes on a special significance in that the curator of the regional pro-
gramme, Yuri Osintsev, is considered to be the main rival of Arkady
Chernetsky at the next election ... [28]

A more fundamental difference lay in the new strategic plan's emphasis on
quality of life and public services, especially the social bloc (education,
health, social services) and housing/utilities. This shift of emphasis away
from a preoccupation with industry reflected Chernetsky's view, expressed at
several conferences and public meetings in 2000–2, that Ekaterinburg had
been developed in the Soviet period as a 'factory-city', a city for production
rather than people, and needed to place a higher priority on the well-being
of the city's inhabitants and the city's development as a multi-functional
internationally oriented 'Eurasian capital'. The strategy's emphasis on the
key areas of education, health and housing were seen to be line with similar
policy shifs at federal level, notably the development of the 'national projects' under federal vice-premier Medvedev.[29]

However, the view was strongly held within the city administration that
the Strategic Plan should not become a theme of the election campaign as
this would undermine its longer-term legitimacy (as a plan in its own right,
as opposed to a sub-division of a regional plan). Legitimacy also required
that the plan be ratified by the City Duma rather than adopted unilaterally
by the Mayor, and that this should take place well before the election, due
for 17 December 2003. There was also to be a gubernatorial election in
September 2003, so to avoid the three-month election campaigning period
for either election the strategy had to be ratified by mid-June.

The Duma was due to debate the strategic plan on 25 April. The day
before, Regional Deputy Premier Osintsev delivered to Yakov Silin, the
Chair of the Duma, a report on the strategic plan by his staff at the regional
ministry of external affairs.[30] The report strongly recommended that the
deputies should not adopt the strategic plan. The next day the Duma session
was inquorate with nearly half the deputies – those belonging to pro-region/
anti-mayor deputies (unofficially) – boycotting the session. The boycott was
a major event in adversarial PR terms – the debate had been scheduled to
take place not in the council chamber but in the great hall of the city
administration building, with a large audience of invited notables and all the
regional and city media present, so that the boycott and its aftermath
dominated the local and regional media.

The fourteen (out of twenty-seven) deputies who boycotted the proceedings consisted primarily of the two pro-regional opposition factions –
Alexander Khabarov's OPS Uralmash (the Uralmash Political and Social

Union created in 1999 by the Uralmash criminal firm: see section on orga-nized crime below) and its allies, the Inter-regional group (seen to have been Osinstev's own creation),[31] led by Maksim Serebrennikov, a former member of OPS Uralmash. The boycott, and the high-profile manner in which it had occurred, projected the strategic plan for the first time into the centre of the political arena between city and region, and led to an escalation of that conflict in public relations terms.

The main arguments in Osintsev's report were that the city strategy should not be approved separately from a regional strategy and that the partnership arrangements associated with the Strategic Plan, and the partnership struc-ture (Programme Council) associated with it, were not workable and that the process should in effect begin again after the election with a new mayor. The report also criticized the emphasis on city marketing and image-making that was seen to inform the city strategy. These points were refuted in a public reply to Osintsev from the bilateral project,[32] which appeared to close this debate, as the original report was no longer referred to.

However following a meeting immediately after the boycott, the bilateral project became embroiled in a dispute with Osintsev's allies in the city duma, the Inter-regional Group of deputies, led by ex-OPS Uralmash Maksim Serebrennikov. After a session was held to discuss why the Inter-regional Group had boycotted the Strategy, the deputies publicized through the regional media a story that the British government was demanding a refund of the project budget from the city administration (the deputies were una-ware that bilateral technical assistance project budgets are not transferred to the beneficiary and therefore could not be refunded by them). This led to a public exchange of open letters that was given prominence by both the pro-mayor and pro-regional media[33] and was for a period the focus of the PR conflict between the two sides. Eventually an agreement was reached with Osintsev that the strategy and the bilateral project should no longer be a focus for political PR. The dispute showed up divisions in the Oblast ranks – not all the Oblast media coverage of the dispute took Osintsev's side:

> The emotional protest by the British side, against the attempts to make the development plan of Ekaterinburg a trump card in a political game, has proved a great help to mayor Chernetsky's team in deflecting the attacks of its opponents. On 25 April the mayor of Ekaterinburg had stated that the deputies' sabotage of the strategic plan was an obedient execution of a political instruction. Duma chair Yakov Silin was more specific, placing the responsibility with the Oblast leadership, whilst Sergei Tushin, head of the analytical section of the mayor's administra-tion, said that behind the scandal was the hand of Yuri Osintsev who hoped to be the next mayor.[34]

This was one of the first indications of a clear split between two PR teams at the Oblast level, one led by Alexander Ryzhkov, reporting to Aleksei

Vorobyev, premier of the Sverdlovsk Oblast Administration, and the governor's PR team, led by Alexander Levin. The governor's team reportedly regarded the strategic plan as non-political[35] and moreover were hostile to Osintsev, preferring to back city duma opposition deputy Jan Gabinsky as their candidate for mayor.[36]

The definitive end to the dispute over the strategy came on 10 June (the last day before the start of the campaign for the gubernatorial election in September), after weeks of behind-the-scenes diplomacy (involving discussions with each deputy in turn) by the Duma Chair Yakov Silin, a quorate City Duma convened to debate the strategy.

At the end of a four-hour debate the final vote was fifteen in favour, four against and four abstentions.[37] The hard core of the OPS Uralmash group continued to oppose the plan (in line with the Governor's position), although some of their allies changed sides and supported the strategy. The four 'interregional group' deputies abstained, thereby confirming that Yuri Osintsev, whilst not supporting the strategy, would no longer oppose it and that the strategy would not be a major theme in the mayoral election campaign in December.

In the event, both the gubernatorial and mayoral elections were dominated by a quite different issue, that of organized crime. Before reviewing its role in the elections of 2003 it is necessary to consider the changing role of organized crime in Sverdlovsk Region over the previous decade.

The rise of OPS 'Uralmash'

In Sverdlovsk Region in the early 1990s criminal gangs could be divided into those that were ethnically Russian ('Uralmash', the 'Central' gang, the 'Blues', the 'Khimmash' and the 'Afghans'[38]), and those that were based on minority ethnicities (Georgians, Chechens, Azeris, Armenians, Tadzhiks and others). The mid-1990s saw a period of violent gang warfare in which Uralmash fought and won a battle for supremacy first against the other Russian gangs in Ekaterinburg and then against the ethnic minority gangs. The battle followed a pattern that was being repeated in other large cities in Russia where, as described by Volkov,[39] the traditional collectivist gangs were sidelined by market-oriented 'violent entrepreneurs' of which Uralmash were an influential prototype. According the security service data, by 1998 OPG Uralmash had established 200 companies, including 12 banks, and were shareholders in a further 90 companies.[40] Up to 30 per cent of the organization's profits were reinvested in production in the region and also into a growing number of social initiatives. These were geared to improving the gang's image sufficiently to enable them to enter the political arena,[41] in alliance with leading regional political forces.[42]

In 1999 Alexander Khabarov, now the lead figure in OPS Uralmash, changed the name of the organization from Organized Crime Society Uralmash to 'Social and Political Union' Uralmash (the Russian acronym

OPS was the same in both cases).[43] This was seen as a key stage in legalization and provided a potentially acceptable under which to be elected to the City Duma. The first of the gang to be elected was Alexander Kukovyakin in 2001.[44] Other members ran for election to the Oblast Duma, and by the time the leader of OPS Uralmash, Alexander Khabarov, was elected to the City Duma in April 2002, he was one of eight Uralmash deputies who, along with five 'inter-regional' deputies, made up an anti-mayor bloc of 14 out of 27 City Duma deputies, the first time since the abolition of the former City Soviet in 1993 that the Mayor faced a majority capable of blocking all decisions.

Thus a certain symmetry was obtained – a pro-Mayor majority on the Oblast Duma complicated regional decision-making, whilst a pro-regional majority in the City Duma would now oppose the city administration. The 'pro-mayor' group on the City Duma did not support the mayor unconditionally, and several of its members were regularly, even routinely, critical of the administration. The difference was that OPS Uralmash and the inter-regionals were opposed *on principle* to the mayor's regime and in this respect they were working to the governor's (or deputy governor's) agenda.

The alliance between the Oblast elite and OPS Uralmash was an open secret. Rumours had long circulated of a pact whereby Uralmash supported Rossel in the election of 1995 onwards, and by 1999 the links had became obvious to the extent that they were a ready source of sensational copy for the federal media.[45] In one press conference Rossel declared that OPS Uralmash no longer had any problems with the law (in fact several of the city Uralmash deputies were facing arrest by the security services for serious crimes, protected only by the immunity from prosecution they enjoyed as elected politicians) and that the organization was making a genuine contribution to the regional economy: 'I ordered them to invest in the region's construction industry.'[46]

The behaviour of the regional media confirmed the alliance. Glowing portraits of leading OPS Uralmash members would appear in glossy region-backed journals,[47] and the media emphasized the charitable and economic roles exercised by OPS Uralmash. Khabarov's election in 2002 was openly celebrated by members of the regional PR team, and there were some who appeared to look forward to Khabarov replacing Silin (the mayor's ally) as chair of the City Duma.[48] In retrospect, however, Uralmash's entry into electoral politics was a major error of judgement on the part of both Uralmash itself and the Oblast authorities.

The election campaigns of 2003

At the start of 2003 Eduard Rossel appeared isolated, being deeper than ever in conflict not only with Chernetsky but also with the President's representative for the Urals, Latyshev. Rossel's ability to lobby the Centre, perhaps aided (paradoxically) by the 'Urals Republic' legacy, together with his popularity in a large a wealthy region, helped him to reverse the position. By July 2003 not only had Rossel received the blessing of the President to run for a third term, but he would be doing so as the candidate from United Russia, the first governor to be elected for United Russia rather than one of its predecessor parties.[49]

Rossel as an incumbent governor now looked unassailable, whereas Chernetsky as incumbent mayor looked potentially vulnerable against a Rossel-backed campaign to unseat him. In anticipation, Chernetsky's campaign team appeared to opt for a two-stage approach: first to establish the theme of organized crime as an issue in the gubernatorial elections in September 2003 (which they had little chance of winning) and then to use the still-warm theme to deadlier effect again in the mayoral election of December 2003 (which they had to win, or see the end of the mayoral regime). The choice of Bakov to stand for governor against Rossel with a campaign theme of organized crime was a bold one. Bakov had the reputation of being an adventurer, to say the very least. He had been involved in a number of scandalous incidents (notably when he had been arrested in 2001 for assaulting the oligarch Fedulev during a forced takeover of the Khimmash plant), and he had been a close associate of Rossel's during the period when the governor and Uralmash had allegedly become allied. However these factors, plus Bakov's undeniable gift for self-publicity, may have been precisely what ensured a large audience for his public accusations, which were outspoken and dramatic even by the standards of Sverdlovsk politics:[50]

> I kept silent, as we all did. And I thought it was normal ... you learn from an early age that there is no justice and....you're not surprised when you see a police chief sharing a table with a known bandit. You're no longer surprised when an underworld '*avtoritet*' is praised on television for his philanthropy or when thieves stand for election as council deputies.[51]

Bakov's bid for the governorship was of course heavily defeated – no one could compete seriously with Rossel's profile across the region. However, it had almost certainly made a big impact on the real electoral battleground, Ekaterinburg.

When it came to the mayoral election in December 2003, the assumption that Osintsev would be the runner-up in the first round proved correct. There had been a number of other candidates, most of whom polled very few votes (OPS Uralmash's Khabarov and Serebrennikov both ran – perhaps to distract attention from their alleged alliance with Osintsev, and received very low votes). The local banker Gusev fought a well-funded campaign but lacked a clear campaign theme. Jan Gabinsky, the duma deputy, had been strongly backed by the governor's team at first, but was mercilessly lampooned not only by the city's PR team but also (allegedly) by the Oblast administration's (pro-Osinstev) PR team, under the combined pressure of which his campaign image collapsed.[52]

The first round showed Osinstev in a close second place. Chernetsky polled 34 per cent to Osintsev's 26 per cent. At this point, three losing candidates, Khabarov, Serebrennikov and Gabinsky, made a joint declaration (known as the 'December agreement') calling upon the population to vote for Osintsev, in what came to be seen as a 'manifesto from OPS Uralmash in favour of Osintsev, and likely to damage his rating'.[53] (OPS Uralmash's own rating had collapsed under pressure from Bakov's 'anti-mafia' campaign.)

The real strength in Osintsev's campaign came from elsewhere. On 10 December, the General Council of United Russia published its decision to support Osintsev, who had not previously been a member of that party.[54] The regional branch of United Russia swung into action, accusing Chernetsky of slander for his statement that criminals supported Osinstev's candidacy. United Russia suspended all local party members who refused to support Osintsev, including Duma Chair Silin and members of both city and oblast dumas.[55] Chernetsky was himself instructed on party grounds to support his opponent or face disciplinary proceedings.

Osintsev's team used the support received from the federal centre and from United Russia to full effect – deploying the slogans 'Putin for President, Rossel for Governor and Osintsev for Mayor' and 'state power is coming to Ekaterinburg'[56] and implying that the president wanted Osintsev to win.[57] The logic was expounded by Franz Klintsevich, who arrived in Ekaterinburg from the party headquarters in Moscow:

> In this country serious changes are occurring. ... no one can deny that Russia is seeing a period of the strengthening of state power ... Now United Russia has become an instrument of the President ... in the autumn of this year we supported Eduard Rossel, who became the first governor to be elected with the support of a federal party. Now it's time to choose a mayor of Ekaterinburg and the general council has supported Yuri Osintsev. That way we will have a logical vertical of power: there is President Putin, there is Governor Rossel. Now there must be Mayor Osintsev.[58]

On the other side, Bakov made a public appeal, reminding voters that Khabarov and OPS Uralmash had called on them to vote for Osinstev, and predicting that if Chernetsky lost, OPS Uralmash would begin a bloody redistribution of city property,[59] and this broadly was the line followed by the pro-mayor campaign.

The organized crime theme had undeniable resonance, particularly in the week leading up to the second round on 21 December. Once public opinion had become exercised by the criminal theme, the Oblast's ability to counter this was limited – after all, everyone had seen the Oblast media backing Khabarov's election to the City Duma the previous year.

In a desperate attempt to deflect the 'organized crime' issue away from Osintsev's campaign, Uralmash leader Khabarov himself made a bizarre statement in which he attempted to argue that in appearing to support Osintsev he had actually been working for Chernetsky all along, thereby helping the latter by discrediting Osintsev who, he stated, had refused to accept his support, unlike (he claimed) Chernetsky.[60] This statement failed to have the desired effect, and the organized crime theme began to tell against Osintsev's campaign.

In the final days before the poll, what were termed the 'heavy artillery' from the federal level were deployed to support Osintsev – Boris Gryzlov the leader of United Russia, Bogomolov the secretary of the UR General Council, the Presidential Administration Head of Internal Policy[61] and leaders of other federal parties including Vladimir Zhirinovsky who contributed a tirade about Chernetsky's Jewish origins ('he is of the race that has tormented and murdered Russia'),[62] while copies of what were said to be Chernetsky's bank accounts were circulated on the web, in an attempt to prove that he had transferred $170 million to a bank in Tel Aviv.[63]

The result must have come as a surprise to the party hierarchy: Chernetsky 54 per cent, Osintsev 39 per cent, with 7 per cent spoilt ballot papers. Moreover, the turnout, at 51 per cent, had been very high by Russian standards.[64] Headlines declaring 'Chernetsky beats United Russia' appeared nationally,[65] although Chernetsky himself was careful to deny that he had any quarrel with United Russia, of which he was still a member.

The mayoral election of 2003 was one the last no-holds-barred PR-intensive elections in Russia and one of the most closely fought. The result and the high turnout suggested either that the crime theme had reached a substantial proportion of the population, or that there had been resentment at the 'hand of Moscow' attempting to depose the mayor,[66] or both. It could be argued that the mayor's campaign sensationalized the issue of organized crime and its links with the governor's camp, but there was sufficient evidence for the public to be alarmed. When they read that, for example, Khabarov and ex-OPS Uralmash colleagues Famiev and Serebrennikov had been promised the departments dealing with property, privatization and utilities reform if Osintsev should win, this might have been a rumour, but it was a rumour that the experience of recent years offered no basis to doubt. Public concern was widespread over organized crime and had strengthened a civil movement 'City without Crime', but the elections of 2003 gave the first opportunity to voice this concern effectively.

United Russia had associated itself with Rossel presumably on account of his proven popularity in the region. However they failed to see that Chernetsky was in an equally strong position with the electorate of Ekaterinburg. The problem was very likely that United Russia officials thought that it would not be possible to work with both Rossel and Chernetsky in the same party and so tried to remove Chernetsky. They had not anticipated the collision between their pro-legality, pro-vertical state message and the fact that their allies in the region had long had a reputation for collaboration with organized crime to the extent of even helping known criminals to get elected. Overall it appeared as though Governor Rossel had been able to push United Russia's leadership towards a position that suited him more than it suited them.[67] United Russia was subsequently to change its position on Chernetsky and, after an attempt to remove him through legal instruments, he was to be restored to the higher reaches of the regional list for United Russia and he was to be the party's candidate for the 2008 mayoral election (endorsed by an overwhelming majority of regional United Russia delegates). The lesson from the election was, first, that public opinion in cities like Ekaterinburg would no longer tolerate the type of alliance with organized crime that had occurred in the past. It also demonstrated an electorate that would willingly vote for Vladimir Putin as President but would not necessarily vote consistently for the 'state vertical', in the sense of voting at all levels for whoever could be portrayed as a pro-Putin candidate. As a result, the winning model for United Russia appeared to be not a simple top-down approach, but a reciprocal alliance between levels of government, including local self-government.

The fall of ex-OPS Uralmash

If the election campaign saved the mayoral regime in Ekaterinburg, it was to have the opposite effect on OPS Uralmash, bringing to an end its decade-long progress[68] towards legitimacy and political power. However, the catalyst for its downfall was a dispute over centralization within the criminal world, between Moscow and the regions. On 15 September 2004 Khabarov called a public rally in the centre of Ekaterinburg of 1,500 members of the Uralmash, Central and Blue gangs. They were called to debate how to resist what was seen as an attempt by the Moscow (Caucasian) underworld to infiltrate their territory, operating through traditional criminal structures, represented in Ekaterinburg by the 'Blues'. The response would be a gang war by OPS Uralmash and OPS Centre to take control of the Blues in order to prevent their becoming a vehicle for takeover by Moscow.[69]

Khabarov's boldness provoked a reaction from the Centre (via the federal district). In December 2004, Khabarov was arrested for extortion and on 27 January 2005 was found hanged in his cell in Ekaterinburg. The death of Khabarov shocked the political elite of the region and contributed to a serious decline in ex-OPS Uralmash's influence. Within months its leading members were either jailed or in hiding abroad. No ex-OPS Uralmash candidates were fielded for the municipal elections of 2005 (apart from anything else, election as city deputy no longer gave immunity from arrest) and of its allies from the anti-mayoral bloc of 2002–3, only Gabinsky was re-elected.

Inside the bear's tent

From 2004 the leadership of United Russia[70] began to work on making peace between Chernetsky and Rossel, presumably in the expectation that each could deliver success for United Russia in federal elections. Rossel and Chernetsky still manoeuvred against each other in the Oblast Duma and City Duma,[71] although each now had a clear majority in their respective dumas.

Much more surprisingly, from 2004 Chernetsky and Rossel began to appear in public, apparently on friendly terms. Cynics held that this became especially noticeable in the run-up to elections, where now both were backing United Russia.[72] There were, however, also major practical benefits for the city and region in their new partnership – projects such as the airport and several large territorial development projects have been completed or launched as a result of investor confidence increasing due to the end of open hostilities and start of genuine collaboration between city and oblast.

There was a brief return of anti-mayor activism in early 2007 (analogous moves were being seen to be made against city mayors elsewhere in Russia), with attempts to remove Chernetsky from the future election (due March 2008) by legal means.[73] With finance-related charges being drawn up against both Chernetsky and Tungusov predictions of Chernetsky's downfall began to appear once again, the implication being that large-scale business (presumably with federal links) would move in. According to one report the position was summed up by Kabanov, the head of the national anti-corruption committee, in the following terms: 'The posts of mayor or governor are now economic posts and they cost a lot of money. There's going to be a new division of property (in Russia) and your mayor's "roof has got thin" as they say in proto-criminal circles.'[74]

In the end the Kremlin appears to have decided that Chernetsky, like Rossel, was a valuable asset or ally in the wider political context. In June, 2007, Vladislav Surkov, Deputy Head of the Presidential Administration, with overall responsibility for political parties and movements, began a series of individual meetings with regional heads, beginning with Eduard Rossel. With other once-powerful Yeltsin-era governors such as Prusak (Novgorod) and Titov (Samara) resigning[75] for (reportedly) not preventing conflict between 'business groups' on their territory and not delivering a sufficiently high vote for United Russia in mayoral, regional duma or federal elections,[76] one might have expected Rossel to be in danger, but the outcome of the discussion was that Rossel would stay in post. Chernetsky was called to see Surkov the following week. The result was confirmation that Chernetsky would be second on the regional United Russia list, after Rossel (this is indeed what subsequently occurred) and that the federal centre would support him as mayor in the March 2008 elections.[77] For his part, Rossel arranged for the Oblast Duma to reduce the number of rounds in the mayoral election to one, which was reported as being a 'present' to Chernetsky, although it would presumably be more in Chernetsky's interest to keep two rounds as no known candidate would be likely to beat him on the second round, whereas if there were a large number of candidates he might not win an outright majority in one round.[78] In the event Chernetsky was endorsed by the vast majority of regional United Russia delegates and was registered as the official United Russian candidate for the 2008 mayoral election which he was to win by a large margin.

Notes

1 The project was funded by DFID and entitled RACE (Russia – advice to the city of Ekaterinburg). The focus of the project was not only the creation of a new type of socially oriented strategy, but the establishment of a large-scale participative partnership structure for decision-making in relation to the strategy. See n. 39.
2 See A. Campbell, 'City Government in Russia', in J. Gibson and P. Hanson (eds), *Transformation from Below*, Cheltenham: Edward Elgar, 1996, pp. 37–56.
3 R. Brunet, *La Russie: Dictionnaire Geographique*, CNRD-Libergeo – La Documentation Francaise, 2001, pp. 349–58.
4 Interview with Alexander Matrosov, Sverlovsk Regional Administration. August, 1993. See also Matrosov's article on the Urals Republic, *Izvestiya*, 10 July 1993.
5 In speech to Kursk veterans, July 1993, Rossel spoke of a Urals Region of 20 million, very similar to the Urals Federal District created in 2000/1. The smaller boundaries after 1993 were referred to as having been a means whereby the Central Committee could practice 'divide and rule'.
6 A. G. Granberg and V. V. Kistanov (eds), *Gosudarsvenno-territorial'noye Ustroistvo Rossii*, Moscow: DeKA, 2003. Granberg and his team welcomed the establishment of the seven federal districts, which they declared to have been based on their own preoject submitted to the presidential administration in 1999.
7 A. D. Kirillov, *Ural: ot Yelstina do Yeltsina*, Ekaterinburg: Urals University Press, 2006, pp. 286–8.
8 See his press secretary's memoir of the run-up to the election: A. Levin, *Kak stat' gubernatorom v sovremennoi Rossii*, Ekaterinburg: Novaya Gildiya, 1995.
9 Conversation with Alexander Bochko, Academy of Sciences, former Party official, Ekaterinburg, March 2003.
10 Interview with Sergei Plakhotin, August 1995.
11 In an interview with the authors in August 1993, Anton Bakov said that Moscow should be careful to avoid monopolizing the country's wealth if it did not wish to meet the same fate as Novgorod under Ivan the Terrible. The theme of Urals autonomy and resentment against a marauding Moscow was the theme of Bakov's 1995 book *Middle Earth*.
12 Conversation with A. Chernetsky, March 2001.
13 Interview with S. Plakhotin, August 1995.
14 Interview with Deputy Speaker of Ekaterinburg City Council, V. Semin, September 1995.
15 S. Tushin and O. Maslennikov in E. Tulisov (ed.), *Ekaterinburg: glavy gorodskogo samoupravleniya 1723–2000*, Ekatarinburg: Y-Factoriya, 2003.
16 Interview with Dr Viktor Rudenko, Institute of Philosophy, September 2005.
17 E. Loskutova, *Biography of Anton Bakov*, http://www.anticompromat.ru/bakov/bakbio.html. The creation of 'May' anticipated the movements launched under the coordination of Surkov (deputy head of the presidential administration) and Anton Bakov in 2004-5.
18 See S. Kuznetsov 'Dviuzheniye "Mai" – rostki grazhdanskogo obschestva ili zachatki ekstremisma?'. For a discussion of the extremism/civil society dichotomy of 'May' see, http:///xxx.svoboda.ural.ru/ch/ch19990522.html
19 According to media reports, 'May' had no genuine activists but consisted entirely of workers from the Serov metallurgical plant (a factory in the town of Serov in the north of Sverdlovsk Oblast that had been given to Bakov during the mid-1990s when he was allied with Rossel). For each attendance at a May rally the workers were

given 1-200 'Urals Franks' to spend in the company shop. The same hired activitists supported Bakov in a mass attack on the Khimmash chemical plant, which ended with Bakov forcibly expelling the previous owner, the oligarch Fedulev (admittedly a highly compromised figure in his own right), from the premises. The May movement transformed the political fortunes of Bakov's associate Burkov, who went from winning 1 per cent in previous elections to winning 28 per cent against Rossel in the 1999 gubernatorial contest. Although Rossel won easily with 78 per cent, Burkov had succeeded in joining the political elite and went on win seats at regional and national levels. See *Kommersant Den'gi*, Vol. 16, No. 471, 26 April 2004.

20 Chenetsky was to lobby consistently for an expansion for the fiscal base of local self-government, for which he made a strong case in front of President Putin at the 2003 annual conference of the Congress of Municipalities.

21 See S. Kondratiev 'The Urals Federal Okrug', in P. Reddaway and R. Orttung (eds), *The Dynamics of Russian Politics: Putin's Reform of Federal-Regional Relations. Vol. 1*, Lanham, MD, Boulder, CO, New York, Toronto and Oxford: Rowman and Littlefield, 2004, pp. 196–9.

22 It would be more accurate to say one of the candidates. Rossel had difficulty in choosing one candidate to oppose Chernetsky, in both 1999 and 2003. Several were backed, with the final choice being made on the eve of the election. For much of the run-up to the election of 2003 Rossel's team had been backing a different candidate, Gabinsky, seeing Osinstev more as a stalking horse to trip up and destabilize the mayor's position.

23 The city administration denied the charges, which were never, to our knowledge, proven.

24 In Russian governance, whether at federal, regional or municipal level, the Economy department has lead responsibility for overall development strategy, a legacy of the Soviet state planning hierarchy of Gosplan. After the fall of the Soviet Union, Gosplan became the Ministry of Economy of the Russian Federation (the Ministry of Economy of Ukraine and several other former soviet republics follows a similar logic). Departments of Economy at municipal level are not hierarchically subordinate to the Ministry of Economy, but are required to collect and submit statistics.

25 Some within the city hold the view that the federal projects presided over by the potential successor to Putin, Dmitri Medvedev (with whom the city's strategists had met in 2003), on which part of the federal budget's oil-generated surplus is being spent, took their inspiration from the Ekaterinburg City Strategy, which placed an emphasis on Education, Health and Housing as strategic areas of improvement in a way that was uncharacteristic of Russian policy in the early 2000s – interview with senior economic manager, Ekaterinburg City Administration, June 2007.

26 Russia-Advice to the City of Ekaterinburg (RACE), DFID (UK Department for International Development, which ran from 2000 to 2003 and was co-ordinated by the authors of this contribution. Elena Denezhkina was project manager and a member of the Co-ordinating Council and of the Board of the Programme Council for the Ekaterinburg Strategic Partnership. Adrian Campbell was project director. See the city strategy web-site http://www.strategy-burg.ru/, also 'The Ekaterinburg City Strategy'. Interview with Adrian Campbell in *Stolitsa Urala*, Issue 3, July 2003 (in Russian) and Russian national radio interview with Adrian Campbell, *Ekho Moskvy*, April 2003 (in Russian).

27 See article by Igor Saveliev 'Ekaterinburg Obraz Goroda XXI veka', http://www. arm-group.ru/rus/talks/articles/citydev/yekaterinburganimageforxxicentury/

28 'Ekaterinburg or Birmingham', by Nikolai Eichler, http//www.politsovet.ru/analy tic.asp?article = 1260, 27 November, 2002. Note : this pro-Osinstev article appeared on a website controlled by Anton Bakov, who was to lead Chernetsky's

campaign against Osintsev the following year. Clearly in 2002 Bakov was not yet fully allied to the mayor's team.

29 Conversation with city officials, June 2007. The strategy had been presented widely, especially through the urban strategy network established by Boris Zhikharevich at the Leontiev Centre in St Petersburg, and had been brought to Medvedev's attention in 2003-4. The participatory structure of the strategy co-ordination council and the partnership principle embodied by the programme council, as well as the arrangements for cooperation between stakeholders, experts and line managers, were also highly innovative in a Russian context.

30 Ministry of Foreign Affairs of Svedlovsk Region, 'Analytical conclusions on the draft strategic plan of Ekaterinburg up to 2015', prepared by the Deputy Chair of the Oblast Government and delivered to the City Duma of Ekaterinburg on 23 April, 2003.

31 Conversation with Ekaterinburg city officials, and with the Inter-regional Deputies's Faction (in April, 2003).

32 A. Campbell and E. Denezhkina, 'Comments on the "Analytical conclusions on the draft strategic plan of Ekaterinburg up to 2015" prepared by the Deputy Chair of the Oblast Government and delivered to the City Duma of Ekaterinburg on 23 April, 2003', 15 pages. Sent to Regional Administration 28 April 2003. Published on (city) API news web-site (in Russian), 26 May 2003 under the heading: 'Britansky experty rekomenduyut Ekaterinburgskoi gordumye prinyat strategichesky plan goroda, nesmotrya na vozrazheniya Yuriya Osintseva.' http://www.apiural.ru/politic/?news_id = 9271

33 e.g. 'Director proiekta RACE obvinyaet nekotopykh deputatov Ekaterinburgskikh deputatov vo Izhi', http://www.apiural.ru/politic/?news_id = 8605, 7 May 2003.

34 'Ekaterinburg. Deputaty gordumy pozhaluyutsya na 'khamskiye deistviya Britanskikh uchenykh'. http:www.regions.ru/news/1101157/, 12 May 2003.

35 'Strategicheskaya Feeriya: rossisskaya deistvitel'nost' v zerkale skandala', *Revizor*, No. 5, May–June 2003.

36 'Britantsi ugodili v omutye Uralskoi PR' – Uralpolit.ru, 15 May 2003, now accessible via http://www.allrussia.ru/nowadays/default.asp?NS_ID = per cent7BF62824DC-F76E-4C8E-B1E1-FBB81BB28267 per cent7D&HN_ID = 2

37 Conversation with pro-Oblast journalists May 2003.

38 'Vtoroi front protiv Gabinskovo', Politsoviet.ru/analytic.asp.article = 5156, 19 September 2003.

39 http://www.egd.ru/index.php?menu_id = 16041&show_id = 8858. The strategic plan itself was seen by some as the precursor for the Russian Federation's national projects, see http://www.pnp-ekb.ru/.

40 In some cases associations and voluntary groups concerned with those who had served in the war in Afghanistan became organised crime groups.

41 V. Volkov, *Violent Entrepreneurs: The Use of Force in the Making of Russian Capitalism*, Ithaca, NY: Cornell University Press, 2002.

42 The main spheres of influence of this group were in copper-related holdings e.g. 'Evropa', petrochemicals 'Uralnefteproduct', mobile services ('Uralvestcom'), car sales, breweries.

43 *Expert*, 15 April 2002.

44 The name OPS (Organized Crime Society) became known in 1993 following the arrest of Konstantin Tsiganov, its then leader. The arrest caused a reaction in the business community. The head of the broker firm 'Eurasia', Andrei Panpurin, referred to OPS Uralmash as being not a criminal group but a 'financial group' with a speciality in socially oriented activities, and referred to their 'civilized and democratic' style of operation, and businesses were not squeezed by them. Thus, Konstantin Tsiganov was a 'stabilizing factor' for the enterprises that came into contact with him. Tsiganov upheld a balance of power within the city that could

be upset following his arrest. Tsiganov was released and the group continued its operations but in a more discreet fashion. Panpurin, it later turned out, was in fact one of the leading members of OPS Uralmash.

45 *Uralsky Rabochy*, 28 December 1999.
46 See 'Chisto ural'skiye umel'tsi', *Vesti.ru*, 12 November 1999.
47 *Nezavisimaya Gazeta*, 11 June 1999.
48 See, for example, the profile of Kukovyakin in *Revizor*, No. 6, June–July 2003.
49 Conversations with regional officials, 2002. In the end it was not Khabarov, but Porunov, the mayor's ally who had previously been chair of the Oblast Duma, who replaced Silin following a cooling of relations between Silin and Chernetsky.
50 *Nezavisimaya Gazeta*, 10 July 2003.
51 Some considered Bakov to be not only a 'scandalously known businessman' but also 'rumoured to be close to criminal groups'.
52 Anton Bakov 'Ne mogu molchat'', http://www.bakov.ru/nemogu.shtml.
53 A video tape was broadcast, showing Gabinsky in the City Duma apparently asking OPS Uralmash Kukovyakin for financial support for his campaign, without realizing the microphone was switched on. The end to his campaign was reportedly brought about by Anton Bakov using federal connections to have his rating in the Party of Life lowered, therefore undermining his campaign stance of being a substantial political figure.
54 *Uralsky rabochy*, 11 December 2003.
55 *Oblastnaya Gazeta*, 16 December 2003.
56 *Kommersant*, 19 December 2003.
57 'Ekaterinburg – na smenu', *Narodnaya Volya*, No. 25 (72), 13 December 2003. Yuri Osintsev, 'Razgovor po Kuschesvu' (Manifesto).
58 *Oblastnaya Gazeta*, 9 December 2003.
59 *Oblastnaya Gazeta*, 16 December 2003.
60 *Vecherny Ekaterinburg*, 15 December 2003.
61 *Kommersant*, 18 December 2003.
62 *Ekaterinburgskaya Nedelya*, No. 52 (512), 25 December 2003.
63 *Nezavisimaya Gazeta*, 23 December 2003.
64 'Sto millionov tuda, sto syuda: i vse iz byudjeta', 4 December 2003. Reproduced on http://www.compromat.ru/main/rossel/chernetskij1000.htm.
65 *Delovoi Ural*, 48 (553), 23 December 2003.
66 *Kommersant*, 23 December 2003.
67 *Ekaterinburgskaya Nedelya*, No. 52 (512), 25 December 2003.
68 *Delovoi Ural*, No. 48 (553), 23 December 2003.
69 In December 2002 Khabarov had formally disbanded OPS Uralmash, although it clearly continued its existence and Khabarov was routinely referred to as the head of ex-Uralmash.
70 http://www.uralpolit.ru, 16 September 2004.
71 The symbol of United Russia is a bear.
72 *Nezavisimaya Gazeta*, 29 April 2004, 2 August 2004.
73 http;www.ura.ru/print/news/25900
74 Conversations with Ekaterinburg city officials, June 2007.
75 Zakat, 'koprporatsiya Ekaterinburg': u Arkadi Chernetskovo 'prokhudilos krysha'. http://www.lenta66.ru/politic/2007/06/26/40-67.
76 In Russian governance there is some reticence about publicly firing senior officials. Instead they go 'of their own volition', typically after being put in a position where this is the logical outcome.
77 'Gubernatorsky pasience: chevo hochet Kreml?', http://www.golossamara.ru/politics/2007/08/28/3802
78 'O chem. Chernetski dogovorilsya s Surkovym – detali vstrechi', http://www.lenta66.ru/politic/2007/08/16/6142 http://www.nr2.ru/ekb/139839.html.

10 Local self-government in Russia

Between decentralization and recentralization

Hellmut Wollmann and Elena Gritsenko

1 Task, scope and concept of the chapter

In this chapter we highlight key features of the recent law on local self-government (LSG)[1] which was ratified on 3 October 2003 under the title 'On the General Principles of the Organization of Local Self-Government in the Russian Federation'[2] (hereafter, 2003 Federal Law).[3] Our account and analysis will be guided particularly by three objectives. First, one of the focal interests of the Article is to place the 2003 Federal Law in a developmental perspective, that is, to explore whether and in which crucial aspects it links up with earlier stages of legislation on LSG and where it deviates from them. Such a historical and developmental approach will allow us to gauge in which direction Russia's legislative and institutional system of LSG is moving – towards greater or lesser degrees of decentralization or (re-)centralization. Thus, reference will be made to: the law, 'On Local Self-Government in the RSFSR' adopted on 6 July 1991 by the Supreme Soviet of the Russian Federation (hereafter, 1991 Federal Law); the Federal Constitution enacted on 12 December 1993; the Federal law, 'On the General Principles of the Organization of Local Self-Government' enacted on 28 August 1995 (hereafter, 1995 Federal Law).[4] References shall also be made to the law 'On the Principles of Local Self-Government and Local Economy'[5] which was adopted by the USSR Supreme Soviet on 5 April 1990 (hereafter, 1990 Law).

Second, the chapter will be structured by sequentially singling out and discussing crucial aspects of the regulation and institutionalization of LSG in order to identify the developmental trajectory within each sequence. Third, where it appears appropriate the chapter will put the legislative development, particularly the 2003 Federal Law, in an internationally comparative perspective, including references to the European Charter of Local Self-Government which was adopted by the Council of Europe in 1985. It was ratified by the Russian Parliament (State Duma) on April 1998[6] and came into force in Russia on 1 September 1998.[7]

2 The competency and scope of legislation on LSG

The history of legislation on LSG in the 'late-perestroika' Soviet Union began with the 1990 Law, which in an unprecedented move broke with the Soviet doctrine of the 'unity of the State' by recognizing and introducing the notions of LSG and 'questions of local significance' as a self-standing level and responsibility. It was obviously conceived as a federal 'frame' law, which was intended to leave legislative scope to member republics and regions.[8] The 1991 Federal Law which was passed by the Russian Parliament (RSFSR Supreme Soviet) on 6 July 1991 was employed by President Yeltsin as a tool of 'nation-building' in that, on the one hand, it was meant to supersede the (rival) USSR Federal legislation and, on the other, to put the establishment of LSG on a common legal footing throughout the RSFSR.[9]

In the wake of Yeltsin's power coup of 3 and 4 October 1993, the National Parliament was dissolved, as were the regional and local councils that had been elected in March 1991, and the 1991 Federal Law was largely suspended. However, the Federal Constitution of 1993 provided LSG with surprisingly progressive rights. With regard to future legislation on LSG, the Federal Constitution incorporated a compromise, which had been struck between the federal level and the regions. In the Federal Treaties of 31 March 1992 legislation on LSG was placed in the category of 'shared legislative powers' to be exercised either by the federal level or by the regions (see Article 72.1 letter n, Federal Constitution). Small wonder that, due to the generality and vagueness of this constitutional provision (typical of such 'dilatory compromises' between rivalling actors) its interpretation was prone to become a bone of contention in the continuing struggle between the federal and the regional levels.[10]

The 1995 Federal Law which was enacted on 28 August 1995 after a protracted legislative process and much controversy[11] can largely be seen as a 'frame law', in that the federal level made noticeably restrained use of its 'shared legislative power' and left considerable legislative scope in the regulation of LSG to the regional administrations.

During the late 1990s, also benefiting from the federal level's power erosion in the late Yeltsin era, the regions (Federal Subjects) made ample use of their 'shared legislative powers' – with a spree of regional legislative provisions on LSG many of which were seen as violating constitutional laws which were[12] meant to protect and guarantee the creation of LSG.[13] Perceived as taking 'the character of a chain reaction'[14] this wave of regional regulations on LSG contributed to what was a kind of 'legal separatism' and there were fears that the Federation would soon fall apart.[15]

Having been elected President on 26 March 2000, Vladimir Putin embarked upon re-establishing the Russian Federation as a 'strong state' by reasserting the federal government's influence and control over the regional and local levels.[16] Hence, in preparing and adopting the 2003 Federal Law, the Federal Government (in stark contrast to the previous 1995 Federal

Law) made extensive use of the 'shared legislative powers', by laying down detailed regulations that left only scarce legislative scope and leeway to the Federal Subjects. The copious use made by the Federal Government of its 'shared legislative powers' (at the cost of the Federal Subjects) has been criticized as 'excessive' and 'exceeding constitutional limits'.[17]

3 Intergovernmental setting and the territorial structure of LSG

3.1 LSG as a self-standing (non-state?) level

The USSR Law on LSG of 5 April 1990 was, as already highlighted, an unprecedented move, to break away from the Soviet doctrine of the 'unity of the State' and to recognize LSG as a self-standing political and administrative level within the state's inter-organizational setting. In Article 12 the 1993 Constitution gave conspicuous expression of the notion that, in the subsequently much-quoted formulation, 'the organs of LSG are not part of the organization of state organs'.[18] In Article 14.5 of the 1995 Federal Law this provision was literally adopted and the stipulation was added that the conduct of LSG functions by state authorities was not permitted.

Not surprisingly the idea to assign the LSG level a status distinct and separate from the State evoked a lively conceptual (and, in its core, political) debate. On the one hand, the cities and their representatives as well as many academics hailed Article 12 of the Federal Constitution as legitimating LSG and its autonomy,[19] and placing local self-government within the 'non-state' and 'societal' spheres.[20] Such a view was reminiscent of that held during the era of the 'zemstvos' in the late nineteenth century.[21] On the other hand, the concept was criticized by some as ushering in 'an artificial distinction between two power channels',[22] and as conjuring up the risk of the State becoming 'ungovernable'.

The 1995 Federal Law has literally adopted this constitutional provision (in Article 14. 5) and emphatically added that the conduct of LSG functions by State authorities was 'not admissible'. The 2003 Federal Law continues to adopt Article 12 of the Federal Constitution (in Article 34.4). Hence, the current legislation upholds the bold claim (and vision) that LSG is 'not part of the State administration'.

In the international comparative debate a conceptual distinction has been made between 'separationist' and 'integrationist' models of local government.[23] While the former hints at a conceptual and institutional 'separation' between the local and the State levels, the latter views local authorities as being institutionally linked with, and 'integrated' into, State structures. Taken at face value, the conceptual claim to the 'non-State' status of LSG envisaged in Article 12 of the Russian Constitution could well be ranked as a 'separationist' scheme. However, as will be shown below, as a result of the 'dual function' scheme (Article 132.2 of the Federal Constitution) under which the local authorities may be put in charge of carrying out tasks 'delegated' to them by the State, the local authorities operate, in the conduct of such 'delegated' tasks, under the tight instruction and control of the State. This brings them close to acting as 'part of the State structures' and of being 'integrated' into them – in sharp contradiction to the 'non-state' vision posited in Article 12.

At this point, it should be noted that a new concept and term, '*publichnyi*' ('public'), has been coined to legally capture the status of LSG. The conceptual and terminological repertoire dating back to the Soviet era was characterized by the dichotomy between 'statist' (*gosudarstvennii*) and 'societal' (*obshchestvennii*) concepts of local government. Under the doctrine of the 'unity of the State', any 'public' sphere outside the State was politically inadmissible and, hence, conceptually unthinkable. In the meantime, Russia's post-Soviet jurisprudence has developed the notion of 'public', particularly with regard to LSG,[24] in order to legally qualify its status as being neither 'State' (in the narrow institutional sense) nor 'society' (as a sphere of 'societal' actors, including 'non-governmental organizations', NGOs).

3.2 Territorial organization

The 1990 Law fell in line with the Soviet tradition of regarding the Federal Subjects (regions) as 'local' entities.[25] By contrast, the 1991 Law ceased to count these as 'local', which mirrored the rapid 'internal federalization' of the Russian Republic. In the Federal Treaties of March 1992 the regions were elevated to the status of Federal Subjects, including the cities of Moscow and St Petersburg, and only the tiers below the subject (regional and republic) level were designated as local.

In the legislative debate about the 1995 Federal Law, the territorial structure of LSG was one of the most controversial issues. Whilst an influential group of deputies advocated (in the so called 'deputatskii variant') that a full-fledged two-tier LSG structure be legally prescribed (thus assigning LSG also to the districts, *raiony*), President Yeltsin (in the 'presidentskii variant') pushed for LSG to be established only on the 'settlement' (*poselenie)* level, while the districts were to continue to be units of state administration. The final version of the 1995 Law showed the ambivalence of a ('dilatory') compromise in which the detailed regulation of the territorial structure was left to the regions.[26] In the ensuing spree of regional legislation on the territorial structure essentially three patterns emerged.[27] In most (that is in forty-six) Federal Subjects the single-tier district (*raion*) type was put in place – with LSG established only in the districts (and some large cities), while the bulk of towns and villages were left without LSG. In about twenty regions the single-tier 'settlement' type was introduced – with LSG established only on the level of the towns and villages, whereas the district level was turned over to the state administration. In a further twenty regions the full-fledged two-tier LSG system was installed (as envisaged in the 'deputy variant'). The great variance which the regional legislation manifested regarding the territorial structure of LSG was a typical feature of the institutional hetero-geneity that has characterized Russia's subnational/regional/local space since the mid-1990s.

This process of territorial and functional restructuring under the imprint of regional legislation resulted in a significant reduction of the number of LSG units. Their number fell, countrywide, to 12,000 by 1998 as compared to 28,000 in 1990.[28] There were a number of reasons for this collapse. First, in thousands of towns and villages there were no elected local governments, as in half of all regions the single-tier district type of LSG was introduced that barred lower-level municipalities from creating LSG. Second, in regions with the single-tier settlement type of LSG, an increasing number of towns and villages decided, for lack of administrative and financial resources, to merge with others to form larger LSG units. Finally, in view of their administrative and financial plight single-tier settlement-based local autho-rities decided to dissolve themselves and to pass their functions on to the district (State) administration.[29]

In view of the extreme heterogeneity of the territorial, organizational and functional LSG structures across regions, and because of Putin's aims to territorially and organizationally streamline and 'unify' local-level structures, thereby making them more amenable to central level guidance and control, the territorial and functional reforms of LSG is a key aspect of the 2003 Federal Law.

The legislative territorial and organizational scheme hinges on three types of LSG units, and on certain organizational criteria to be applied throughout the Federation:

- Lower-level municipalities,[30] either rural municipalities (*selskie posele-niya*) and urban municipalities (*gorodskie poselenya*), are to be established as lower-level LSG units, whereby in all settlements with a total of at least 1,000 inhabitants such LSG units (with an elected local council etc.) must be formed (Article 11.1(6) of the 2003 Federal Law). In view of the fact that since the mid-1990s elected local authorities at town and village levels had disappeared in half of the regions due to the establishment of single-tier districts, the 2003 Federal Law makes it obligatory for these regions to install a two-tier LSG system with elected LSG authorities.[31]
- At the upper level, *municipal districts* (*munitsipal'nye raiony*) are to be formed as a (two-tier) local authority, the territory of which comprises the lower-level rural and urban municipalities and is often identical with the former administrative districts (*raiony*). They can be institutionally and functionally compared to the German *Kreise* and to the British/English *counties*.
- Moreover, at the upper level, in urban and metropolitan contexts city districts (*gorodskie okruga*) are to be established as (single-tier) elected local authorities, which combine district and municipality functions. The

status of city districts has in most cases been granted to regional capitals and similarly large (industrial) cities. In comparative terms, they have an equivalent in the German (single-tier) *kreisfreie Städte* ('county free cities') as well as in the English (single-tier) unitary local authorities.

• Standing in remarkable contrast to its basic thrust to pre-empt and curb the legislative powers of the regions within the constitutional concept of 'shared legislative powers', the 2003 Federal Law puts the regions explicitly in charge of implementing these massive territorial, organizational and functional reforms (see Article 85.1).

In setting a legislative schedule with binding deadlines for the various steps and components of territorial and organizational reforms, the 2003 Federal Law gave the regions 'extraordinary' powers during the initial 'founding' period to suspend the 'ordinary' legal provisions (relating, for instance, to the rights of the local population to create local boundaries by referendum[32] or the right of the local councils to settle, by way of local charters (*ustavy*), the composition of their councils, their duration and the type of local leadership).[33] These 'extra-ordinary' powers of the regions pertain particularly to the 'newly created municipalities' that are to be established 'from scratch' (see Article 85.1(2) of the 2003 Federal Law). At the end of the restructuring period some 12,000 out of 24,000 LSG units were 'newly formed', with their boundaries and institutional setting, having been decided 'single-handedly' by the regional authorities.

In the meantime (as of 1 October 2006) a total of 1,757 legislative acts have been passed by regional assemblies to restructure the LSG levels and units under the mandate of Article 85 of the 2003 Federal Law, resulting in: 19, 904 rural settlements (*selskie poseleniya*), 1,745 city settlements (*gorodskie poseleniya*), both constituting the lower-level of the two-tier LSG structure, 1,801 municipal districts (*munitsipal'nye raiony*) which make up the upper level of the two-tier LSG system, and 522 city districts (*gorodskie okruga*) which are the (single-tier) local authorities in urban/big city/metropolitan areas.[34] There are also 236 'inner-municipal areas' in the two 'cities of federal status', Moscow and St Petersburg. As a consequence of these developments the number of local authorities has about doubled from some 12,000 in 2000 to 24,210 in October 2006. This sharp increase is mainly due to the creation of new municipalities in regions and rural areas where lower-level elected local authorities had not been put in place, or had been eliminated during the 1990s.

The great number of 'newly formed' municipalities hints also at the magnitude of the administrative, personnel and financial challenges posed by this massive institutional transformation at the local level. The fact that the deadline by which the 2003 Federal Law should be operative in all its provisions has been postponed several times (from 2006 to 2009) mirrors the (administrative, financial but also political) difficulties which this mammoth restructuring project has encountered.

4 Functional model of LSG

Dating back to the RSFSR Law of 1991, Russia's LSG system has been characterized by the 'dual function model' according to which, besides being responsible for 'questions of local importance' in their own right, the local authorities can be put in charge of carrying out tasks 'delegated' to them by the State. In adopting the 'dual function' model of LSG, Russia's legislation fell in line with (and probably consciously drew on) a strand of (West) European local government tradition, which has been part and parcel of the German-Austrian system of local government since the early nineteenth century, and was also a characteristic of local government in Central Eastern Europe until 1945.[35]

4.1 (Genuine) local government tasks

In line with the concepts of LSG and 'question of local importance', which were first introduced by the 1990 Law, the 1991 Law took up the concept of LSG as a self-standing legal body at the local level, which marked a rupture from the Soviet concept of the 'unity of the State'. At the same time, by assigning these tasks exclusively to LSG, it broke with the 'Russian doll' ('Matryoshka') principle that allowed the higher government levels to intervene in and take over any (local) matters.[36]

In accordance with 1995 Federal Law, the 2003 Federal Law puts forward a differentiated concept and understanding of 'questions of local importance'. On the one hand, it puts forward a general definition of 'questions of local importance' (Article 2.1) which largely corresponds with what is understood in (West) European (particularly Continental European) countries as the (traditional) 'general competence clause'.[37] On the other hand, it spells out lists of specific tasks assigned to the three types of LSG. This enumeration approach shows some resemblance with the British/England *ultra vires doctrine* according to which the local authorities may only exercise those powers that have been explicitly ascribed to them by Act of Parliament.[38] The mix of these two principles in the 2003 legislation (as well as in the previous 1995 legislation) has given rise to legal controversies since the 'enumeration' approach has been criticized for making the assignment of tasks 'inflexible', and for obscuring the scope of 'questions of local importance' as a self-standing source of task definition.[39] In fact, the repeated amendments to the 'list of competencies' hints at the legislative uncertainties they harbour.

It should be noted, however, that the list of 'competencies' spelt out in the 2003 Federal Law show a significant conceptual advance in that some differentiation is made particularly between the tasks ascribed, within the two-tier structure, to the lower-level LSG units (settlements), on the one hand, and to the upper LSG units (municipal districts), on the other (see articles 14 and 15) – with the latter being assigned tasks that go beyond the borders (*vne granits*) of the 'settlements'. Whereas in the antecedent 1995 legislation such a differentiation between the LSG level was not made, the 2003 legislative scheme marks still another step, away from the Soviet-era 'matryoshka doll' principle.

4.2 Delegated (State) tasks

The Federal Constitution of 1993 explicitly mandated the 'dual function' model of LSG when it declared that 'organs of LSG can be endowed, by law, with specific state tasks'[40] (Article 132.2) – with the crucial addendum and proviso that such transfer of tasks should/must proceed alongside 'the transfer of the material and financial resources required for the discharge thereof'.[41]

In an important organizational innovation and shift, the 2003 Federal Law has linked the prescription of the Federation-wide two-tier LSG system to the provision that only the upper LSG units, that is the (two-tier) municipal districts and (single-tier) city/metropolitan districts, carry out 'delegated (State) tasks'. Thus, it is local authorities in the 522 city districts (which are essentially constituted by the regional capitals and other big – industrial – cities), and the 1,081 municipal districts (which are largely identical with the earlier administrative districts), which are charged with carrying out the delegated (state) functions.

4.3 'Statesization' (ogosudarstvlenie) through the delegation of functions?

Under the constitutionally confirmed 'dual function' model, Russia's LSG system has been exposed to similar tensions and contradictions to those found in western European states (such as Germany) which employed the 'dual function' model of local government.[42] In this model:

- The ('genuine') LSG matters fall to the responsibility of the elected councils. In exercising them the local authorities stand under the legal review of State authorities as a 'mild' form of state control (in German: *Rechtsaufsicht*). One may also speak of a 'separationist' model[43] that institutionally and functionally distances the LSG levels and units from the State. Article 12 of the Federal Constitution that declares LSG not to be 'part of the State' would express the 'separationist' idea.
- By contrast, with regard to 'delegated' (State) tasks the elected local councils have no or minimal influence, while their conduct lies with the local administration and executive. At the same time, the discharge of 'delegated' tasks is subject to a comprehensive ('administrative') control by the upper State authorities, pertaining to the 'expediency' and appropriateness of local decisions (in German: *Fachaufsicht*).
- Since it is categorically stipulated in Article 132.2 of the Federal Constitution that the 'implementation of delegated tasks (takes places)

under the control of the State'[44] and as local administration, in the conduct of 'delegated' tasks, is significantly tied into and 'integrated' with the State administration, one can see this as an *integrationist* model with a tendency to 'statesize' (*ogosudarstvlenie*) the local authorities.[45]

5 The political institutions and procedures of LSG

5.1 The rights of the local citizens

Dating back to the 1991 legislation the political rights of the local citizens have been given key importance. From the beginning, besides electoral rights, other participatory forms of direct democracy have been highlighted. Accordingly, the Federal Constitution of 1993 assigns local democracy a high constitutional rank. After referring to LSG as a basic form in which 'the (multi-national) people' realizes its 'sovereign right... also through organs of LSG' (Article 3), and after emphatically stipulating that local citizens 'must not be deprived of their right to have LSG' (Article 12. 1), the Constitution goes on to spell out that LSG 'is exercised by the citizens through referendums, elections, and other forms of direct expression of its will, through elected and other organs of local self-government' (Article 130.2).

Falling in line with these sweeping democratic proclamations, the 1995 and 2003 Federal Laws have both gone to great lengths to codify the democratic rights of the citizens. In fact, judging by the formal letter of the law the repertoire of local citizen rights is more extensive than in many (West) European countries. Thus, for example, binding local referendums are not provided for in Sweden and Great Britain. In a similar vein, the direct election of mayors introduced in Russia, as a principle, in 1991 (see below) has made its entry in (West) European countries only since the early 1990s and has so far been adopted only in Germany and Italy and England.[46] The same applies to the 'direct democratic' right of citizens to 'recall' the sitting mayor/head of administration (see below) which has so far been introduced, among (West) European countries, only in Germany,[47] after having been traditionally in place in some US States. It needs to be added, however, that in the current reality of Russia's local politics the practical exercise of these democratic local citizen rights often falls woefully behind such legal prescriptions.

5.2 Local councils

(a) Status, composition

In the 1991 legislation an all but paradigmatic change was effected in the (horizontal) arrangement of functions and powers between the elected local council and the local executive position-holders.[48] In what, with some caution and not without controversy,[49] can be regarded as local variants of the concept of the 'division of powers' and 'checks and balances', the local elected council is seen as the supreme local representative organ that essentially acts as a deliberative, rule-setting and scrutinizing body, while the administrative function is assigned to a local administration directed by the 'head of administration' (*glava administratsii*) acting as a 'chief executive' with a monocratic (*edinonachalie*) role.[50]

While, as a general principle, all LSG councils are elected directly by the local citizens, an exception has been introduced by the 2003 legislation (Article 35.4(1)) for the councils of municipal districts. Instead of being directly elected the municipal district councils may be indirectly elected (depending on approval by a local referendum) from the deputies and heads of the member settlements. This modality of composing municipal district councils by way of delegation has been criticized in a legal debate as violating the constitutional guarantees of LSG (and also the pertinent Article 3 European Charter). Currently the composition of 220 district councils (which make up 14 per cent of the 1,801 district councils) has been formed through this indirect delegation method.[51]

(b) Powers and responsibilities of the local councils

According to Article 35.10 of the 2003 Law the elected councils possess remarkably broad powers. Among these looms large the adoption of the local charter ('ustav') (see Article 35.10(1), and Article. 44), in which the local council can determine a broad spectrum of questions – in an array of matters which, *nota bene*, are wider than in most (West) European countries. Thus, for example, within the limit of legal thresholds, they have the power to determine the number of council members and the duration of the elective mandate of the council. Interestingly the 'norm-setting' power of the local councils pertains even, under certain conditions, to 'delegated' matters (see Article 7.2) – which is different, for instance, from the German practice of the 'dual function' model on which the elected council does not have any influence.

In addition to these decision-making powers the local council is assigned the pivotal function to exercise 'control over the discharge, by organs of local self-government and its position-holders, of their local level responsibilities' (Article 35.10(9)).[52] But when it comes to delegated functions administered by the municipal and city districts, in comparison with the German practice of the 'dual function' model, the Russian councils have to function under much tighter control from the State.

5.3 Head of municipality and head of administration

As was already pointed out, in an all but paradigmatic rupture and shift from the previous Soviet State model, and in a move premised on a local variant of the 'division of powers' concept and the 'checks and balances' principle,[53] the position of the 'head of administration' was introduced as a local ('monocratic') chief executive in juxtaposition to the elected local council.

The directly elected 'head of administration' made its spectacular entry to Russia's local government system when, in June 1991, Gavriil Popov and Anatoly Sobchak were elected mayors of the cities of Moscow and Leningrad, respectively. Their election was seen, at the time, as signalling a victory by democratic reformers over members of the Soviet elite (*nomenklatura*).[54]

The 1991 Law on LSG, bearing the handwriting of Yeltsin's reformist camp, followed suit and introduced the post of directly elected 'head of administration' as a centrepiece in the new post-Soviet local government system with some resemblance to a 'local presidential system'. The first round of direct elections of the new 'mayors' was scheduled to take place on 1 November 1991. However, as part of his power-struggle with the ('old communist') majority in the Supreme Soviet and in an attempt to enforce his policy of 'radical economic reforms', Yeltsin, while retaining the mayors as 'monocratic' local position-holders, suspended their election and, instead, appointed them, thereby turning them into local cogs of his 'vertical power' machine.[55]

In the wake of Yeltsin's power coup of October 1993, the local heads of administration continued to be strictly appointed 'from above', first, within Yeltsin's 'power vertical' and second, under the sway of the increasingly powerful regional governors. The 1995 Federal Law held on to the 'monocratic' position of the head of administration, whereby it was left to the local council to decide (by way of the local charter) whether the head of administration be elected directly by the local citizens or indirectly by the local council. As a result of these provisions, for the first time in Russia's history a large number of mayors were directly elected. These popularly elected and self-confident local leaders were soon to pose a challenge not only to the regional governors, but also to the central government.[56]

The 2003 Federal Law inaugurated a significant institutional innovation by introducing the distinction between function (and possibly position) of the 'head of municipality' (*glava munitsipal'novo obrazovaniya*) and the 'head of administration' (*glava administratsii*) (articles 36 and 37), the latter directing the local administration, in a 'chief executive' function, on the 'single actor' (monocratic) principle which, as was already mentioned, made its entry into Russia's LSG legislation in 1991.

According to the 2003 Law the function of the 'head of administration' can be filled in two ways:

• Either, the 'chief executive' function is exercised by the 'head of municipality' himself/herself. In case the 'head of municipality' resumes the 'chief executive' function it is stipulated (mirroring some local variant of 'division of power' concept) as a rule that he/she cannot be chairperson of the local council (see Article 36.2(4)). However, in rural settlements the chief executive and the chairing the council functions may be combined by the head of municipality (see Article 36.3). Such a combination of functions has been laid down in the charters of 48.3 per cent of all settlements.[57]

- Or the 'chief executive' function is assigned to the newly introduced position of the 'contractual' 'head of administration', appointed by the local council. The 'head of municipality' plus 'head of administration' arrangement is analogous to the '(elected) mayor plus (appointed) city manager' scheme which is in place in some 'Western' countries (such as in some US States[58] and since 2000 in the 'elected mayor plus city manager' variant in England).[59] One of the main aims behind the 'contractual' head of administration was to 'professionalize' the conduct of local administrations.

As a rule, the selection and appointment of the contractual head of administration is to be effected by the local council on the basis of a competition that is carried out by a 'competition committee', the members of which are chosen by the municipal council (see Article 37.5).

Reflecting the fact, that under the provisions of the 2003 Federal Law, the 'delegation' of State tasks essentially pertains to, and focuses on, the municipal districts (*munitsipal'nye raiony*) and city districts (*gorodskie okruga*), the regional authorities are given special powers to exert their influence on the competition and selection process (see Article 37). This shows particularly in the provision that one half of the members of the crucial 'competition committee' must be representatives of the regional authorities, in addition to the other half, elected by the local councils.

The influence, thus opened to the regional authorities over the politically sensitive selection of the contractual heads of administrations is just another example of the institutional mechanisms through which the upper level LSG units are meant to be 'integrated' into the State administration. Small wonder then, that when the time came to carry out their mandate (under Article 85) to massively restructure the levels and units of LSG, the regional authorities preferred to prescribe and impose the 'head of municipality plus head of administration model', that is, the 'city manager model', upon the local authorities. About three quarters of all LSG units currently operate under the contractual head of administration ('city manager') scheme.[60]

5.4 Removal of the head of municipality and/or head of administration

As we noted above, local citizens have the right to 'recall' the local elected position-holders by local referendum – a provision which was first introduced in the 1991 Federal Law and which has been extended, in the 2003 Federal Law, to all elected local positions, including members of the elected council (71.2). As was already said, such (formally extended) 'recall' procedures can be found only in a few 'Western' countries (such as some US States and more recently in Germany).[61]

The right of the regional and central government authorities to remove an (elected) local 'head of administration' has always been a politically particularly touchy issue as it was right at the heart of the central–local level relations. Under Article 49 of the 1995 legislation the removal from office of a local head of administration could be decided by the regional assembly only on narrowly defined legal grounds and needed to be confirmed by a court decision.[62] Subsequently, on 8 August 2000 this Article was amended, significantly broadening the reasons for which regional (and now also federal) local authorities could take the initiative to dismiss local heads of administration from office.[63]

The 2003 Law continued on this course of making the status of local position-holders (including heads of municipalities as well as heads of administration) even more precarious by widening the reasons for their removal to include for instance the violations of federal and regional legislation, as well as of local charters; again these are subject to a court decision (Article 74).

6 State control over the levels and units of LSG

In total, the 2003 Federal Law has laid down a number of legal procedures and levers that, in being mutually supportive and complementary, add up to a formidable repertoire of top-down guidance and control.

To just briefly sum up:

- In the conduct of their 'normal' LSG responsibilities the local authorities operate under the 'ordinary' legality review by the upper level State authorities – whereby the power of the regional authorities to initiate a removal procedure against a local position-holder (under Article 74) acts as a permanent threat and sanction.
- In discharging the delegated functions, the municipal districts and urban areas are subject to a much more extensive supervision by the upper level State authorities, pertaining not only to a legality review, but also control over the expediency and appropriateness of their activities. In most of these units the chief executive function is in the hands of a contractual head of administration. The strong hand which the regional authorities have in the latter's selection, contract, qualification, etc., accentuates and reinforces the tendency of local units being subjugated and 'integrated' into State structures – in clear defiance of Article 12 of the Federal Constitution.
- The generality and vagueness of the reasons stated in Article 74 (2003 Federal Law) which allow regional authorities to start dismissal procedures against local position-holders has led to a situation whereby local heads may be politically and psychologically intimidated by regional authorities.

- Still another avenue of top-down intervention (and potential intimidation) has been included in Article 75 of the 2003 Law, according to which the regional authorities may temporarily intervene by suspending the power of the local authority and by acting in their stead, in cases where the budget deficit exceeds the local authority's own revenues by 30 per cent. The threat to the status of the LSG levels and units, lurking in this provision, lies in a budgetary 'vicious cycle'. Federal and regional authorities have been eager to shift expenditure-intensive responsibilities (infrastructural, social policy, etc. tasks) to the local authorities while failing to live up to their obligations (formally entrenched in Article 132.2 of the Federal Constitution) that such transfer of tasks should go hand in hand with the transfer of the required 'material and financial resources'. Thus, the local authorities find themselves in a budgetary trap, which all but forces them to drive up their budgetary deficits. This, however, conjures up the spectre of a 'top down' intervention under Article 75. Moreover, Article 75 provides the context for political manoeuvering and 'arm-twisting', as federal and regional authorities may employ a financial lever to withhold grants to politically opposed local authorities, wilfully driving them further into the budgetary 'vicious cycle'. Furthermore, an interventionist measure under Article 75 may allow regional 'raid-type' actions against local authorities, with the aim of dividing up municipal property, including real estate, following a similar pattern to the hostile take-over of companies by other enterprises.[64]

7 Local government finances

Parallel to the territorial, functional and institutional changes predicated in the 2003 Law, which was intended to make LSG more amenable to central and hierarchical guidance and control, the entire tax and budgetary system has also been revamped to buttress and support the centralist thrust. Without going into details at this point[65] it should suffice to highlight the following points. On the expenditure side of the LSG level it should be recalled that in recent years the federal government has been pouring out legislation which has led to LSG being overburdened with delegated tasks, particularly in the infrastructural and social policy fields. Hence, the local-level expenditures have seen a steep growth.

On the revenue side, it is stipulated, it is true, in Article 132.2 of the Federal Constitution, as well as Article 19.5 of the 2003 Law, that the transfer of tasks should be accompanied with the necessary funds to carry out these tasks. Yet, in recent years the federal government has far from heeded this constitutional and legal obligation. Insofar as grants were assigned, they have been given as narrowly 'ear-marked' (categorical) grants, often based on a short-term formula which allows the upper government levels flexibility and also political discretion, whilst depriving local government of the possibility to plan its expenditure on a long-term scale.

Furthermore, through changes in the overall taxation system, the share of the local authorities' own (local) taxes as compared to the total amount of public tax revenues has been reduced, while the share of the federal taxes has increased. This shift reveals a massive re-centralization of the country's tax and fiscal system with a pattern of top-down distribution and flow of money which increasingly resembles the 'fan scheme' that was characteristic of the centralist Soviet State model.[66] Thus, for example, the share of the federal revenues of the entire public revenues grew from 40 per cent in 1998 to 66 per cent in 2006, while that of the local authorities fell from 27.6 per cent in 1999 to 18.7 per cent in 2002. Correspondingly, the share of government grants in the local government revenues grew from 26.7 per cent to 40.9 per cent.[67]

8 Summary: Pendulum of LSG swinging back towards re-centralization and 'statesization'

Since the collapse of communism in the Soviet Union in 1991 the LSG system has experienced a conspicuous sequence of ruptures and shifts. Remarkably radical moves were already made by the 1991 Law on LSG, particularly on two points. First, in abandoning the 'Stalinist' concept of the 'unity of the State' the local authorities were recognized as being endowed, in the vertical dimension, with self-standing LSG powers. Second, in the local horizontal dimension a kind of local 'division of powers' was acknowledged, with an elected local council (as the local 'legislative' decision-making body), and the elected, monocratic 'head of administration'. Although the concept of the local 'head of administration' fell immediately prey to Yeltsin's decision to turn this position into a local appointee in his 'vertical power' hierarchy, the basic concept of the 'duality' of local council and local executive has become a permanent feature of the institutionalization of Russia's LSG.

Between 1991 and 1993, under the new legislative scheme (despite its truncation by the suspension of the direct election of the mayors) Russia's towns and villages saw an unprecedented upsurge of local politics and LSG activities. The elections to the local councils which were held nationwide on 3 March 1990 were premised, for the first time in the Soviet Union's history, on a competitive, multi-candidate, quasi-democratic formula. These elections proved to be a turning point, in that, through them, cohorts of reform-minded people (largely reform communists) were elected to the councils and found themselves confronting 'old guard' communists, still entrenched in the 'executive committees'.[68] In short, this period saw an 'active transformation of life in the localities',[69] most noticeably in the larger cities, less so in rural areas.[70] Without much exaggeration one might speak of a political and institutional (albeit, alas, short-lived) 'springtime' of Russia's LSG.[71]

However, the institutional and political development of Russia's LSG was profoundly disrupted when President Yeltsin resorted to violence to resolve his power struggle with the Khasbulatov-led majority of the Russian

Parliament. The Parliament was forcibly dissolved through the use of military force on 3 and 4 October 1993. In addition, the entire structure of regional and local councils that had been elected in March 1990 for four years was also dissolved and the development of LSG suffered a severe set-back.

The adoption of the Federal Constitution of December 1993 and the enactment of the 1995 Law provided the legal basis for new developments in local politics. It was particularly during the late years of the Yeltsin era – when federal power was eroding and the power of the regional governors was rising – that, local self-government in some regions experienced a significant revival, at least in larger cities. Some observers, such as Sergey Mitrokhin (who, as a Yabloko deputy of the Russian State Duma, was one of the chief promoters of the 1995 Law) went so far as to speak of a 'municipal revolution'.[72]

After Vladimir Putin became President in 2000 he embarked on a 'federal reform' which hinged on a decentralization of political and financial powers at the federal level and which aimed at bringing the regions as well as local government back under federal control. Against this backdrop, the 2003 Law contains a number of ambivalent propositions. On the one hand, it continues to subscribe to the political and institutional principles of local self-government, which have been part and parcel of Russia's local government schemes since 1991. As far as the stipulation of democratic and participatory rights of local citizens and the scope of decision-making powers of the elected local council are concerned, the 2003 Law not only falls in line with (West) European local government systems (and with the *European Charter*), but in some respects gives even wider rights and powers to the citizens and the councils. On the other hand, however, the 2003 Law is imbued with the centralist logic of Putin's 'federal reforms', which aims to 'streamline the Federation's entire political and administrative system. Local government is now much more amenable to political, administrative and financial controls from the centre. An array of provisions and mechanisms have been inserted in the 2003 Law, which are directed at 'integrating' local government structures into (federal and regional) state structures. This applies particularly to the upper level of municipal districts and city districts and their responsibilities to carry out 'delegated' state functions. In this context, it should be stressed, that with regard to the newly introduced position of a 'contractual' ('city manager') head of administration, as distinct from the head of municipality, regional authorities have now been given a powerful voice in defining the 'contracts', the professional qualifications required for such posts, and details of the recruitment and selection process. Somewhat pointedly, these 'city managers' might be seen as 'Trojan Horses' whose role is to provide additional state influence, particularly on the upper levels of LSG, thus fostering the 'statesization' of local government.

Among the mechanisms that are meant to place local authorities under state control and possibly discipline and sanction them, mention should also be made of the comprehensive state control over 'delegated' tasks, the extended right of state authorities to remove (albeit still depending on a court's approval) the heads of municipalities, heads of administration and elected councils, and, in temporarily suspending the local authorities, to act in lieu of them. The centralist thrust of the institutional design has been complemented and enforced by similar centralist changes in the overall fiscal and budgetary regime, through which federal control over the local authorities has been financially buttressed.

Within the recent territorial and functional reform of the local government structures (which is probably the key piece of the 2003 Law) additional powers have been given to the regional authorities to decide on the organizational and institutional setting of the newly created local government units (a task normally left to local councils to decide). By way of these regional legislative acts, for instance, the 'contractual head of administration' model has been put in place in the majority of the cases.

The centralist levers that are at work in provisions of the 2003 Law, as well as in the budgetary system, are political enforced in many localities by the dominance of President Putin's party, United Russia ('Edinaya Rossiya'), and by the regional and local 'parties of power' which, while revolving around regional and local political leaders and their political (and economic) 'families', are often closely linked, if not identical with the presidential party.[73] As these regional and local networks of political parties and groups are, in many cases, closely tied to the President and often hold overwhelming majorities in the local councils, decisions on the application (or non-application) of the formal rules are often made in compliance with orders from above. In addition, the independence of court decisions (where such decisions are still required, for instance for the removal of local position-holders) may be in jeopardy, in view of the fact that local power elites also control the process of nominating and appointing judges.

Hence, in sum, the available evidence paints a fairly bleak picture of the present state of local government in Putin's Russia, which bears traces, as it was caustically put, of a 'municipal counter-revolution',[74] a dismantling of the (incipient) 'municipal revolution' of the mid-1990s, and a general decline in the powers of LSG, with the exception of some big cities.[75] At the same time the chorus of voices questioning the feasibility of LSG, given Russia's centuries-old statist tradition and the weakness of civil society, has been gradually been gaining salience.[76] Whether the 'revival' of LSG units, in the wake of mammoth territorial and organizational reforms under Article 85 of the 2003 Federal Law, has the potential to reverse these centralist trends and to belie the growing number of sceptic voices, remains to be seen.

Notes

1 In the Russian legal and legislative parlance since 1990 the term '*mestnoe samoupravlenie*' has been employed which, in the literal translation, means 'local self-*administration*'. This is analogous to the relevant terminology which is used in

Continental European countries, for instance in Germany ('kommunale Selbst*verwaltung*' = 'municipal *self-administration*') and in France (' libre *administration*' = 'free *administration*'). Although it may be more appropriate to speak, with regard to Russia, also of 'self-*administration*', we shall use the term 'local self-government' which, derived from the British tradition, is the more familiar term employed by international scholars.

2 'Ob obshchikh printsipakh organizatsii mestnovo samoupravleniya v Rossiiskoi Federatsii'.

3 In the official registration of Russian Federation legislation this act is identified as Federal Law, No. 131, which points at the sequence of legislative enactments during the State Duma's respective legislative period. Accordingly, in the relevant Russian literature it is mostly referred to as (Federal) Law 131. Because of the historical and developmental approach we pursue in this chapter we prefer to speak of the 2003 Law in order to set it sequentially apart from earlier pieces of legislation.

4 In the official registration of Russian Federation legislation this legislative act is identified as Federal Law No. 154.

5 'Ob obshchikh nachalakh mestnovo samoupravleniya i mestnovo Khozyaistva v SSSR'.

6 'The European Charter of Local Self-Government' was adopted by the Council of Europe on 15 October 1985. The RF State Duma ratified the Charter in April 1998 by adopting Federal Law No. 55, 'O ratifikatsii khartii mestnovo samoupravleniya'. NB: in the official Russian legislative wording the Charter's original (English language) term, 'local self-government', has been translated as 'local self-administration'.

7 Among Russian legal experts there is some disagreement on whether, through its ratification by the Duma, the European Charter has, within the Russian Federation legal order, become a directly binding and applicable law (as might be inferred from Article 15.4 of the Federal Constitution and Article 4 of the 2003 Federal Law). However most agree that, by virtue of the ratification, the Federal Parliament and authorities are duty bound to comply with its principles. For a detailed discussion see, Elena Gritsenko, 'Universal'nye evropeiskie standarty mestnovo samouprvaleniya v rossiiskoi pravavoi sisteme', *Sravnitel'noe Konstitutionnoe Oborzenie*, Vol. 52, No. 3, 2005, pp. 127–34.

8 For a case study of the City of Vladmir, see Sabine Kropp, *Systemreform und lokale Politik in Rußland*, Opladen: Leske + Budrich, 1995, p. 245 ff.; Hellmut Wollman and Natasha Butusowa, 'Local self-government in Russia: precarious trajectory between power and law', in Harold Baldersheim, Michael Illner and Hellmut Wollmann (eds), *Local Democracy in Post-Communist Europe*, Wiesbaden: VS Verlag für Sozialwissenschaften, 2003, pp. 211–240.

9 See Hellmut Wollmann, 'Institution building of local self-government in Russia: between legal design and power politics', in Alfred B. Evans and Vladimir Gel'man (eds), *The Politics of Local Government in Russia*, Lanham, MD, Boulder, CO, New York, Toronto and Oxford: Roman & Littlefield, 2004, p. 108.

10 See n. 16 below.

11 For details and references see Wollmann 2004, p. 113 ff.

12 In an analysis conducted by the Russian Federation Ministry of Justice in 1996 only 4 of 68 regional laws regulating LSG were in full agreement with the Constitution, the rest were considered to be in blatant or partial contradiction: see Aleksandr Veronin, 'Poka lish chetyre zakonnykh zakona', *Rossiiskaya Federatsiya Sevodnya*, No. 6, 1997, p. 30; Valerii Kirpichnikov, 'Aktual'nye problemy formirovaniya mestnovo samoupravleniya v RF', in *Gosudarstvo i Pravo*, No. 5, 1997, p. 30; see also Wollmann and Butusowa, p. 231 for further references.

13 In its much-quoted decision of January 1997 on the 'Udmurtiya case', the Russian Federation Constitutional Court took an ambivalent position in reviewing a legislative act passed by the Udmurtiya Republic according to which the local organs of larger cities and districts were to become part of the state administration. For details of the Court's reasoning see, Wollmann 2004, p. 119. See also n. 24 below.

14 See Leonid Polishchuk, *Rossiiskaya Model' Peregovornovo Federalizma: Politico Ekonomika v Regional'nom Izmerenii*, Moscow and St Petersburg: Letnii Sad, 2000, pp. 88–108.

15 See Wollmann and Butusowa 2003, p. 231.

16 For details on the exercise of the legislative powers by the Federal Subjects (which cannot be pursued in this chapter) see Federal Law No. 184 of 6 October 1999, 'On the General Principles of the Organisation of Legislative and Executive Organs of State power in the Federal Subjects of RF'.

17 See Elena Gritsenko, 'A new stage of local self-government in Russia and the German experience', in *Kazan Federalist*, No 4, Autumn 2003, p. 12. On the distribution between the Russian Federation and the Federal Subjects and the legislative competence of LSG, see also Elena Gritsenko, 'Problemy razgranicheniya polnomochii v sfere pravovovo regulirovaniya organisatsii mestnovo samoupravleniya v RF na sovremennom etape federativnoi i munitsipal'noi reformy', in Kazan *Federalist*, Nos. 1–2 (17–18), 2006, pp. 111–20.

18 'Organi mestnovo samoupravleniya ne vkhodyat v sistemu organov gosudarstvennoi vlasti'.

19 See, Nina Mironova, 'Vlast'' v Rossii edinaya, no funktsii i kazhdovo ee urovnya raznye', in *Rossiiskaya Federatsiya Sevodnya*, Nos 8–9, 1998, p. 44.

20 See Konstantin F. Sheremet, 'Aktual'nye problemy formirovaniya mestnovo samoupravleniya v RF', in *Gosudarstvo i Pravo*, No. 5, 1997, p. 38.

21 See Kirk Mildner, *Lokale Politik und Verwaltung in Rußland*, Basel and New York: Birkhäuser 1996, pp. 15 ff.

22 Suren Avak'yan, 'Obosnovannaya kritika luchshe navesivaniya yarlykov', in *Rossiiskaya Federatsiya Sevodnya*, Nos 8-9, 1998, p. 37.

23 See A. R. Leemans, *Changing Patterns of Local Government*, IULA: The Hague 1970; Hellmut Wollmann, 'The development and present state of local government in England and Germany', in Hellmut Wollmann and Eckhard Schröter (eds), *Comparing Public Sector Reform in Britain and Germany*, Houndmills: Ashgate 2000, pp. 125 f.

24 See, Resolution of the Russian Federation Constitutional Court of January 24 1997, No. 1–P, 'Po delu o proverke konstituyionnosti Zakona Udmurtskoi Respubliki', "O sisteme organov gosudarstvennoi vlasti v Udmurksoi Respublike"', *Vestnik Konstitutsionnovo Suda RF*, No. 1, 1997. In the decision LSG was categorized as a form of 'realizing public power' (*spsob osushchestvleniya publichnoi vlasti*).

25 See Wollmann and Butusowa 2003, p. 215.

26 For details see Wpllman 2004 op. cit., p. 113 with references.

27 For date and comment see, 'Kruglyi stol, problemy i perspektivy razvitiya territorial'nykh osnov mestnovo samoupravleniya', in *Materialy Kruglovo stola Soveta Federatsii, Vypusk 14*, Moskva: 2001; Wollmann 2004, p. 117 ff.

28 See, Wollmann 2004, p. 120 f.

29 See, Vsevolod Vassil'ev, 'Munitsipal'naya geografiya', *Rossiskaya Federatsiya Sevodnya*, No, 16, 1999, p. 29.

30 As was already mentioned, the term 'municipal formations' was first introduced by 1995 Federal Law as the generic term for LSG units. In order to avoid the linguistic clumsiness of this term, we shall use 'municipalities' as the generic term.

31 See Gritsenko 2003.

32 See Article 11, 2003 Law, see also Article 131.2 of the Federal Constitution.

33 See Article 34, 2003 Law.
34 Data from, Ministerstvo regional'novo razvitiya 2006; for slightly earlier figures see also Vladimir Gel'man, 'Ot mestnovo samoupravleniia – k 'vertikali vlasti', *Pro et Contra*, No. 1 (35), January–February 2007.
35 See Wollmann 2000, p. 118.
36 See Wollmann and Butusowa 2003, p. 216.
37 See Wollmann 2000, p. 116. The 'general competence clause' has also been stipulated in Article 3 of the European Charter.
38 See Wollmann 2000, p. 108.
39 See Gritsenko 2003.
40 'Organi mestnovo samoupravleniya mogut nadelyat'sya ispolneniyami gosudarstvennymi polnomochiyami'.
41 For an overview on the regional legislation regarding the delegation of State functions to local authorities see, Anna Madyarova, 'Ob obshchikh nachalakh opredeleniya perechnya gosudarstvennykh polnomochii, peredamykh organam mestnovo saoumpravleniya', in *Konstitutsionnoe i Munitsipal'noe Pravo*, No. 2, 2007, pp. 27–32.
42 See Wollmann 2000, p. 117 f.
43 See Leemans, Wollmann 2000, p. 125 f.
44 'Realizatsiya peredannykh polnomochii podkontrol'na gosudarstvu'.
45 As to the 'integrationist' and 'statesising' implications of 'delegated' tasks in the German setting, see Hellmut Wollmann and Geert Bouckaert, 'State organisation in France and Germany between territoriality and functionality', in Vincent Hoffmann-Martinot and Hellmut Wollmann (eds), *State and Local Government Reforms in France and Germany*, Wiesbaden: V. S. Verlag, 2006, p. 22 f.
46 For an overview see Hellmut Wollmann, 'Changes, ruptures and continuities in European local government systems between government and governance', in Fred Lazin, Matt Evan, Vincent Hoffmann-Martinot and Hellmut Wollmann (eds), *Local Government and Governance in a Globalised World*, Lanham, MD: Lexington Press, 2007. For Germany see Hellmut Wollmann, 'The directly elected executive mayor in German local government', in Rikke Berg and Nirmala Rao (eds), *Transforming Local Political Leadership*, Houndmills: Palgrave, 2005, pp. 29 ff.
47 See Wollmann, 'The directly elected executive mayor', 2005, pp. 35 ff.
48 See Vladimir Kryazhkov, 'Mestnoe samoupravlenie: pravovoe regulirovanie i struktury', *Gosudarstvo i Pravo*, No. 1, 1992, p. 20.
49 Mention should be made, at this point, of the controversial debate as to whether the concepts of 'division of power' and 'check and balances' can be applied to the LSG level. From a (strictly) legal point of view it has been argued that these concepts should be only employed with regard to the state (as the 'sovereign' holder of legislative, executive and judiciary powers) and not with regard to the sphere of LSG whose functions, according to this legal reasoning, are essentially *administrative* and standing separate from 'the State'. From a more political science-guided perspective these concepts can be interpreted and applied in a broader functional meaning and understanding which could comprise the State as well as the LSG spheres. See, for instance, Vladimir Fadeev, *Munitsipal'noe Pravo Rossii*, Moscow: Yurist, 1994, who speaks, *inter alia*, of a 'system of checks and balances'('systema sderzhek i protivovesov'). Interestingly, a similar controversy can be observed in Germany between the (traditional) legal doctrine reserving and restricting these (and related) concepts to 'the state' proper, on the one hand, and a political science view which prefers to take a broader functional stance, thus encompassing the LSG level, on the other. See Hellmut Wollmann, 'Kommunalvertretungen: Verwaltungsorgane oder Parlamente?', in Hellmut

Wollmann and Roland Roth (eds), *Kommunalpolitik*, Opladen Leske and Budrich, 1999, pp. 50–67.

50 See Wollmann and Butusowa 2003, p. 216.

51 See *Itogi monitoringa realizatsii Federal'nogo Zakona ot 6 oktabrya 2003 No. 131*, Moscow: Ministerstvo Regional'novo Razvitiya, 2006, p. 15.

52 'Kontrol' za ispolneiem... polnomochii po resheniyu voprosov mestnovo znacheniya'.

53 For a discussion of the controversy whether the 'division of power' concept can be applied to the LSG level, see n. 49 above.

54 See Mildner 1996, pp. 87 ff., Wollmann 2004, p. 108.

55 See Wollmann 2004, pp. 109 ff. for details and references.

56 See Wollmann and Butusowa 2003, pp. 230 ff for details and references

57 See *Itogi moniforinga*, 2006, p. 19.

58 See James H. Svara, 'Institutional form and political leadership in American city government', in Rikke Berg and Nirmala Rao (eds), *Transforming Local Political Leadership*, Houndmills: Palgrave 2005, pp. 131 ff.

59 See Nirmala Rao, 'From committee to leaders and cabinets: the British experience', in Rikke Berg and Nirmala Rao, p. 45. Out of 386 English local authorities the 'mayor plus city manager' option has been put in place only in one case, ibid., p. 50

60 See, *Itogi monitoringa realizatsii*, p. 19.

61 For references see Wollmann 2007 (see n. 51 above).

62 See Sergey Mitrokhin, 'Osobennosti realizatsii munitsipal'novo proekta v Rossii: nekotorye aspekty federal'noi politiki', in Sergei Ryzhenkov and Nikolai Vinnik (eds.), *Reforma mestnovo samoupravleniia v regional'nom izmerenii. Po materialam iz 21 regiona Rossiiskoi Federatsii*, Moscow: Moscow Public Science Foundation, 1999, p. 21.

63 See Peter Reddaway, 'Will Putin be able to consolidate his power?', in *Post-Soviet Affairs*, 17, No. 1, 2001, pp. 23–44.

64 See note Gel'man 2007.

65 For an overview see ibid.

66 Ibid., p. 5.

67 Ibid.

68 See Wollmann 2004, p. 108.

69 See I. I. Ovchinnikov, 'Aktual'nye problemy formirovaniya mestnovo samoupravleniya v RF', *Gosudarstvo i Pravo*, No. 5, 1997, pp. 31–33. See also, Vladimir Gel'man and Olga Senatova, 'Political Reform in the Russian Provinces. Trends since October 1993', unpuplished manuscript, 1995.

70 See Mildner 1996, p. 115.

71 See Wollmann 2004, p. 111.

72 See Mitrokhin 1999,

73 See Wollmann and Butusowa 2003, p. 235; Tomila Lankina, 'The central uses of central government in Russia', 2001, unpublished manusript. For a recent case-study-based analysis see Tomila Lankina, Anneke Hudalla, and Hellmut Wollmann, *Decentralisation and Local Performance in Central and Eastern Europe,* Houndmills, Basingstoke: Palgrave Macmillan, 2007.

74 Gel'man 2007

75 For case studies on (Siberian) big industrial cities ('one company towns') see John C. Webb, 'Energy development and local government in western Siberia', in Alfred B. Evans, Jr. and Vladimir Gel'man (eds), *The Politics of Local Government*, pp. 235–73.

76 K. V. Aranovskii and S. D. Knzazev, 'Munitsipal'naya reforma v Rossii: razvitie mestnovo samoupravleniya ili detsentralizatsiya gosudarstvennoi administatsii', in *Pravovedenie*, 271, No. 2, 2007, pp. 3–20.

11 Russia's elusive pursuit of balance in local government reform

John F. Young

Local governments are vulnerable in all varieties of state organization, and their autonomy and capacity are especially vulnerable in federal systems.[1] Subordinated to two levels of government, the development of local government in the Russian Federation can be constrained by intergovernmental dynamics as well as other political, economic and social forces. Despite the latest round of local government reform – the third such effort in Russia in two decades – at best there are legitimate grounds for only guarded optimism that local governments can gain a minimal capacity to regulate and manage a share of public affairs under their own responsibility and in the interests of the local population.[2] This chapter examines the historical, political, economic and social contexts of local government in contemporary Russia with the intent to illuminate dimensions of Russian federalism.

Writing in the early twentieth century, British education reformer E. Salter Davies noted the challenge of finding a balance between central authority and local government. 'The supreme problem of local government', he declared, 'is to achieve the golden mean between over-centralization and excessive decentralization.' The former may lead to a soulless uniformity and to a lack of interest on the part of those most affected, while the latter, at its worst, leads to chaos.[3] This challenge not only captures the conundrum of local government reform in Russia, it also underscores how universal the challenge is in administration generally. Comparative perspectives on local government highlight the various democratic arguments for both centralization and decentralization. Centralized authority, for example, can ensure compliance with the implementation of policy, promote equality of services, provide an antidote to parochialism or local corruption, coordinate administration, offer cost effectiveness, and draw effectively from expert and professional experience. In contrast, it is argued that decentralized authority promotes innovation, improves responsiveness to local interests, provides checks and balances to the abuse of power, and fosters both public participation and opportunities for leadership training.[4] Neither centralization nor decentralization are inherently undemocratic. Such debates from public administration theory become more relevant with the realization that erring towards one side inevitably comes at the expense of the other. An apt metaphor would be Dolittle's pushmepullyu – the fictional two-headed creature. Unless it walked sideways, movement forward for one half required the other half to retreat.[5] In terms of local government, efforts to centralize authority in the name of order or equality require concessions that are likely to undermine meaningful participation or local responsiveness, and vice versa: decentralized authority may provide schools of democracy and innovation, yet foster localism and raise the risk of corruption.

Local government reform in post Soviet Russia perpetuates a pursuit for an elusive golden mean. In all political systems, a perfect balance can only be approached rather than captured. Economic, social and political dynamics constantly impact the equation, and if an effective equilibrium is found at one moment, or in one policy arena, the equilibrium can become quickly outdated or inapplicable in another context. To chronicle the many challenges for Russian local government since 1991, we begin with the recognition that Russia possessed little experience with pursuing such balance, and historically erred on the side of central control rather than local autonomy. Second, the political, economic, and social flux of the past two decades makes it impossible for any one solution to satisfy all interests.

The historical context for local government extends well beyond the legislative framework of the post Soviet era. Local government reform has been an enduring theme of Russian politics for most of the past 150 years. Historians often highlight local government reform to cast light on the challenges of reforming autocracy and on Russian social development. Counterfactual history posits the 'what if' question, suggesting that *zemstvo* reforms of the second half of the nineteenth century, or the Stolypin reforms of the early twentieth century, might have provided a solid foundation for a liberal and democratic Russia.[6] Yet local reforms in pre revolutionary Russia were well described by Gradovskii in 1907, when he suggested that in the hands of (state) offices and officials 'remained power without competence; in the hands of the *zemstvo* institutions were concentrated competence without power'.[7] Although liberal values were part of the motivation for local government reforms, the primary purpose for decentralization was the promotion of state interests, extending and strengthening the reach of the state throughout the territory it purported to govern. The consequences of such reform reflected the tension inherent in extending the reach of the state through decentralization. Reforms were thus matched by counter-reforms, seeking to repair administrative disorder by tightening central authority.[8]

Similar tension between decentralization and administrative order was found during the Soviet period.[9] In the early years of the Bolshevik regime, the very coherence of the state was threatened by *mnogovlastie*, power fractured into smaller pieces, each struggling against the other. Vertical authority was best asserted through the ranks of the Communist Party, yet Soviet administration and inner Party politics also wrestled with the tension between centre and periphery. Efforts to invigorate local soviets and local party committees in any meaningful way challenged the authority of the centre. This is one reason why the collapses of the Tsarist and Soviet states were through implosion. Top-heavy administrative structures lack effective foundations at the local level, the proverbial giants with feet of clay.

Historical perspectives encourage us to examine local government reform from the perspective of the priorities dominant at the point of departure. Seventeen years after the reforms of 1990 and 1991, it is tempting to forget that many of those reformers and politicians then engaged in creating the legal architecture for local government were focused on dismantling a unitary system of power that had so dominated Soviet society. The creation and approval of a societal model for local government was perceived to be a critical development for the emergence of civil society, public participation, and local autonomy. Local *self*-government, outside the reach of the state apparatus, with a locally elected executive accountable to an elected local council, was considered a bold initiative and a new foundation for a democratic state. Meaningful public participation, responsiveness to local interests, and the division of power and authority trumped concerns for order, efficiency, or equality. That executive–legislative relations were not clearly defined, or that the financial resources of local government did not match their enumerated responsibilities, became more apparent, and more important, after the implementation of the law rather than during its drafting.[10]

In the aftermath of Yeltsin's war against the Supreme Soviet in 1993, the context for local reform changed. Local governments were then situated in two storms: first, in the conflict between executive and legislative bodies; and second, in a centrifugal storm that threatened the viability of the Russian state. On the one hand, the federal government wanted to ensure a tighter degree of control over executive power throughout the Federation, and sought to play a greater role in the determination of principles for local self-government. On the other hand, local governments were potential allies to the federal government in the centre–regional dynamic. Stronger local government would place regional administrations between the proverbial hammer and the anvil, achieving a more effective balance of power within the federation.[11] While federal strategy aimed to enlist local government support against regional autonomy, Moscow proved to be a fair-weather friend to local government: federal–regional agreements often came at the expense of local self-government. Additionally, local governments played an important supporting role as a buffer against political criticism directed towards both regional and federal governments. Politicians from these higher levels of government could pass legislation or decrees guaranteeing various subsidies and social services, knowing full well that local politicians were charged with the delivery. When the needed funds were transferred either too late or not at all, regional and federal officials were insulated from the reaction. They could blame local politicians for the failure, maintaining some measure of credibility with the public at the expense of local deputies and mayors.

Such purposes and priorities of reform are often temporary rather than enduring. By the last years of the Yeltsin era, local government as guarantor against hypercentrism or as leverage for the federal government against the regions was overshadowed by greater needs to provide much-needed services and foster administrative order. In this light, calls for administrative efficiency and the reassertion of central authority did not originate with the ascent of Vladimir Putin in 2000, but were increasing in volume and in frequency well before President Yeltsin resigned at the end of 1999. Putin's reforms were hardly an illegitimate response to the needs of Russian society and the Russian state. That the reforms required a diminution of local autonomy and the concomitant negative consequences of centralization is as much a consequence of the realities of public administration as a manifestation of Russian political culture.

Perhaps a snapshot of local government at the end of the Yeltsin era can provide further perspective on Putin's reforms. Three elements of this snapshot draw our immediate attention. First, federal efforts established general principles of local self-government and left some important details to regional legislatures. Thus, different structures were the direct result of regional governments exercising their prerogatives in designing local administration, responding to socio-cultural factors and local political interests. Throughout the Russian Federation, a wide variety of models and regional practices emerged. Among eighty-nine regions of Russia, thirty-seven regions established a single tier of local government at the district (*raion*) level. Six regions based local government at the settlement, or village level. Thirty regions developed a two-tier system of local government, but only seventeen of those had budgets for both tiers. Another sixteen regions, including Moscow, St Petersburg, and nine national republics, had more complicated versions of local government that do not fit with the simpler categories noted above.[12] In all cases however, local executives were accountable locally. Mayors were elected either by direct elections by the public, or indirect elections through an elected council. Not all regional decisions concerning local government structures and practices were always in accordance with federal guidelines, but federal and local governments could appeal to the Constitutional Court to defend the principles of self government, such as the right of citizens to elect their local leaders.[13] In all, the 1995 law led to 24 resolutions (*postanovlenie*) and 137 decisions (*opredelenie*) by the Constitutional Court.[14]

These various structures and practices coupled with disparate dynamics in intergovernmental relations to blur some of the images of local government and make it very difficult to engage in comparisons across the Federation. In terms of elections, for example, the manipulation of elections by regional or local actors could be manifest through either high or low voter turnouts, or the postponement of elections altogether, depending on the time and place in question. Other factors, such as multiple- or single-member electoral districts, the incumbency of candidates, rural and urban voting patterns, electoral fraud, and the candidates themselves, led to huge variations in voter participation, even among local communities within the same region. Most commonly, however, electoral turnout for local elections in the Russian Federation averaged about one-third of registered voters, with higher turnouts reaching 70 per cent and low turnouts falling below 20 per cent.[15]

Second, despite any measure of political independence for local governments fostered by law, there was an acute lack of local capacity to deliver much-needed services.[16] Efforts to strengthen the financial base of local governments through legislation, such as the tax code of 1991, or the budget laws of 1993 and 1997, failed to compensate for the realities of economic decline and inflation or the use of intergovernmental transfers as undue political leverage. Additionally, the privatization of enterprises and diminished industrial output meant that many services previously provided by employers were cancelled or transferred to local governments, placing greater stress on local budgets. By one estimate, local governments experienced a 65 per cent increase in the demand for the provision of social services such as day cares and health clinics, and a tenfold increase for the provision of municipal housing.[17] As a result, local financial resources were woefully insufficient to provide such services as health care, public education, social benefits, and public housing. One mayor described the situation: 'It is no secret that budgets are the most difficult sphere in the relations between the regions of the Federation and organs of local self-government. Yes, we have a municipal budget. It is a strange thing. We have numbers, and we have accountability. But as for money, we have none.'[18] While local governments were charged with the delivery of services, the financing, standards, and objectives of such policies were determined by federal ministries and regional administrations. In this regard, local governments were agents of higher-level administrations, a role that was in direct conflict with their legal status as organs of self-government. Such mismatched revenues and responsibilities are not uncommon in the practice of multi-level governance.[19] In Russia, however, no level of government had the resources to pay for the promised public services. Dmitrii Kozak pointed out in 2003 that the estimated cost of fulfilling the social obligations of the state were more than twice the total state budget.[20]

Third, the implementation of federal laws was a mess at the local level. This was not merely a consequence of insufficient financial resources, but also a reflection of parochialism and insufficiently qualified personnel. The latter characteristic followed from high turnover rates, lack of training, and susceptibility to corruption. Stalin once infamously remarked that 'cadres decide everything', and local governments were not only conceptually and financially adrift from regional and state administrations but also constrained by the limited abilities of their own personnel. Discussing local efforts to register and supervise religious associations in accordance with Federal law, for example, Nina Volodina has highlighted the ways in which federal agencies and ministries relied on local governments to perform functions outside local purview. Seemingly innocuous measures, such as property use, construction permits, and registration of religious organizations allowed local governments either to recognize or to ignore organizations already recognized by federal authority and local groups or individuals. Many local officials were either ignorant of their responsibilities, exercised personal bias, or were influenced by private interests to violate civic rights in their decisions, something more often the norm than the exception. The easiest solution to such predicaments required increased supervision by federal ministries over local officials – a weird paradox where federal authorities were forced to violate principles of local self-government in order to promote civic rights.[21] Weak administration became more problematic as public security and terrorism became a more critical policy arena for the federal government, particularly in light of Russia's conduct in the Chechen War and terrorist activities in Russia and abroad. Policing, the registration of citizens, and public security all became directly linked to effective public administration at all levels of government.

These three characteristics from this snapshot of local government are very much interconnected. While the differences in structure and processes of administration across regions testified to the regional and local influence in self-government, they also left the federal government in an administrative quandary. The transfer of federal funds to local governments, and the supervision of federal policies and regulations at the local level, were both made exceptionally challenging due to the varied structures and organizations of local administration dotting the country. A federal ministry relying on local delivery or implementation, for example, might have to deal with district level local governments in one region, and settlement level local government in another. Regardless of whether or not the regional administration was in compliance with federal directives, the differences among local governments across regions muddied the process of administration. The lack of uniform local administration might be considered by some to be a positive consequence of the 1995 law, but since important social policies were shared between federal and regional governments, some measure of consistency in local administration seems to be a reasonable expectation.

In light of these very real deficiencies in local government and administration, the decision to draft new federal reforms can be characterized as both responsible and necessary. Critics of the status quo on the eve of reform could highlight inequality of services across communities, the limited capacity of most local governments in terms of personnel and financial resources, and the failed implementation of federal standards. They could also point to concerns of parochialism and the limited reach of the state. Of course, the actual details of legislation and implementation of reform determine the real impact and final assessment of how well reform responds to these criticisms. But it ought to be widely recognized that the status quo prior to Putin's ascent to power was a poorly governed state. The public had grown weary of slogans and promises, weary of democracy and blurred accountability. Local government reforms passed into legislation in 2003 are thus best characterized as reform of a reform, which is something altogether different from a counter-reform. The latter would be an effort to turn back the clock to a pre-1991 administration era. The former, in contrast, is a legitimate response to real circumstances caused by reforms. The 2003 reforms were meant to re-establish administrative order and promote a functional, well governed state, while holding true to some of the principles that motivated the earlier reforms.

The question that then surfaces is the degree to which the 2003 reforms strengthen any gains made towards self-government. Can administrative efficiency complement principles of local self-government, or are the two mutually exclusive? President Putin charged trusted colleague Dmitrii Kozak with leadership of the Presidential Commission for the Demarcation of Powers Between the Federal, Regional and Municipal Levels of Government. The Commission was comprised of one main body of twenty-two members (two of whom represented local governments) and several working bodies, where local representation was more actively involved.[22] The Commission had two primary tasks: bringing regional laws in line with the federal constitution; and reforming the system of local self-government. It is the fulfilment of the latter of these two tasks that led directly to Federal Law No. 131, 'On the general principles of organization of local self-government in the Russian Federation' (2003).[23]

What does the new law do? In Chapter 10 in this volume Hellmut Wollmann and Elena Gritsenko highlight many specific features of the law. Among other things, the law establishes two tiers for local government, in an attempt to address the tension that flows from local governments functioning as both agents of the state and as self-governing institutions. By establishing a foundation for two distinct tiers of local government, the federal law relegates to the higher tier authority over the costlier social services delivered by local government. Public education, health care, and social benefits are primarily reserved for the higher of the two tiers, leaving settlements to deal primarily with local issues rather than state policies. Although both levels will possess their own budgets, it is clear that state transfers will flow predominantly to the district rather than the settlement level. This ensures that local governments at the settlement level will work with smaller budgets, but will have fewer mandates to implement state policy and greater autonomy in minor local affairs. This same dynamic holds in relation to the higher tier of local government and regional governments. In public education, for example, local governments will now only carry the responsibility to maintain property and buildings, and teacher salaries will fall under the responsibility of regional governments. The trimming of local jurisdictions is meant to reflect more accurately the limited financial capacity that local governments posses. In short, the law seeks to realign authority in conformance with fiscal capacity, rather than vice versa. The law also tightens local executive accountability on the vertical axis, undermining horizontal accountability to the local council. Local government charters must chose between two models: an elected mayor and a contracted administrative manager, or an elected head of administration. In either model, as Wollmann points out, the regional administration has increased capacity to influence the local executive, including broader powers over dismissal.

Critics of the reform, both foreign and domestic, routinely describe the law as a step backwards for democracy, the 'emasculation of local democracy'.[24] Without attempting to obfuscate, it is clear that the theoretical foundation of local self-government is weakened by the new law. But what is yet unclear is whether the practice of local government will also be weakened. Surely, the actual status of local government in Russia never matched its early promise. Absent a history of divided power, Russia wrestled with reconciling political differences across administrative boundaries. Economic decline and private interests intensified such differences. And society grew increasingly impatient with paeans of optimism about democracy and improved quality of life – the notion that more local self-government would usher in a radiant future ceased to resonate with government and society. Instead, the new law on local government and the reforms that have followed have attempted to do more with local government by granting less autonomy and less authority – or, in the words of comrade Lenin, better, fewer but better. It would be too hasty to pass judgment on the consequences of the law while the law has not yet been fully implemented. We can, however, look at some of the trends and early returns, and then offer an interim assessment. We examine here six major issues and concerns.

The first concern stems from ongoing reforms of the reform of reform. Since being passed in 2003, the new law on local self-government has been amended and been impacted by more recent legislation that intersects with local government, and not consistent with what was established in law No. 131. The implementation of the local government reform, originally targeted for January 2005, was first postponed until 2006, and then pushed back further until 2009. This second postponement occurred as late as September 2005, even though more than half the regions had implemented the law by the end of that year.[25] These postponements reflect both the challenges of reform, and the persistent reluctance in a number of different regions to alter administration. Besides buying more time, however, the postponement also altered the process, granting regional governments greater influence in local matters until 2009, and, perhaps, beyond. In the original design, the budget was intended to help force a realignment of authority in accordance with federal guidelines. But the postponement allows those regions that have yet to reform a freer hand in local budget decisions, influence that will prove difficult to overcome.[26] Other laws, such as Federal Law No. 198, which introduced changes to the Budget Code (dated 27 December 2005), reduced the coefficient that determined a maximum for local budget autonomy. Prior to the amendment, local budgets could be up to two times higher per capita than the regional average. The new law reduced that factor to 1.3, after which 50 per cent of excess funds could be confiscated by higher levels of government. Federal Law No. 199 (on introducing changes to certain legislative acts of the Russian Federation concerning the improvement of the division of powers check title, passed 31 December 2005) blurred the distinction between settlement and district local government, allowing the latter to pursue intersettlement infrastructure such as libraries, athletic facilities, and cultural organizations. On the surface, these alterations might seem banal, but they suggest a drift away from the principles of budget autonomy and local self-government enunciated in 2003.[27]

A second concern also flows from the distinction between theory and practice. The 2003 law promotes a two-tier system to reconcile the tension between administration and self-government. By design, municipal districts would lean more to the purposes of administration, while settlements would lean more to self-government. It should not be a surprise to know that in the implementation of the model, functions follow form. Since the district level has greater budget resources, the transfer of jurisdiction and authority allowed by the law tends to flow upwards rather than in the other direction. Coupled with tighter control from higher-level administrations, local self-government benefits only if the lowest tier, at the settlement level, also flourishes. Yet early returns, both in the transition period for those regions lagging behind in implementation, and in those regions where reforms have been implemented, suggest that the lowest tiers often transfer what meaningful authority they have to the district level, and receive instead the less meaningful clerical tasks.[28] Additionally, state functions transferred downwards to municipal districts include such matters as health, social support, care for orphans and disabled children, and physical sports, while state functions transferred to settlement administrations are limited to the registration of marriages and preparations for the census.[29] There is a danger in such developments that municipal districts will eventually emerge solely as agents of state administration, and that the two-tier system of local government will eventually develop into a two tier system of regional government, with only a very diminished role for settlement administrations.

A third concern with local government reforms, especially from the perspective of administrative coherence, is the mushrooming of municipalities and the need for qualified personnel to staff these offices. Early estimates on the number of local governments in Russia suggested that Law No. 131 would almost triple the number of municipalities, from 11,560 to more than 31,000.[30] Although full implementation has not yet occurred, a doubling has already taken place.[31] One significant consequence is that the number of people required to work in these institutions is also growing. Nikolai Petrov has suggested that hundreds of thousands of new civil servants are needed to staff new municipalities.[32] Given that qualified personnel were difficult to find prior to the new law, there is little reason to believe that this challenge will be easily resolved. An estimated 60 per cent of people elected to local governments are inexperienced in local government and administration.[33] Additionally, one wonders about the overall cost of local government, given the increased number of full-time employees. This predicament might explain why smaller settlements are willing to transfer authority to the district level. While federal and regional authorities are devoted to training local officials, those who perform well are often enticed out of municipal government to regional administration or the private sector. Increased pay scales and real authority might encourage more officials to continue their employment in local governments, but these changes are not on the immediate horizon. It is also clear that a rotation of cadres is also re-emerging, where effective administrators at one level are promoted to higher positions, even from one local government to another. So, for example, the mayor of Tobolsk, Evgenii Kuivshev, was recently approved as the new head of the Tyumen' City Administration.[34] Such lateral moves, from one local government to another (with greater stature), will likely become more common with the contracting of city managers. It also threatens to undermine the concept of local self-government, where a local community resolves its own concerns rather than be managed by a professional staff from elsewhere.

A fourth concern is with the role of mayors in the new system of local government. One of the foundations of the municipal revolution of the 1990s was the assertion of local accountability of mayors and an end to the Soviet principle of 'dual subordination'. Darrell Slider has highlighted the subsequent conflict between governors and mayors throughout the 1990s, and the various federal efforts to resolve the conflict.[35] The new law not only provides two ways to elect a mayor, but also presents two very different types of mayor. The most common structure adopted in Russia has been the emergence of a contracted city manager to lead the administration, and to resurrect the principle of dual subordination. Such an office is promoted by Igor Kokin as a more effective way to employ experts and qualified personnel, smooth out administration and executive–legislation relations, and overcome deficiencies such as weak local political and legal cultures, and limited opportunities for the training of professionals.[36] Such a change, of course, also serves to tighten vertical administration and weaken local accountability. At the same time, elected mayors enjoy far less local authority. These changes come at a time when the federal government appears to have targeted elected mayors who continue to lead local administrations. Mayors can now be more easily removed from office with legal cause, although some allegations in 2007 appear to be the result of political machinations rather than the pursuit of justice. It is interesting to note that many of the mayors threatened with dismissal or charged with criminal conduct are those who are in conflict with governors or federal agencies.[37] A notorious letter dated 18 November 2006 from the presidential administration to the General Procurator of the Russian Federation, Yuri Chaike, included a list of five mayors from each of the seven federal districts. The letter vaguely accused each of activities unbefitting their office, as alleged in the Russian media. Criminal charges were laid against a number of those on the list, although the line between real criminal conduct and political opposition seems to be quite blurred.[38] While there are too many local factors in play behind these circumstances to make specific conclusions, it is apparent that the role of independent mayors, so dominant during the 1990s, has now been radically diminished.

Fifth, the question of financing local government continues to dominate reforms. The large increase in the number of municipalities does not begin to match the huge increase in the number of local budgets now integrated in the consolidated state budget. Prior to 2003, budgets existed in many regions at only the district level. Now, however, the number of governments with their own budget has blossomed by a factor of 5.7.[39] Bringing all these budgets together in any meaningful way would require Herculean effort. Effective, results-based budgeting will most likely succumb to far simpler mandates concerning the amounts transferred from regional and district level budgets to each subordinate local government. The good news is that Russia's public finances are far healthier now than during the 1990s, and there is much more money to go around. Unfortunately for local governments, the amount that filters down to the local level will still be minimal, and local revenues, as a share of total government revenues, will fall to about 5 per cent.[40] Strengthening local revenues and budgets does not appear to be a priority or even a concern of federal and regional officials. One necessary step would be to move forward with the transfer of property from federal and regional governments to local governments. But this process has been stalled until legislation expected in 2008.

As noted above, one of the fundamental challenges to local government in the recent past has been unfunded mandates, where local governments were expected to finance services mandated from above without any additional resources. One intent of the reform was to resolve this predicament. In this context, however, a recent ruling by the Constitutional Court suggests that much is yet to be done. The case was brought to the Court by the city administration of Tver', which complained that social services guaranteed by the state and delivered by local governments must come with funds adequate to meet those standards imposed by the state. Day-care services that came out of local budgets, for example, ought not be required to meet all state standards unless there is adequate compensation from the state. The Constitutional Court, however, disagreed, arguing that equal standards throughout the country require commitments from local governments rather than the federal government. The Court obliged the Tver' municipality to comply with state regulations with or without adequate funding, and added that the state *might*, rather than must, transfer funds accordingly.[41] In other words, even with diminished responsibilities, it seems as if unfunded mandates will continue at the local level.

Lastly, public perceptions of local government are also a concern, particularly as they relate to participation and trust. The early enthusiasm for local democracy was largely extinguished by the chaos of administration. Early in his first mandate, President Putin spoke favourably of local government and suggested that local government ought to be closer to the people.

Puzanov and Ragozina have argued that, instead, the public has become increasingly estranged from local government. In their examination of 217 cities from 64 different regions in 2004, and then subsequent study of 84 cities from 44 regions in 2006, the authors found a marked decline in assemblies and modest declines in citizens' meetings and local public opinion surveys. They also noted, however, more than a doubling of public hearings, which suggests some ambivalence towards their conclusion that public estrangement follows reforms of local government.[42] Another way to examine the level of engagement is through electoral turnout to local elections. Levels of participation appear to have held constant, or even improved in many different regions where the latest round of reform has been implemented. Perhaps most interesting is the wide variety of variation within these same regions. In Novgorod Oblast, voter participation in recent local elections ranged from 12 per cent to 89 per cent. These differences cut across the different tiers of local government and across elections for executives and local councils. A by-election for the Oblast Duma on 11 March 2007, for example, drew 25 per cent of registered voters, while three district heads of administration drew between 41 per cent and 45 per cent. Heads of administration for two settlements drew 49 per cent and 67 per cent, by-elections for district councils attracted between 12 per cent and 38 per cent, while general elections for three different districts drew between 52 per cent and 89 per cent.[43] In Kemerovo Oblast district council elections varied from district to district, and from electoral district to electoral district within municipal districts as well, with ranges between 23 per cent and 100 per cent.[44]

Samples from other regional electoral commissions confirm a tremendous variety of turnouts, suggesting there are a number of potential explanations for such variations, some of which have been noted above. While it is difficult to draw direct conclusions, both the wide variety of turnouts and the averages reflect some measure of vibrancy in local elections despite diminished local authority. Perhaps the Russian public is not adverse to local governments being charged with less responsibility. More relevant to the purposes of this discussion, however, is the variety of support for local governments within and across regions. This gives a hint of a predicament that existed before the most recent reforms, namely that there were winners and losers among local governments, not just regions. Some communities did well, politically, economically, or both. While the new law levelled many of these differences, it is very likely that such differences will again emerge.[45] How they will be dealt with under tighter central tutelage remains to be seen.

Taken as a whole, these six concerns reflect ongoing and future tensions within local government. Delayed reforms are already mutating: the role of municipal districts as agents of state policy, the need for professional cadres and temptation for rotation, limits on strong local leadership, and the continuation of unfunded mandates all suggest that local self-government will not bear meaningful fruit. In this sense, it is clear that local government has been weakened in its capacity to regulate and manage a share of public affairs under its own responsibility and in the interests of the local population. Yet Putin's mandate has been to cultivate order and administrative efficiency, a reasonable, if imperfect, response to the political, economic, and social context in Russia. Reforms in local government are less the consequence of the assertion of a top down administrative model than the pursuit of a well-governed state. And they have not been unpopular, as harsh as some critics might be. As Putin's second term draws to a close, it is likely that, in time, future leaders will begin to address the consequences of this latest reform in local government rather than the chaos of the 1990s. The variation that will endure in political and economic outcomes will provide some motivation for future reform. More importantly, the gains made in the interest of administrative order are likely to have been at the expense of accountability and responsiveness. The 2003 law on local government and how it has been implemented will thus become a new point of departure for future reforms, as Russia continues its pursuit for a golden mean between centralization and decentralization.

Notes

1 Harvey Lazar and Christian Leuprecht (eds), *Spheres of Governance: Comparative Studies of Cities in Multilevel Governance Systems*, Montreal: McGill-Queen's University Press, 2007. This comparative study notes the ubiquitous top-down process under which municipal governments the world over are forced to operate.

2 The language derives from the European Charter on Local Self-Government, Part I, Article 3. See http://conventions.coe.int/Treaty/EN/Treaties/Html/122.htm. The Russian Federation signed the Charter in 1998.

3 As cited in the *Royal Commission on Education in Ontario*, Toronto: Baptist Johnston, 1950. Known also as the Hope Commission, ch. 7. The full text of the report is available on the web, http://www.canadianeducationalpolicystudies.ca/ (accessed November 4, 2006).

4 See the classic exchange between two authors, Georges Langrod, 'Local Government and Democracy', *Public Administration*, Vol. 31, No. 1, Spring 1953, pp. 25–33; and Keith Panter-Brick, 'Local Government and Democracy – A Rejoinder", *Public Administration*, Vol. 31, No. 4, Winter, 1953, pp. 344–8.

5 The creature is also familiar to Russians, who know the pushmepullyu as the *tyanitolkai*.

6 See, for example, Terence Emmons and Wayne Vucinich (eds), *The Zemstvo in Russia: An Experiment in Local Self-Government*, Cambridge: Cambridge University Press, 1982; Mary Schaeffer Conroy (ed.), *Emerging Democracy in Late Imperial Russia*, Niwot, CO: University Press of Colorado, 1998.

7 A. Gradovskii, 'Pereustroistvo nashego mestnago upravleniia", *Sobranie sochinenii*, St Petersburg, 1907, p. 540.

8 John F. Young, 'Parallel Patterns of Power? Local Government Reform in Late Imperial and Post Soviet Russia", *Canadian Slavonic Papers*, Vol. 42, No. 3, September 2000, pp. 269–94.

9 A. O. Dement'ev, 'O sisteme sovetov i zemskikh uchrezhdeniiakh v Rossii: vozmozhnye istoricheskie paralleli", *Gosudarstvo i Pravo*, Vol. 8, 1996, pp. 112–20.

10 See John F. Young, 'Zakonodatel'stvo Rossii po mestnomu samoupravleniyu', in Kimitaka Matsuzato (ed.), *Tret'e zveno gosudarstvennogo stroitel'stva Rossii*, Sapporo: Slavic Research Centre, Hokkaido University, 1998, pp. 109–29.

11 See, for example, Vladimir Kuznechevskii, 'Komu ne po dushe edinaia Rossiia, *Rossiiskaya Gazeta*, 6 April 1995, pp. 1–2; Sergie Shakhrai, 'Federalizm i novaia regional'naia politika', *Rossiiskaya Gazeta*, 4 February 1995, pp. 1, 4.

12 See Irina Starodubrovskaya, *Problems of Reforming Local Self-Governance: Structural and Financial Aspects*, Moscow: Institute for the Economy in Transition, 2005, pp. 60–4. The vast differences in structures are not shaped by any one factor, as national republics, oblasti and autonomous okruga are found in each category. There was, however, a surge of republics in the last category, those too complicated to fit into the simpler classifications.

13 The case of Udmurtia is best known. The Republic of Udmurtia nullified local self-government in 1996, subordinating local administration to state authority. The Constitutional Court defended the right of citizens to elect their local governments, but also conceded that the republic could legally create local organs of state power parallel to local governments. See 'Aktual'nye problemy formirovaniia mestnogo samoupravleniia v Rossiiskoi Federatsii', *Gosudarstvo i Pravo*, Vol. 5, 1997, pp. 24–45; Young, 'Parallel Patterns?'. The Constitutional Court also ruled in favour of local elections in the Republic of Komi. See 'Postanovlenie Konstitutsionnogo Suda Rossisskoi Federatsii', 15 January 1998.

14 'Kollizii zakonodatel'stva o MSU', *Mestnoe Samoupravleniia* No. 5, May 2007, http://emsu.ru/lg (accessed, 24 September 2007).

15 For a statistical overview, see *Formirovanie organov mestnogo samoupravleniia v Rossiiskoi federatsii, 1995–1998: Elektoral'naia statistika*, Moscow: Ves' mir, 1999.

16 Vladimir Gel'man and Alfred B. Evans, Jr., 'Conclusion: Toward a New Politics of Local Government in Russia', in Alfred B. Evans Jr. and Vladimir Gel'man, *The Politics of Local Government in Russia*, Lanham, MD, Boulder, CO, New York, Toronto and Oxford: Rowman and Littlefield, 2004, pp. 274–87.

17 See Andrei Poliakov, 'Vlast' bez deneg – fiktsiia', *Malye goroda*, No. 6, 1998, pp. 5–11. Poliakov was the chair of the Duma Committee on local self-government.

18 Aleksandr Koliadin, 'Zazerkal'e gorodskogo biudzheta', *Rossiiskaya Federatsiya*, No. 14, 1999, pp. 39–40.

19 See Roger Gibbins, Antonia Maioni, and Janice Gross Stein, eds., *Canada by Picasso: The Faces of Federalism*, Ottawa: The Conference Board of Canada, 2006; and Janice Gross Stein, 'Networked Federalism', in John F. Young (ed.), *Federalism, Power, and the North: Governmental Reforms in Russia and Canada*, Toronto: Centre for European, Russian and Eurasian Studies, University of Toronto, 2007, pp. 77–106. The references to Picasso suggest that his art is an apt visual demonstration of the distortions and imbalance between financial capacity and political accountability among different levels of government.

20 As cited in Gel'man and Evans, 'Conclusion', p. 275.

21 N.V. Volodina, *Gosudarstvenno-Konfessional'nyi Otnosheniia: Teoretiko-Pravovoi Analiz*, Moscow: Shchit-M, 2005, pp 157–69. Another example is noted by Tomila Lankina, who referred to the 70,000 violations by local governments of federal statues concerning permits for such things as publishing, vocational training, and investment management. See her *Governing the Locals: Local Self-Government and Ethnic Mobilization in Russia*, Lanham, MD, Boulder, CO, New York, Toronto and Plymouth: Rowman and Littlefield, 2004, p. 157.

22 John F. Young and Gary N. Wilson, 'The view from below: local government and Putin's Reforms', *Europe-Asia Studies*, Vol. 59, No. 7, November 2007, p. 1077.

23 Federal'nyi Zakon No. 131 (2003), 'Ob obshchikh printsipakh organizatsii mestnogo samoupravleniia v Rossiiskoi Federatsii', Moscow: Grossmedia, 2006.

24 Vladimir Gel'man, 'Ot mestnogo samoupravleniia – k vertikali vlasti', *Pro et Contra*, Vol. 11, No. 1, January–February, 2007, pp. 6-18; Cameron Ross, 'Putin's federal reforms and the consolidation of federalism in Russia: One step forward, two steps back!', *Communist and Post-Communist Studies*, Vol. 36, 2003, pp. 29–47.

25 Forty-six regions had implemented Law 131 by 1 January 2006. Another eleven regions had implemented the law by 1 January 2007. As cited by S. N. Samoilev, at a round table discussion at the Institute for State and Law, 'Kollizii zakonodatel'stva o MSU', *Mestnoe Samoupravleniya*, No. 5, May 2007.

26 Starodubrovskaya, pp. 26–30.

27 Starodubrovskaya and Tomila Lankina noted that the postponement created 'a morass of complication and legal confusion for both local and federal officials because now laws are out of sync.'. See 'New system weakens municipalities', *Russian Regional Report*, Vol. 10, No. 17, 19 October 2005.

28 'Kollizii zakonodatel'stva o MSU', *Mestnoe Samoupravlenie*, No. 5, May 2007.

29 Starodubrovskaya, p. 254.

30 P. Dul'man, 'Munitsipalitety ishut kadry', *Rossiiskaya Gazeta*, 15 February 2005, p. 3.

31 V. Gel'man, 'Ot mestnogo samoupravleniia – k vertikali vlasti', *Pro et Contra*, Vol. 11, No. 1, January–February 2007, p. 11.

32 N. Petrov, 'Local self-rule on the line', *Moscow Times*, 24 January 2007.

33 S. Migalin, 'Arbitrary government instead of self-government', *Nezavisimaya Gazeta*, 27 January 2006, as cited in *Johnson's Russia List*, No. 26, 28 January 2006.

34 'Naznachen bez problem', *Mestnoe Samoupravlenie*, No. 7, July 2007.

35 D. Slider, 'Governors versus mayors: the regional dimension of Russian local government', in Evans and Gel'man (eds), *The Politics of Local Government*, pp. 145–68.

36 I. Kokin, 'Naznachet ili vybirat'?', *Mestnoe samoupravlenie*, No. 5, 2007.

37 'Kto izbavlyaetsya ot slabogo zvena v vertikali vlasti?', *Obshchaya Gazeta.Ru*, 24 May 2007.

38 Claire Bigg, 'Russia: mayors in the crosshairs as power vertical gains force', Radio Free Europe/Radio Liberty, *Newsline*, 21 June 2007, and *Johnson' Russia List*, No. 138, 2007.

39 Starodubrovskaya, *Monitoring*, p. 68.

40 Tomila Lankina, 'New system weakens municipalities'.

41 Postanovlenie Konstitutsionnogo Suda RF ot 15 Maya 2006g. N 5-P 'Po delu o proverke konstitutsionnosti polozhenii stat'i 153 federal'nogo zakona ot 22 avgusta 2004 goda No. 122-F3'.

42 Aleksandr Puzanov and Liudmilla Ragozina, 'Otchuzhdenie mestnoi vlasti', *Pro et Contra*, Vol. 11, No. 1, January–February 2007, pp. 72-84.

43 'Aktivnost' izbiratelei na vyborakh, sostoyavshikhsya v Novgorodskoi oblasti, 11 Marta 2007 goda', http://novgorod.izbirkom.ru/diagr_akt1_2_version.xls. Novgorod has been the focus of study by Nicolai Petro and is considered among the lead regions in fostering local democracy. See N. Petro, *Crafting Democracy: How Novgorod has Coped with Rapid Social Change*, Ithaca, NY: Cornell University Press, 2004.

44 See 'Vybory deputatov Anzhero-Sudenskogo gorodskogo Soveta narodnykh deputatov tret'ego sozyva', 8 October 2006, http://www.kemerov.izbirkom.ru/way/932194.html.

45 O. Savranskaia, 'The implementation of local government reforms in remote and underpopulated regions', in Young (ed.), *Federalism, Power and the North*, pp. 175–96.

12 Vertical or triangle? Local, regional and federal government in the Russian Federation after Law 131

Adrian Campbell

Introduction

This chapter examines the thinking behind the Russian local government reform of 2003 (Law 131) in the context of the evolving relationship between the three levels of authority in the Russian Federation. Law 131's critics have tended to see the law as part of a straightforward policy of centralization, aimed at integrating local government into the 'state vertical'. This chapter argues that the motives behind the reform were more complex and may genuinely have included the aim of creating a stable triangular distribution of power between federal, regional and local institutions.

In addition to published sources, the chapter draws on the author's participant observation of the work of the Federal Commission for the Division of Powers between Levels of Government in the Russian Federation (Kozak Commission), at intervals over the period 2002–4, including attendance at sessions of the commission, participation in seminars and conferences related to the Commission's work, and discussions with members of the Commission and its working group on local self-government.

The chapter briefly reviews the role of the Law 131 in the work of the Kozak Commission and then considers the wider theoretical aspects of the reform, before considering whether the reform represented a genuine opportunity to establish a triangular balance of power between federal, regional and local levels, and why this opportunity was not fully exploited.

Law 131 and its critics

Since its appearance of its first draft, in October 2002, through its adoption by the State Duma in October 2003, and its coming into force in January 2006 (and frequent amendments), the Law 'On the General Principles of Local Self Government in the Russian Federation' (Law 131)[1] has been the focus of sustained debate and controversy, to a degree matched by few other laws initiated by the Putin administration.

The law was seen by some as bringing local government into the structure of the state, in contravention of Article 12 of the Constitution, through alleged misapplication of the term public authority .[2] It was seen to emphasize the administrative-territorial aspects of local government, rather than economic development.[3] It was seen to centralize power, concentrating financial resources at federal level while seeking to place the burden of meeting social guarantees on the local level.[4] It was seen as giving governors more extensive powers over mayors and seeking to integrate Russia s local government into Russia s hierarchical state structure.[5]

Recentralization of power from regional to federal level has been one of the defining policies of the Putin administration. However, it does not follow that the policy towards local government should be interpreted as a straightforward extension of the same principle of centralization. Were this the case then it would have been logical for the principle of appointment rather than election, applied to regional heads since October 2004, to have been extended to mayors. Such a step has been seen by some as entirely in keeping with the administration's outlook:

> To a product of the Soviet system the elimination of checks and balances appears to increase the manageability of the political system. ... the same striving or clarity and order will encompass the sub-regional level ... and may result in the direct subordination of mayors to governors.[6]

The option of substituting mayoral elections with a system of appointment from above was openly considered by President Putin as early as 2000 and was the subject of much high-profile debate in early 2005, before becoming the subject of a draft amendment to Law 131 in November 2006. On each occasion the principle appeared close to adoption only to be brushed aside at the last minute – a vocal federal constituency in favour of appointed mayors was obliged to give way to another in favour of elected mayors.

Were Law 131 primarily about integrating local government into the state vertical, and if this were all that federal policy on local government amounted to, this repeated recoiling from the idea of appointing mayors would be inexplicable. This chapter sets out to explain why the refusal (so far) to appoint mayors was consistent with the principles underlying Law 131, and how the latter was the result of a more complex set of aims.

The Kozak Commission

Law 131 was one of the main outputs of the Federal Commission on the Distribution of Functions between Levels of Power in the Russian Federation, which was convened by the President in 2001. The first chair of that commission was Dmitry Nikolaevich Kozak, deputy head of the Presidential Administration, who had just competed an overhaul of the Russian Federation's judicial system.[7] Although the Commission revised over 300 federal laws in its programme of federal reform, most of these were sectoral laws. Two new laws, however, had a special status as they dealt with the powers of institutions. The second was Law 95 of 2003, which dealt with Executive and representative arrangements in subjects of the federation (regions), and which included for the first time a closed list of regional competences.[8] On the basis of these laws all the sectoral legislation that covered the shared competences set out in articles 72 of the Constitution were altered.

The reform of local government thus needs to be seen in the context of the wider reform, in which its role was, initially, to be a means of achieving a wider reform of federal–regional relations, not an end in itself. The reform of local government was not even on the agenda of the Kozak Commission at its inception in 2001. At that stage the emphasis was on altering sectoral legislation, and the idea of revising the law on local self-government of 1995 only came to the fore During 2002, once it became clear that a closed list of regional powers was not possible without also clarifying local government's powers. It was not anticipated then that Law 131 would become the most visible and most widely debated of the changes initiated by the Commission (with the exception of Law 122 on the monetization of benefits, although here the Commission played a secondary role in a government-led reform).

At the same time it would be misleading to link Law 131 with all federal policy initiatives regarding local government, as if there were some elaborate conspiracy to centralize power away from local government. Different groups within the federal centre have entirely different agendas regarding local government. Broadly these may be divided into those who wish to see an unbroken vertical hierarchy running from the presidency to the sub-regional level, and those who saw local self-government as a basis for the development of a democratic state.

The Commission's Approach

The Commission was convened to provide a rational solution to the broader problems of Russian federalism as it had developed, including:

1 Overlapping jurisdictions and responsibilities, originating in Article 72 of the Constitution.
2 Unfinanced mandates created both by ill-informed or vague federal legislation, and by unclear responsibilities at each level of government.
3 Distribution of finance, and sources of finance, unconnected with functions and responsibilities at each level of government.
4 Excessive inequality between subjects of the federation (real and perceived), and unsustainable anomalies (such as subjects being located on the territory of other subjects).
5 Lack of checks and balances at the level of the subjects of the federation – local authorities over-dependent on subjects financially, and federal agencies numerous but (allegedly) operationally weak.

The Kozak Commission sought to counter these problems by ensuring the following:

1 All functions contained in the competences listed under Article 72 are assigned to a specific level of government (avoiding the need for an amendment to the Constitution).
2 All sectoral legislation to assign responsibilities, including financial responsibilities, to a specific level of government.
3 All functions to be allocated to specific sources of finance (as far as it is practicable to do so).
4 Special agreements between the federal centre and the regions were to be kept to a minimum, and none to have 'treaty' (*dogovor*) status, except in the most exceptional circumstances. The Commission's work has also contributed towards the removal of territorial anomalies in terms of subjects being situated on the same territory, and is thereby supporting the emerging consensus in favour of regional mergers in order to arrive at a more workable number of subjects of the federation (see Chapter 4).
5 Strengthening of local self-government as a political entity and as a properly financed level of government delivering a substantial range of services.

Observation of the sessions of the Commission showed debates to be remarkably frank, open and informal and characterized by genuine debate. Valery Kirpichnikov, Chair of the Board of the Congress of Municipalities, stated that in fifteen years he had not seen such a qualified team or such an intense work programme as on the Kozak Commission:[9]

> The concept was simple. Take existing legislation, literally every second law, and you will find that one or another service to the public, or obligation, is to be fulfilled by the executive of the subject of the federation and by local self-government. Everyone is responsible for everything and when everyone is responsible for everything, this is the main and fundamental sign of irresponsibility. The task of the Commission was to remove these difficulties, draw up three columns and under each write who does what and what resources they have for this.[10]

The commission was extremely productive, and managed the revision of over 200 laws in less than two years. There is no space to reflect the scale of the Commission's work here, where we are concerned with the more specific issue of local government and whether, how and why the Commission's Law 131 did or did nor serve the interests of local government as an institution.

It is useful to summarize the main points and rationale of the reform via Kirpichnikov's account, as a member of the Commission:

> The first major change was the territorial structure of local self-government – one third of subjects do it one way, one third another way

and in the last third there is no local self-government at all … In Tyumen (Governor) Roketskii was for the settlement model, and then in his place came (Governor) Sobyanin who was for the territorial model and changed everything. The same in Orenburg and Kursk. The new law brings local self-government closer to the people via two types. The first type is settlement – if its population is over 1,000 it should be a municipal formation. The second type brings together these settlements, currently in rural raions (districts), and makes these municipal raions (the existing boundaries are taken so as not to break things but make maximum use of what is currently there). Each type is given its powers, a closed list, which can only be added to by a law of the subject. Why? In seven years of the current law, not one subject has added a single local function, but regions have been adept at renaming their state powers as local and passing them down, naturally without funds.[11]

Composition of the Commission and the working group on Local government

The commission has been criticized for its composition,[12] which included only two regional and two local government representatives, but drew instead on the presidential administration, government ministries and specialist institutes. This has created the impression that the law was put together by persons wholly removed from municipal reality, and with a predetermined centralist agenda – in contrast to the more localist law of the same title of 1995. This is a misleading view on both counts.

Although there would have been strong arguments in favour of including more serving governors, mayors and councillors, this should not obscure the fact that the working group which prepared the text of Law 131 (and all subsequent Kozak and Shuvalov[13] Commission legislation on local government) was dominated by people strongly identified with local government, and specifically with the Congress of Municipalities throughout its post-1991 history. The working group was chaired by Vitaly Shipov, formerly mayor of Kaliningrad and Chair of the Congress of Municipalities of the Russian Federation; Igor Babichev, secretary of the Congress; Oleg Syssuev, former mayor of Samara, President of the Congress; Vitaly Chernikov, formerly Mayor of Kaluga and a leading expert of the Congress. Valery Kirpichnikov, founder of the Congress, was a member of both the working group and the Kozak Commission.

Second, the other members of the working group had been heavily involved with the 1995 reform – including Alexander Shirokov, also a former mayor, a key author of both texts, Leonid Gil'chenko, deputy president's representative of the Volga region (also a former mayor and a well-known expert on local government), and Alexander Zamotaev, an expert on local government from the presidential administration.

Those who had been involved in the previous law did not (as a rule) share the idealized view of that law that has subsequently become common among critics of Law 131. Shirokov in particular came to the view that the previous law needed to be altered substantially and in a paper, written before the Kozak Commission was formed, the changes he outlines read like an early draft of Law 131.[14] Igor Babichev describes how the authors of the 1995 law agreed that they would revise it within five years and that this work had commenced in 2000, again before the Commission was set up.[15]

It might be argued that the working group was obliged to follow the concept set out by Kozak. Whilst formally correct this ignores the degree to which Kozak's concept of a two-tier local government system was itself derived from critiques of the existing law by the members of the working group and others in the local government policy network that had become established in connection with the 1995 Law and its aftermath. Babichev, in the paper cited above, regards the introduction of the two-tier structure as the most revolutionary innovation of the new law, ending the 'artificial uniformity' of municipalities under the previous law. Vladimir Mokriy, the chair of State Duma Committee on Local Self-Government,[16] considered that it had been clear from the start that the 1995 Law would not be implemented in most parts of the country, since it did not deal with the relationship between local self-government and the state at a territorial level, and ignored the existing system of raion state administration which continued to exist under the guise of local self-government in many regions. The introduction of municipal raions was seen to provide territorial basis for cooperation between local self-government and the state.

A similar analysis was presented as early as 1998 by a team from the (then) Ministry of Nationalities, responsible for local self-government,[17] who noted the widespread use of pre-existing state administrative raions as the first level of local self-government under the 1995 Law. At the same time the authors understood that to avoid discrediting the new system of local self-government the organization of municipal formations on the level of villages and rural councils in most cases, and at the level of small villages and hamlets in all cases, is unrealistic and pointless. This implied that a two-tier system might work better, although the authors appeared to go one stage further and consider letting local government develop via a two-stage process – establishing it first in larger territorial units (e.g. raions) and then extending the principle to smaller settlements over time. This would suggest that the error in Law 131 was not the establishment of a two-tier system (without which the system would not work) but that it attempted also to introduce a strongly settlement-oriented principle from the start, which could only lead to large numbers of small municipalities.[18]

The reform becomes enmeshed in the monetization of social guarantees

At first the Commission's aim appeared to be to reduce the dependence of the federal state on the regional level, by transferring powers either up to the federal level or down to local government (by creating a formal system for delegation of powers and local government units at district level capable of carrying out delegated functions). Transferring powers and responsibilities to the federal level encountered a major obstacle, however. The Commission became aware that successive laws (mostly from the late 1990s) had lead to a position where accumulated expenditure responsibilities on social guarantees were twice as great as the amount of budget funds available for that purpose. This led to what appeared to be a change in strategy. Shared responsibilities (which were not being met by any level) were to be divided between levels of government according to the proportion of actual expenditure currently incurred at that level. It would then be incumbent on the level concerned to decide what level of guarantees it would meet and on what basis, out of its own resources.[19]

The regional representatives on the Commission were less than enthusiastic about this approach, preferring that more social responsibilities might stay at the federal level, at which Dmitry Kozak commented:

> When we talked about earth's resources then we heard all about the principles of federalism; now we're talking about social responsibilities we are hearing less ... This is about decentralization of powers and of money. No function should be devolved without decentralization of the corresponding revenue resources. This is the principled position of the President. Of course there will always be too little, but we have to distribute real money and send it to the right level.[20]

The Commission's approach, driven by the need to pay off external debts as well as the desire to rationalize state spending, led ultimately to Law 122 on the monetization of state benefits which provoked street protests the like of which had not been seen since the early 1990s. The policy may have been the government's rather than the Commission's but it was to have significant knock-on effects for the policy of strengthening local government as an institution. In order to delegate the hard choices on social guarantees down to regional level, a greater proportion of funds than previously envisaged were transferred to the regional level (which had previously been hit by budget cuts).

This had two effects as far as local government was concerned. The Commission had repeatedly stressed that the aim of its activity was to divide powers and responsibilities between levels and then ensure that adequate 'own' revenue sources were made available through amendments to the Tax and Budget Codes, thereby avoiding the chaotic practices of the 1990s, when subjects had routinely re-designated their responsibilities (under Article 72 of the Constitution) as local responsibilities and passed them down to local authorities as unfunded mandates. This is probably the most justifiable criticism that may be made of the reform – that it did not lead to the expansion in local tax income that would have been expected from the outset and would be necessary for its success. Instead it proved necessary to increase the subject's budgets to meet expanded social expenditure (the transfer did not lead to the anticipated reductions).

This led to a vicious circle whereby local government's role in large multi-level functions such as education, health and social support were reduced in favour of the subjects, on the basis that local authorities did not have sufficient budget.[21] There were debates within the working group and the Kozak and (later) Shuvalov Commission over the risks in allowing the long-term policy of division of power between levels of government to become intertwined with a deeply unpopular rationalization of social guarantees, but considered that there was no option – this was the largest issue arising from the overlapping jurisdictions of Article 72, and therefore had to be confronted. This underlines the importance of seeing the local government reform in the larger context of the reform of the federal–regional division of competences.

For its part the Ministry of Finance does not appear to have envisaged a massive transfer of funds to local government. The head of the budget department of the Mininstry of Finance, Alexei Lavrov, saw the priorities as being first to establish a local government structure where functions were clearly assigned according to a two-tier structure, then to ring-fence local budgets from regional interference, then standardize the system for delegating state competences to municipal districts. Only then could any serious expansion of local budgets take place (part of a wider system of introducing results-based budgeting across the state sector).[22]

The intertwining of the Kozak reform agenda with that of the monetization of social benefits thus led to unintended consequences and suggests that there were limitations to what could be achieved by a systematic and rational reform programme, despite the very substantial scale of legislative changes carried through. This brings us to consider the reform campaign concerned can be incorporated into a theoretical understanding of the current evolution of the Russian state.

Russian federalism between *Gemeinschaft* and *Gesellschaft*

In order to analyse the changes brought about in the early years of the Putin presidency Robinson[23] proposed a framework derived from two sets of opposed ideal types: *absolutist* versus *constitutional* (whether power is concentrated or divided) and *bureaucratic* (in the Weberian sense) versus *patrimonial* (whether or not officials are selected through patronage and have personal access to the state's resources. Robinson sees the Yeltsin period, particular the late 1990s, as characterized by constitutional patrimonialism, that in which the state has the least capacity and the least organizational integrity, and the injustice and inefficiency of patrimonial regimes, without the certainty and authority of absolutism or the accountability of democracy.

Of the four possible combinations constitutional patrimonialism is the least stable and the least likely to endure. For all Yeltsin's brinkmanship,[24] it was clear that any successor would need to move the state in a different direction.[25] In terms of the framework there are three possibilities – constitutional-bureaucratic (the Western model), absolutist-patrimonial (the Third World authoritarian regime) or bureaucratic absolutism. Putin's modernization project from 2000 onwards could be seen as to move Russia away from the weakness and uncertainty of constitutional patrimonialism and towards either constitutional bureaucracy or absolutist bureaucracy The oscillation in foreign policy in Putin's first term between European and Chinese reference points reflected this,[26] although in the first term the long-term aim of a European-style constitutional-bureaucratic model dominated, so that if absolutism were to be used, it would be a means of moving towards the Western model. This was the basis of the alliance between economic reformers and strong state advocates that supported Putin. The argument for this two-stage approach would run as follows:

(a) it is not possible to move from the chaos of constitutional patrimonialism directly to constitutional bureaucracy, as the weakness of the state has removed the capacity to create a rule-based bureaucracy (or, by extension, a law-based *Rechtstaat*).
(b) this transition can only be done via absolutist bureaucracy. Constitutional bureaucracy requires the rule of law, and this can only be achieved by reasserting the power of the state. Power must be re-centralized. Then, once the rules have been established and are being observed, power can be decentralized once again (see Figure 12.1).

This would involve moving from quadrant 1 and entering quadrant 3 as a precondition for entering the final destination, quadrant 2. In some respects this may be seen as the trajectory of Russia's modernization, at least as it appeared during Putin's first administration, absolutist bureaucracy (quadrant 3) being seen as preferable to absolutist patrimonialism (quadrant 4), which would be antithetical to modernization.

It would be misleading to consider quadrant 3 as a return to the Soviet Union, since absolutist bureaucracy need not imply control of the entire economy, only control over the political system and machinery of government. It would involve some of the form of the Soviet system, but not its ideological content. The movement from quadrant 1 to 3 may still be seen as modernization in that it involves (at the level of federal–regional relations) a shift from *gemeinschaft* (the informal power of quadrants 1 and 4) to *gesellschaft* (the law-based authority of quadrants 2 and 3).[27]

This logic is not without plausibility, although it is clear there are two potential problems. First, the move from quadrant 1 to quadrant 3 entails the removal of the checks and balances that operate (however imperfectly) in quadrant 1. Second, the movement from one quadrant to another may be carried out by judicial (and legislative) means and by administrative pressure.[28] If administrative pressure predominates, movement to a democratic law-based state could be impeded,[29] although a purely legal approach without development of wider support and engagement might be too weak.

A weak change coalition can prevent the values underlying the change from being institutionalized and normalized, leading to a return to rule by power rather than law.[30] Anything other than an optimal balance between judicial, administrative and political could, in the absence of a system of checks and balances, lead to slippage in the direction of absolutist patrimonialism (quadrant 2). Centralizing power without changing the principles by which it is exercised may amount to exchanging one form of patrimonialism (differentiated) for another (integrated). This lay behind the perception (in late 2006) that the monocentric system established by President Putin could, on his departure, or even earlier, revert into a polycentric system of 'feudal pluralism'.[31] The problem is, as before, a lack of state capacity, or rather insufficient state capacity for the strategy adopted, leading some to question whether the vertical hierarchical approach associated with the current administration is necessarily more effective than the discredited decentralized approach of the Yeltsin period.[32]

A further theoretical dimension may be provided by placing the model in the context of the romantic–baroque distinction developed by Chunglin Kwa.[33] The first quadrant implies acceptance of a degree of (baroque) complexity in the governmental system and the idea of each element and each situation requiring special arrangements and deals. Quadrant 4 also involves a baroque type of complexity behind apparent unity – the type of incipient feudalism liable to emerge in the event of a weakening of an autocratic regime. The right-hand quadrants are both, by this definition, romantic, in that they attempt to apply an overarching rationalist conception to deal with complexity (quadrant 2 – although this may be seen as overlaying baroque elements) and eliminate it altogether (quadrant 3 – which has no trace or tolerance of the baroque). The Kozak Commission may be seen as having been split between these two approaches, that of creating a system to deal with complexity and that of seeking to eliminate it. This may be seen as reflected in the choice of a dual local government system – the small settlement

Figure 12.1 Robinson's (2002) framework of state transition in Russia (notes in brackets added)

Constitutional Patrimonialism	Constitutional Bureaucracy
1	2
(Yeltsin Era/1990s fragmentation, private oligarchs)	(Western Pluralist *Rechtstaat*)
Absolutist Patrimonialism	Absolutist Bureaucracy
4	3
(regional regimes, official oligarchs)	(dictatorship of law)

Source: N. Robinson, *Russia: A State of Uncertainty*, London and New York: Routledge, 2002, pp. 2–6.

model being a unit of 'baroque' complexity and specificity, preserving difference and localism, whereas the territorial district reflects a more 'romantic'
view of state bureaucracy uniting the nation through standardization.

The framework, understood in this way, helps to explain the otherwise
curious nature of the political/professional alliance that supported the Putin
administration – ex-secret service personnel, economic liberals and 'St
Petersburg lawyers'.[34] All three groups might be expected to regard the
combination of fragmentation at the centre and entrenched quasi-sovereign
regimes in the regions with displeasure, albeit for different reasons. The alliance may be seen to derive from the St Petersburg Mayoralty post-1991 (where
Vladimir Putin served as Deputy Mayor for External Affairs and Dmitri
Kozak as head of the legal department) where a widening split appeared in
what had been a broadly united liberal opposition in the late 1980s. On the one
hand were those attached to the late 1980s ideas of democracy from below, and
on the other, those who had come to the view that reform required strong
executive rule.[35] Those who had supported the council against the executive in
St Petersburg and elsewhere were generally strong supporters of the principle
of local self-government as a popular rather than state institution.[36] Thus the
schism that occurred after 1991 in St Petersburg within what had been the liberal intelligentsia was to focus in the longer term around the issue of local self-
government, which, as a result, took on major symbolic as well as practical
significance, as the terrain on which a compromise was still sought between
state pragmatism and the democratic ideals of the late 1980s.

However, the significance of the Robinson framework, as far as local
government is concerned, lies more in the degree to which Russian regional
interests tend to be based on the left-hand *gemeinschaft* of the framework, as
subjects of a pluralistic constitutional patrimonialism (quadrant 1) or (as in
the case of the more autocratic titular republics of the Federation) in quadrant
4 as domains of absolutist patrimonialism in their own right.

In terms of this framework, Law 131 with its emphasis on rationalizing
and clarifying the division of powers and responsibilities between levels (and
with clarifying the rules for delegating functions between levels) was clearly
aimed, as was the entire project of the Kozak Commission, at moving the
system of intergovernmental relations from the left (*gemeinschaft*) side of the
framework to the right (*gesellschaft*) side, substituting rules for informal
arrangements. As one senior federal official put it:

> The problem was the habit of 'living by unwritten rules' rather than by
> laws, these unwritten rules being neither in local government's nor the
> public's interest, but in the interests of internal departmental procedures.
> This is the first law of its kind.[37]

The paradox of the Kozak Commission is that the more the law's authors
sought to contain regional power through clarification and rationalization of
the division of powers between federal and regional government, the more

difficult it became to use traditional (i.e. more patrimonial) counters to regional power. In the end the most effective counterweight to a tough regional patrimonial regime may well be a strong mayoral regime. However, the reform itself was, through the reinforcement of rational rules, to render the establishment or maintenance of such mayoral regimes more difficult than before.

Local–regional conflict

Where Subjects of the Federation (regions or republics) operate within quadrant 4 local government is largely or entirely subservient to the regional authority.[38] It would be wrong to imply that patrimonialism was more prevalent at regional level than at federal or local level. However, the more a regional authority inclined towards patrimonialism (especially of the absolutist type) the more local authorities were likely to be under pressure. As one senior federal official commented: 'If the subjects of the federation had the power, there would be no local self-government at all.'[39]

There were regions such as Vologda and Tambov where the regional administrations were supportive of local autonomy, but there were many others where local autonomy was kept to the absolute minimum. Larger cities, typically regional capitals, were as a rule caught in a zero-sum struggle for power and resources against regional heads,[40] exacerbated by the lack of clarity between local and regional (and federal) jurisdictions.

The struggle for supremacy between mayors and governors has in many ways been analogous to the power struggle between regions and the federal centre. There is a fundamental difference, however. Although the federal centre has often targeted individual regional heads, centre–regional tensions have tended to be manifested and mediated through collective institutions such as the upper house of the Russian Parliament, the Federal Council (especially prior to 2001 when regional heads were still *ex officio* members of that body). Even in the late Yeltsin period, when special agreements with individual regions were the federal authorities' preferred method of dealing with conflict, and according to some the most effective,[41] it could be said that it was the collective bargaining power of the regions as a whole that kept the federal authorities on the defensive.

Local–regional tension, by contrast, has tended to manifest itself through individualized conflict between governors and mayors, with usually only the regional capital involved – the pattern of Russian urbanization is such that in most regions there is only one city substantial enough to challenge or resist the regional authority.[42] This conflict appears to be endemic to the system – some have suggested that it would exist even under a system of appointments:

> Prussak (former governor of Novgorod region) got his own person elected when Kursunov (mayor of Novgorod city) died, but within six months they were enemies. The conflict is in the structure not the personalities or whether they are elected or appointed.[43]

Conflict between municipalities and the state thus tends to be on a one-to-one basis, involving the state at regional rather than federal level, and does not directly involve federation-wide collective institutions such as the Congress of Municipalities or the Union of Russian Cities. Although the Congress of Municipalities was closely involved in the process of developing Law 131, the lack of a tradition of federal lobbying of municipal interests was to put the municipal point of view at a disadvantage when it came to passing the draft law through the Federal Council, and regional interests began to make their presence felt.

The degree to which, in Russian federalism, tensions have been common between federal centre and regions and between regions and the larger municipalities, but not directly between federal centre and municipalities (until very recently), raises the question of whether a common interest in containing regional power existed between federal and municipal authorities.

In terms of the Robinson model, discussed above, this question takes on considerable significance. The federal centre cannot bring about the modernization of the state and its constituent regions by legislation alone. Its attempt to compensate for this by using administrative methods runs the risk of undermining the whole modernization project through the accumulation of unaccountable power at the centre. If, on the other hand, pressure was exerted on the regions through the development of municipalities as a countervailing force, this would lessen the need for administrative methods to be applied from above, and would enable the reassertion of federal authority and modernization to take place in accordance with the principles of pluralism and constitutionalism, rather than risking their abandonment and with it the integrity of the modernization agenda.

Vertical or triangle?

The notion of deploying local authorities as a political counterweight against the regions dates back to the nineteenth century councils (*zemstvos*) – seen as part of a system of 'constrained autocracy'[44] – and it may be seen as a natural consequence of Russian adversarial political culture and geographical expanse. As Sakwa has observed, 'Local self-government has the potential to become a powerful third tier, something fostered by the central authorities as a way of undermining the trend towards the regionalization of Russia.'[45]

The drive for greater local self-government has rarely been supported with any sustained commitment from the federal centre, due to the lack of a sufficiently strong pro-local government group at the federal level, where there are also groups which are wholly unsympathetic to local autonomy. The Yeltsin administration did attempt to revive the strategy, particularly through the localist local self-government law of 1995, but the abolition of local councils in 1993, in the wake of the clash with parliament, sapped the ability of local government (even once reconstituted) to fulfil this role.[46] The idea of local government as a 'second front' in the struggle between the centre and the governors was considered, but the speed with which Putin was able to establish the seven federal districts to oversee and coordinate the regions was seen to reduce the necessity of this second front.[47] Early in his first term it appeared that Putin supported this strategy, but even at that stage (in 2000) he seriously considered doing the reverse – allowing mayors to be appointed by governors - in exchange for concessions from the governors. This was the bargain that was implicit in Putin's statement:

> If the head of a territory can be dismissed by the country's president under certain circumstances, he should have a similar right in regard to authorities subordinate to him ... This is not just a right thing to do, but simply necessary in order to restore the functional vertical structure of executive power in this country ... It would mean we are living in one strong country, one single state called Russia.[48]

In the event the Duma agreed with the proposal on condition that it should be the President and not regional heads that would have the power to sack mayors. This was unacceptable to the Federal Council (upper house of regional representatives) and the proposal was dropped.[49]

It is clear that the main aim of restoring the vertical is to strengthen Russia as a state, a *derzhava* or power, and that it is the regions that provide the potential threat to unity, with the sub-regional level being (apparently) offered as a concession to secure the loyalty of the regions. The tendency for the Putin administration, despite its rhetoric, to strike bargains with regional leaders, giving them monopoly of power in their own regions provided they were loyal to the centre, has been noted by Matsuzato[50] and contrasted with the Yeltsin administration's approach. Yeltsin feared separatism where regional leaders were too well entrenched and backed challengers to unseat them. Putin has been more inclined to use the party United Russia and other means to exact loyalty from regional leaders, but has apparently been content to leave them with their regional monopoly of power intact where they are loyal. This approach supports the *derzhava* rationale for centralization, but runs counter to the constitutional rights argument for centralization that was often used during Putin's first term. If the aim of centralization is to ensure that citizens enjoy the same rights regardless of where they live within the Federation, then supporting authoritarian regional regimes cannot long remain a feature of that policy.

The idea of a local counterweight does have an enduring residual acceptance in the federal centre, such that each time proposals for appointment or dismissal have been raised they have been opposed successfully, whether in the Duma or (even) in the Federation Council of regional representatives. This may reflect a recognition that a structure based on checks and balances (what we have here termed a triangular structure) may be more robust than a simple vertical structure, due to limitations placed on any vertical hierarchy by principal-agent theory.[51]

It is worth considering why the debates on local government reform have tended to be polarized between those the 'statists' who see local government as part of an unbroken vertical line of authority and accountability and those who see it as entirely disconnected from that line. The alternative, which we have referred to here as the 'triangle' option, would draw on the original Florentine notion of the balance of power,[52] whereby three or more parties in potential conflict prevent any one of their number from becoming too powerful. Thus all stay in the game and none wholly dominate the game. However the participation in this approach would imply the recognition that complete control over other actors is not possible, and this would run counter to the tendency in Russian political culture to maximize rather than optimize control.

However, it is not necessary for local government actively to pursue this role for it to be effective. Simply by virtue of being autonomous, municipalities can exert restraint on the growth of regional power, as I. V. Babichev, the secretary of the Congress of Municipalities argued: 'If local autonomous self-government is absent from the federal state, the self-sufficiency of the Subjects would threaten the existence of the Federation.'[53] This view is seen by some to be understood by all sides:

> There will be no appointment of mayors for political reasons. There needs to be a counterweight to governors, and the Subjects (regions) know that. The talk of appointment of mayors was only to soften the blow of the appointment of governors.[54]

The 'triangle' under strain

The problem of the 'triangle' or 'balance of power view of federal–regional–local relations is that it comes under pressure in the run-up to federal elections, when the loyalty and support of regional heads comes at a premium. As one commentator put it, 'Now that the Kremlin is "perfecting" local self-government by means of turning it into a system of opposition to the gubernatorial power … can the Kremlin rely on governors' support at the parliamentary or presidential election?'[55]

What premium could the Centre offer to regional heads in the approach to national elections? The choice appeared to have been between extra or preferential resources (which cannot by definition be granted to every region) or political support against sub-regional rivals (which is potentially available to all regions).

One interviewee saw the electoral cycle as influencing the ebb and flow of the centre's support for local government, at the cost of destabilization of the local governmental system:

> Local self government has ended up as an instrument of political struggle – between elections – each president starts by developing local-self-government, then makes peace with governors. This is wrong – it should be about people's needs not politics.[56]

Given that the progress of Law 131 from its genesis in early 2002 through to its adoption in October 2003, with amendments beginning almost immediately (and becoming a regular feature as the implementation of the reform progressed), straddled most of the electoral cycle, right up to the presidential election of 2004, it should be possible to test this hypothesis regarding whether the evolution of the law became more pro-regional as the election approached. Some commentators saw this effect at work as the draft law was being finalized in late 2002.

> Why make people angry before an election? The fate of Dmitry Kozak's municipal reform is a very convincing example – first the reform was carried out fast enough, however of late its tempo has considerably slowed down. At present there are numerable consultations with regional leaders.[57]

This comment was proved wrong regarding tempo, but there did seem to be a perceptible change in the style with which the reform was approached after mid-2002. In early 2002 the rhetoric was very strongly in favour of local government as a constitutional principle that was being denied by a substantial proportion of the Subjects of the Federation.[58] The impression was very much of a joint campaign by an alliance of the Presidential Administration (or rather a section of it – and not including the legal division) and the Congress of Municipalities, with the aim of promoting local government and containing the power of regions to interfere with local authorities. As a member of the working group on Law 131 put it,

> Municipalities will have fewer powers of their own than with the existing (1995) law – under which they already have more than in Europe. Delegated powers will be increased – so they will have more power overall. Small municipalities will lose those that they cannot deliver. However, it is hard to imagine greater dependence on the regional level than at present. We have tried to remove any dependence on the regional level altogether … We can judge by the reaction of the regions. They're not happy, so therefore what we're doing must be right. Yes, they will be distributing more money, but they will be having to do it according to new rules.[59]

However, by the autumn of 2002 there were signs of strain in this alliance. On a number of issues the Commission appeared to have different views from some of those (though not all) in the Congress who had previously supported the reform wholeheartedly. By June 2003, when Vladimir Putin attended the annual conference of the Congress of Municipalities, there was no disguising the discontent of municipal leaders including leaders of the Congress and the project of building up local government as a counterweight to regional government seemed to have fallen into at best a reserve option (though clearly retained, as described above).

Conclusion

Why did what we have termed the 'triangle' concept of federal–regional–local relations not take hold in the course of the local government reform of Law 131? The reason may have been electoral considerations, as suggested above, but an even simpler explanation is possible. From September 2002 Dmitri Kozak and his team were preoccupied with getting the law through the Federal Council. This brought him into contact with a much better-organized lobbying body than the Congress, and compromises (although more in style than substance) were necessary to win support. The Congress, on the other hand, had never managed to evolve into a genuinely powerful representative body, partly because of its own internecine political pro-blems[60] and partly because, as described earlier, it lacked an established interlocutor/relationship at the federal level.

Following the establishment of the seven federal districts in 2001, the territorial directorate in the Presidential Administration was abolished. The other main central interlocutor was the Ministry of Nationalities, which was reorganized and re-created under various names before being incorporated into the Ministry of Economy, soon after which its local government related functions were transferred to the new Ministry of Regional Development, which is only gradually developing a curatorial role for local government.[61] This lack of an institutional dialogue meant that the cities and towns that were in conflict with regional heads had no standard means of dealing with the federal state as corporate bodies. It also meant that federal officials derived their information about the situation on the ground from regional heads, with whom they were more likely to have official contact.

In 2001, when the Kozak Commission was established, the President of the Association of Russian Cities (which forms part of the Congress), the Mayor of Ekaterinburg, Arkady Chernetsky, asked Kozak personally whether he might fill the vacuum and be, in effect, the federal curator for local government,[62] and although this arrangement was never formalized there was a period during which Kozak appeared to be acting in the capacity of champion of local government.

Kozak at that stage professed the view that local government should not be coordinated by a central ministry but through a network or association coordinated from the centre.[63] This was the role that clearly seemed to have been marked down for the Congress of Municipalities, and in early drafts of the Law, the Congress was referred to by name as being responsible for organizing local authorities, which would be obliged to join the Congress (which may help to explain some of the Congress's enthusiasm in the early stages of developing Law 131). Late in 2002 this was changed as it became clear that this role would deprive the Congress of its voluntary non-governmental status, even if it were to increase its influence. Instead, Law 131 has led to obligatory associations being established in each Subject of the Federation, leaving the Congress in an ambiguous position.

In conclusion, one may state first that the centralization campaign of the Putin administration was never uniform regarding local and regional government, and that the notion of local government as a counterweight to regional power has survived. On the other hand, it remains largely undeveloped as an idea, and lacks mechanisms and resources to give it greater application. This is not, it is argued, due largely to any conspiracy by the federal centre, but more to as yet weak capacity in local government's own federal-level institutions. This in turn may be explained by the absence of any substantial and continuous institutional dialogue between the federal centre and local government.

In terms of the evolution of the Russian state, the limited degree to which the 'triangle' of federal, regional and local power has developed has led to the development of what may prove to be a brittle 'state vertical' once again vulnerable to the development of patrimonialism both at the centre and in the regions. Support for a balance of power between the three levels would have helped to secure movement towards constitutional democracy. The experience of the Kozak Commission suggests, however, that a rational approach to establishing a law-based state may have unintended consequences, and a more pragmatic approach may after all be required.

Notes

1 Federal Law *'Ob obschikh printsipakh organisatsii mestnovo samoupravleniya v Rossiiskoi Federatsii'* (131/2003). 26th edition, Moscow: Yurait, Pravovaya Biblioteka, 2007.
2 'Eshche odno ogosudarstvlenie'. Interview with N. B. Kosaryeva, President of the Foundation 'Urban Economics Institute', *Konservator*, 25 October 2002. This view is disputed by A. Campbell, 'State versus Society? local government and the reconstruction of the Russian State', *Local Government Studies*, Vol. 32, No. 5, 2006, pp. 659-76. According to V. A. Lapin and V. Y. Lyubovniy, *Reforma Mestnovo Samoupravleniya i Administrativno-Territorial'noe Ustroistvo Rossii*, Moscow: Izdatel'stvo Delo, 2005, 'publichnaya vlast'' is defined (p. 134) as 'power derived from the people', and the 'system of public power' as having as elements bodies of state power and bodies of local self-government. This accords with international usage and in no way contradicts the constitutional principle of separation of local self-government from the State.
3 Institut Ekonomiki Goroda (Institute of Urban Economics Moscow). 'Positsiya Fonda "Institut Ekonoiki Goroda" po proektu FZ "Ob obshchikh printsipakh organizatsii mestnovo samoupravleniya v RF."' http://www.urbaneconomics.ru, 21 January 2003.
4 Marina Liborakina, 'Atribut vertikai vlasti ili osnova grazhdanskogo obschestva', *Perekryostok*, No. 1 (Winter 2003) (executive director of the Foundation Institute of Urban Economics): 'The attempt to make local self-government part of the vertical of public authority in a country as large and diverse as Russia is bound to fail.'
5 R. Orttung, 'Key Issues in the Evolution of the Federal Okrugs', in P. Reddaway and R. Orttung (eds), *The Dynamics of Russian Politics, Vol. 1. Putin's Reform of Federal-Regional Relations*, Lanham, MD: Rowman and Littlefield, 2004, pp. 43-5.
6 N. Petrov and D. Slider, 'Putin and the Regions', in D. L. Herspring (ed.), *Putin's Russia*, Lanham: Rowman and Littlefield, 2005, pp. 237-58.

7 D. N. Kozak had headed the legal department at St Petersburg City Adrministration, when Vladimir Putin had been head of external affairs. Kozak was to manage Putin's re-election campign in 2004, and headed the secretariat of the RF government from where in 2004 he led the reform of federal administrative structures of 2004 which separated ministries, services and agencies. Since November 2004 he has been presidential representative in the Southern Federal District, which includes the North Caucasus.

8 Federal Law 'Ob obshchikh printsipakh organisatsii zakonodatel'nykh (predstavitel'nykh) i ispolnytel'nykh organov gosudarstvennoi vlasti sub'ektov Rossiiskoi Federatsii' (Law No. 95/2003).

9 V. A. Kirpichnikov (Chair of the Board of the Congress of Municipalities), 'Planiruyemiye izmeneniya v zakonodatel'stvye po mestnomu samoupravleniyu', in V. B. Zotov (ed.), *Mestnoye Samoupravleniye v Rossii*, Moscow: Os'-89, 2003, pp. 45–50.

10 Kirpichnikov, p. 46.

11 Ibid., pp. 46–8.

12 T. Lankina, *Governing the Locals*, Lanham, MD: Rowman and Littlefield, 2004.

13 Alexander Shivalov replaced Dmitri Kozak as chair of the Commission on the division of powers between levels of government in late 2003, when the latter moved to the *apparat* of central government (in the process replacing Shuvalov as chair of the commission on administrative reform.

14 This has been discussed in A. Campbell, 'Local Government and the Russian State', *Local Government Studies*, Vol. 32, No. 5, 2006, pp. 659–76.

15 V. Babichev (secretary of the Congress of Municipalities), 'Mestnoe samoupravlenie v postsovietskoi Rossii: nekotoriye itogi i prognozy', in A. V. Ivanchenko (ed.), *Konstitutsionniye i zakonadatel'nye osnovy mestnovo samoupravleniya v Rossiiskoi Federatsii*, Moscow: Yurisprudentsiya, 2004, pp. 175–220.

16 V. S. Mokriy 'Mestnoe samoupravleniye: vchera, sevodnya, zavtra', in V. B. Zotov (ed.), *Mestnoe Samoupravleniye v Rossii*, Moscow: Os'-89, 2003, pp. 36–44.

17 Yu. V. Yakutin (ed.), *Samoupravleniye v Rossiiskoi Federatsii*, Moscow: Vneshinform, 1998.

18 This issue has been dealt with in Campbell, 2006, so is not discussed further here.

19 Session of the Kozak Commission, 18 June 2002. Authors included Leonid Giltchenko (then head of the Terrorial Directorate of the Presidential Administration), and Aleksandr Mal'tsev (then vice-chair of the Duma Commission on Local Self-Government).

20 Session of the Kozak Commission, 25 June 2002.

21 Discussion with senior federal official, 14 December 2005.

22 Alexei Lavrov, presentation at Gorbachev Foundation, 19 February 2004.

23 N. Robinson, *Russia: A State of Uncertainty*, London: Routledge, 2002, pp. 2–6.

24 In an interview with the author in June 2006, a representative of the Social Democratic Party of Russia, usually highly critical of Yeltsin, nonetheless argued that had Yeltsin been President of the Soviet Union rather than the Russian Federation, the Union would have survived the crisis in its relations with the constituent republics.

25 This view coincides with J. L. Linz and A. Stepan's concern (in, *Problems of Democratic Transition and Consolidation*, Baltimore: John Hopkins Press, 1996) that in Russia economic reform had been privileged over democratic reform (p. 392), and also their inclusion of a functioning state administration as a precondition for successful democratic transition.

26 M. Thumann, *Das Lied von der russischen Erde*, Stuttgart: Deutsche Verlags-Anstalt, 2002.

27 See C. Lever-Tracy 'A civilised gemeinschaft – ally of civil society in capitalist development', in *Szelenyi*, No. 60, Rutgers University, 1998, http://hi.rutgers.edu/

szelenyi60/lever-tracy.html for the view that in China Gemeinschaft has been the driver of development.

28 We may note that the Kozak Commission sought to integrate the Federation primarily through judicial means. The Commission did not appear to regard the federal districts as having a key role in federal–regional relations and did not seek to strengthen their role. Following Kozak's appointment as head of the Southern Federal District his approach to this institution may be seen to have changed.

29 See G. Hahn, 'Putin's "federal revolution": the administrative and judicial reform of Russian federalism', *East European Constitutional Review*, Vol. 10, No. 1, Winter 2001.

30 See H. Wollmann and N. Butusowa, 'Local self-government in Russia: precarious trajectory between power and law', in Harold Baldersheim, Michal Illner and Hellmut Wollmann (eds), *Local Democracy in Post-Communist Europe*, Wiesbaden: VS Verlag für Sozialwissenschaften, 2003, pp. 211–240.

31 A. Ryabov, 'Feudal pluralism', http://www.gazeta.ru/comments/2006/12/19_a_1170672.shtml.

32 http://gazeta.ru/comments/2006/12/20_e_1173210.shtml.

33 C. Kwa, 'Romantic and baroque conceptions of complex wholes in the sciences', in A. Mol and J. Law (eds), *Complexities*, Duke University Press, 2002, pp. 23–52. See also J. Law, 'And if the global were small and incoherent: method, complexity and the baroque', *Environment and Planning D: Society and Space*, Vol. 22, 2004, pp. 13-26.

34 Presentation by pro-Kremlin political analyst Vladimir Markov, European University Institute, Florence, 23 April 2004. The term 'St Petersburg lawyers' may be taken as a reference to Dmitri Kozak, among others.

35 A. Campbell, 'Local government policymaking and management in Russia: the case of St. Petersburg (Leningrad)', *Policy Studies Journal*, 21 January 1993, pp. 133–42. For the re-emergence of strong executive rule, see: A. Campbell, 'Democracy versus efficiency? The conflict between representative and executive rule in Russian local government 1991–2', *Administrative Studies*, No. 4, 1991, pp. 210–18, and A. Campbell, 'The restructuring of local government in Russia', *Public Money and Management*, October–December 1992, pp. 19–25.

36 See V. Gel'man, 'Federal policies towards Local government in Russia', in A. B. Evans Jr. and Vladimir Gel'man (eds), *The Politics of Local Government in Russia*, Lanham: Rowman and Littlefield, 2004, pp. 85–103. Gel'man distinguishes between managerial pragmatists (with a state-oriented view of local government) and self-governmentalists (*samoupravlentsy*) who see local autonomy as a social (political) rather than state institution.

37 Comment by Sergei Samoilov, presidential administration, working group meeting on Novosoibirsk regional laws, 5 February 2005. The Russian phrase meaning 'to live by unwritten rules' – *zhit' po ponyatiyam*, has negative, underworld connotations.

38 See Tomila Lankina, *Governing the Locals*, Lanham, MD: Rowman and Littlefield, 2004.

39 Comment by senior federal official at working group meeting, Moscow, December 2001.

40 See D. Slider, 'Governors versus Mayors: the regional dimension of Russian local government', in Evans and Gelman, pp. 145–68.

41 G. Easter, 'Re-defining centre-regional relations in the Russian Federation: Sverdlovsk Oblast', *Europe-Asia Studies*, Vol. 49, No. 4, 1999, pp. 617–35.

42 V. Gel'man, 'The politics of local government in Russia: the neglected side of the story', *Perspectives on European Politics and Society*, Vol. 3, No. 3, 2002, p. 502; also, K. Matsuzato, 2004, cited in A. Campbell, 'State versus society: local

government and the reconstruction of the Russian State', *Local Government Studies*, November 2006.

43 Interview with federal official, Miniustry of Economy, 15 May 2005.

44 N. Petro, *The Rebirth of Russian Democracy: An Interpretation of Political Culture*, Cambridge, MA: Harvard University Press, 1995, p. 153.

45 R. Sakwa, *Russian Politics and Society*, 3rd edn, London and New York: Routledge, 2003, pp. 250–1.

46 Gel'man, 'Federal Policies towards local government', in Evans and Gelman, pp. 85–103.

47 K. Simonov 'Dilemma gossovieta. Komissiya Kozaka obmenivayetsya mneniyami s gubernatorami', *Vek*, No. 32, cited in R. H. Abdulatipov, *Federalogiya*, Moscow: Piter, pp. 257-8.

48 Cited in J. Kahn, *Federalism, Democratization and the Rule of Law in Russia*, Oxford: Oxford University Press, 2002, p. 267.

49 R. Sakwa, *Putin: Russia's Choice*, London and New York: Routledge, 2004, p. 149.

50 K. Matsuzato, preface to Kimitaka Matsuzato (ed.), *Fenomen Vladimira Putina i Rossiskiye Regioni*, Moscow: Materik, 2004, pp. 6–13.

51 G. Satarov, 'Demokratura vertikal: the illusion of control', *Novaya Gazeta*, 2004, p. 62.

52 M. Sheehan, *The Balance of Power: History and Theory*, London: Routledge, 1996.

53 Babichev in Ivanchenko, pp. 175–220.

54 Interview with federal official, Ministry of Economy, 14 May 2005.

55 O. A. Salov, *Soviety: Forma Samoupravleniya i Osnova Politicheskoi Sistemy Sotsializma*, Moscow: Ekonomika, 2004. Note that Salov, an advocate of returning to the soviet model of local government, regards Law 131 as using local government to undermine the position of the regional heads.

56 Interview with former expert of State Duma, 13 May 2004.

57 'Russian Political Plots "'Not one step back!"' – all sides position themselves for campaign battles', *Politruk* Issue No. 45, 11 December, 2002, http://elist.com/archive/media.politics/200212/11102805.html.

58 Dmitri Kozak, closing speech to conference of Joint Working Group of the Federal Commission on the Division of Powers between levels of government in the Russian Federation, Tauride Palace, St Petesrsburg, 22 April 2002.

59 Interview with member of working group on local government, 26 June 2002.

60 Urban Institute, 'Analytical report on the inter-municipal movement in Russia', Moscow, 2004.

61 This may change following Dmitri Kozak's appointment as Minister of Regional Development in September 2007.

62 Conversation with Arkadi Chernetsky, Mayor of Ekaterinburg, November 2001.

63 Conversation with Dmitri Kozak, 17 July 2002.

13 Municipal elections and electoral authoritarianism under Putin

Cameron Ross

In 2000 Putin initiated a series of federal reforms whose primary aims were to create a unified economic, legal and security space across the Federation. Over the last seven years we have witnessed a concerted attack on the powers of the regions and localities and a recentralization of economic and political power in the hands of the Kremlin. Through the instigation of what he terms a 'dictatorship of law', Putin has sought to reign in the anarchic and feudal powers of the regions, and to bring an end to the 'negotiated federalism' of the Yeltsin era.

More recently the president has turned his attention to politics at the sub-regional level. In July 2001 Putin set up a Commission, chaired by Dmitry Kozak (the Deputy Head of the Presidential Administration), which was charged with drawing up new proposals on the distribution of powers between federal, regional and local governments. Proposals from the Commission have led to amendments to nearly 200 Federal laws. In 2002 the Commission drafted a new law on local self-government, which was ratified by the Duma on 16 September 2003 and signed by the President on 6 October. The Law, 'On the Principles of Organizing Local Self Government in the Russian Federation' (hereafter, the 2003 Law),[1] was originally scheduled to come into force on 1 January 2006 but in October 2005 the Duma passed legislation postponing full implementation until 2009, that is, until after the completion of the 2007-8 cycles of parliamentary and presidential elections.

The 2003 Law seeks to establish a uniform and universal system of local government throughout the country. It calls for the creation of a two-tiered system, comprising upper level 'municipal districts' and their constituent 'settlements' (city and rural). There is also a third type of municipality, the 'city districts' (city okrugs), which stands outside the jurisdiction of the municipal districts. Since the adoption of the 2003 Law the number of municipalities has doubled to 24,210. Before discussing the first round of elections to these new bodies of local self-government municipalities we need to examine Putin's recent radical reforms of party and electoral legislation. As I shall demonstrate, Putin has now instigated an 'electoral vertical' which stretches from the Kremlin through the regions to the grassroots.

Party and electoral reforms under Putin

In a highly complex serious of manoeuvres in the wake of the Beslan Hostage Crisis of September 2004, Putin cynically pushed through a number of key amendments to election and party legislation that has dealt a serious blow to the development of grassroots democracy in Russia. A new version of the 2001 Law 'On Political Parties' was ratified in December 2004 with further amendments in July 2005,[2] a new version of the 2002 Federal Law 'On Basic Guarantees of Electoral Rights and the Rights of Citizens of the Russian Federation to Participate in a Referendum' was ratified on 21 July 2005,[3] and further important amendments to key laws on election and parties were introduced in 2006.[4] According to the Chair of the Central Electoral Commission, Alexander Veshnyakov, the main aims of these revisions were 'to stimulate the development of political parties, strengthen their role and raise their responsibility in the electoral process'.[5] However, far from improving the opportunities for electoral participation, Putin's electoral and party reforms have made it much more difficult for opposition parties, and particularly small regional-based parties, to contest elections, and to win seats at the regional and local levels.[6] The main provisions of Putin's new legislation on elections and parties are as follows:

(a) According to the latest version of the Law 'On Political Parties', in order to register for elections, parties (from 1 January 2006) had to have a total of not less than 50,000 members (previously according to the original 2001 law it was 10,000). Moreover they were required to have regional branches in over half of the federal subjects, each with a minimum of 500 members (previously 100 members), and the number of members of other regional branches had to number not less than 250 members (previously 50). Moreover, only parties which have been registered for one year prior to an election can register for that election.[7]

(b) There was also a total ban on electoral blocs at all levels. Formerly, on 4 June 2003, election blocs were restricted to a maximum of two or three political parties, then in further amendments it was declared that after the December 2003 Duma elections they were to be banned altogether. Having earlier benefited from being able to form an electoral alliance, United Russia has now denied the same rights to other parties.[8]

(c) From July 2003 regional councils have been obliged to elect at least one half of their members by proportional representation in a party list system. Whilst this could be seen as a positive move which will encourage the development of parties at the regional and local levels, viewed alongside the other changes discussed above, it is more likely to simply increase United Russia's domination of regional legislatures. In 2005 the electoral threshold was raised from 5 to 7 per cent, another factor that will make it more difficult for small parties to win seats, and independents will no longer be able to contest regional elections.[9] According to

Putin the new PR system has increased the number of parties in regional assemblies and it has weakened the governor's ability to control the elections,

> Practice shows that the proportional system gives the opposition greater opportunities to expand its representation in the legislative assemblies ... In the three years since the system has been used at regional level, the number of party factions in local parliaments has increased almost four-fold. Today they account for almost two-thirds of all members of the regional parliaments.[10]

However, it would appear that the changes to the electoral system have benefited one party in particular – United Russia. Over the period December 2003–March 2006 elections took place in fifty-two regions. United Russia gained the largest number of seats in forty-seven regional assemblies (with an absolute majority in twelve) and they took second place in five regions.[11]

(d) The weakness of Russian Federalism is graphically illustrated by the fact that the Law 'On Parties' also prohibits regional parties from competing in elections. Such a ban is clearly designed to prevent regional governors and republican presidents from building local political machines in order to capture control of their legislatures. This is especially important now that (since January 2005) regional legislatures have been charged with approving Putin's nominees for regional chief executives. In a further, amendment to legislation governing the presidential appointment of governors, the party that wins the most party list seats in a regional legislature has the right to nominate a candidate for the post of governor. It is perhaps no coincidence that this new ruling coincides with United Russia's newly acquired electoral success in the regions.

(e) The percentage of signatures that an individual or party needs to gather in order to contest an election has been set by federal legislation as 'no greater than 2 per cent' of the number of electors, up from 1 per cent in previous legislation, and the number of invalid signatures that are permitted has been lowered. Up until 2005 registration for elections could be refused if 25 per cent of a candidate's signatures were declared invalid. This has now been reduced to 10 per cent for regional and local elections and 5 per cent for federal elections. As Wilson notes, 'this could be used to deny virtually any party registration, as it is almost impossible to collect so many signatures with so few mistakes'.[12] The verification of nomination signatures has been subject to widespread abuse by regional and local administrations with scores of opposition candidates being ousted from election campaigns (see discussion on this below). The deposit required for candidates and parties to register for elections has also been increased. Moreover, parties which have party list seats in the

Duma (currently CPRF, LDPR, Motherland, United Russia) do not need to gather signatures or pay a deposit in order to register for any level of election, and the amount of state funding to these parties has also been substantially increased.

(f) In July 2005 the maximum share of state officials and members of political parties that were permitted to serve in electoral commissions was increased from one-third to one-half. Parties with party list seats in the State Duma also have a privileged positions through their nomination of the members of electoral commissions. This has led to a situation whereby supporters of United Russia now dominate the electoral commissions at all administrative levels (see below). Under Putin we have witnessed the development of a new 'power vertical' of electoral commissions, with higher-level commissions now granted the right to appoint heads of lower-level commissions. Thus, for example, the Russian Federation Central Electoral Commission has the right to appoint the chairs of regional commissions. These changes, it has been argued by members of the Central Electoral Commission, were motivated by the need to create regional and local commissions that would be independent of regional and local powers. Under Yeltsin, regional electoral commissions were captured by regional powers, and municipal commissions in turn were under the tight control of regional commissions. The situation is now much more complex, especially given the fact that Putin since January 2005, has been granted the power to nominate and dismiss regional executives.

(g) In July 2006 the Duma adopted legislation removing the 'vote against all' category from ballots. No longer will citizens have the opportunity to show their disapproval of the election system, the lack of real choice, or of individual candidates, by voting against all candidates. In a similar vein from January 2007 minimum turnout requirements have been abolished.

For Wilson, the above developments are part and parcel of Putin's 'centralizing project'. The Law 'On Political Parties' 'prohibits national ethnic and religious parties and prevents the formation of regional parties', whilst 'the introduction of Proportional Representation in the regions has given parties a foothold in regional legislatures that were previously the almost exclusive preserve of regional interests'.[13]

Municipal elections 2004–5

The first round of elections to the newly formed municipalities was held over the period March 2004–December 2005. During this period elections were held (for both old and new bodies of local government) in 19,266 municipalities.[14] By the end of this election cycle, in December 2005, 198,815 deputies had been elected to the local councils (including 119,358 to the newly formed councils), and 13,655 heads of local administrations were elected (including 8,644 in newly formed municipalities).

Elections of chairs of councils and heads of municipalities

The 2003 Law continues the practice (first established in the 1995 Law) of allowing heads of municipalities (in municipal districts and city okrugs) to be indirectly elected from members of their local assemblies, or directly elected by their citizens. It also calls for a separation of executive and legislative powers. No longer will the chair of a council be allowed to hold the additional post of head of municipality. This means in effect that there are will be two heads of municipalities: the chair of the council (who may be indirectly or directly elected) and an 'executive manager', to be hired by a special selection committee. According to the original provisions of the 2003 Law, one third of the members of the panels charged with appointing the new executive managers were to be chosen by regional administrations (Article 37.5) and the others by the local councils. However, in an amendment adopted in April 2005, the percentage of representatives from regional administrations was raised to 50 per cent, thereby significantly enhancing regional control over the appointment process. This new dual system has the potential to generate conflict between heads of the local councils and appointed managers, especially in cities where the latter are nominees of regional governors.

There have been numerous complaints by local politicians and officials of pressure being put on them to adopt the indirect method of electing their council heads. According to the Ministry of Regional Development, by July 2005, thirty-six of Russia's federal subjects (e.g. Vladimir, Voronezh, Tver', Ul'yanovsk, Sverdlovsk and Chelyabinsk) had changed to this system. However, in numerous municipalities (e.g. in Kaluga, Kostroma, Perm, Vladimir and Leningrad oblasts) citizens have appealed to the local courts to have direct elections reinstated. Thus, for example, in January 2005 deputies of the City Assembly of Obninsk (Kaluga Region) adopted a decision to cancel the direct election of the city mayor. This was despite the fact that a decision on the introduction of direct elections had already been decided by a local referendum in 1995. The City Court on 8 February 2005 declared that the cancellation of direct elections was illegal; however, the Kaluga Regional Court on 14 March revoked the decision of the City Court.[15] It is clear that the indirect method is preferred because it is much more open to manipulation and control from the regional authorities than popular elections. It is much easier for regional executives to gain control over local councils than to control local electorates.

Type of electoral system

Regions are free to determine their own electoral system for municipal council elections. However, in 2005 the Central Electoral Commission produced a Draft Model Law which proposed that in the future all municipal elections should adopt a mixed electoral system with a high level of proportionality.[16] However, the Draft Model Law was not published in time for the 2004-5 round of municipal elections where a first past the post majoritarian electoral system was by far the most common system employed. A mixed, majoritarian/PR system was adopted in only fifty council elections, in seven regions (Kransnoyarsk Krai, Volgograd, Nizhegorod, Tomsk, Tula, Sakhalin and Chita oblasts).[17] Only one municipality – the city of Volzhskii (Volgograd Region) – adopted a fully proportional party list system.

The 2003 Law allows for the indirect election of deputies to the municipal districts. Thus, for example, in Stavropol' Krai the councils of municipal districts are made up of the ex-officio heads of the settlements situated within their jurisdiction, plus two deputies from each settlement council.[18] This, provision conflicts with Article 130 of the Russian Constitution which states that local self-government 'shall be exercised by citizens through a referendum, election, or other forms of direct expression of the will of the people, through elected and other bodies of local self-government'.[19]

Candidates

Outside the capital cities of the regions competition for posts as deputies and executives was very low. Over the period March 2004–December 2005 a total of 283,811 candidates competed for the 198,815 seats in local councils which was an average of just 1.42 candidates per seat. For the 13,655 posts of heads of municipalities there were 37,715 candidates, an average of 2.76 candidates.[20] As Lankina notes, 'In many areas, particularly in the countryside, the locals' lack of interest in voting or running for local positions has been a great source of concern, even panic, for regional officials and electoral commission members keen on demonstrating that the reform is going smoothly.'[21]

In Tatarstan 80 per cent of all candidates ran unopposed, as was the case in many of the rural settlements in the Republic of Yakutiya, and the Ust'-Ordinskskii Buryatskii Autonomous Okrug. In Arkhangel'sk Oblast five days after the beginning of the election campaign there were still only 16 candidates who had registered for the 202 posts of heads of local administrations and just 481 candidates for the 1,861 local council seats: in Plesetskii and Nyndomskii districts no candidates had come forward at all! It would appear that the heads of district administrations in the region were not enthusiastic about creating new representative bodies to challenge their powers.[22]

In Rostov Oblast 7,795 candidates put their names forward for 4,273 council seats (1.8 candidates per seat), and 1,640 candidates competed for the 408 posts of head of municipalities (4.0 per post) in the September 2005 municipal elections. In the run-up to the campaign Rostov Regional Assembly adopted legislation making it much easier for candidates to register for the elections. Thus, for example, in those districts where the population numbered less than 10,000, candidates were allowed to register without having to submit a list of signatures, or pay a monetary deposit. In districts with less than 5,000 inhabitants, candidates were not obliged to provide information about their income and property. Moreover, in an even more radical move the region approved uncontested elections in city and rural settlements. Such elections took place in 15.8 per cent of the electoral districts. By holding these uncontested elections (which are provided for in federal electoral legislation) the region undoubtedly saved millions of roubles, which it would otherwise have had to spend on holding repeat elections. However, such a policy is hardly a positive recipe for developing grassroots democracy.[23]

Turnout and 'Votes Against All'

For the 2004-5 elections a minimum turnout of 20 per cent was required to validate the elections, compared to the previous norm of 25 per cent (as noted above, from January 2007 turnout thresholds have now been abolished). Overall, the average turnout in local elections held over the period 2004-5 was quite healthy from a comparative perspective. As Table 13.1 shows, turnout varied from a low of 38.45 per cent for city district council elections, to a high of 56.6 per cent in the elections for deputies of rural settlements. One significant factor which sets Russia apart from many other countries is the fact that turnout has been consistently higher in the rural areas than in the cities. The explanation would appear to be that citizens in rural areas are more easily mobilized (or coerced) by local officials to participate in elections than their counterparts in the cities. Turnout levels are also generally higher in elections for executive bodies than for local councils, and participation in elections at the local level is considerably lower than at the regional and national levels.

In those cases where we find much higher than average levels of turnout there are good reasons to believe that these are 'managed elections' – that is, elections which have been manipulated and controlled by regional and local administrations. Thus, for example, average turnout for elections to rural settlements councils was, as we noted above, 56.4 per cent. However, it was 97.44 per cent in Bashkortostan, 81.6 per cent in Sakha, 84.6 per cent in Chukotka AO, 81.2 per cent in Orenburg, and 80.1 per cent in Aginskii-Buryatskii AO.[24] In Tatarstan there was an average turnout of 87.6 per cent, but in some districts it reached 99 per cent! (Atninskii and Apastovskii) – figures which are reminiscent of the manufactured rates of the Soviet era.[25] As Sharafutdinova notes, 'Officials exerted considerable pressure to achieve such numbers. Directors of publicly financed institutions, such as hospitals and schools, and industrial managers used their influence among employees to mobilize voters.'[26]

As Table 13.2 demonstrates there was considerable variation in turnout levels across the municipal districts of the Saratov region, ranging from an average of 27.55 per cent in the city of Engels to 78.74 per cent in the

Tatishchevskii rural settlement. In the Tula Region average turnout in municipal districts varied from a low of 15.81 in the city of Efremov (which was below the 20 per cent minimum) to a high of 38.99 in Kamenskii raion.

Votes 'Against All'

Low turnout in many cases may not simply reflect the apathy of the electorate but rather the belief on the part of citizens that: (1) the elections are corrupt, (2) there is no meaningful choice of candidates or parties, and (3) local government has no real power. Here, the percentage of votes cast 'against all candidates' is an excellent additional guide to the levels of political dissatisfaction amongst the electorate. Indeed, the 'vote against all' can be viewed as an excellent barometer of the integrity of elections. Where the percentage of votes against all is unusually high, it is usually for a reason – Russian citizens are showing their disapproval in the only way permitted. Overall, in the local elections conducted in 2004-5 an average of 18.8 per cent of the participants chose to voice their protest by this method. However, in many municipalities the figure was much higher and in some cases new elections had to be called, as the 'votes against all' received the highest support.[27] In Saratov Oblast the level of such protest voting varied between a low of 2.51 per cent in Ivanteevsk raion to 16.92 per cent in Balakovsk raion. In Tula Oblast there were more protest votes, which ranged from 10.27 per cent in Kamenskii raion to a high of 22.5 per cent in the city of Kimov (see Table 13.2).

Where there are low levels of turnout combined with high percentages of 'votes against all', the legitimacy of the election is much more sharply brought into question. Thus for example, in Balakovsk raion (Saratov Region) there was a relatively low turnout of 36.86 and a relatively high percentage of protest votes of 16.92 per cent. In Tula in almost every district there were low turnout rates combined with sizeable percentages of protest votes. In the city of Kimov there was a low turnout of 21.57 per cent combined with a protest vote of 22.5 per cent (see Table 13.2). Likewise, where turnout was high, protest voting was low. Thus, for example, in Piterskii

Table 13.1 Average turnout in Russian local elections 2004–05 (%)

Average turnout (per cent)	*Local councils*	*Heads of municipalities*
Rural settlements	56.4	54.8
City settlements	40.63	41.86
Municipal raions	50.46	51.65
City districts	38.45	41.75

Source: L. F. Dem'yanchenko (ed.), *Reforma Mestnovo Samoupravleniya v Rossiiskoi Federatsii: Itogi Munitsipal ' Nykh Vyborov v 2004-2005 Godakh*, Moscow: Tsentral'naya Izbiratel'naya Komissiya Rossiiskoi Federatsii, 2006, p. 8.

Municipal Raion in Saratov, turnout was 72.85 per cent and protest votes comprised just 5.76 per cent. As we noted above, citizens no longer have the right to cast a 'vote against all', and minimum turnout thresholds have been abolished.

Party membership of municipal councils and administrations

In the territory of the Russian Federation in 2004, 1,538 regional and 5,328 local branches of political parties were registered. However, parties played a relatively minor role in the 2004-5 round of municipal elections. The most active parties were United Russia (UR), the Communist Party of the Russian Federation (CPRF), the Liberal Democratic Party of Russia (LDPR), and Motherland (Rodina). Also taking part to a lesser degree were the regional branches of the Russian Party of Pensioners (RPP), the Russian Party of Life (RPL), the Agrarian Party of Russia (APR), Yabloko, and the Union of Right Forces (SPS). There were also a host of other minor parties, which fielded less than 1 per cent of the total number of candidates. However, only 17 per cent of candidates to local councils and 8.9 per cent of those standing for posts as heads of local municipalities stood on a party ticket.[28] Moreover, of the 198,815 elected deputies just 18.6 per cent were party members and of the 13,655 elected heads of local municipalities, only 20.2 per cent declared a party affiliation.[29]

Party competition at the settlement level was particularly low and in some cases almost non-existent. Thus, for example, in elections in Khabarovsk Krai for heads of 217 city and rural settlement councils, held on 3 April 2005, 7,000 of the 7,006 candidates were independents. Of the tiny number of candidates (just six) nominated by a political party, two were from United Russia, two from the CPRF, and two from the LDPR. Moreover, only one of the six party contestants was successful (from the CPRF).[30]

The dominance of United Russia

Where parties did compete, United Russia was by far the most active and successful. In total, as Table 13.3 demonstrates, in the elections to municipal councils it won 15.2 per cent of the seats in rural settlements, 17 per cent in city settlements, 15.4 per cent in municipal raions and 17.5 per cent in city okrugs. In elections for heads of municipalities the percentage of votes for United Russia were all slightly higher: 16.7 per cent in rural settlements, 20.1 per cent in city settlements, 20.8 per cent in municipal raions, and 21.0 per cent in city okrugs. As can be seen the Communists (CPRF) came a very distant second with figures ranging from 0.6 to 4.24 per cent. All the other parties had a token representation of less than 1 per cent.

In Tver' Region 94 per cent of all party-nominated candidates for local councils and executive heads were nominated by United Russia,[31] in Saratov (87 per cent). In Kareliya, United Russia dominated the elections contesting

Table 13.2 Turnout (average per cent) and Votes Against All (average per cent) in the electoral districts of municipal raions in Saratov Region and Tula Region

Saratov Municipal Raions	Saratov turnout	Saratov votes against all	Tula municipal raions	Tula turnout	Tula votes against all
Aleksandro-Gaiskii	66.06	6.29	Aleksinskii Raion	36.15	13.36
Arkadatskii	64.36	5.73	City Aleksin	34.24	13.15
Atkarskii	47.05	9.08	Belevskii Raion	34.39	11.41
Bazarno	77.77	3.80	Bogordintskii Raion	27.37	13.89
Karabulakskii					
Balakovskii	36.86	16.92	City Bogorodinsk	22.95	15.07
Balashovskii	32.34	12.26	Venevskii Raion	25.42	14.94
Baltaiskii	68.58	9.99	Yefremovskii Raion	22.19	12.47
Vol'skii	42.89	9.40	City Efremov	15.81	17.4
Voskresenskii	64.10	7.44	Kamenskii Raion	38.99	10.27
Dergachevskii	62.22	5.10	Kimovskii Raion	30.74	14.98
Dukhovnitskii	78.34	5.66	City Kimov	21.57	22.5
Ekaterinovskii	49.01	5.73	Kireevskii Raion	27.76	16.92
Ershovskii	56.51	7.76	Novomoskovskii Raion	25.74	14.71
Ivanteevskii	73.02	2.51	City Novomoskov	23.34	13.71
Kalininskii	52.14	8.48	Plavskii Raion	32.73	17.35
Krasnoarmeiskii	38.27	9.06	Suvorovskii Raion	27.99	12.27
Krasnokutskii	50.27	6.23	Uzlovskoi Raion	20.11	11.96
Krasnopartizanskii	61.05	3.38	City Uzlov	16.13	13.61
Lysogorskii	63.96	3.65	Shchekinskii Raion	31.07	17.55
Marksovskii	39.75	7.47	City Shchekino	28.55	11.3
Novoburasskii	63.26	5.90	Yasnogorskii Raion	27.73	18.57
Novouzenskii	73.05	9.58			
Ozinskii	53.22	5.51			
Perelyubskii	55.19	6.49			
Petrovskii	35.44	10.12			
Piterskii	72.85	5.76			
Pugachevskii	39.55	5.76			
Rovenskii	52.17	7.04			
Romanovskii	62.79	4.03			
Rtishcheveskii	37.08	7.51			
Samoilovskii	61.01	4.59			
Saratovskii	61.00	4.70			
Sovetskii	36.29	9.02			
Tatishchevskii	78.74	4.46			
Turkovskii	63.00	5.46			
Fedorovskii	56.53	6.39			
Khvalynskii	54.10	10.74			
Engel'skii	27.55	11.35			
Saratov Oblast	45.93	8.52			

Source: For data on Saratov see, 'Svodnaya Statistika po Vydvizheniyu i registratsii kandidatov na vyborakh deputatov predstavitel'nykh organov pervovo sozyva vo vnov' obrazovannykh munitsipal'nykh obrazovaniyakh Saratovskoi Oblasti, 9 Oktryabrya 2005 goda', p. 15 downloaded from http://www.saratov.izbirkom.ru/informacia1. For data on Tula, see http://www.izbirkom.ru/way/929936.htm

80 per cent of the seats in local councils and 75 per cent of the contests for the posts of heads of municipalities. In second place, far behind, was the Liberal Democratic Party of Russia (LDPR) which took part in just 2.5 per cent of the elections, and in third place were members of the CPRF with a negligible number of candidates. United Russia swept the board winning 76 per cent of the council seats and 62 per cent of the posts of heads of municipalities.[32] In Volgograd Region, United Russia nominated 2,000 candidates for local council elections, whilst the Communists, the main opposition party in the region, could only muster 359, the LDPR 112, Rodina 184 and the Agrarian Party of Russia 144. However, 60 per cent of the electorate who turned out to vote gave their support to parties of the left (Communists, Agrarians, Rodina) in this traditional stronghold of leftist parties.[33]

However, many parties declared that their actual electoral support was much higher than the above official data would suggest. Many of the so-called 'independent candidates', it is claimed, were in fact party members. Thus, for example, in Arkhangel'sk Oblast according to the official data, only three parties took part in the elections (UR, CPRF and LDPR), which were held on 2 October 2005 and less than 1 per cent of the total number of candidates were nominated by parties.[34] However, United Russia later declared that of the 1,035 candidates for local councils, 806 were party members, and of the 153 candidates for heads of municipalities, 122 supported the 'party of power'. For the Communists the figures were thirty deputies and five heads of municipalities; for Motherland fourteen and eight respectively, LDPR (seven deputies).[35]

In Tatarstan, opposition candidates were threatened with 'criminal investigations and other forms of harassment' if they did not withdraw their names from the ballots.[36] This may explain the fact that 97 per cent of candidates (approximately 5,000) came from United Russia and its close ally 'Tatarstan – a New Century', whilst the number from the opposition numbered only 300 (3 per cent).[37] These two 'parties of power' won over 70 per cent of the votes. The remaining parties, including the CPRF, LDPR and SPS, together received less than 1 per cent. Candidates from the democratic opposition, supported by the public associations 'Equality and Legality' and 'Our City', failed to win a single seat. Moreover, all but one of the district heads, who had previously been appointed by the Republican President, won re-election.[38]

Party representation was, as we would expect, much higher in those very few municipalities which used a mixed electoral system. Thus, for example, in elections for Tomsk City Okrug Council, eleven parties participated in the elections and six of these are represented in the new assembly.[39] In Tula Region United Russia won 79 of the 211 seats in the local council elections. The CPRF was second with 44 seats, followed by Rodina with 39 and the LDPR with 9. The Russian People's Party won a total of 18, the Agrarian Party of Russia 11, and the Union of Right Forces 8.

Table 13.3 Party membership of municipal councils and heads of municipalities in December 2005. (Number of members and (per cent))

	Rural Settlements Councils	City Settlements Councils	Municipal Raions Councils	City District Councils	Rural Settlements Heads of Municip.	City Settlements Heads of Municip.	Municipal Raions Heads of Municip.	City District Heads of Municip.
Total No of Deputies	148708	19776	21637	7322	11626	1172	982	314
United Russia	22629 (15.2)	3380 (17.0)	3340 (15.4)	1287 (17.5)	1950 (16.7)	236 (20.1)	205 (20.8)	66 (21.0)
CPRF	1410 (0.9)	507 (2.5)	918 (4.24)	200 (2.7)	285 (2.4)	24 (2.0)	26 (2.6)	2 (0.6)
LDPR	187 (0.1)	102 (0.5)	79 (0.3)	44 (0.6)	34 (0.2)	18 (1.5)	12 (1.2)	6 (1.9)
Rodina	126 (0.08)	93 (0.4)	93 (0.4)	47 (0.6)	3 (0.02)	2 (0.1)	1 (0.1)	0 (0.0)
Yabloko	15 (0.01)	1 (0.005)	9 (0.04)	16 (0.21)	1 (0.008)	0 (0.0)	0 (0.0)	0 (0.0)
SPS	11 (0.007)	3 (0.015)	11 (0.05)	10 (0.1)	1 (0.008)	0 (0.0)	0 (0.0)	1 (0.3)
Others	1385 (0.9)	116 (0.5)	311 (1.4)	154 (2.1)	76 (0.6)	7 (0.5)	16 (1.6)	2 (0.6)

Source: *Vestnik Tsentral'noi Izbiratel'noi Komissii Federastii*, No. 2 (193), 2006, p. 260. Does not include data for Chechnya and Ingushetiya. Key: CPRF=Communist Party of Russian Federation; LDPR=Liberal Democratic Party of Russia; SPS=Union of Right Forces. Percentages added by author.

Party competition was also much greater in the capital cities of the federal subjects where there were fierce battles for power.[40] Thus for example, in Izhevsk, the capital city of Udmurtiya, 223 candidates contested the 42 seats for the City Council in the elections of 16 October 2005. Party membership is also much higher amongst the mayors of capital cities. Thus, for example, in my study of seventy mayors of capital cities (in post as of March 2007), sixty-two were members of a political party, and of these, fifty-nine were members of United Russia: two were members of 'A Just Russia', and one was a member of the 'People's Will' party.

Appointment of mayors of regional capital cities

Over the last few years there has been a vigorous debate within the Russian political establishment over the vexed question of granting regional leaders the power to appoint the mayors of their capital cities. In November 2006, the Governor of Sverdlovsk, Aleksandr Levin, stated that:

> sooner or later mayors would be chosen in the same way as governors. Governors would nominate candidates for mayors in local representative organs, deputies would vote on their choice. If we build a power vertical it should not be interrupted at the level of the governors. It should penetrate all structures – from the president to the heads of rural settlements.[41]

As Coalson notes, public support for such a policy has also come from a number of high-ranking politicians, such as: Lyubov Sliska, the First Deputy Chair of the Duma (and a member of United Russia); Vladimir Zhirinovsky, Deputy Chair of the Duma (head of the Liberal Democratic Party of Russia); Vladislav Surkov, Deputy Head of the Presidential Administration. However, other key politicians, such as Boris Gryzlov, Chair of the Duma (head of United Russia), have declared their opposition to such a move.[42]

Critics of the proposed amendments also argue that the elimination of mayoral elections would require changes to the Russian Constitution. Article 32.2 states that: 'Citizens of the Russian Federation shall have the right to be elected to bodies of state governance and organs of local self-government.' Furthermore, Article 130.2 declares that 'local-self government shall be exercised by the citizens through referendums, elections, and forms of expression of their will, through elected and other bodies of local self-government', and Article 131.1, states that 'the structure of bodies of local self-government shall be determined by the population independently'.[43] The appointment of mayors would also violate the 'European Charter of Local Self-Government' to which Russia is a signatory. Article 3.2 of the Charter stipulates that rights in the field of local self-government must be exercised by democratically constituted authorities.[44]

At a meeting of an All-Russia Inter-municipal Forum in Novosibirsk in November 2006, fifty mayors of Siberian cities sent an appeal against the appointment of mayors to the State Duma and Federation Council. Aleksandr Sokolov, the Mayor of Khabarovsk, noted that 'a vertical chain of command is, of course, not a bad thing, but then one needs to stop dreaming of initiatives on the part of the public, of possibilities for self-government, and of engaging everyone in active constructive endeavours'.[45]

However, it would appear that the direct appointment of mayors by regional governors has been put on hold until after the 2007–8 round of parliamentary and presidential elections. At a session of the Congress of Local and Regional Authorities of Europe which took place in Moscow in November 2006, top United Russia officials spoke out against the direct appointment of mayors. At the meeting Igor Shuvalov rejected the appointment of mayors stating that such an initiative was 'an attempt to role back municipal reform in this country.' The law was branded as a 'private initiative' rather than an official policy of United Russia. Shuvalov's position in turn has been supported by Dmitry Medvedev, one of the favourite candidates to succeed Putin.[46]

One of the key changes to power relations within the regions is the fact that Putin since January 2005 has the power to directly appoint regional governors (see Chapter 5). This has led to a situation whereby governors are viewed by the public more as representatives of the centre in the regions rather than vice versa. Regional chief executives may have been granted more powers over mayors but now that they are appointed from above, they have lost much of their authority and democratic legitimacy. In contrast, directly elected mayors can still claim to have a popular local mandate to govern. It may be for this reason that we have recently witnessed a concerted attack on the probity of mayors. Governors have launched a series of criminal investigations against mayors accusing them of squandering their cities' budgets and engaging in corrupt practices. Thus, for example, in Krasnodar region, over thirty mayors were forced from office during 2002–4, after being charged with trumped-up criminal offences.[47]

In December 2006 Aleksandr Makarov, the Mayor of the city of Tomsk was arrested and imprisoned after police accused him of taking bribes 'in exchange for lucrative construction contracts'. He later suffered a heart attack when police allegedly found large sums of money in his home. Makarov rejects all the charges brought against him and he has lodged a complaint with the European Court of Human Rights. As Bigg notes, this is not an isolated incident. Over the period 2005–6 'a dozen mayors in Russia [were] detained and taken to court on corruption-related charges'.[48] As Oreshkin notes, often the charges against the mayors are 'simply ridiculous'. Thus, for example, the Mayor of Arkhangel'sk, Aleksandr Donskoi,

> fell from grace in February [2007], when prosecutors indicted him on four counts – faking a university diploma, using it to obtain a second higher education, using budget funds to pay for his son's bodyguards, and authorizing a company to build a shopping centre without government clearance.[49]

Donskoi has stated publicly that he is being persecuted because of his intention to stand for office in the 2008 presidential elections. 'I declared in October that I would run for president', Donskoi said,

> After this, criminal cases were opened. What's more, I was made to understand that these criminal cases are connected to my declaration that I planned to run. The people who commissioned these criminal cases are federal officials, together with the governor of the Arakhangel'sk Oblast.'[50]

In June 2007 the Mayor of Volgograd, Yevgeny Ishchenko was sentenced to one year in prison after being charged 'with possessing ammunition and engaging in illegal business activities'. Ishchenko 'had repeatedly clashed with the local branch of United Russia and with the regional Governor'.[51] Six members of Ishchenko's administration have also been arrested.[52]

Manipulation and falsification of elections

During the Putin era there have also been countless instances of opposition candidates and parties being ousted from elections because of so-called infringements in their nomination documents, and there has been widespread manipulation and falsification of elections in favour of United Russia. Governors and mayors command significant 'administrative resources', which have 'often included compliant regional assemblies, courts and electoral commissions'.[53] In some cases, compromising materials may be collected by regional police forces to 'persuade' incumbent mayors to voluntarily withdraw from elections.[54] As Buzin demonstrates, in the Moscow municipal elections of March 2004, 1,100 out of the 4,500 candidates were refused registration! Registration was often denied to candidates simply because they signed their name or wrote the date in the wrong columns of their nomination papers or for other similar trivial reasons. Similarly, in the elections to Klimov City Council (Moscow oblast) in 2005, thirty-three of the seventy-seven candidates were denied registration, because of supposed infringements in their registration documents. None of the ousted candidates were members of United Russia.[55]

Another favoured method of manipulating the vote is to persuade members of the electorate to vote ahead of schedule or to vote not at the polling station but at home using portable ballot boxes. Portable ballot boxes are only meant to be used where citizens are too ill or frail to travel to the polling stations. Often these early voters are enticed to vote in such an unorthodox manner with promises of gifts, money or the provision of local services. Those who vote at home may also come under subtle pressures to vote in the 'right way'. Thus, as Oreshkin notes, in the March 2007 elections for regional and local councils in the Orel Region, 14.6 per cent of the electorate voted by means of portable ballot boxes, and in the raion elections in the City of Orel, the figure was 30 per cent. United Russia won 53 per cent of the votes where portable ballot boxes were used and 39 per cent in the polling stations. In the Pskov region, 20.1 per cent of the electorate voted at home (in the Nevelsk District the figure was 49.5 per cent). As Oreshkin concludes, 'a clear pattern is observable: wherever over 30 per cent vote from home, the turnout is 15 per cent higher than average for the region, and United Russia receives 10 per cent above the average result'.[56]

As we noted above, minimum turnout thresholds have now been abolished. One of the reasons for this is that regional leaders have often had to resort to falsifying turnout figures to validate their elections. Thus, for example, in local elections in March 2007 in the city of Hasavyrut (Dagstan Republic),

> Turnout by two o'clock was approximately the same in all districts – between 34.99 and 35.18 per cent. And notably, the turnout in all 26 districts changed in step: by 4 p.m. it fluctuated between 61.98 and 62.41 per cent, while two hours later it was 77.98-78.03 per cent.[57]

The turnout figures here were clearly fabricated according to the wishes of the Republican leadership.

Outright falsification of elections is also widespread. Thus, for example, in 783 electoral districts in Dagestan, where a total of 395 thousand people voted in the 11 March 2007 regional and local elections, there was not a single invalid ballot paper. Not one single voter made a mistake and spoiled his or her ballot paper, which as Oreshkin notes, 'is simply, in practice, impossible'.[58] Furthermore, 'In 124 districts, United Russia won 100 per cent of the votes; in 36 districts there was a 100 per cent turnout, and all of them, without exception, voted for United Russia.' Moreover, 'in one electoral district, United Russia won 100 per cent of the votes in the republican level ballots, but only 7 per cent in the municipal ballots'[59] However, citizens have already begun to fight back by spoiling their ballot papers, which is now the only method they have left to voice their discontent. Thus, for example, instead of the normal average of about 1 per cent, wasted ballots made up 6.1 per cent in the March 2007 local elections in the Komi Republic; in the city of Velikhie Luky 8.9 per cent were wasted, whilst in electoral district No. 158 of the Pskov Region, the figure for spoilt ballot papers was 31 per cent![60] In his Study of the Moscow Municipal Elections of 2004 Buzin gave this pessimistic assessment,

> it is necessary to stress that in many of Moscow's polling stations (there are 3,200) there were no skilled observers. The impudence of the way in which the falsifiers were covered from the rear by the Moscow Prosecutors' Office, and in some cases the courts, allows us to assume that the falsification of elections was conducted on a massive scale.[61]

Politicization of electoral commissions

One of the reasons why the manipulation of elections is so prevalent is the fact that election commissions are financially dependent on the state and are dominated by members of United Russia. Thus, as the former Chair of the Central Election Commission, Ivanenko, observed in 2005,

> in our country the electoral commissions themselves are entirely within the complement of the system of executive power. In the Soviet period, there were also elections, people came to the polls, took ballots and marched along a clear straight line, without deviating to the right or left. And we are returning to this now.[62]

In July 2005 the maximum number of state officials and members of political parties that were permitted to serve in electoral commissions was increased from one-third to one-half.[63] Only those parties which have party list seats in the State Duma are permitted to nominate members for posts in regional and local electoral commissions. In the elections to rural and city settlements in 2004-5, 25 per cent of the voting members of municipal electoral commissions were members of political parties and this figure rose to 42 per cent in the electoral commissions of municipal districts and city okrugs.[64] Members of United Russia had the largest number of representatives, comprising 40.3 per cent (of the total number of party members) in rural and city settlements commissions; members of the CPRF were second (with 25 per cent) LDPR (14 per cent), Rodina (3.7 per cent). Yabloko and SPS both had approximately 3 per cent.[65] It should also be stressed that the electoral commissions also have a sizeable number of members who come from posts in the state administration, many of whom will have no choice but to support United Russia.

On 27 July 2006 the Duma adopted a new 'Law on Combating Extremist Activity' which gives the government new powers to ban parties from elections if any of their members are charged with extremist activities. Even Aleksandr Veshnyakov, who at the time was the Chair of the Central Electoral Commission, spoke out against this Law. In an interview conducted in the summer of 2006, he warned, 'I will mention that attempts are now being made to modify legislation in order to get more ways to cut out disliked candidates using administrative resources', and furthermore,

> What frightens me is that if these amendments are adopted, we will have elections without choice, as it was in fact in Soviet times … It is simply a different ideology of elections where everything must be regulated and in that way no candidate the government does not like will be permitted to participate in an election. It resembles Soviet times.[66]

Veshnyakov also spoke openly of 'several cases in which local or regional election officials in the Russian Federation falsified results, only to receive small fines or have criminal investigations closed without prosecution or conviction', and he went on to argue that, 'inappropriate light punishments discredit the authorities and give the opposition serious arguments for discrediting elections in Russia'. He concluded by calling on 'prosecutors and courts to toughen the criminal and administrative penalties for violating election laws'.[67] Soon afterwards, Veshnyakov was fired from his post as head of the Central Electoral Commission and replaced by one of Putin's protégés, Churov.

Conclusion

For elections to be considered democratic all citizens and parties must be provided with equal opportunities to stand for elections and the rules for the registration of candidates must be open and transparent. Supervision of the elections must be carried out by independent and impartial electoral commissions whose decisions are backed up by independent courts. However, as we have seen, this is far from the case in Russia where in many regions United Russia and the regional governments have effectively merged and there is no longer any meaningful separation of legislative, executive and judicial power, and no impartial electoral commissions. Municipal elections in many of Russia's regions are now largely 'decorative', with no real contestation and no level playing field. Of particular concern is the politicization and state domination of the courts, procuracy, police, and electoral commissions, and the extensive use of administrative resources to manipulate elections in United Russia's favour. Putin's 'electoral vertical' has now been extended from the regions to the municipalities and what Schedler calls 'electoral authoritarianism'[68] is slowly but surely taking root.

Notes

1 Federal Law, No. 131, 6 October 2003, 'Ob obshchikh printsipakh organizatsii mestnovo samoupravleniya v Rossiiskoi Federatsii', Moscow: Os' 89, 2005.
2 Federal Law, 11 July 2001, No. 95, 'O politicheskikh partiyakh', *Sobranie Zakonodatel'stva RF*, No. 29, 16 July 2001.
3 Federal Law, 21 July 2005, No. 93, 'Ob vnesenii izmeneniiv zakonodatel'nye akty Rossiiskoi Federtatsii O vyborakh i referendumakh i inye zakonodatel'nye akty Rossiiskoi Federtatsii', 21 June, 2005. In *Rossiiskaya Gazeta*, No. 161, 26 July, 2005.
4 For an excellent dicussion of the new legislation see, A. S. Avtonomov, A. Yu. Buzin, A. V. Ivanchenko, V. I. Krivtsov, A. V. Kynev, A. E. Lyubarev, *Rossiiskie Vybory v Kontektste Mezhdunarodnykh Izbiratel'nykh Standartov*, Moscow: Nezavisimaya Institut Vyborov, 2006. http://www.vibory.ru Accessed 9 July 2006.
5 A. A. Veshnyakov, 'Address of Chairman of the Central Election Commission of the Russian Federation, to the Users of the Web Site of the Central Electoral Commission of the Russian Federation', http://www.cikrf.ru/cikrf/eng/, July 2006, p. 1. Accessed August 2006.
6 For an excellent dicussion of the new legislation see, A. S. Avtonomov, A. Yu. Buzin, A. V. Ivanchenko, V. I. Krivtsov, A. V. Kynev, A. E. Lyubarev, *Rossiiskie vybory v kontektste mezhdunarodnykh izbiratel'nykh standartov*, http:/www.vibory. ru, accessed July 2006
7 Federal Law, 20 December 2004, 'O vnesenii izmeneni'.
8 Lev Levison, 'Political monetization', *NGO Newlsletter*, Issue 87, May–June 2005, p. 1.
9 Regional councils could orginally choose their electoral threshold, with a maximum of 7 per cent.

10 Vladimr Putin, 'Annual Address to the Federal Assembly', http://www.president. kremlin,ru/eng/text/speeches/2007/04/26/1209_type70029_1254, p. 2, Accessed 1 May 2007.

11 Ivanchenko and Lyubarev, *Rossiiskie Vybory*, p. 181.

12 Kenneth Wilson, 'Party-system development under Putin', *Post-Soviet Affairs*, Vol. 22, No. 4, 2006, p. 340.

13 Ibid., p. 342.

14 L. F. Dem'yanchenko (ed.), *Reforma Mestnovo Samoupravleniya v Rossiiskoi Federatsii: Itogi Munitsipal'nykh Vyborov v 2004–2005 Godakh*, Moscow: Central Electoral Commission of the Russian Federation, 2006, p. 8.

15 A. S. Avtonomov and A. Yu. Buzin, *et al.*, p. 26.

16 See, *Vestnik Tsentral'noi Izbiratel'noi Komissi Rossiiskoi Federatsii*, 17 October, 2004, No. 157, pp. 1–4.

17 Dem'yanchenko, p. 379.

18 'Analiticheskaya zapiska o nekotorykh voprosakh praktiki organizatsii munitsi-pal'nykh vyborov v khode reformy mestnovo samoupravleniya v Rossiiskoi Federatsii', *Vestnik Tsentral'noi Izbiratel'noi Komissii Rossiiskoi Federtatsii*, No. 6 (185), 2005, p. 11.

19 M. I. Liborakina, 'We need a law for a free people', *NGO Newsletter, Legislative Process in the State Duma*, Issue 55, Short Version (special), 23 April 2003, p. 6.

20 A further 6,000 heads of municipalities were elected indirectly by their local councils. For the contested posts there were run-off elections for the top two candidates, if none of the candidates received over 50 per cent of the votes in the first round.

21 Tomila Lankina, 'New system weakens municipalities', *Russian Regional Report*, Vol. 10, No. 17, 18 October 2005, p. 1.

22 Natal'ya Senchukova, 'Aktivnee vsevo golosovali v nebol'shikh selakh', *Vestnik Izbiratel'noi Komissii Arkhanglel'skoi Oblasti*, No 2 (12), 2005, p. 11.

23 S.V. Yusov, 'Realizatsiya pervovo etapa reformy mestnovo samoupravleniya na territorii Rostovskoi Oblasti', in *Vybory organov mestnovo samoupravleniya gorodskikh i sel'skikh poselenii munitsipal'nykh raionov Rostovskoi Oblasti, sentyabr'–oktyabr' 2005 goda*, Rostov-on-Don, IAITS: 'Mestnaya Vlast', 2006, p. 7.

24 Dem'yanchenko, pp. 312–29.

25 Gulnaz Sharafutdinova, 'Municipal elections in Tatarstan: old wine in new bottles?', *Russian Regional Report*, Vol. 10, No. 18, 3 November 2005, p. 1.

26 Ibid., p. 4.

27 Dem'yanchenko, p. 388.

28 Ibid., p. 10.

29 Calculated by the author from data presented in Dem'yanchenko, pp. 8, 10, 310–11, 376–7.

30 V. I. Fadeev, N. I. Rautkina, N. M. Mironov, *Munitsipal'nye Vybory v Rossiiskoi Federatsii*, Moscow: Norma, 2006, p. 324.

31 M. I. Titov, Ob itogakh munitsipal'nykh vyborov v khode reformy mestnovo samoupravleniya v Tverskoi oblasti v 2004-5 godakh', in Dem'yanchenko, p. 457.

32 http://www.karel.izbirkom.ru/way/9030659.html. Accessed July 2007.

33 G. S. Shaikhullin and D. N. Kuts, 'Munitsipal'naya mnogopartiinost'', in Dem'yanchenko, pp. 435-6.

34 Fadeev, et al., pp. 406, 408.

35 Kseniya Dymova, 'Partiinoe predstavitel'stvo v munitsipal'nykh poseleniyakh', in *Vestnik Izbiratel'noi Komissii Arkhangel'skoi Oblasti*, No. 2 (12), 2005, p. 22.

36 *Nezavisimaya Gazeta*, 6 October 2005. Quoted in Tomila Lankina, 'Local government reform: new system weakens municipalities', *Russian Regional Report*, Vol. 10, No. 17, 18 October 2005, p. 3.

37 S. A. Sergeev, 'Tatarstan 2005', p. 24. Moscow Carnegie Centre Website, http://www.carnegie.ru.

38 Gulnaz Sharafutdinova, 'Municipal elections in Tatarstan: old wine in new bottles?', *Russian Regional Report*, Vol. 10, No. 18, 3 November 2005, p. 1.

39 Fadeev, Rautkina, Mironov, pp. 317-18.

40 Sergei Sergievskii, *Nezavisimaya Gazeta*, 11 October 2005, p. 6.

41 Aleksei Makarkin, 'Mery: bor'ba za nezavisimost'', *Pro et Contra*, No. 1 (35), January–February, 2007, p. 28.

42 Robert Coalson, 'Mayoral elections: democracy's last stand', RFE/RL, *Russian Political Weekly*, Vol. 5, No. 9, 4 March 2005, p. 2.

43 Ibid.

44 See, 'Russian mayors a matter for concern in the Council of Europe's Congress of Local and Regional Authorities', Strasbourg: Council of Europe Press Division, 22 March 2005.

45 Polina Dobrolyubova and Natalya Gorodetskaya, 'Local self-justification', *Komersant*, 13 November 2006, p. 3. Translated in *CDPSP*, Vol. 58, No. 46, 2006, p. 5.

46 Valery Vyzhutovich, 'Power without money', *Rossiskaya Gazeta*, November 17, 2006, p. 3. Translated in *CDPSP*, Vol. 58, No. 46, 2006, p. 6.

47 East West Institute, *Russian Regional Report*, Vol. 9, No. 15, 31 August 2004, p. 1.

48 Claire Bigg, 'Russia: mayors in the crosshairs as power vertical gains force', Radio Free Europe/Radio Liberty (RFE/RL), *Newsline*, 21 June 2007, p. 1.

49 Ibid.

50 Ibid., p. 2.

51 Ibid.

52 *RFE/RL Newsline*, Vol. 11, No. 4, Part 1, 9 January 2007, p. 1.

53 Slider, p. 157.

54 Nikolai Petrov, 'Regional elections under Putin and prospects for Russian electoral democracy', *Ponars Policy Memo*, 287, February, 2003, p. 2.

55 Aleksandr Kynev, 'Munitzipal'nye vybory po novym pravilam', *Pro et Contra*, No. 1 (35), January–February 2007, p. 40.

56 Dmitrii Oreshkin, in 'Opinions, Comments' section of vibory.ru. website, pp. 2–3. Accessed in July 2007 at, www.en.pravonavibor.ru/comments/65.php.

57 Dmitry Kamyshev and Viktor Khamraev, Interview with Dmitrii Oreshkin, head of 'Merkator analytical group', in 'Opinions and Comments' section of the vibory. ru website, http://en.pravonavibor.ru/comments/65.php, p. 2, accessed July 2007.

58 Ibid., pp. 2–3.

59 Ibid., p. 3.

60 Ibid., p. 3.

61 A. Yu. Buzin, *Moskovskie munitsipal'nye vybory 2004 goda: istoriya fal'sifikatsii*, Moscow: RDP 'YABLOKO', 2005, p. 41.

62 Aleksey Levchenko, 'Russian elections official Ivanchenko on potential for election fraud', *Gazeta Ru*, 8 July 2005, reprinted in *Johnson's Russia List*, No. 9196, 10 July 2005, p. 12.

63 Avtonomov, Buzin *et al.*, p. 44.

64 Dem'yanchenko, pp. 9–10.

65 Calculated by the author from, 'Zapiska ob itogakh munitsipal'nykh vyborov v khode reformy mestnovo samoupravleniya v Rossiiskoi Federatsii v 2004–5 godakh', *Vestnik Tsentral'noi Izbiratel'noi Komissii Rossiiskoi Federatsii*, No. 2 (193), 2006, pp. 21–60.

66 Interview conducted by Natalya Kostlenko, 'Why electoral commission head Veshnyakov opposes election law amendments', *Nezavisimaya Gazeta*, 21 July 2006, p. 1.

67 Laura Belin, 'Election commission chairman calls for crackdown on election fraud', *RFE/RL Newsline*, Vol. 9, No. 125, 1 July 2005, p. 1.
68 Andreas Schedler, 'Elections without democracy: the menu of manipulation', *Journal of Democracy*, Vol. 13., No. 2, April 2002. See also my discussion of 'electoral authoritarianism', in Cameron Ross, 'Federalism and electoral authoritarianism under Putin', *Demokratizatsiya*, Vol. 13, No. 3, Summer 2005, pp. 347–72.

Index

Abkhasiya 59, 60, 62
Afanasyev, Mikhail N. 55
Aspaturian, Vernon 27

Bermeo, Nancy 25, 50
Beslan 1, 106, 109, 116, 285
Birch, Anthony 25
Bunce, Valerie 50
business associations 187–8
business elites 184, 185, 187, 190, 191, 192, 194, 198, and governors 191–205; in regional assemblies 189, 191

Chechnya 8, 43, 44, 46, 61, 62, 63, 68, 72, 75, 76, 107, 135
city districts 231–2, 238, 242, 284
communitarianism 153
corporatism 189-91

Dahl 190

Ekaterinburg: data on 207–8; Stategic Plan 213–16
Elazar, Daniel 59
electoral commissions: 140, 259, 287; politicization of 299–301
electoral deposits 129, 138
electoral systems 12, 120, 122, 126, 155, 156, 162–3, 170, 176, 285–6, 288–9, 297; *see also* municipal elections, regional elections
electoral vertical 284, 301
ethnic groups: 43, 55, 57, 58, 60–64; autochthonous 60, 67, 70, 71.
elitism 190–1
étatism 189–91

federal bargain 26, 35–7, 49
Federal Treaty 32, 33, 89, 208

Federalism: asymmetrical 3, 8, 18, 46–9, 55, 56, 60, 86; Austrian 39–40; Belgian 43-44, 47-48; Canadian, 46, 47; De-federalization 55, 72, 75, 78; and democracy 55, 72–6, 106, 116–17; and ethnicity 68–72; fiscal 86–7; German 47, 48; Indian 40, 43–4, 47, 48; Malaysian 40–1, 43, 44, 45; Nigerian 40, 41, 43, 45-6; Soviet legacy 26–9, 32, 43, 49
Federation Council 9, 54, 64, 69, 82, 96, 106, 108, 120, 140, 174, 276, 297
Fillipov 44, 62
Friedrich, Carl 29

Georgia 59, 60
Gligich-Zolotareva, Milena 101
Goble, Paul 55
Governors: appointed by Putin 4, 9, 38, 76, 82, 106–117, 202-3, 264, 286; biographies of 193–5; businessmen 191–5; and mayors 117, 207–23, 257–8, 264, 274–5, 276, 296–8

Hahn, Gordon 73–4, 82
Heinemann-Grüder, Andreas 33, 36, 38, 42, 43
Historic institutionalism 122
Hough, Jerry F. 16

King, Preston 34
Konitzer, Andrew 108
Koniuchova, Irina 59
Kozak, Dmitry 13, 59, 200, 252, 264, 268–70, 273, 278–9, 284
Kozak Commission 254, 263, 264–70, 278–80, 284

Lankina, Tomila 289
Law on Combating Extremist Activity 137
Law on Political Parties 130, 285
Leksin, Vladimir 86, 88
Local elections: turnout 259
Local-self government; delegated tasks 234-5; European Charter of 242; finance of 240–41, 252, 258; head of municipality 236–9; local councils 235–6; numbers of 232, 256; powers of 228-9, 232–4, 254–5; public perceptions of 258-9; rights of citizens in 235; statesization 234–5, 239–40; societal concept of 250; structure 231–2;

managerialists 7, 8, 11, 15
Matheson, Thornton 86
Matsuzato, Kimitaka 276
Mayors: 106, 158, 186, 210, 298; appointment of 112, 117, 276; election of 235, 237, 238, 241, 251, 257–8; and governors 210-211, 257–8, 264, 274, 277-8; harassment of 222, 257–8, 297–8; in Kozak Commission 267; party membership 296
merger of regions: ethnic dimensions of 97–8; law on 83; list of 84; prerequisites for 87-8;
monetization of benefits 14, 265, 268–70
municipal districts 98-9, 231–4, 236, 239, 242, 256, 259, 270, 284, 288, 289, 290–1, 300
municipal elections: 221, 287; candidates in 289–90; dominance of United Russia 292, 294–6; electoral systems 288-9; manipulation of 298-9; party membership of 292; turnout 290, 291, 293; votes against all 291–3

national-cultural autonomy 66
neo-institutionalism 155, 186
new centralism 5
North Osetiya-Alaniya 61, 62, 73, 109

OPS Uralmash 209, 214–21
Ordeshook 15

political representation 150, 154, 163, 168, 176
polpredy 10, 74, 200
Puzanov, Aleksandr 259

Ragozina, Liudmilla 259
rational choice theory 151, 154, 157, 184–6
regional elections: blocks in 124–5, 129, 135–6, 285; gubernatorial 106–11, 113, 116; managed 109–10, 134; ousting of party lists from 126, 134, 139–42; PR electoral system 120, 122–3, 285-6; registration of candidates 129, 138; terms 110–11, 113, 114, 180; turnout 137-8, 287; in Sverdlovsk 209–10, 217–21; thresholds 120, 129, 137, 285; votes against all 135, 287
Riker, William 29, 35, 36, 37, 49.
Robinson, Neil 270, 272, 273, 274, 275.

Sakwa, Richard 31, 49, 275.
Schedler, Andreas 301
Schumpeter 155, 185, 190
self-governmentalists 7, 8, 11–12, 14.
Shvetsova, Olga 15, 62
Slider, Darrell 257
South Osetiya 59, 60, 62
Sovereignty: 19, 31, 32, 46, 55, 56, 58, 67, 76; divided 58
Smith, Graham 31, 36, 43.
Stepan, Alfred 36
Stoner-Weiss, Kathryn 8, 49
Sverdlovsk Region: data on 207–8

Turovskii, Rostislav 87

Urals Republic 208-9
Utilitarians 7, 8, 12, 13

Veshnyakov, Aleksandr 285, 300, 301

Wheare, K. C. 40
Wilson, Kenneth 286, 287

Zemstvos 13, 14, 229, 249, 275
Zubarevich, Natalia 92, 101